Religion in Mississippi

Heritage of Mississippi Series
Volume II

Religion in
Mississippi

Randy J. Sparks

University Press of Mississippi
for the Mississippi Historical Society
Jackson

Unless otherwise noted, images contained in this volume are provided courtesy of the Mississippi Department of Archives and History.

www.upress.state.ms.us

09 08 07 06 05 04 03 02 01   4 3 2 1
♾

Library of Congress Cataloging-in-Publication Data

Sparks, Randy J.

   Religion in Mississippi / Randy J. Sparks.
     p. cm. —(Heritage of Mississippi series ; v. 2)
   Includes bibliographical references and index.
   ISBN 1-57806-361-2 (cloth : alk. paper)
   1. Mississippi—Church history.   2. Mississippi—Religion.
I. Title.   III. Series.

BR555.M7 S68 2001
277'.62—dc21   00-051362

British Library Cataloging-in-Publication Data available

Contents

Acknowledgments

I would like to express my appreciation to the editors of the Heritage of Mississippi Series for the opportunity to be a part of this ambitious reexamination of the state's history. Elbert Hilliard, Ray Skates, and Christine Wilson have been especially helpful and supportive of the project. I also thank Carol Cox, who copyedited the manuscript for the University Press of Mississippi. My debts to the many dedicated and capable librarians and archivists across the state continue to mount. I am grateful to Anne Webster and the entire staff at the Mississippi Department of Archives and History and to the archivists at the Cain Archives (Millsaps College), the Mississippi Baptist Historical Commission (Mississippi College), the Special Collections Department at Mississippi State University, and the Southern Historical Collection, all of whom have done much more than their jobs required.

I am also pleased to acknowledge the assistance of my colleagues, who, in their willingness to comment on portions of this work, have not only made it a better book but have also helped to make our profession an intellectually exciting one. Fitzhugh Brundage and Michele Gillespie generously read the bulk of the manuscript, and John B. Boles, Anne Boylan, David Chapell, Paul Harvey, Jane and Bill Pease, and Clarence Walker read portions of it. All of them had insightful suggestions that greatly improved the book; however, I alone am responsible for any shortcomings that remain. Finally, I would like to thank Judith Lee Hunt, whose encouragement, support, and healthy skepticism are a constant source of inspiration.

I dedicate this book to the congregation of Palestine United Methodist Church in Montpelier, Mississippi, where members of my family have worshiped for over a century and a half. They gave me my earliest and best lessons in the importance of religion in Mississippi.

Introduction

This book explores the symbiotic relationship between religious and secular life in Mississippi over its turbulent three-hundred-year history. Understanding how religion has shaped Mississippi's culture and society is a complex undertaking, one made more challenging by the dramatic changes over time, by the state's particular class divisions, and, most significantly, by the race factor, which has played such a crucial role in shaping Mississippi culture. This study looks beyond religion as a private and personal system of belief and explores religious and theological concepts in the society at large. For example, what is the relationship between the eschatological message and the social and political life in various historical periods? An exaggerated and stubborn opposition is often falsely erected between spiritual life and social life, between what religious folk actually believe and what they live by. The predominant faith in Mississippi is Christianity—particularly evangelical Christianity—which affirms the promises of God in the New Testament: freedom, peace, justice, and reconciliation. These precepts cannot be entirely individualized, internalized, and spiritualized, especially if the believer finds himself or herself in a society that negates these core values. If religious and sociocultural values conflict, as they so often do, then religious institutions and their members must either try to make their faith conform to social and cultural norms or act as critical agents for change. Religious people and institutions can take a critical attitude toward society; they can and sometimes do contest sociopolitical conditions, and occasionally these may take the form of revolutionary protest. This critical gospel stance can be a powerful force for positive social change, though its potential is often overlooked in the scramble for conformity.

This study begins at a time of remarkable religious transformation, a time when the upheavals of the Protestant Reformation were still under way. When Christianity became the faith of the Roman Empire, it helped legitimate the absolutist state of the emperors, a role that reappeared with the emergence of the great nation-states during the Renaissance when religion became closely tied with nationalism. The concept of the Christian State and the attempt on the part of European rulers to use religion as one instrument of empire explains much of the history of religion in Mississippi's colonial period. The dramatic revolutionary protests of the European Reformation had a powerful impact on early American history as well; Reformers retained their revolutionary zeal and their critical attitude toward society, whether they were New England Puritans or New Light Baptists on the Mississippi frontier.

Once Mississippi passed into American hands, however, a new period of religious history began, one marked not by state control of religion but by the supremely American concept of voluntarism. With the disestablishment of the churches after the American Revolution, religion competed freely in the marketplace of ideas; in theory, a wall of separation divided religious and political life. Initially it appeared that religion would attract few buyers in the new marketplace, as the once-established churches, like the Anglican Church in some former British colonies or the Catholic Church in Mississippi, all but collapsed. The recently planted evangelical sects, particularly the Baptists, Methodists, and Presbyterians, had only a few hundred members scattered across the new republic but concentrated in the South.

Evangelicalism began in the eighteenth-century South as a revolutionary movement among the plain folk who consciously created their culture in opposition to the dominant culture of the gentry. As a part of this evangelical revolt, converts challenged the hierarchical structure of their society and all the cultural trappings of the elite. So powerful was their critique that they attracted large numbers of people alienated from that culture, including women and blacks, who joined in large numbers. Fueled by the Great Revival, these sects expanded rapidly among the plain folk and enslaved African Americans in the early nineteenth century. The typical church was a biracial one, and the African American converts greatly influenced evangelical ritual and practice. In these biracial churches a remarkable process of cultural exchange took place between blacks and whites.

The large and growing number of enslaved African American converts brought the evangelicals face-to-face with America's greatest moral dilemma, the central paradox of American history, the institution of slavery. Early evangelicals, given their stance as committed critics of societal evils, opposed slavery, a position that almost doomed them in the South. It was a bitter test of their commitment to their most cherished beliefs. By the time they arrived in Mississippi, the evangelicals had largely abandoned any real opposition to the institution, though they continued to criticize abuses within the system.

The 1830s marked a major turning point in the history of evangelicalism. As the Mississippi economy boomed and the plain folk moved up the economic ladder to join the ranks of the slaveowners, more and more wealthy converts came into the churches. With the evangelicals abandoning their stance as cultural revolutionaries and social critics and with small sects growing into major denominations, evangelicals became the most ardent defenders of a hierarchical social system grounded in slaveholding, patriarchal households—a dramatic shift mirrored in the churches, where ritual and practice relegated women and blacks to more subordinate positions.

Evangelicals, wedded to their orderly, hierarchical slaveholding republic, contributed to the disastrous civil war that destroyed it. Their impassioned defense of slavery, their own division along sectional lines, and their vision of southern whites as God's chosen people served to undermine their commitment to the Union and helped propel the state into secession and war. The Confederate government attempted to harness the evangelical vision of a virtuous republic to build Confederate nationalism, and ministers led that crusade by preaching that God would not abandon the South in a just cause. That message became a double-edged sword as defeat loomed on the horizon. African American Christians had a far different vision of the war and its message. For them, it resonated with the deliverance of the children of Israel from bondage and came in answer to heartfelt prayers from enslaved evangelicals. A century of biracial worship came to an end as black and white evangelicals divided along racial lines, marking a major turning point in the history of religion in Mississippi.

During Reconstruction blacks created their own religious denominations, and churches became the largest institutions under black control and the bedrock of the black community. For white denominations the decades after the war also saw dramatic growth; indeed, only in the postbellum period can the South be considered the nation's Bible Belt. Mississippi Christians embraced many of the humanitarian and social reforms associated with the Social Gospel movement, and they attempted to use the power of the state to redeem society. The postwar years saw, however, a steady worsening of the racial climate, and white Christians were not fully able to bring the power of their faith to alter social practice, though they represented practically the only voices of moderation. For black Christians, their theology, firmly grounded in the doctrine of Christian equality, served as a powerful antidote to racist ideology.

The growing institutionalization of worship among members of both races, part of a process that theologian H. Richard Niebuhr described as an all but inevitable "institutionalization and secularization of the king-dom," left the established churches open to challenges from below.[1] The tension inherent in Christianity between conformity and revolt reemerged in the postbellum period in the Holiness and Pentecostal movements, per-haps the most dynamic religious movements to appear since the Great Revival. Like the early evangelicals, these movements were egalitarian and biracial. Members of these sects emphasized the charismatic gifts of the Holy Spirit, relied on biblical primitivism, and disdained material wealth. Though dwarfed by the mainline denominations, these churches un-leashed enormous creative and spiritual energies.

The period from World War I to World War II was one of dramatic change. The prosperity of the war years and early 1920s and a growing rapprochement between the South and the rest of the nation opened the region to an influx of outside influences, perhaps best symbolized by the phenomenon of the Scopes trial. Like the continuing growth of the funda-mentalist sects, the Scopes trial demonstrated that many southerners viewed the rapid social changes with misgivings. The Great Depression and World War II ushered in changes that fundamentally reshaped the southern landscape, changes that were, in the view of many historians of the region, even greater than those brought about by the Civil War. The demise of the sharecropping system marked a revolution in the state's eco-nomic system with equally important implications for the state's social system, particularly Jim Crow and white supremacy, which had, in part, been buttressed by the sharecropping system. The Depression saw some highly visible, though largely ineffective, efforts on the part of outsiders to bring the Christian religion to bear on the conditions of the state's dispossessed croppers and on racial injustice. Their failure indicated that change, when it came, would have to come from within. By the 1930s, the state's white population embraced a homogeneous social and cultural system supported by a fundamentalist faith that kept doubt and skepticism to a minimum. Very few white Mississippians were compelled by their faith in a mighty, righteous, and vengeful God to question the racial status quo. Black Christians heard a different message, one that emphasized mercy, love, and hope, particularly the virtues of brotherly love and nonviolent racial justice, concepts noticeably absent from the white Christian message.

The horrors of World War II and Nazi Germany had revealed the terrible tragedy that racial hatred and injustice could produce, and black *and* white Christians pointed out the contradictions between American rhetoric and reality. During and after the war, Christians of both races called for an end to racial injustice in the state. In the postwar years blacks began to mount an aggressive challenge to the Jim Crow system, and the Supreme Court's 1954 decision in *Brown v. Board of Education* gave that challenge a significant boost. While religion was a major part of the civil rights movement for blacks and for whites, churches as institutions failed to provide moral leadership in the midst of twentieth-century America's greatest moral struggle. Outside the institutional setting, however, individuals of both races and all political persuasions relied on Christian doctrine as they sought support for their beliefs. Eventually, and with much terror, bloodshed, and heartache, the doctrine of Christian equality, that silver thread running through centuries of church history, proved to be the basis for a consensus among the majority of Mississippians that the day of racial injustice had ended.

The huge preponderance of evangelical Protestants among religious folk in Mississippi almost obscures the presence of other religious groups in the state, but nonevangelical religious groups represented important alternative belief systems. Three of the largest of these groups, Catholics, Jews, and Mormons, provide examples of how outsider religious groups function within such a setting. The Catholic and Jewish presence in the state dates back to the colonial period, and an examination of their histories reveals that these two groups, so often the object of violent persecution elsewhere, used their religion actually to overcome their outsider status. In a place where race prejudice overwhelmed all other kinds, Catholics and Jews could conform to the state's racial code, define themselves as white, and thereby integrate into society. Mormons, acting in a way that was more characteristic of earlier movements of religious cultural revolt, set themselves apart from society, but their challenge did not extend to an attack on racial mores. Through their adherence to Jim Crow, all these outsider religious groups passed the state's ultimate litmus test as trustworthy white southerners whose religious beliefs were no threat to the majority.

Since the upheavals of the 1960s, evangelical religion has further cemented its hold on the region, though with some noticeable changes. As elsewhere across the nation and around the world, fundamentalist churches have expanded most rapidly since the 1970s. Buffeted by drastic social, cultural, and economic changes, Mississippians of both races have sought the comfort offered by fundamentalist churches. Battles over the teaching of evolution, public prayer in schools, abortion, and homosexuality have divided Mississippians and provide further evidence that the state is very much a part of the national religious scene.

Religion in Mississippi

Religious worship is not performed with dignity in this country. . . .
The majority of the inhabitants do not attend mass on Sundays and
feast days. Impurity is conducive to irreligion.

—Sieur Hubert, 1717[1]

[T]he least considered persons of the colony have always been the
priests. . . . [S]ince the majority of those who have hitherto governed
the province have been people without religion they have done what
they could to annoy and to displease the missionaries and by that
means get rid of these censors of their impiety and scandalous lives.

—Father Raphael, 1725[2]

Religion is the first object that his Majesty proposes in the establish-
ment of the colonies. . . .

—King Louis XV, 1732[3]

I Religion and Empire: Colonial Mississippi, 1682–1796

From the opulence of the Palace of Versailles, Louis XIV and his ministers laid plans for an expansive empire in the Americas worthy of a Sun King. The immense domain stretched in a vast arc from Canada in the north to south along the Mississippi River and out into the Caribbean; every instrument of empire would be required to conquer, settle, and control such a region. Religion was one of the many instruments of empire that the French, along with other European powers, employed in their colonization schemes. Religion had many uses for European conquerors: it legitimated their claims to the land they occupied; its agents, particularly missionaries, could be employed in a variety of ways useful to the empire; and it helped sustain the settlers in their hardships and suffering and imposed order on a wild and dangerous frontier and its unruly inhabitants.

In April 1682, René-Robert Cavelier, Sieur de La Salle, and his party arrived at the mouth of the Mississippi River from the French colony of Quebec, the first Europeans to travel the length of the great river. At the river's mouth, La Salle erected a column dedicated to the Sun King, and in a solemn ceremony, "The whole party chanted the *Te Deum*, the *Exaudiat*, the *domine salvam fac Regem* . . . ," and France laid legal claim to the territory that would become Mississippi. A series of European wars prevented the French from following up on their claim until 1698 when they dispatched an expedition from France to the Gulf of Mexico under the command of Pierre Le Moyne, Sieur d'Iberville. Iberville's party sailed to the new Spanish settlement at Pensacola, then along the coast to the bay of Biloxi, which he chose as the site for his settlement and where the French hastily built a wooden fort. Among the men who accompanied Iberville was Father Du Ru, a Jesuit, who immediately began to work among the Native Americans. Even before this expedition, missionaries from Canada quickly followed La Salle's route and began to work with Native Americans along the river, and, with the establishment of the colony at Biloxi, then other settlements at Mobile, New Orleans, and Natchez, missionary work began in earnest.[4]

As agents of empire, missionaries were unsurpassed in their diligence, dedication, and usefulness. Along with traders, missionaries acted as cultural mediators, as conduits who carried European culture to Native Americans and knowledge of Native Americans back to Europeans. In 1705 the Count de Pontchartrain, Minister of Marine and Colonies, wrote Jean-Baptiste Le Moyne, Sieur de Bienville, Iberville's brother and the governor of Louisiana since 1702, that "[t]he gentlemen of the Foreign Missions are sending two priests to Louisiana who are to go and settle at the Choctaws and at the Chickasaws in order to preach there the enlightenment of the faith. It is necessary that you do everything in your power to assist them in the accomplishment of this intention by having these Indian nations assemble as far as possible in order to put them in a position to be instructed. Inform these priests of the order that I am giving you and confer with them about everything that there is to do to attain this good end." The minister's orders suggest that the French intended to follow the Spanish model and have the Native Americans settle in villages centered around a church, where their lessons in religion would only be part of a larger socialization process. On another occasion, Pontchartrain wrote that missionaries should "make large villages" of Native Americans.[5]

Native converts could be very useful. The English launched a successful expedition from Charleston against Spanish Florida in 1703 and decimated not only the Spaniards but also their Indian allies. Thousands of captured natives were taken to Charleston and sold into slavery, but a few hundred Apalachees escaped and asked to settle in French territory. The French government approved of Bienville's decision to allow them to settle. "As they are Christians and Catholics they can more easily become accustomed to us than the others whom they will be able also to attract by means of them to the knowledge of the faith. . . ." The French expected these converts to assist them in bringing others into the faith and into the French orbit. In the early years of the colony when supplies were scarce, the French had to rely on native sources for food. In 1700, De Sauvole de La Villantray, first governor of Louisiana, "asked a missionary who left this place to return to the Natchez please buy us some corn and put it in a cabin so that it may be all ready when we pass by them."[6]

Of course, missionaries were expected to convince natives of the glory, goodness, and power of the European God, but another duty was to convince them that the French king shared at least a substantial portion of those attributes. This could be a particularly difficult undertaking when the natives saw only a few hundred bedraggled settlers in their squalid villages. In 1706 the Chitimachas captured and killed several Frenchmen, including Jean François Buisson de St. Cosme, a seminarian from Quebec who had been missionary to the Natchez for six years. The French officials attributed these and other assassinations to the "low opinion" and "small fear" the natives had of the French. Choctaw and Chickasaw chiefs once asked Bienville if it were true that "there were really as many people in France as here. . . ." If there were, the doubtful chiefs argued, then some of them would come to avenge the deaths of their countrymen unless "you have no courage at all." The wily chiefs, having also seen the terrible death rate among European immigrants, said, "You have been here for six years. Instead of increasing you are diminishing. The good men are dying and only children come in their places." In a similar vein, a native medicine man recognized the threat that missionaries posed to traditional worship practices and encouraged his fellows to attack a priest who was severely wounded. Father Antoine Davion, one of the earliest missionaries in Louisiana, who arrived in 1698 to work among the Tunicas, barely escaped with his life when he destroyed the idols of the Yazoo Indians.[7]

Despite the example of hostile tribes like the Chitimachas and attacks from individuals, most tribes welcomed missionaries. Indeed, Bienville reported that "[t]hey ask me earnestly for missionaries." Still, he warned that "[t]hey must be careful to select priests of strong constitution and without any infirmity. There is one here [Father Alexandre Huve] who is very near-sighted and has a very bad pronunciation. The Indians make fun of him." No doubt the natives found much to laugh at among the band of Frenchmen set down among them, but once European colonists pulled various tribes into alliances with them, European goods, particularly guns, became a necessity if they were to defend themselves. When Bienville asked the Apalachees why they wanted to desert the Spanish and live near the French, they replied that the Spanish "did not give them any guns at all, but that the French gave them to all their allies." For a people who had just seen thousands of their tribe carried off into slavery by the English, weapons were no small matter. The French knew that many Native American "converts" "receive baptism in order to please and . . . are Christians only in name and without inclination."⁸ The presence of a missionary, even a nearsighted one, must have seemed a small price to pay for weapons and other goods.

Missionaries were a vital source of trade goods for Native Americans; indeed, their role as merchants caused criticism and debate. Bienville complained that "few missionaries remember the vows that they take in France. No sooner are they here than they keep open shop, sell and buy like ordinary individuals." Missionaries complained, however, that they could not live on the meager allowance given to them. In 1726, Father Raphael, Capuchin Vicar General of Louisiana, wrote that of eight missionary posts in the colony, only those at New Orleans, Mobile, and Natchez had parsonages. He acknowledged that priests "took what they thought proper from the warehouses and carried on a trade which brought them in a great deal beyond their salaries," but what choice did they have when their salaries were too small to live on and imported necessities were so dear? He continued, "For myself, . . . I should leave the mission rather than carry on or permit commerce of this sort which is not at all proper for our profession." If only officials would "take an interest in our needs and procure us the means for subsistence," he insisted. Apparently, however, missionaries like Father Petit, a Jesuit who worked among the Choctaws, continued to engage in trade with the knowledge of secular officials. Indeed, officials defended his right to do so since *"this priest is the first settler of that place, because he is residing there and because if he wishes to get a living he simply must trade. . . ."*[9]

Officials knew that Native Americans sometimes valued trade goods over missionaries and used merchandise to ingratiate priests with natives who were otherwise hostile to such overtures. In the early years of the colony, Bienville notified his superiors that "in order to facilitate [the way] for missionaries he will be obliged . . . to make presents to each nation. . . ." Even though Bienville assured the officials in France that these measures would not be necessary for long, such inducements continued. For example, in 1729 officials doubted that the Kawitas would accept a missionary, and so "it was agreed that this father should go to them in secular dress with an interpreter and a servant and that he should remain three or four months in order to dispose them to receive him in another costume," namely that of a Jesuit priest. The priest hoped "to succeed in it by means of some little presents."[10]

The government was willing to engage in such stratagems not only to swell the ranks of the converted, but also to put priests in useful positions where they could facilitate communication and provide information on Indian activities. The most successful missionaries were those who learned the native languages. For instance, in 1706 Bienville reported that a priest in Mobile would "have difficulty in becoming accustomed to the life of the Indians and in learning their language without which it is impossible to succeed among them." Missionaries who mastered the language and earned the trust of a tribe could be useful indeed. For example, in 1732 Bienville consulted the Reverend Father Beaudouin, a Jesuit missionary to the Choctaws, who knew the natives "perfectly" and "whose language he likewise understands." Beaudouin provided a detailed description of that tribe to Bienville and to French officials in which he estimated the number of warriors they could field, explained the intricacies of diplomacy between the English and the Choctaws and Chickasaws, told where forts and storehouses might best be constructed, and gave advice on war against the Chickasaws. A year later Bienville asked Beaudouin to follow up on disturbing reports that the Choctaws might be involved in negotiations with the English. The Jesuit conferred with the "principal chiefs of the nation," who assured him of their deep and abiding loyalty to the French, but because of his intimate knowledge of the tribe the priest was able to elaborate on this report. The truth of the matter was that "the nation in general is murmuring. . . ." There was growing dissatisfaction with the French alliance over a shortage of trade goods "which has brought them to a general want of all things." Meanwhile, the English had sent word that their French foes would never be able to supply the Indians with the goods they desired. The jockeying among the Choctaws, the French, and the English continued for years, and Bienville continued to rely on the efforts of Father Beaudouin who acted as his eyes, ears, and voice.[11]

Given the many obstacles facing European missionaries and the difficulties in finding capable and talented men, Father Raphael in 1725 devised a scheme to train Indian missionaries. Since "[w]e have neither the sufficient number of missionaries nor the necessary means to establish ourselves in their villages . . . ," he proposed training "several young Indians" at a school in New Orleans. He reported that "[t]here are already some of the nation of the Natchez who have presented themselves of their own accord attracted by a young Indian of the same nation whom we have had with us for about twenty months." While he suspected that these young men were drawn by "the curiosity to learn to speak and to live like the French . . . ," he felt sure that the Capuchins would soon make "good Christians of them." The priest added, "I see nothing impossible in this undertaking for I know several Indians of both sexes who are good enough Christians to make me wish that our Europeans resembled them." Some might doubt that natives were the spiritual equals of Europeans, but Father Raphael had no such qualms. He wrote, "God has his elect everywhere and I should think that I lacked faith in the general redemption of the human race if I doubted that the salvation of these poor unbelievers in the midst of whom we live is possible."[12]

If some Indians chose to live like Europeans, some Europeans chose to live like Indians, much to the consternation of the missionaries. How could priests enforce religious order on a population "accustomed to live the free life of the Indians . . ."? The fear that life in the wilderness of the Americas would lead to moral degeneracy was widespread among Europeans of the colonial era, and colonizers at home saw the enforcement of religious morals as one means of avoiding such a catastrophe. As early as

1704, Pontchartrain ordered Bienville to "see to it that divine worship is conducted with as much decency as the place can permit [and] that the impious blasphemers and people who cause scandal are repressed according to his Majesty's intentions." Symbolically, churches stood at the very center of French settlements, facing an open square, or *place d'armes*, as indicated on a 1721 plan for New Biloxi. Over and over again French officials issued religious decrees. In 1732 Bienville received a memoir from the king informing him that "[r]eligion is the first object that his Majesty proposes in the establishment of the colonies. . . . He also recommends to him to give particular attention to maintaining the inhabitants in the practice of religion by suppressing debauchery and scandal, and still more by giving an example of orderly conduct in keeping with the authority with which he is vested."[13]

Repressing scandal and debauchery was no small task among the French colonists. In keeping with the king's orders, the colonists erected a church house sixty-two feet long and sixteen feet wide, and the Reverend Henri Roulleaux de La Vente arrived from Normandy on July 24, 1704, and was formally inducted into his parish on September 28 of that year. His efforts to impose order on the infant colony brought him into immediate conflict with Bienville, who complained that the priest "opposes him in everything that he can and . . . forgets nothing to disparage his authority." Bienville and La Vente engaged in an ongoing struggle over matters large and small. La Vente explained that he had been "obliged to warn him [Bienville] about a too great familiarity that he had with a woman which scandalized the entire colony, and although this woman has died, this commandant has not become pacified in regard to these missionaries."[14]

Whether or not this charge was true, sexual relations were among the most disorderly aspects of colonial life. Though colonization is often thought of as a male enterprise, women, whether by their presence or their absence, had a profound influence on colonial development. With the great disparity in sex ratios, French men quickly took Indian women. Bienville complained in 1706 that La Vente "has had several marriages of Frenchmen with Indian women performed by the missionaries who are among the Indians although he [Bienville] has warned these missionaries that was not his Majesty's intention because it was important to bring in

all the Frenchmen who are scattered among the Indians and not to autho-
rize them to live there as libertines under the pretext that they have wives
among them." Antoine de La Mothe Cadillac, who replaced Bienville as
governor and arrived in 1713, described the residents of Louisiana as "jail-
birds without subordination for religion and for government, addicted to
vice principally with the Indian women whom they prefer to French
women."[15]

Cadillac attempted to force the Frenchmen to give up Indian women,
but with little success. He wrote, "The Canadians and the soldiers who
are not married have female Indian slaves and insist that they cannot dis-
pense with having them to do their washing and to do their cooking or to
. . . keep their cabins." The governor was not convinced that these women
were kept only as domestics. "If this reason were valid," he said, "it ought
not to prevent the soldiers from going to confessional, or the Canadians
either." Outraged, the governor thundered, "[T]he glory of God and the
service of the King demand a remedy for such disorder. . . ." Father La
Vente had also attempted to stop the practice and in 1708 wrote Pontchartrain that "[i]t is necessary to issue an ordinance to forbid the French of
Mobile from taking Indian women as slaves and especially from living with
them under the same roof in concubinage." According to Bienville, the
priest "is attempting further to annoy the officers and the colonists to the
extent of [preventing them from] having any women slaves." Bienville
tried to solve the problem by having the slaves sent "to sleep in the houses
in which there are Frenchwomen, which does not fail to be a very great
inconvenience for them." Apparently, the masters found it a great inconvenience, indeed, for the enslavement of Indian women continued un-
abated. In 1717 Hubert of Saint-Malo arrived at Dauphin Island to fill the
post of commissary general. Deeply shocked by the state of the colony, he
reported that "[r]eligious worship is not performed with dignity in this
country. . . . The majority of the inhabitants do not attend mass on Sundays and feast-days. Impurity is conducive to irreligion. The public commerce of the Indian women is in part a cause of it." Cadillac suggested
that the practice could be stopped by moving all the troops inside the fort
and allowing them to own only male slaves. The practice declined with
the arrival of more Frenchwomen after 1717, though it did not stop.
Father Raphael wrote in 1726 that "although the number of those who

maintain young Indian women or negresses to satisfy their intemperance is considerably diminished, there still remain enough to scandalize the church and to require an effective remedy." The Code Noir, promulgated in 1724, outlawed sexual unions between slaves and masters, but it was far from an effective remedy.[16]

Even the presence of more Frenchwomen did not mean an end of scandals, but without them the colony could not succeed. Leaders of the colony pleaded with French officials to send women. In 1709 one colonist reported that Bienville had tried to convince a group of Canadians to settle down and farm, but they "replied with a common voice that they could live without that and that further, being unmarried, they would not settle down. . . ." If forty girls could be sent from France, the officials believed that the Canadians "would first get married and being married would work to support their families in mutual rivalry." Diron d'Artaguette, commissary of the king, wrote Pontchartrain in 1710 that "[t]here are here . . . young men and soldiers who are in a position to undertake farms. They need wives. I know only this one way to hold them." Without women, the young men simply would not become farmers or even permanent residents. As another observer wrote, "[T]he hunters and backwoodsmen who are of strong and vigorous age and temperament and who like the sex, not finding any who can hold them, are wanderers among the Indian nations and satisfy their passions with the daughters of these Indians, which retards the growth of this colony." French officials agreed that such interracial unions, and their offspring, endangered the colony. The ministry of marine feared that "the colony would be populated with half-breeds who are by nature idle, loose and even more rogues such as are those of the Spanish colonies."[17]

The government tried to respond by sending women from the prisons and poorhouses of Paris, which was hardly a solution to the problem. Occasionally, such women refused to marry at all or caused other scandals. One officer pleaded with the company to "send us girls who have at least some appearance of virtue." In 1725 the Superior Council of Louisiana noted "the necessity of purging the colony of . . . a number of women of bad life who are entirely lost." Again in 1728 officials complained that "there are many women and girls of bad life here. These wenches become pregnant and afterwards they will not give the name of the fathers of the children so that to-day the Company is obliged to feed five or six nursing children whose fathers are not known." New laws were passed which ordered women to name fathers of their children under threat of corporal punishment. Colonial officials also asked for "a house of correction here in order to put in it the women and girls of bad lives who cause public scandal." Instead of women such as these, colonial officials instead urged their superiors in France "to send families of farmers, selecting those in which there are many girls who would be married. . . ."[18]

Repeatedly, women challenged the priests' authority and disrupted worship. Father Raphael complained that a group of young women "laughed and talked very immodestly at the beginning of parochial mass. . . ." Despite warnings from the schoolmaster and the officiating priest, the young women continued their merriment, and the priest refused to say mass until they left the church. At that, one of them cried out, "The devil! I am not going out like that." The father of one of the young women, who also served as attorney general, then filed a complaint against the priest with the council. Apparently the problem of talking during services was so common that in 1725 the Superior Council of Louisiana issued a decree prohibiting it. Exasperated by the whole affair, Father Raphael mourned that so many people "seek only to contradict us in everything we do for the service of God and . . . render us odious and contemptible to the people."[19]

Perhaps the colony's greatest scandals involved allegations of homosexuality. Sieur Du Tisne, commandant of the post at Natchez, was repeatedly charged with this offense. In 1726 Father Raphael visited the settlement and found "no church at all" there. Mass was conducted in a "very indecent" building that had no ceiling, floor, or windows and that held only twenty people when two hundred communicants lived nearby. Services had been carried out in a more spacious building until Du Tisne took it as his lodgings. The priest reported that "[t]his officer has long been accused of abominable crime. There is certainly evidence against him." Years before, a young man under Du Tisne's command accused the officer of homosexuality in a petition to the council. Father Raphael also noted that "Sieur de Montigny, lieutenant of the garrison of the Natchez, likewise sent me his last summer, both offering to prove the fact, and a short time ago a young German boy came down who deposes the same thing and says that he left Sieur du Tisne whom he was serving, only because of this abomination." The priest protested "the scandal of his post and . . . the persecutions to which he has subjected the missionary who performs the functions of curate."[20]

Another infamous example involved Captain Beauchamp, who commanded a ship called the *Bellone* that suddenly and mysteriously sank off the coast of Dauphin Island in 1725. The ship, scheduled to depart for France, was heavily loaded with goods and passengers when it went down. Several people drowned, and all the goods were lost, including a valuable cargo of indigo. Father Raphael surmised that "a monstrous crime committed on this vessel by the captain . . . may have been enough to bring on this effect of the vengeance of the Lord." According to the priest, "The abominable relations of this wretch with a cabin-boy was so well established that the cabin-boy was taken from him and transferred to another vessel." The cabin boy had reported the captain's crime in writing, and the ship's surgeon, who had treated him for injuries suffered "in connection with this infamy," could provide additional evidence; many crew members also had knowledge of the affair. Despite the strong evidence against the captain, he suffered no punishment, and was only narrowly prevented from taking the boy away with him in violation of orders to the contrary. The episode caused great scandal. "In short the thing had become public; the entire town was filled with it." Though some people suspected foul play caused the shipwreck, Father Raphael wrote, "I am content to adore the conduct of divine providence and to think that in whatever way the thing may have happened our sins are the principal cause of it. . . . Without pretending to fathom the secrets of Heaven this can be attributed to the great disorders that prevail among us and which hitherto have been punished very little."[21]

If the priests and missionaries did not have enough problems attempting to impose order on such a disorderly colony, they compounded their problems by arguing among themselves. The most serious conflict was between the Jesuits and the Capuchins, who competed with one another for posts and influence within the colony. An effort was made to settle the dispute in 1722 by dividing the province of Louisiana into two spiritual jurisdictions, one in the south, for the Capuchins, with its seat at New Orleans, and one in the north, for the Jesuits, with its seat at Kaskaskias in the Illinois country. The company agreed to build churches and parsonages "in the places where it shall think it advisable" and provide funds for mission chapels, lodgings, and a salary for Indian missionaries. The company would pay for these expenses with a capitation tax on slaves. In 1728 the Capuchins had twelve members of their order in the colony, including posts at Biloxi and Natchez. The Jesuits operated a mission among the Yazoo, the southernmost point of their domain.[22]

Certainly the missionaries and priests had served the purposes of the kings of France in their efforts to create a vast empire in Louisiana, but the colony was far from successful. As late as 1715 only about four hundred French people lived in the colony, though the colony grew more rapidly once the royal government turned it over to John Law's Compagnie des Indies in 1717. By the mid-1720s the population of the Louisiana colony, excluding Native Americans, stood at about five thousand people, including thirteen hundred African slaves. Almost everyone in the colony agreed that its success depended on the institution of African slavery; indeed, cries for African slaves were second only to those for women. As early as 1706 Bienville noted that "[t]he colonists are very earnestly asking for negroes to cultivate their fields. They will pay cash for them." Native Americans allied to the French were willing to supply them with other Native Americans captured in war, but "the ease that they find to desert prevents the inhabitants from burdening themselves with them." Bienville suggested sending Indian slaves to slaveholders in the Caribbean who would send back black slaves, a plan that French officials seriously considered but found unfeasible. Instead, Pontchartrain promised in 1709 "in the future to induce French vessels to bring them there." Within less than a decade a few large parcels of African slaves were sold in the colony, but according to Bienville, it was "only in 1718 that serious thought was given to establishing Louisiana." Between 1717 and 1721, seven thousand Europeans and two thousand Africans flooded into the colony. Almost twenty-five hundred of the Europeans were bound laborers, engagés, who served three-year terms of indenture; over twelve hundred fifty of them were criminals, and about thirteen hundred were German recruits. The skewed gender ratios continued, for only twelve hundred fifteen of the total number were female. Despite the numbers, death took a high toll. Of seven thousand whites, at least half had either died or deserted the colony by 1725, and by

1723 only nine hundred African slaves labored in the colony. The Code Noir required that slaves should be taught the tenets of the Roman Catholic faith and further said that only Catholics could own slaves. Priests urged that it be enforced, but in reality how could a handful of priests serve as missionaries to the Indians and Africans *and* minister to the scattered European settlements? Father Raphael urged "that the ordinances of the black code against masters who abuse their slaves and make them work on Sundays and feast days . . . be put in force. . . . The profanation of Sundays and feast days is counted as almost nothing. . . ."[23]

The chronic population shortage was exacerbated by the exclusiveness of the Catholic Church. The idea of "one state, one church" was deeply ingrained in the very concept of the European nation-state. Even at home such a policy could be costly, as Louis XIV discovered when he expelled the French Huguenots in 1685 and lost hundreds of thousands of useful and prosperous merchants, artisans, and farmers. But while Louis was unwilling to tolerate French Huguenots within his kingdom or his empire, the chronic shortage of settlers for Louisiana induced the king to allow German Lutherans to settle there. John Law, the Scot who served as French minister of finance during the first two decades of the eighteenth century, aggressively recruited Germans and Alsatians to settle in Louisiana, and often entire villages relocated there. Most of them settled about thirty miles above New Orleans in an area called the German Coast. Catholic priests in the colony, however, resented the presence of the Lutherans among them. The commandant at the German Coast was Lutheran, and missionaries complained that "his religion . . . was an obstacle to the conversion of several of the inhabitants who are of the same sect." Priests were constantly on the lookout for non-Catholics. For example, Father Raphael complained that Mr. Perry, a member of the council, "has not attended the sacraments . . . and I am not quite sure what his religion is. There are some who are inclined to think that he is a Huguenot and his talk sometimes causes him to be suspected of being one." On another occasion Father Raphael criticized the commander at Natchez, Mr. de Merveilleux, "who makes public profession of the so-called reformed religion, so that this poor parish . . . is greatly to be pitied." The same priest complained about Mr. de Louboey, a highly decorated and capable officer, a Knight of the Order of St. Louis, but one who "had no religion at all, although he has renounced the Calvinism in which he was born." The priest referred to him as "an avowed heretic," for he lived openly with a woman not his wife who bore his children. Father Raphael thought "that disorders of this sort would be less prevalent if some exemplary punishment of them were inflicted." The priest reminded officials that "his Majesty does not permit the least officer of justice who does not profess the faith of the Roman church." To persecute and drive out non-Catholics may well have been the best way to create a pure church, but certainly not to build a successful colony. These disputes put the officials and priests at loggerheads; as Raphael reported, owing to "the manner in which we are treated by several members of the Council our ministry becomes almost useless."[24]

Because of the many problems plaguing the colony, in 1725 Bienville was recalled to France under a cloud. Back in France, he defended his administration in a lengthy history of the colony. As he surveyed the colony in 1726 after twenty-seven years as its commander, he recorded that the region had been "the most densely populated with Indians" in America, but that there now remained only "pitiful remnants . . . that are diminishing every day because of the different diseases that the Europeans have brought into the country and which were formerly unknown to the Indians." After carefully reviewing all the many tribes within the vast boundaries of Louisiana, he congratulated himself for "being in absolute control of so many different nations of such a barbarous disposition. . . ." He had won that position of control, he informed his superiors in France, by learning many native languages, manners, and customs, and by winning the natives' confidence and friendship. So successful was he, he boasted, that he became "the arbiter of all their disputes," and he even "governed despotically, so to speak, these nations . . . born in independence . . . to the point of dismissing even chiefs at my pleasure . . . and of obliging them whenever any of their number insulted a Frenchman . . . to bring me their heads and to come and ask me for peace which I never granted to them except on that condition."[25] How satisfying it must have been to relate his "absolute control" and despotic powers to the ministers of the king of France! Not even the Sun King could have his enemies' heads for merely insulting a Frenchman. It was a document filled with hubris befitting a character from Greek tragedy, and soon a tragedy struck that left his proud boasts in tatters.

Despite his claims, Bienville knew well that relations with the Indians were not as quiet and peaceful as he described them. In 1722 a quarrel at Fort Rosalie, situated up the Mississippi in the Natchez lands, had resulted in the deaths of several members of that tribe. In retaliation, Natchez from the White Apple village launched raids against French settlements; they killed an African slave, injured other residents, killed cattle, and stole livestock. Bienville "marched against them, burnt two of their villages and had twelve heads of the assassins brought to him and imposed upon them laws. . . ."[26] An uneasy peace ensued until 1728, when Sieur de Chepart became commandant at Fort Rosalie. He quickly alienated the Natchez, especially those at White Apple village, whom he planned to relocate entirely in order to take their valuable farmland.

Now set on revenge, the Natchez laid careful plans for an attack on the French settlement on November 28, 1729. They so humored Chepart, who was apparently drunk, that when seven men warned him that an attack was imminent, he locked them in irons. The Natchez scattered throughout the settlement, sometimes even borrowing guns from unsuspecting colonists with promises of venison in return. They also sought the support of the African slaves in the settlement by promising that "they would be free with the Indians . . . and that our wives and our children would be their slaves. . . ." Reportedly, the chief of the Natchez fired the first shot that killed Chepart at about eight o'clock in the morning, the signal that began the slaughter, which lasted until four o'clock in the afternoon. A total of a hundred forty-four men, thirty-five women, and fifty-six children died in the attack while about fifty French women and children were captured and some three hundred Africans apparently joined the Natchez. Among the dead was the Reverend Father Dupoisson, Jesuit missionary to the Natchez. After the carnage, the Natchez "had all the heads of the French brought to the public square with the booty that they had taken in order to divide it among themselves." According to one source, the heads of the officers were in one row opposite those of the colonists, a grim repayment for all the heads Bienville had demanded from them. The horrors of the slaughter must have led the missionaries to wonder what they had accomplished in the thirty years they had worked among the Natchez.[27]

More subtle clues about the Native Americans' attitude toward the European God appeared in the months that followed. The French persuaded the Choctaws to attack the Natchez. The victorious Choctaws recovered almost all of the women and children and about one hundred Africans who fought bravely against them beside the Natchez. The Choctaws held onto some of their captives, including most of the Africans, until they were rewarded by the French for their efforts. Father Beaudouin was a member of the French delegation that went to negotiate with the Choctaws. At a feast and dance, supposedly held in the Frenchmen's honor, the Choctaws engaged in a macabre ritual of their own: "The Indian who was leading had a paten hanging about his neck, another a sacred ciborium at his side, this one with a maniple on his arm and all the others were adorned with the clothes of the French that they had won. . . ." The paten is a flat dish used to hold the consecrated bread in the eucharist, the ciborium a covered cup used for the same purpose, and a maniple one of the eucharistic vestments, a piece of cloth a few feet in length suspended over the left arm by the celebrant. It seems difficult to believe that the Indians were ignorant of the importance of these sacred objects to the French, most particularly to Father Beaudouin, who had to use trade goods to recover the sacred vessels adorning the native dancers. Did the Choctaws fully appreciate the multiple layers of meaning involved in dressing themselves in the sacred vessels linked with the sacrificial blood and body of the Christian God, vessels stolen in a bloody massacre that very likely held sacrificial symbolism for the Natchez, who carried out the slayings? It is impossible to know, though the scene seems too carefully contrived to be accidental. The Choctaws told Father Beaudouin about a chalice belonging to another priest who died in the massacre that was in other hands, suggesting that they knew very well what such objects were. Later that evening one of the chiefs came to him at bedtime and said "that he had a coat like his and at once he went and got a front cloth of a funeral altar which the Reverend Father Beudouin [sic] obtained from him by trading."[28]

Bienville had tried to dismiss the Native Americans in Louisiana as a pitiful remnant, but they were strong enough to fatally weaken France's hold over the region. As a result of the disastrous massacre at Natchez, the Company of the Indies surrendered its monopoly, and Louisiana became a royal colony. In 1733 Bienville, once again restored to royal favor, returned to resume his post of governor. The later decades of French rule were dominated by wars and Indian troubles growing out of the colonial contest between France and England. Bienville conducted two disastrous campaigns against the Chickasaws in 1736 and 1739–40. The colony was still underpopulated, and, while the colonists carried on a limited commerce in deer skins, naval stores, tobacco, indigo, and rice, prosperity eluded them. Religion was no more prosperous. When Bienville returned in 1733 he noted that religious life languished in the colony because of a lack of priests, perpetual bickering between the Jesuits and the Capuchins, and inadequate finances. "It is disgraceful for religion," he wrote, "that from . . . ten leagues above New Orleans as far as ten leagues below there is only the single curacy of the city. How many inhabitants [there are] who pass entire years without hearing mass and who forget, so to speak, that they are Christians!"[29]

French rule came to a rather ignominious close when Louisiana was made a bargaining chip in the negotiations ending the Seven Years War in 1763. French territory west of the Mississippi, including the Isle of Orleans, became the Spanish colony of Louisiana, and territory east of the Mississippi became the British colony of West Florida. In what could be considered his final official act, the aged former governor Bienville, approaching ninety, joined a representative from Louisiana to lodge a formal protest against the transfer.[30]

The British were not greatly impressed with their new province; one English official referred to it as "a useless territory," and, upon his arrival, Lieutenant Governor Montfort Browne described its "melancholy and deplorable situation." At the time of the transfer, the entire colony had a population of about seven thousand whites and six thousand African slaves, heavily concentrated around New Orleans. Browne was, however, struck by the potential of the western portion of the province around Natchez. He surveyed the area on a 1766 expedition and afterwards devoted "considerable attention" to its development. His efforts were rewarded, and the Natchez region became the most rapidly growing part of the British province. The district had few settlers in 1770, but by 1774 about three thousand people resided there, and in 1777 these settlements were in a "flourishing condition." Religion was not of paramount concern for the British, though Governor Peter Chester proposed to offer free transport to all Protestants who would settle in the province. According to the terms of the Treaty of Paris of 1763, England agreed to extend religious toleration to Catholics in the colony, but when French Catholics requested the appointment of a priest, the English made it clear that there was no provision for that in the treaty. The bishop of London, through the Church of England's missionary arm, called the Society for the Propagation of the Gospel in Foreign Parts, selected Anglican priests for West Florida, who were paid by the state. Given the scattered and sparse population, only two Anglican priests came to the colony, one to Mobile and one to Pensacola, though both places were often without ministers. There is no record of organized Protestant worship in the territory that became Mississippi until 1773, when Richard and Samuel Swayze moved from New Jersey and settled near Natchez in an area that became known as the Jersey Settlement. Samuel Swayze was a Congregational minister, "and most of the adults who came with him were communicants."[31]

With the outbreak of the American Revolution, West Florida became an official asylum for British Loyalists, and a steady stream of prosperous new settlers arrived, "families of wealth and distinction," many of them with slaves. In 1779 British officials in Pensacola learned that Spain had joined France in the war against Britain. Although the military commanders at Natchez and other garrisons prepared for an invasion from Spanish Louisiana, those preparations were inadequate to resist the force launched by Don Bernardo de Galvez, governor of the Spanish colony, who quickly captured the Natchez district and by 1781 had all of West Florida. As a result, as many as a third of the residents fled the colony, particularly those Loyalist emigrants, some of whom had resisted the Spaniards with force of arms.[32]

The Spanish learned from the French example and knew that their colony could not flourish without a larger population, which was not available in Spain. Given the peculiarities of the colony, the Catholic religion could not serve as an instrument of empire as it had for the French and as it did for the Spanish in other parts of the Americas. Instead, Catholicism was a serious obstacle to overcome in the eyes of Protestant immigrants.

As early as 1785 the governor-general of Louisiana, Esteban Rodriguez Miró y Sabater, proposed establishing a parish in Natchez staffed by Irish priests who could then teach and convert non-Catholics in the region. Viceroy Conde de Gálvez approved the plan, and the call went out across Spain for suitable priests. In 1787 Miró appointed an immigration agent in Kentucky and published broadsides inviting immigrants to Louisiana. Petitions flooded in, but over and over again those petitioners demanded religious freedom as a precondition for their settlement. Such demands help account for Miró's proclamation issued on April 20, 1789, that immigrants would "not be molested on religious matters, although no other public worship will be permitted to be publickly exercised than that of [the] Roman catholic Church." Once immigrants settled in the colony, the governor hoped to convert them. A later decree explained that once the English-speaking population grew, a number of Irish priests would be brought in to "teach and attract the colonists, their children and families to our Religion with the suavity and good method which the Church counselled."[33]

Manuel Gayoso de Lemos, governor of the Fort of Natchez, supported the plan, which got off to a promising start. Four young men answered the call for Irish priests and arrived in New Orleans in 1787, when they were promptly assigned to their respective posts, including Natchez and Nogales (now Vicksburg). William Savage served in Natchez from 1787 until his death in 1793, the first of several Irish priests to hold the post. One of Gayoso's additional duties was to supervise construction of churches, which he did with great energy. He approved plans drawn by a New Orleans military engineer and architect in 1790, and on June 12, 1791, Father Savage held the benediction ceremony in the new church, the first church in what would become Mississippi since the French buildings in Biloxi, grandiosely named Iglesia Parroquial del Salvador del Mundo de Natchez (Parish Church of Our Savior of the World in Natchez) by the priest. The governor held a celebration afterwards.[34]

On the surface, at least, the plan seemed well under way. The call for Irish priests had been answered, and everyone agreed that Savage was a gifted preacher, well suited to attract a Protestant congregation. Conflicts between Gayoso and Savage soon arose, as so often happens when politicians attempt to use the church to further their own ends. Spanish governors had wide powers over church affairs; any area other than dogma—the creation of new dioceses and parishes, the choice of priests to fill positions, for instance—was approved by church officials but in reality implemented by governors. Gayoso, as proud as any proverbial Spaniard, guarded his powers over the church jealously. When Father Savage announced the date for the consecration of the church without having cleared it with Gayoso, the governor changed the date. Savage responded by arriving an hour late while the governor sat and stewed in front of the assembly. To add insult to injury, the following week he began his sermon an hour early. Gayoso, now furious, demanded that the vicar general of Louisiana reprimand Savage.[35]

Despite these petty conflicts, Gayoso recognized his loss when Savage died. Father Francis Lennan, another of the Irish priests, followed Savage, but his overt hostility to Protestants threatened to drive them away and foil Gayoso's well-laid plans. The Protestants, many of them wealthy and well educated, composed the bedrock of the district. As Gayoso complained, Catholics were few, "mainly Irish and not the best people of their nation . . . of turbulent and intriguing spirits." Despite Lennan's hostile stance, Gayoso continued his remarkably tolerant policy toward non-Catholics. In one case in 1769, a prominent resident, Benjamin Monsanto, a Jewish merchant, planter, and lumber dealer, was expelled from the colony, though whether or not his religion was a factor is debated, since he was also accused of smuggling. It appears that other members of the family remained in Natchez. Certainly, Spanish law, like the French Code Noir, prohibited Jews from emigrating to Spanish colonies, though Gayoso might well have turned a blind eye.[36]

Lennan's opposition to Gayoso's tolerant policy soon caused major problems for the governor. The policy strictly prohibited the public exercise of any religion other than the Catholic faith, but Gayoso did not rigorously enforce this measure. Samuel Swayze, for example, continued to hold his services in the Jersey Settlement. Swayze reportedly hid his Bible in a hollow sycamore tree and abandoned public services for secret ones until his death in 1784, though the meetings were certainly an open secret. His son carried on the services for a few years, but, when he died, the church was not reorganized. Perhaps the fact that these services took place outside town in a self-contained settlement made them easier to ignore.

Violations in Natchez were a different matter. Under pressure from Lennan, Gayoso ordered the arrest of John Bolls, a Presbyterian elder who preached in Natchez, though Bolls's strong republican sympathies may have also played a part. The governor himself was said to have attended a sermon by Adam Cloud, an Episcopalian who lived at Villa Gayoso on Cole's Creek, where the governor maintained a summer residence. According to one source, as Gayoso left the service, he expressed his support for toleration of them, but added, "You know I have a master." It soon became evident that the governor had a master, for Cloud's enemies complained to Governor-General Francisco de Carondelet, Gayoso's superior, who ordered Cloud's expulsion over Gayoso's protests.[37]

Another problem was brewing on Cole's Creek, where Richard Curtis, Jr., a gifted Baptist preacher, was gaining converts. In 1780 the family of Richard Curtis, Sr., and Phoebe Jones Curtis had moved from South Carolina to the Spanish territory. The family included five sons and three daughters, along with John Jones, Jr., Phoebe's son by a previous marriage, and his wife, all committed Baptists. After a dangerous trip through Indian territory, they arrived safely in Mississippi and settled about twenty miles above Natchez. Given the Spanish regulations, they met secretly in their homes for services, but their meetings, probably an open secret like the earlier Jersey Settlement services, "soon attracted the attention of the American portion of the population. . . ."[38]

Here Gayoso confronted an entirely new breed of Protestant heretofore unknown in the colony, an evangelical. The governor only dimly perceived the revolutionary potential of these settlers, who more than any others challenged his view of what shape the community should take. Implicit in the early Baptist movement and deeply embedded within it was a form of social revolt. Gayoso envisioned a settlement where various religious beliefs would be tolerated, but only one church, the Catholic Church, would meet. With other religions thus marginalized, settlers would be attracted by English-speaking services to the only church, their children would be educated there, and, within a generation, Catholicism would emerge triumphant. Baptists challenged this vision in a variety of ways. First, at the heart of Baptist theology lay a belief in the spiritual equality of all believers; the only authority they recognized was that exercised by brothers and sisters in Christ meeting in fellowship. Their preachers were not selected by a governor but raised up from within the congregation after receiving a "call" to exercise that gift before others. Such a call could fall on any man, black or white, from any station in life without reference to family connections, status, or education. They recognized no parish lines, and there was no suggestion that their churches encompassed everyone with certain boundaries. This was a community based on faith, a community that quite consciously separated itself from the larger community, in ways completely antithetical to Gayoso's vision.

Perhaps Gayoso could have ignored even these meetings, but problems developed when new converts, including a Spaniard, wanted to be baptized. Curtis, who was licensed but not ordained, could not perform the rite of baptism, so central to his sect. In an effort to resolve this dilemma, Curtis wrote his church in South Carolina, which advised him to have his congregation elect a member to perform the ritual. Naturally, Curtis was chosen and began to baptize converts, probably in Cole's Creek itself, since the ritual was a highly public one. As their numbers grew, the Baptists became more bold. "[B]elieving their cause was the cause of God, . . . [they] bid their opponents defiance, and even went so far as to have their places of worship guarded by armed men, while they denounced in no very moderate terms the 'image worship' and other unscriptural dogmas and ceremonies of the Catholic Church." Despite Gayoso's leniency, he could not ignore such flagrant challenges. In a letter to Gayoso, Ebenezer Drayton, a Presbyterian, dismissed the Baptists as "weak men, of weak minds, and illiterate, and too ignorant to know how inconsistent they act and talk . . . too weak and undesigning to lay any treasonable plans. . . ." But he warned Gayoso, quite correctly, that "they would call any chastisement from Government for their disobedience, persecution, and suffering for Christ. . . ."[39]

In April 1795 Gayoso wrote Curtis ordering him to curb his activities. When Curtis refused, he was arrested and taken before the exasperated Gayoso, who threatened to expel him. For a time, the Americans accepted the prohibitions, but, as their numbers grew, they became "more and more clamorous for religious, as well as civil, liberty." Carondelet warned that the Curtis case demonstrated that "if disputes and quarrels over religion are not cut off at their roots . . . they will have the most perverse and evil results." As if to verify his prediction, the Baptists resumed their meetings, and Gayoso ordered the arrest of Curtis and two others, one of them Spanish, who fled to South Carolina where Curtis was regularly ordained.[40]

The Baptist challenge to Spanish authority did not end with their flight. In 1795 Spain and the United States signed the Treaty of San Lorenzo, highly favorable to the United States, which transferred Natchez to the Americans. The number of Americans in the territory had increased in anticipation of the Spanish evacuation, an event they continually delayed, much to the annoyance of the Americans. Under the watchful eye of American officials on the scene to carry out the transfer, evangelical ministers preached under the Stars and Stripes to "immense congregations." Barton Hannon, an itinerant Baptist preacher, delivered inflammatory anti-Catholic sermons, and "being a weak man, was extremely puffed up with the attention he received. . . ." A native of Virginia who arrived in the territory in 1795, Hannon was a shoemaker who first emigrated to Alabama where he raised livestock before moving to Natchez. Emboldened by his newfound popularity and "a little heightened by liquor," he rashly "entered into a religious controversy in a disorderly part of town" inhabited by Irish Catholics, who "gave him a beating." Hannon demanded that the Irishmen be punished and threatened to do the job himself if Gayoso refused to have it done. Clearly, Hannon knew as little about Gayoso as about Irishmen, for the governor ordered Hannon placed in stocks inside the local fort.[41]

Armed guards escorted Hannon through town toward the fort. The preacher tried to escape and called on his fellow Americans to help him. Quickly recaptured and placed in stocks, Hannon became a symbol of American resistance; three hundred armed settlers, including a group at Cole's Creek, threatened to attack Natchez, capture Gayoso, and exchange him for Hannon. Meanwhile, Gayoso appealed to Carondelet for troops, and violence appeared imminent. Gayoso's calm but firm response and the efforts of more level-headed Americans prevented conflict, though the angry men at Cole's Creek were the last to lay down their arms. Gayoso's generous treatment of the rebels persuaded the discontents to obey Spanish law until the transition to American rule was completed the following year.[42]

Mississippi's evangelical revolt came at the close of the age of empire.

At the end of the period as at the beginning, the relationship between faith and government was a conflicted one. As an instrument of empire, religion had been tried and found wanting. For the empire builders, particularly the initial conquerors, religion did serve to legitimate their claims to the land they occupied and the means they employed to subdue the inhabitants. The French found that missionaries could be useful agents among the Native Americans; their role as cultural mediators, as conduits of information and cultural exchange, was extremely significant during the colonial era. From a religious perspective, however, their impact among the Native Americans was marginal. Only the Apalachees, who had been converted by the Spanish, seemed to have genuinely embraced the faith. Paradoxically, religion may have been most unsatisfactory as a tool of empire *within* the European colonial communities. As a locus of power often at odds with the secular authorities, the church was more a source of conflict than consensus. In addition, the exclusive nature of state churches hampered settlement and trapped European officials in a maze of inconsistencies. As Gayoso discovered, the contradictions between a state church and religious tolerance were practically irreconcilable, and his efforts to reconcile them ended predictably in disaster.

The state of society in this Territory is truely deplorable. Most of the emigrants to this country came here for the purpose of amassing wealth, and that object seems to have absorbed their souls.

—JOHN F. SCHERMERHORN
AND SAMUEL J. MILLS[1]

I fear religion is at a low ebb in the Mississippi Territory. When cotton bore a price, the people had enough to talk about their large crops & riches, now its [sic] their poverty. . . .

—LAURNER BLACKMAN[2]

2 "Religion Is a Fortune": Frontier Culture Wars, 1797–1830

Probably the first poem published in Mississippi outside the newspapers was a ribald satire called *Rab & Jane: A Legendary Tale, (and True)*. The poet aimed his doggerel at readers of "good breeding." Set in Washington, the story opened when Burwell awoke at 1:00 A.M. suffering with "chronic dysentery." After relieving himself, he heard voices coming from the nearby church (which had to be an evangelical church since no others existed in the town). When Burwell peeked between the logs, he saw Rab and Jane engaged in sexual intercourse on the church floor! The author described Rab as a prominent politician, one of the territory's "*great ones.*" When Jane was overcome by guilt, Rab attempted to allay her fears:

> P'rhaps reason or philosophy
> May furnish some relief.
> When nature made the human race,
> She male and female made them—
> With inclinations warm for love,
> Which to indulge she bade them;

There were no cursed *parsons* then;
With fears of hell to frighten—
. . . Thus nature led mankind of yore,
And happiness abounded—
Till crafty priests enslav'd the mind—
And nature's plans confounded:
They lucre-led, first target the weak—
Enjoyment was an evil—
And . . . common sense decay'd—
No soul could wed, be born, or die—
But Mr. Priest was paid![3]

Repeatedly, the author asserted that these religious sentiments had spread among "the vulgar race," and "the rabble." The poem was clearly written half in jest and might easily be dismissed as a bit of foolery, but it opens a window onto the culture wars then under way in territorial Mississippi.

The poem's theme of illicit sex, its libertine monologue, and its classical allusions are drawn directly from a type of burlesque verse popular in the British world since the early eighteenth century.[4] Unlike earlier examples, however, this piece targeted the evangelicals, ridiculed their incessant attacks on the pleasures of the flesh, and portrayed their preachers as money-grubbers. In keeping with the conventions of that cultured and mannered society they so closely imitated, worldly gentlemen took delight in ridiculing their inferiors in prose.

Early Mississippi society was composed of diverse cultures, among them those of the planter elite, the plain folk, and enslaved Africans and African Americans. These cultural systems sometimes overlapped, sometimes reinforced one another, and sometimes conflicted. One of the most dramatic of the cultural wars that erupted in the early South pitted the planter elite against the evangelicals, who drew their strength primarily from the plain folk. It is impossible to separate the evangelical movement in early Mississippi from the plantation revolution under way at the same time. The formative power of the plantation revolution can scarcely be overestimated; it brought sweeping demographic, economic, political, social, and cultural change to Mississippi. This period was one of dramatic transformation during which ambitious and resourceful "borderland gentlemen" laid the groundwork for their economic, social, and political mastery.[5] But that domination did not come without resistance, and religion provided cultural constructs through which nonelites expressed their opposition to their elite opponents.

When the United States took possession of the Natchez District in 1797, there were about five thousand people in the Mississippi Territory, 40 percent of them enslaved Africans and African Americans. Already, the future contours of Mississippi society had largely taken shape, and the elements that would dominate the region throughout the antebellum period—plantation agriculture, slavery, and cotton—were firmly in place. Cotton had become an important crop by about 1793, the first public gin opened in 1796, and by 1798 the region had produced 1,200,000 pounds of the fleecy white staple. The region's first governor, the phlegmatic Massachusetts native Winthrop Sargent, described Natchez as "*a most abominable place*," teeming with Catholics, Spanish criminals, Africans, and Indians. Though still a frontier, the territory was already producing great riches; in 1797, for example, one prominent planter, Stephen Minor, sold his cotton crop for $51,200. A wealthy planter elite dominated the territory's economic and political life, but a population boom following the United States's takeover brought thousands of small farmers into the region.[6] Here, as in other parts of the South, the plain folk challenged planter supremacy, and evangelical religion helped define this challenge.

Natchez, with a population of about fifteen hundred, was the only town of any consequence in the territory, the center of trade, and the primary seat of the planter elite. Neither the wealthy planters who resided on the bluffs nor the riverboat men and gamblers who congregated below the hill were much interested in religion. Evangelicals lamented the town's wickedness much as Old Testament prophets had invoked Nineveh or Babylon as icons of worldly evil. In 1803 Methodist evangelist Lorenzo Dow reported that "there were not three Christians in the town, either white or black" and called it the center of "irreligion and every form of vice." His fellow Methodist, Jacob Young, looked aghast at "Americans, French, Spaniards, English, Irish, Dutch, negroes, and mulattoes—all mingling as 'fellows well met.' Many Kentuckians were lying in their flatboats, along the wharf, drinking, fighting, swearing, and acting like demons."[7]

While the riverboat men drank, fought, and whored in the shanties below the hill, the self-styled "nabobs"of Natchez and the plantation region could afford to live luxuriously, and beginning about 1810 they built imposing mansions as symbols of their wealth and social dominance. In 1812 the architect Levi Weeks described one of these mansions: "The brick house I am now building . . . is designed for the most magnificent building in the territory. The body of this house is 60 by 45 feet with a portico of 31 feet projecting 12 feet supported by 4 Ionic collums with the Corinthian entabliture [sic]. . . . The site is one of those peculiar situations which combines all the delight of romance, the pleasures of rurality and the approach of sublimity." These elegant edifices, filled with imported furnishings, polished silver, family portraits, and other trappings of wealth and status, stood in such contrast to the humble farmhouses of the plain folk that they referred to the planters as the "pillared folk," a reference to the mighty columns that dominated the facades of many of these residences like the one described by Weeks.[8]

Along with the mansions and furnishings came the other trappings of wealth and civility that defined cosmopolitan, genteel culture in the period. Aspiring planters did their best to imitate polite society as it existed in the cities of the eastern seaboard, and by extension, in Britain. When Andrew Ellicott visited Natchez in 1797 he wrote: "The natives of the southern part of the Mississippi are generally a sprightly people, and appear to have a natural turn for . . . painting, music, and the polite accomplishments. . . . Many of the planters . . . enjoy life not only in plenty but affluence, and generally possess the virtues of hospitality. . . ."[9] The virtues of hospitality included polite conversation, or what another visitor called "brisk and cheerful Conversation," and a well-laden table. One grateful guest complimented his host's "talent for entertaining" and described a "superb dinner" in 1798 "of game and fish, dried fruits, and madeira fit for the gods." Such feasts were often followed by parties enlivened with drinks and dances. So common was the practice that one writer suggested that "their conduct in general was drinking and dancing." Drinking required no special skills, but dancing masters operated schools to bring the latest steps to those wealthy enough to afford lessons. Horse racing was the favorite sport among the pillared folk. A track called Fleetfield was laid out in 1795, where nabobs like William Dunbar and Stephen Minor raced their horses and bet on the outcome. Elite planters organized the exclusive Mississippi Jockey Club, bought expensive thoroughbreds, and laid out the track. The sport provided an outlet for planters to publicly display their self-assertion, their competitiveness, and their liberality.[10]

The theater was another popular entertainment among the pillared folk, and, in Natchez, as in other parts of the Anglo-American world, "plays mapped the fashionable terrain. . . ." The Natchez Theatrical Association, organized in the early 1800s by elite young men, had staged twenty-eight performances by 1817. The city council praised its "laudable purpose of improving the manners and morals of the citizens." A prologue delivered at the opening of the 1816 season also praised the theater as "[t]he nurse of morals and the school for men . . ." and concluded that "The *Theatre* has been, is now, will always be, / Virtue's resort, the *throne of sympathy*." The idea that the theater was the "nurse of morals" outraged evangelicals, but it was the nabobs' determination to segregate themselves from those below them on the social ladder that caused trouble. Laurner Blackman, a Methodist preacher, rejoiced in 1812 that "[i]n the city of Natchez the Devils Kingdom is divided against itself. They have had one playhouse burned down by the mechanics. They have erected a new one. Mechanics are not allowed to attend . . . it is supposed that they burnt down the former & that they will burn the latter likewise. So we may hope the Devils Kingdom will fall." As this case suggests, another feature of the "virtues of hospitality" was exclusivity. One visitor reported that "[a]s there are no publichouses, a spirit of hospitality is kept up between neighbors. This hospitality . . . is only shown amongst neighbors, or the friends of neighbors. . . ."[11]

This exclusive society was reinforced through a variety of private clubs and societies. For example, in 1803 a group of influential gentlemen established the Mississippi Society for the Acquirement and Dissemination of Useful Knowledge, only one of the several reading societies established in the town. Such clubs were an integral part of the process of social refinement under way in American and British towns and cities. Prominent men also joined the Ancient Order of Free and Accepted Masons, whose secrecy and quasi-religious origins and rituals (they claimed descent from the builders of Solomon's Temple) earned them the evangelicals' special scorn. Baptist churches, for example, prohibited their members from joining secret societies and expelled members who joined the Masonic Order.[12]

Another elite institution, Jefferson College, trained the sons of the planters. Established in 1803, the college came under fire from evangelicals in 1818 when an evangelical religious convention resolved that "Jefferson College was conducted on principles, in which 'an almost total dereliction' of Christian duties was obvious." After an editorial in the local press condemned the resolution as "an assumption of power over the minds and consciouses of the people," the evangelicals shot back with a pointed statement of their own mandate. In their view, "The members of the convention are under the command of the 'Captain of the Lord's Host.' It is theirs to assail with holy and yet kindly violence, every thing that exalteth itself 'against the Lord and the Annointed.' " This conflict may help explain why evangelicals formed a Sunday school in Natchez in 1819, reputedly the first south of Philadelphia.[13]

The lifestyle of the plain folk stood in sharp contrast to that of the pillared folk. Instead of stately mansions, hastily erected log cabins served as houses for the plain folk. As William Winans reported, pioneers built "a mere shelter, their most important business was to bring their lands into cultivation, that they might provide subsistence for themselves and for those dependent on them." Winans himself built such a cabin, then added another room, and finally built another cabin parallel to the first and connected them with an open hallway. This was the typical plain-folk dwelling—"the usual term applied to such a structure was that it was 'two pens and a passage.' " According to one resident, "In no country that ever I have seen, is so little attention paid to comfortable living, as among the common people of Louisiana and Mississippi." He reported that "[t]he men are generally idle, devoted to hunting, and the attention of their numerous herds. . . . The poorer sort work some, are fond of drinking, gambling and horse racing. . . ." In contrast to the groaning dinner tables of the rich, the poor subsisted on "a mess of *mush* and milk" or a "mess of fish fried in bear's oil."[14]

In Mississippi the plain folk challenged the pillared folks' virtues of hospitality with the ascetic virtues of their evangelical faith. Only in this context can evangelical rules against dancing, drinking, luxurious dress, gambling, horse racing, attending the theater, and joining secret societies be properly understood. Drawn primarily from the lower orders, the evangelicals attacked almost every aspect of the refined culture the gentry had created, and the elite stage settings for ritual displays of social dominance became cultural battlegrounds. Ruffles and silks became emblems of sinful vanity and indulgence, drunkenness, dancing, and gambling evidence of worldliness and dissipation. The evangelicals defined themselves as a "counterculture," and in their close-knit communities they embraced an egalitarian fellowship. They called one another brother and sister and recognized no superiority except that of the spirit, with some even questioning slavery as they welcomed slaves into their fellowship. Emboldened by the transforming effects of the New Birth, evangelicals entered a new religious community with values dramatically at odds with those of the elite. Methodists enforced a strict dress code among their congregants and rebuked members who drank to excess. James Axley, a minister of humble origins, "declaimed earnestly against superfluous ornaments, and the passions, pride and vanity which occasion them." At an 1808 camp meeting, "The congregation was unusually large . . . and some of them splendidly dressed." Axley caused a major disturbance as he hammered home "his favorite theme, the pride and vain-glory of the people of that territory. . . ."[15]

The worldly symbolism of rich attire carried over even to church members, and evangelical prohibitions against elaborate dress were one part of their ongoing crusade to discredit the virtues of hospitality. Winans reported in 1821, for example, that he "[r]ead and enforced the Rules dwelling with peculiar emphasis on those respecting dress and dram drinking." On another occasion he complained of Sister Vick, who "fashionable in dress and independent in spirit will not conform to M[ethodist]. Discipline tho' in society." In 1820 the members of Salem Church resolved "that wearing of earrings shall not be admissible in Church members." Churches disciplined their members for drinking, dancing, gambling, and horse racing—in short, for virtually all the pastimes associated so closely with the pillared folks' hospitality, individual competitiveness, and display of wealth and status.[16]

The evangelical movement has been described as a "counterculture" because it shaped an ideal vision of society in opposition to that of the pillared folk and challenged the virtues of hospitality with the ascetic virtues of evangelical faith. Evangelicals staged a "revolt" against the traditional rituals of the more conservative churches—a dynamic part of a broader process of "democratization" under way across the young Republic. Their new forms of worship, their camp meetings, and even their language reflected their hostility to elite culture. The rise of evangelicalism in Mississippi, then, was a powerful movement of social and cultural change. More than any other event, the Great Revival defined that revolt. From its hearth in central Kentucky, the revival blazed across Mississippi as it swept the frontier and brought thousands of converts into the evangelical fold. Increasingly, the lower classes challenged gentry domination and the hierarchical social structure that supported it. Deference gave way to competition and individual autonomy. Religion was an important battleground between the gentry and the plain folk, and evangelicals won that battle through the camp meeting revivals, helping to lay a foundation for the young Republic.[17]

On the surface, the early Mississippi evangelicals looked like Davids engaged in a struggle with mighty Goliaths; they were primarily from the lower class, they were poor, and they did not control the government. Appearances could be deceptive, however. The rock in their sling was an ideology with enormous appeal in their society. Like any successful ideology, theirs brought converts, in this case through a dramatic and life-altering "New Birth" that completely changed the lives of evangelicals who experienced it. The New Birth was an integrative experience, one that brought converts a sense of empowerment that prepared them to do battle with the local elites. That ideology spread through words—through sermons, songs, and voices, which were now given new powers of social definition. Through their emotional services, especially in the camp meetings, evangelicals created new identities for themselves, their region, and ultimately for the entire nation.

In territorial Mississippi, society was more stratified than in other frontier regions, and the plain folk and pillared folk were divided by wide cultural, economic, and ideological gulfs. James Pearse, a young emigrant from Vermont, published an account of his residence in early Mississippi for other "men of ordinary life" who might consider moving there. His narrative bristled with revolutionary democratic idealism and expressed a yeoman class ideology based on agrarian virtues and a belief that small, independent farmers were the bedrock of the Republic. The nabobs' acquisitiveness and ostentatious displays of luxury had no place in a republican society. He described the "great distinction between the different classes" in the Natchez District and wrote that "[f]ew, who are raised to affluence, have any feelings for those below their rank. . . . The master is proud and overbearing on all below his imaginary greatness, whether white or black; often cruel, and pleased with a display of needless power."[18]

But were their displays of power "needless"? The planter elite were engaged in a quest for mastery: mastery of their physical environment, of their emerging society's social and political systems, and of their own households, including thousands of enslaved African Americans who resisted them at every turn. As one gentleman poet phrased it in 1805, "Pow'r is . . . a glorious thing— / From common rules it frees one, / And gives a liberty to act, / Just as it best may please one."[19] Implied in that statement of the liberating effects of power was a repudiation of the evangelical lifestyle, the limits it placed on individual behavior and its strict code of conduct.

Evangelicals struggled to gain a foothold in Natchez. The Methodists built a little meeting house there in 1807, but for the first ten years it barely survived. The Baptists did not even manage to establish a church there until after the territory became a state in 1817. In 1815 the Presbyterians had a new church, but no preacher. Prospects looked grim indeed; a preacher who visited the town in 1812 found the people "very rich, very proud and very polite," but with "little humility, little religion and little piety."[20]

Natchez's position as a freewheeling river town made it unusually irreligious, but across the country in the decades following the American Revolution churches fell into decline. The disestablishment of churches, the destruction of church property during the Revolution, the massive westward migration, a widespread economic depression, and the focus on creating new governments diverted attention away from worship. Without state support, religion was left to fend for itself in the marketplace of ideas. Despite the Protestant missionaries' best efforts, evangelical churches attracted only a few hundred members before 1810. There were hopeful

signs, however, even on the Mississippi frontier. The rising tide of immigration brought more and more converts into the region. In fact, the communal nature of evangelical churches provided the basis for entire
congregations to migrate to the territory. Richard Curtis, Sr., and his fellow Baptists provide an early example of such communal emigration patterns, but many other cases exist. In 1804, for example, a group of one
hundred Baptists began a dangerous journey from the Beaufort district of
South Carolina. They arrived in the territory in 1805 near the future town
of Woodville and built Bethel Baptist Church.[21]

The Baptists at Cole's Creek built the territory's first Protestant meeting house. When Curtis and his friends returned from South Carolina
after Natchez passed into American hands, they found a church already
built. Curtis officially organized the church in 1798; appropriately, after
years of conflict, the Baptists called their church Salem, meaning
"peace."[22] The Methodists organized their first church in 1799 in Washington, the territorial capital, under the ministry of the Reverend Tobias
Gibson, an unmarried, handsome, well-educated South Carolinian who
had relatives in the Natchez area. He was described as "cheerful enough
when spoken to but generally very serious and solemn and much retireing.
His preaching was [a] little alarming but mostly inviting." The Methodists
sent several other missionaries to the territory, but their task was a difficult
one; when Gibson died in 1804, only 132 whites and 72 blacks belonged
to Methodist churches.[23]

The Presbyterians, plagued by a shortage of ministers because of their
high educational requirements, were even slower to establish themselves
in the territory. In 1801 three missionaries sent by the Synod of Carolina
arrived in the Natchez District, where they collected congregations but
did not establish churches. In 1804 the Presbyterians organized their first
church near Uniontown, in the Natchez region. One of their most prominent early ministers, the Reverend James Smylie, a North Carolinian of
Highland Scots ancestry, arrived in the territory in 1805 as a missionary
from the Synod of Carolina. He established several churches in Amite and
Adams counties, and became one of the most influential ministers in the
Old Southwest.[24]

Adam Cloud, who had been banished from the territory in 1790 for
preaching in violation of Spanish law, returned and in 1820 established

the first Episcopal church, Christ Church, at Church Hill in Jefferson County. The Episcopalians catered to the planter elite, but they also found that the wealthy planters were more interested in the virtues of hospitality than the virtues of Christianity. The Episcopal Diocese of Mississippi was organized in 1826 with only four churches, five priests, and about a hundred members.[25]

The evangelicals found their greatest strength outside Natchez among the farmers and plain folk. Laurner Blackman, a Methodist missionary who arrived in the territory around 1804, wrote that many of the "Old Settlers" were "so rich they are above religion and religion is above them." The poor, on the other hand, were "mostly very ignorant," and he found it "difficult to make impress on their minds about religion. . . ." Blacks, he wrote, were numerous but "mostly very wicked." Only "[a] few of the old inhabitants that hold a mediocrity in life embrace religion and do honor to the cause. . . ."[26]

The pillared folk, who saw themselves above religion, could hardly have been prepared for the challenge to their exalted positions posed by the revolutionary camp meetings. Methodist bishop Francis Asbury described the camp meeting as "[t]he battle ax and weapon of war . . . ," a military metaphor that reflected the intensity of the struggle and the effectiveness of the meetings as a weapon. Camp meetings were held in clearings in the woods, which isolated people from the world around them. A preachers' stand—a raised structure, sometimes roofed and partially walled, from which the sermons were delivered—dominated the meeting ground. The open area directly in front of the stand was padded with straw to receive those converts who experienced the dramatic "physical exercises" that quickly became the hallmark of a successful meeting. Services began early and continued all through the day and late into the night. Meetings were notoriously noisy, for the evangelicals flouted their society's norms of acceptable behavior as a part of their revolt against elite culture.[27]

Camp meetings began in the early 1800s and quickly became institutionalized. The famous but eccentric Methodist evangelist Lorenzo Dow, who claimed to have been carried up to heaven in a whirlwind at the age of thirteen, held the first camp meeting on Mississippi soil in 1805. Critical articles in the Natchez press created considerable public interest, and

the big event was scheduled for the town of Washington, outside the nabobs' citadel at Natchez. Dow wrote that the meeting took a serious turn
when "[a]n old backslider, who had been happy in the old settlements,
with tears came forward and fell upon his knees, and several followed his
example. A panic seized the congregation, and a solemn awe ensued. We
had a cry and a shout. It was a weeping, tender time. The devil was angry,
and many without persecuted, saying, 'Is God deaf, that they cannot worship him without such a noise?' " The meeting continued for four days,
and over fifty people converted.[28]

The evangelicals' opponents enjoyed disrupting their services. At an
1823 meeting Winans was in his tent ready for a quiet evening when he
"was informed that a mob had commenced . . . cutting bridles and saddles;
and, hearing the devils charge sounded by a singing at or near the spring
I hastened to rise. . . ." He stood guard until three o'clock in the morning,
when the mob gave up. Ministers were a frequent target for abuse. James
Pearse "heard some young gentlemen observe, that if there was not better
order in the Methodist meeting-house, they would be willing to see a certain exhorter led out and whipped; and if any would assist, they would
have it done. . . ." In 1829 the Reverend George Moore, a Presbyterian,
was preaching in Vicksburg when "a group of drunken rowdies came into
the building and noisily proclaimed that they had come to stop such silly
doings as preaching." When they ordered Moore to step out of the pulpit,
he pulled off his coat, marched down the aisle, and began "to pummel
them right and left." The intruders fled, and Moore "went calmly back to
the pulpit . . . put on his coat and began again to preach the glad gospel."[29]

Some preachers like Moore took matters into their own hands, but
others relied on divine punishment for those who mocked evangelicals.
When yellow fever hit the Natchez District in 1817 "five men gathered
together at Washington & agreed to brave the judgement of God—they
came & drank—& in one week they were all in their graves." Evangelicals
held up their example as a warning of the punishment due those who in-
dulged in the so-called virtues of hospitality. During another outbreak of
fever in 1823, "11 young men, some fathers of families held a mock prayer
meeting & in derision of the Lords Supper—administered Sacraments—
before the Epidemic left every one was dead."[30] The godless might attack
ministers, disrupt meetings, and mock evangelical rituals, but converts

took comfort in the fact that a terrible judgement awaited them. As Governor Gayoso had discovered decades earlier, any attempt to persecute evangelicals only increased their determination.

The camp meeting movement intensified with the arrival of veterans from the revival movement in Kentucky. William Winans, a Pennsylvania native and Methodist minister, arrived in the territory in 1810 and became a leading revivalist. In Kentucky, Winans first attended camp meetings and heard celebrated revivalists including Dow. Winans was a man of humble origins who had received only two weeks of formal education. One participant at an early camp meeting described him as "a tall, thin, raw-boned and awkward young man—arrayed in homespun pants, with a long, brown, straight-breasted coat, no neck handkerchief, and a coarse pair of boots." Such men were objects of ridicule to the elegant nabobs in their silks and ruffled shirts, but a simple background and homespuns were advantages on the frontier where he labored among men much like himself. "There was nothing prepossessing about him," the writer continued, "and nothing to remark but his small, burning eyes that glowed like coals of fire. His manner was . . . slow, deliberate, self-possessed, but the first sentence he uttered arrested the attention of the audience, and told them that he was no ordinary man."[31]

From the importance attached to preachers' dress, it is clear that their appearance was an important symbol. Anthropologist Mary Douglas noted the "distinctive appearance of prophets" who "tend to arise in peripheral areas of society, and . . . tend to be shaggy, unkempt individuals. They express in their bodies the independence of social norms which their peripheral origins inspire in them." Like Winans, Dow—or "Crazy Lorenzo" as he was sometimes called—was known for "his bizarre appearance—long hair parted like a woman's, weather-beaten face, flashing eyes, harsh voice, crude gestures, and disheveled clothes." Clothing served as an outward form of identification and a highly visible marker of status. The evangelicals' opponents often ridiculed their somber, antiquated style of dress. For decades, Methodists required their preachers to wear the severe, outmoded clothes associated with their first generation of divines. Some younger ministers hesitated to give up current fashions. Thomas Griffin, for example, "had a short but severe struggle about . . . donning the old-fashioned, round-breasted, colonial coat and vest, which

were . . . adhered to with great tenacity by the Methodists of those days."
In 1816 the Reverend Roswell Valentine was brought before the Mississippi Methodist Conference for "his principle to continue . . . his conformity to the world particularly in the article of dress. . . ." William
Winans once infuriated a bishop when he jokingly asked if he should leave
a ruffled shirt for the bishop's use.[32]

For skeptics, the most shocking aspect of the camp meetings was the
loss of bodily control or inhibitions among those converts overcome by
the Holy Spirit. Their "physical exercises" became the most notorious
aspect of the camp meetings. Here, too, evangelicals cast aside rules of
elite behavior. Mary Douglas wrote that, under certain circumstances,
"people . . . seek, in the slackening of bodily control, appropriate forms of
expression" for their newfound spiritual independence. Shouting was the
most common expression among evangelical converts. Repeatedly,
preachers like Samuel Sellers, a Methodist, described such outbursts; in
1816 he noted in his diary that "we had a sweet time in Love feast & a
Shouting time as Sacrament. . . ." Weeping was also common. William
Winans described the ministry of Lewis Hobbs, who, by his preaching,
"would make his audience weep, very often, when they could have given
no rational account of the cause of their weeping." These mourners, as
they were called—sorrowful salvation seekers—were brought forward
toward the meeting's close. More dramatic was the "falling exercise," in
which some converts fell to the ground—hence the importance of the
straw—and all their apparent bodily functions except for a faint respiration
stopped for hours. Their extremities and faces became cold to the touch,
and their pulses decreased. John G. Jones, who experienced this phenomenon as a young convert, described himself as a "willing captive" to "a
rushing mighty wind." "It was unpleasant to be touched, or spoken to,"
he recalled. "But O! the joy, the rapture, the dissolving and absorbing love
felt in the 'inner man.' "[33]

The elite code of conduct emphasized bodily control, including practiced, polished speech and elegant, graceful movements—rules that stood
in sharp contrast to the remarkable displays at the camp meetings. In the
jumping exercise, for example, "the subject would bound from the floor
twenty or thirty times in quick succession, with a countenance beaming
with holy joy." Witnesses reported that "the feats performed in jumping

over benches, and bounding from place to place without injury . . . were extraordinary." Women overtaken by the dancing exercise "would suddenly spring to their feet, and with countenances beaming with extatic [*sic*] joy, and their eyes turned upwards, they would gracefully jump up and down with a quickness, nimbleness, and apparent ease, not easily imitated. . . ." How different this was from the graceful cotillions so popular at the elite dances! Critics called such behavior nothing more than animal excitement, but those who experienced the exercises described them as deeply moving expressions of spiritual joy.[34]

If in their dramatic physical exercises evangelicals flouted society's rules of acceptable behavior, they issued yet another challenge to their opponents with their speech. The preachers consciously rejected elite conceptions of language and authority. Methodist minister Benjamin Drake said in an 1825 sermon, "What gives efficacy to the preaching of the gospel in these days? It is generally adorned with none of the trappings of art. It is frequently proclaimed by men of plain talents and slender pretensions to learning. But in their mouths is the power of God to the salvation of the hearers. The most giddy and thoughtless, the most gay, and proud are cut to the heart and made to cry God be merciful to me a sinner."[35]

According to Winans, most early evangelical preachers were illiterate men drawn from the "laboring class." Formal education was not required; as one preacher said, "Itinerancy was the *best* school. . . ." Such men, ignorant of elite rules of rhetoric and grammar, spoke the dialect of the plain folk and thereby validated that culture to the listeners who shared it. The idea that some language was vulgar and some refined was an elite construct. By creating a hierarchy of language, the pillared folk dismissed the language of the plain folk as "vulgar" and therefore irrelevant. Preachers capitalized on the hierarchy of language by turning it against its elite creators.[36] The evangelicals dismissed polished, practiced speech as artificial. For them, only spontaneous speech that flowed from the heart was evidence of divine inspiration. For this reason, early evangelicals actually distrusted ministers who prepared written sermons rather than relying on divine guidance in their discourse; a Methodist bishop boasted that he "never wrote a sermon before he preached it. . . ."[37]

The most successful preachers were impassioned performers. One critic attended a service during a meeting of the Methodist conference and was stunned by the preacher's "hallowing, Crying, screaming, starting, shaking hands, jumping, groaning & c & c. . . ." Similarly, James Pearse attended a service where a Methodist preacher became "wild, disconnected, and furious. . . ." Sermons became endurance tests; one minister, for example, preached for three hours nonstop. Preachers frequently used the same biblical texts over and over, but obviously in sermons of such length delivered without notes, no two performances were the same. Preachers employed "oral formulas," or phrases that could be manipulated and combined with spontaneous phrases to produce a lengthy sermon.[38]

The preaching style common in the early churches was called the "heavenly tone," the "holy tone," or "holy whine," characterized by "the cadences of whining, mourning, lamentation and wailing, . . . intended to arouse the sympathies of both preacher and auditors." Because of its rhythmic quality, one listener asked, "Brother . . . did you preach us a song or sing us a sermon?" It lives on today as "spiritual preaching" among blacks and among whites in Appalachia and other rural areas.[39] The level of the congregation's response influenced the preacher's timing, his performance, and the length of the sermon. Preachers encouraged such antiphonal responses, which signified the presence of the Holy Spirit, as spiritual preachers still do today. William Winans described one 1812 meeting where "Bro. Johnson and Bro. Hobbs set the people on fire with exhortations. We had considerable disturbance." Such services reinforced the democratic nature of the movement; one modern scholar's description of the congregation's role applies equally well to the early camp meetings: "They are all a part of the sermon, and every bit as much as is the preacher."[40]

Evidence suggests that camp meeting sermons had a musical quality, a preaching style referred to as "chanting." This camp meeting preaching style evolved through the remarkable interaction between blacks and whites during the Great Revival. The origin of the chanted sermon cannot be traced definitively, but clearly elements within it derived from both African and European oral culture. This preaching style is evidence of the significant religious exchange between blacks and whites, a process under way in the South since the evangelical revivals of the eighteenth century. The mingling of blacks and whites in camp meetings and other evangelical services challenged their society's racial mores. The evangelical emphasis on the equality of believers led whites toward an acceptance of blacks as individuals with souls equal to their own, a concept with revolutionary potential so great that many masters refused to allow evangelicals to preach to their slaves. The evangelicals' willingness to accept enslaved African Americans into membership was especially significant because, as Mississippi Baptists pointed out, "[T]here are men even in this, our own country, who look upon slaves with no more respect than upon a dumb beast. . . ."[41]

This cultural exchange between blacks and whites revolutionized American music. The chanted sermon evolved alongside the spiritual, a close affinity that clearly points toward a common origin. Chanted sermons and spirituals show the same repetitious structure, and sermons often borrow lines directly from the spirituals. Rhythmic sermons and revival hymns shared the pentatonic scale and the same rhythms. Central to both is the antiphonal performance, for camp meeting songs encouraged an active congregational response. Evangelical worship services began with prayer and song, blended into a sermon where musical influence remained strong, and finally closed with singing and prayer. This blending speech and song is related to "the common use in Africa of recitative styles of singing, and the frequent transitions between a speaking and singing delivery." The songs were as important as the sermons in arousing the congregations. As one Methodist journalist wrote, "In revivals, it is well known that singing is an essential and powerful agent in awakening devotional feelings." William Winans described the closing scene at an 1823 camp meeting: "Bro. Harper offered up the concluding prayer; after which farewell songs were sung accompanied by much feeling and much noise and, indeed, the former is never known here without the latter."[42]

The development of gospel music was a part of the larger "democratization" of religion. Between 1780 and 1830 evangelicals broke with traditional church music and developed "indigenous folk alternatives." Unlike those in more liturgical churches or the New England Puritans, evangelicals did not limit their songs to biblical texts and psalms; they agreed with the popular eighteenth-century English songwriter Isaac Watts that the purpose of singing was to "speak to our own experience of divine things. . . ." Beginning during the Great Revival in Mississippi and in other parts of the country, preachers and converts composed gospel songs derived from their own experiences. Singing was one of the numerous gifts that God bestowed on the faithful, and many early ministers were talented singers and songwriters. Prominent Mississippi Baptist preacher Thomas Mercer published a hymnbook and composed at least some of the songs himself. So great was the difficulty in acquiring hymnals from outside Mississippi that in 1816 the Mississippi Methodist Conference printed a pamphlet of the most popular songs for distribution at camp meetings.[43]

Members quickly "learned the tunes, and memorized many of the most commonly used hymns. . . ." The tunes were already familiar, since composers frequently borrowed popular secular melodies. Another means of compensating for high illiteracy rates and the shortage of hymnals was the practice of "lining out" the songs, described as follows:

> When the people had all assembled, the pastor arose, in the old high pulpit, and read a hymn through from beginning to end. And then, because hymn books were few, he would line it out for the congregation, couplet by couplet thus:
>
> > 'How firm a foundation ye saints of the Lord
> > Is laid for your faith in His excellent word.'
>
> And then the people would sing, and as they reached the last word of the couplet, he would continue:—
>
> > 'What more can He say than to you He has said
> > You, who unto Jesus for refuge have fled.'
>
> And again all the people sang.[44]

In Europe, the practice of lining out songs dates back to the dissolution of choirs during the Protestant Reformation, and it was in practice in England and Scotland by the seventeenth century. But here again, this vital part of evangelical worship had African roots as well, for it also embodied the call-and-response structure of African music.[45]

Congregational singing emphasized the equality of all believers and encouraged participation from blacks and women. One scholar observed that "democratized" singing "brought women their first significant liturgical role" in churches. Women not only sang but often led the song service; one Mississippi evangelical recalled, "My mother was a fine singer. She often had to lead the music in our little church when the men's hearts failed them. I can almost hear her voice as it rose above the volume of song as she sang the 'top line' of old Pisgah or New Brittain."[46]

Many preachers operated singing schools, where they taught a form of notation called "shape notes," in which the shape of the note head corresponds to notes on a scale. Designed for untrained singers, the method enabled people to read music on sight and was especially popular among the Baptists (and later the Primitive Baptists, who continue the practice today). Singing was so important to Baptist churches that some churches' Rules of Decorum required that services open with prayer and song. As one writer commented, "Their meetings are models of musical democracy." Singing contributed to the spread of evangelicalism. One church member wrote that "[a]lthough the preaching service did not begin until eleven o'clock the young people always gathered about half past nine and for an hour or more, engaged in singing, the music and songs in the old 'Sacred Harp' . . . because of the entertainment they afforded, many older people and children came to hear them. . . ." Singing became an important social event even apart from services. Henry J. Harris recalled that often "friends . . . meet at each others houses and spend evenings . . . in social singing and prayer." The evangelicals revolutionized American music, as they "wrested singing from churchly control," wrote historian Nathan O. Hatch. "The music created a spontaneous, moving medium, capable of capturing the identity of plain people."[47]

Fueled by popular singing, emotional and dynamic services, and ever-larger numbers of converts, camp meetings provided evangelicals with an ideal means to spread their message on the frontier. By attracting huge crowds, these meetings provided the perfect solution to the problem of a widely scattered population and too few ministers. In 1823, for example, William Winans estimated that four thousand to six thousand people attended a camp meeting; the crowd included a large number of blacks. Methodists held the first camp meetings, but the Baptists and Presbyterians also employed them in these early years. Often preachers from several denominations would preach at the same meeting. Jacob Young recalled a meeting where "five or six Methodist preachers" and "five Calvinist preachers . . . some Presbyterians—some Baptists" hotly debated the merits of their faiths.[48]

The camp meetings brought hundreds of converts into the churches, where the regular worship services continued with the same emotional intensity as the camp meetings. In an 1814 service Samuel Sellers noted that "I had considerable liberty. Many wept & some shouted." Services might be held on any day, since Methodist and Baptist itinerant ministers met with worshipers throughout the week. In 1811 and 1812, for example, William Winans served on the Wilkinson Circuit, which he covered in four weeks. He preached at twenty-four meeting places, most of them private homes, to one hundred eighteen members. At one point he preached every day except Monday. On a four-week circuit, for example, congregations saw the preacher only once during that period. These infrequent visits encouraged lay participation and independence. Lorenzo Dow Langford recalled that he and a few other Methodists built a log church and "agreed to meet every other Sunday one of us would read a chapter in the Testament sing and Pray after which sing & call on another we would have about 3 prayers some . . . conversation and all go home. . . ." He observed that "[i]t was not an uncommon thing for souls to be converted in night meetings in private houses."[49]

Evangelicals did not "compartmentalize" their religion and broke with the convention that confined religious worship to a Sunday morning church service. The strong personal bonds that grew up among members of such congregations could be a powerful attraction for new converts. Norvelle Robertson, Sr., who brought his Baptist congregation from Georgia to Mississippi, recalled that among the Baptists he felt "that love, of which I had never before had the most distant idea. And to me it proved contagious. Fortunately I felt my affections run out to that people, and from that time I felt an anxious desire to become as they were, and to have a name and a place among them."[50]

Evangelical brothers and sisters reinforced their intimacy and shored up their faith through a variety of remarkably personal and deeply emotional rituals and practices. The Methodists' class meetings and love feasts, both initiated by John Wesley, were intimate gatherings of spiritual renewal. Every week a lay leader took the members of the class through a series of questions intended to reveal "how every soul of his class prospers:

not only how each person observes the outward rules, but how he grows in the knowledge and love of God." Class meetings opened with hymns and prayer, after which the class leader might exhort before examining each member. As each member rose and discussed his or her trials and tribulations, doubts and fears, or confidence of salvation, the meetings often became very emotional. In 1812 William Winans "met class, had a considerable shout. . . ." Another preacher reported, "I have been able to raise a class . . . of fifteen tender souls. Bro. Maberry, class leader." He added affectionately, "Uncle Winans scolds the class and preaches awfully, the Lord bless him." Leaders recorded attendance, and absences could be cause for dismission.[51]

Love feasts, which were sacramental meetings, often accompanied quarterly conference meetings among the Methodists. Love feasts could also be very emotional; Winans described an 1821 love feast where "many spoke to the purpose particularly old Sister Hampton. She spoke with an eloquence wholly irresistible for she spoke from the heart in the strong language of feeling." Winans also conducted separate love feasts for black Methodists. In 1823, for example, he wrote, "At half past 8 we met the Blacks at the M[eeting]. House and held love feast. This was quite a re-freshing season . . . and some whites that were present were very happy also." A. C. Ramsey recalled that "[l]ove feasts, Class meetings, and com-munion service were in those days and for a long time afterwards seasons of refreshing, of joy, of spiritual strength to the church and often produced convictions among the people of the world. People . . . regarded it a privi-lege, yea, a great privilege to testify to the truth of our holy christianity."[52]

Presbyterian services were much less emotionally demonstrative, but their biannual communion seasons shared some characteristics of the class meeting and love feast. Communion season lasted from three to five days and included a day of fasting and prayer followed by sermons and examina-tion of members. The communion season was a time of soul searching for Presbyterians, and it was the time when new members were added to the churches. Before Presbyterians abandoned camp meetings and revivals, these were generally associated with communion seasons, and, indeed, the camp meetings very likely grew directly out of these meetings.[53]

Among the Baptists the most intimate ceremony was the "washing of the saints' feet." The ceremony was a common one, and in 1810 the Mississippi Baptist Association declared it to be a "christian duty." For example, the records of Salem Baptist Church in 1819 reveal that "after due deliberation—Resolved that washing of feet be done at our Next Augt meeting in course and that it be adopted as a rule. . . . Bro. John Wells Purchase for the Church a Wash Pan, & 2 Towels. . . ." The Salem church held the ceremony annually, but in other churches it was a biannual event. This solemn, deeply moving ceremony still occurs across the South among some black and some white Baptists.[54] Through these emotional and personal services, evangelicals created their communities of faith. Here ties of Christian brotherhood and sisterhood were forged and strengthened, and the hallmark of all of these services was the shared religious experience among the laity. By these means, evangelicals created communal bonds unheard of on the frontier.

The strength of the revival can be measured in part by the explosion in church membership and the establishment of new churches. Methodist membership increased from 132 white and 72 black members in 1805 to 1,551 white and 410 black members in 1816, a dramatic 1,075 percent increase in white membership and 469 percent increase in black membership. In 1807 five Baptist churches in the territory organized the Mississippi Baptist Association, and by 1818 the association had forty member churches. Their membership increased from 196 in 1807 to 1,072 in 1818. Add to these figures the people who attended churches and camp meetings but were not yet ready or qualified for membership, and the number of individuals under the evangelicals' sway swells considerably.[55]

Evangelicals had advantages over their elite opponents. One of the sharpest contrasts between the virtues of hospitality and evangelical doctrine was the exclusivity of the former and the universality of the latter. Evangelicals reached out to all members of society, but especially those most alienated from elite culture. In a wide variety of ways, then, evangelicals challenged social stability by upsetting the prevailing hierarchical social relationships. Their message of spiritual equality resonated with women and blacks, who joined in large numbers. The typical evangelical church had a female majority of about 65 percent, and blacks composed 36 percent of the Methodists' membership in 1805 and 21 percent in 1818. Husbands and fathers often opposed the conversion of the women in their households and sometimes pressured women in their families to stay away from religious services or to withdraw their memberships. Evangelicals also targeted young people, whom they regarded as "the dearest hope of our rising churches," a wise choice given the youthfulness of the Mississippi population. Most of the preachers were young men themselves and often found their authority challenged by older gentlemen. For instance, when William Winans rebuked someone for intoxication, the older man was infuriated at being called to account by a mere boy (Winans was then in his twenties), and other preachers faced verbal abuse, whippings, and worse from the gentlemen who opposed them.[56]

The evangelicals made a few wealthy converts in these early years, but, as the Reverend Daniel De Vinne put it, "Riches and worldly honours are so unfriendly to taking up the cross daily and following a lowly Savior. . . . [L]ove of gold! how many does it send to hell." Despite the occasional convert among the pillared folk, the real strength of the evangelicals continued to lie with the "moderately poor," as De Vinne described them. The dangers of the things of the world continued to be a refrain among them. One evangelical convert wrote a relative that "Mississippi is the place for making money, but not the place for making happiness. . . . I am forced to prize virtue & happiness above wealth & vice . . . to make Gold & silver & Negroes the . . . incessant objects of pursuit I consider a violation of the Gospel & derogatory to the Christian name." One hymn was titled "Religion Is a Fortune," while a different one painted a more graphic image:

> Lord what a thoughtless wretch was I,
> To mourn, and murmur, and repine,
> To see the wicked placed on high,
> In pride and robes of honour shine,
> But, oh, their end; . . .
> On slipry [sic] rocks I see them stand,
> And fiery billows roll below.[57]

For evangelicals, worldly riches were not the road to honor, but rather the slippery path to hell. Through the popular camp meetings, they fashioned a countercultural movement and a community of faith built not on a celebration of wealth, competitiveness, and displays of power and status, but on brotherhood and sisterhood born of spiritual equality, on simple dress and godly deportment. Their conviction grew out of their faith, born from their own individual experience and deeply felt conversion.[58] The New Birth gave converts this sense of personal empowerment, a faith in their own convictions, and a sense of mission to carry the Word throughout the land. Evangelicals challenged traditional patterns of deference and thereby called into question the very foundations of the social system. Their emphasis on the equality of believers allowed blacks to enter a sacred space within which a remarkable and lasting cultural exchange took place. Through evangelicalism, the plain folk and enslaved Africans and African Americans defined a new popular culture. For them, wealth, social position, education, and the virtues of hospitality became symbols of all that was wrong with their society, stumbling blocks on the road to salvation. As Lorenzo Dow put it, "[I]n the sight of God there is no respect of persons. With him the righteous are noble, however poor and despised in the world. . . ."[59]

[L]ove is the first duty of a man, and submission the chief duty of a woman.

—Mississippi Baptist Association[1]

He . . . has chosen the weak things of the world to confound the mighty. . . . [I]t was right and proper, and perfectly in accordance with that "decency and order" recommended by the apostle, for women to exercise their gifts in singing, prayer, and Christian conversion or exhortation.

—James Bradley Finley[2]

3 "The Duty of Sisters": White Women and the Evangelical Experience

In the struggle between the plain folk and the pillared folk, evangelicals attacked the traditional hierarchical structure of their society, but the weapon they chose—the doctrine of Christian equality—was a double-edged sword, for, while it struck effectively at hierarchy, it implicitly undercut patriarchy as well. White male evangelicals, however, had no intention of carrying the doctrine of the equality of all believers so far as to threaten the domination of white men throughout southern society. For white women and for blacks of both genders, then, churches would be contested terrain. Despite reluctant or resistant men, white women played a vital and active role in the churches. Mary Douglas proposed that groups denied power and authority in their society—blacks and women in the Old South, for example—often expressed that marginality through religious worship. Women's response to the evangelical message of equality was enthusiastic, and they struggled to carve out a role for themselves in churches. So important was that role that historian Donald Mathews suggested that "women made southern Evangelicalism possible."[3]

Women responded to the evangelical message in such numbers that they composed a majority in virtually every church—a crucial but under-appreciated factor in the evangelicals' success. An analysis of membership figures from approximately fifty churches around Mississippi over the period from 1845 to 1876 reveals that women made up a majority of members in 82 percent of the churches in that sample, and the average ratio of women to men was 62:38. A religious newspaper estimated that the number of women actually in the churches was double or quadruple the number of men, and in a handful of cases women organized churches themselves.[4] For example, in 1832 nine women organized the Unity Presbyterian Church in Amite County and signed the church's charter. Given the patriarchal structure of the Presbyterian Church, the Unity women had to appoint a temporary male elder from a nearby church until men joined later in the same year.[5]

No church in Mississippi extended the ideal of Christian equality to include the ordination of women, who were universally barred from the pulpit. Women did, however, exercise a wide variety of public "gifts." As noted in the previous chapter, many women employed the gift of song and thereby acquired their first major liturgical role in worship services.[6] Women frequently employed the gift of public prayer, and long, highly emotional prayers could have the same impact as a sermon. Hannah Swayze, the daughter of Samuel Swayze, the first Protestant minister in the territory, was noted for her religious zeal. After the death of her first husband, she wed Richard Curtis, Sr., of Salem Church. She joined the Methodist Church under the preaching of Tobias Gibson in the 1770s. She was remembered as "a wise and safe counselor in religious matters, but her greatest excellence, perhaps, was in the eloquence and power of her public prayers. . . . [S]he seemed to have 'power with God and with men' in her approaches to the throne of grace." Her daughter, Hannah Coleman Griffing, "was also greatly gifted in extemporaneous prayer, and was often called on . . . to exercise her gifts." Martha Thompson Hoover, also the wife of a Methodist preacher, was so gifted in prayer that "her prayers contain more theology than some preachers' sermons." Women's prayers and exhortation did sometimes function as sermons, and women could be real crowd pleasers even when prominent male preachers failed. Elizabeth Hannah Osteen, the daughter of an early Baptist preacher in the territory, "was, in every true sense of the expression, one of the most influential and useful female members of the Church." At one camp meeting the preachers received a cold reception from the crowd until "Elizabeth Osteen arose and began to rehearse in glowing terms what wonderful things the Lord had done for her. She became inspired with the Spirit of God, and, turning to the congregation, gave a powerful impromptu exhortation, called for mourners, and soon had the altar crowded."[7] One Methodist responded to those who criticized women's active involvement in services by reminding them that "we see in this, as in other similar manifestations, that God's ways are not as our ways and that He . . . has chosen the weak things of the world to confound the mighty."[8]

Many of the early evangelicals strictly enforced gender segregation in their churches and in camp meetings. Churches frequently even separated members by gender (and race) in the roll books. Women often had separate prayer meetings or class meetings, and, even during regular worship services, men and women were likely to sit on different sides of the church—men on the right, women on the left. Many churches had separate entrances for men and women, since "every seat was reserved for a special purpose, one side for the men and the other for the women, and there was no mixed seating." Many Baptist churches in their Rules of Decorum even required members to call one another "Brother" and "Sister."[9] The concept of Christian "sisterhood" had real meaning among evangelical women, and, through segregated seating, separate services, and terms of address, women's separate sphere was acknowledged and reinforced.

As the predominance of women in the churches suggests, wives often converted without their husbands, daughters without their fathers. Given the revolutionary potential of the concept of Christian equality and the women's claim to a public role in worship, women's assertiveness could sometimes cause strains within their families. Husbands and fathers sometimes opposed their wives' or daughters' conversions. For example, Samuel Sellers described a family divided by religious differences. After a young girl joined the Methodists, her father "treated her very cooly which rendered her situation disagreeable." "The Family," he continued, "at least the Female part of it is very Friendly disposed toward religion," but this was not the case for the father. He concluded, "I am truely [sic] sorry for some girls[;] I believe they wish to be Religious but are violently opposed by their Relatives." Such opposition seldom turned to physical violence, but in Vicksburg, John B. Fisher, an angry husband, shot the Reverend Peter E. Green after the minister converted Fisher's wife, Ann. Fisher met Green on the road near the preacher's home in Warren County, "abused him terribly, and finally pulled out a pistol and shot him." Fisher, a native of Virginia, was a young man in his twenties who worked as an overseer. He claimed that his "pious parents" taught him to revere "the Church and its worthy members," but he confessed that he was "no Christian, but a sinner." Fisher was held on bail "in the immense sum of $1,000." The records of the court case have been lost, so the legal outcome of the case is unknown. The census records of 1860 reveal, however, that while John Fisher and Ann still lived in the neighborhood, they resided in separate houses.[10]

A more common reaction from husbands was simply resignation. Timothy Flint described such an encounter: "I was directed to a young lady, whose husband had something of the appearance of a dandy, and who answered my inquiries about the profession of his wife, with a shrug, and a half-suppressed smile, informing me that she was a Methodist . . . . He gave me clearly to understand that it was no affair of his and that I must converse with her alone." For other couples, religion became a topic of ongoing debates and discussions. Throughout their lives together, Isham and Elizabeth Howze explored religious matters, and she labored for years, without success, to convert her husband. In 1847 he wrote:

> Would to God we all could . . . join together as you still seem so anxious we should—The time *may* yet come. . . . I love you above all earthly things, and . . . I would not hurt your tender feelings, or be in the way of your christian privileges for the world. But for myself I *must* be the judge—and if I perish for my obstinacy, I cannot help it. . . . I *know* you love me, and are honest in your opinions, and in your desires for me to join the church (any church). . . . [M]y inability to go with you, gives me pain. . . . I am as the aged oak, hard to be bent—No human power can do it—not even the wishes and persuations [*sic*] of my earthly idol.

Howze filled volumes with his religious musings, but he never found the salvation that his wife so desperately hoped he would. After he died in

1857, she wrote in his journal, "How long O Lord shall this painful separation exist! My Soul is weary of his absence! My heart longeth for his beloved presence, as the hart panteth for the water-brook—I cannot be satisfied without him." What she most feared was eternal separation, and the thought that her beloved was lost for eternity. She wondered if her own prayers had been too feeble or her own sins too great to gain for him the pearl of great price. In desperation she cried, *"Thou alone knowest the whole weight of this great affliction upon me. Wilt Thou not hear the constant cries of my desolate heart?"*[11]

For all Christians, the promise of eternal life brought solace in times of sorrow and affliction, but, particularly for women, that promise could be a source of joy or sadness, as Elizabeth Howze's desperate case illustrates. With an infidel husband, she faced eternity alone. Many women hoped to spend eternity in the company of their loved ones, if only they could be brought to Christ. In 1854 Sophia Boyd Hayes wrote, "How much could I wish to see my brothers and sisters all claim the promise of eternal life, that we might have the sweet hope at some future day of being reunited in a home of ineffable and never ending happiness."[12]

"Our people die well," said John Wesley. Evangelicals exhibited an obsession with death and dying that is perhaps the most difficult aspect of their faith to recapture, so far removed is it from the taboo about such topics in contemporary America. Women had a crucial part to play in the rituals surrounding death and dying. As one religious newspaper put it, "[T]he couch of the tortured sufferer, the prison of the deserted friend, the cross of a neglected Savior—these are the scenes of a woman's excellence." By the 1850s, evangelicals spoke less of conversion as a New Birth and more often of it as a death. For example, at an 1859 revival, "Seven were buried with Christ in baptism . . . ," and in another, "Thirty-one Died—26 Buried!" Like conversion and baptism, death was an event to be treasured, not feared. According to an article in the religious press, one of the statements most often heard at class meetings and love feasts was "I Thank God That I was Born to Die."[13]

Death was not a solitary affair, but rather a very public one, where the dying person was surrounded with friends and family. Some of the most effective calls for repentance came not from the pulpit but from the death bed. The evangelical press was dominated by death-bed scenes, articles and poems on death and dying, and lengthy obituaries like the following one for Mary Ann Raney, wife of David Raney and a thirty-four-year-old member of Friendship Baptist Church in Newton, who died in 1859: "She spoke of her journey through the valley of the shadow of death, as men often speak of contemplated visits to near and dear relatives. . . . This was one of the most triumphant and deeply impressed departures of life I have ever witnessed. She often exhorted her husband to live for God and meet her in heaven, and to train up the only little pledge which they had living, (a daughter, two years of age) in the nurture and admonition of the Lord. She continued, while she had strength, to exhort friends, neighbors, servants, all to meet her in heaven." Many people could "trace their first serious [religious] impressions" to such scenes, "to the time when death entered their family circle. . . ." Given the predominance of women in the churches and the fact that women died earlier than men during this period, it is not surprising that women's obituaries dominated the pages of the religious press and that converts were more likely to recall a mother's exhortation than a father's.[14]

The worst death was a sudden, solitary one. The obituary of Emily Dowsing of Columbus, who died suddenly, alone in her room at the age of thirty-three, mourned the fact that "she died alone, so far as earthly friends are concerned; her beloved father and mother were not permitted to minister to her in the last moments; her dying couch was not surrounded by her affectionate brothers and sisters; no praying circle of pious ministers and brethren bore her up. . . . [S]he was not permitted to give her parting blessing to her weeping friends and kindred and to assure them of her happy exit." It was a powerful faith indeed that allowed Christians to face death with joy, as they so often did.[15]

Fellow Christians could take heart that death was not an end, but the beginning of eternal life. William Winans reminded the congregation at one funeral that "[w]e should rejoice in death as the means employed by our best friend to bring us near to Himself." Sometimes, dying relatives promised to watch over those they left behind or to return as guardian angels if possible. The belief that loved ones lived on, that they were near, and that an eternal reunion awaited gave great comfort to bereaved Christians. John G. Jones and his wife, Jane Oliphant Jones, were married for almost fifty-five years. He recalled their lives together and the power of faith not only to bring two people together but to allow them to part. He wrote:

> As we advanced in life we had become more and more blended together . . . until we were seldom separated more than a few hours at a time. We never tired of each others company but enjoyed ourselves together as much as two congenial Christians ever did. . . . We often passed off our evenings pleasantly and profitably all alone, by our room fire in the cold months, and on our upper gallery in warm weather, recounting the reminiscences of our long pilgrimage together. Ours was more than earthly love; it partook largely of the sweet foretastes of heavenly union and communion of the spirits of the just made perfect.

When she died of a heart attack on July 14, 1883, her final words were "My Dear, pray for me!" Racked with grief, he asked, " 'How can I possibly live without the companionship of my Dear Wife?' . . . At the close of the burial service my bereaved heart prompted me to say audibly, 'Farewell my ever Dear and Faithful Wife, but not forever! This parting is not final. We will meet again at our Dear Redeemers feet and then shall we ever be with the Lord.' " He felt her spirit near him, and he knew that some people would "sneer at this, and nominal Christians will call me a fanatic, but such visitations, unseen but felt, add greatly to the alleviation of my loneliness." He welcomed such visitations when he mourned and wept alone, as he often did. As he approached death himself in 1888, he wrote in a trembling hand, "I live and move and have my being in a boundless ocean of love, peace and joy. I have glory begun below and expect soon to have it consummated above. All glory be to the Father, Son and Holy Ghost." He died October 1, 1888, at the age of eighty-four, still confident of his approaching reunion with his beloved Jane.[16] Perhaps the example of John and Jane Jones can illustrate why women (or men) whose spouses were not Christian feared so deeply for the nonconverted, and why such unions could be so especially painful.

In cases where women braved their men's displeasure by joining churches, they often sought solace from the preachers who had converted them. However understandable and innocent such associations might be, they could open up both parties to ridicule or worse. In 1852 Elizabeth C. Irion described a case in which a woman in her congregation seemed overly attached to the minister; she wrote, "It is really amusing to see Sister Corne with Mr. Schosler—she loves him dearly—she feels that he is almost her spiritual father." Many preachers were clearly uneasy with these new demands and with the women who played such an important role in their churches. The Reverend Lewis Hobbs's comments about women were made more revealing by a Freudian slip; he remarked that "too great a familiarity is disgusting especially from the fear [fair] Sex." Another minister, John G. Jones, wrote, "As a means of self preservation, and to keep the devil from tempting, both myself and others, I kept at a great distance from females, especially young females." He added, "Those young ministers who are so fond of displaying their gallantry by . . . association with young women, are continually tempting the devil to tempt them." Jones faced a most unusual challenge in Natchez and appealed to a fellow minister for advice: "I am more at a loss to know what to do in Natchez on the subject of calling up mourners than any other place I ever laboured. . . . We have here . . . a parcel of illfamed women who, at every call are the first to come to the altar—the most noisy while at it—and the last to go away—and what is most to be lamented—is they are mourners by profession *indefinitely*—for they never get religion." Few ministers confronted problems with prostitutes, but they had to be constantly on guard, for temptation awaited them at every turn. William Winans experienced just such temptation; he was surprised when a young woman "expressed a desire to inveigle me by the arts of coquetry, nor can I easily resist the temptation." Recognizing these dangers, the Methodist *Discipline* warned ministers to " '[c]onverse sparingly, and conduct yourself prudently with women.' "17

Such warnings were justified, because not all preachers resisted temptation. Academy Baptist Church was almost destroyed when the preacher, J. S. Morton, was accused of having a sexual relationship with a woman not his wife. The charges were initially dismissed, but rumors persisted, so that another committee was appointed and thirteen other churches were asked to help. This time, Morton was found guilty of "unlawful intercourse with said girl." Still others took advantage of their position and the trust placed in them. One preacher, Mr. Leftwich, was blatant in his abuse of young women. According to a fellow minister, "He is passionately attached to young girls and hugs and kisses them, feels their thighs and takes liberties which were to say the least very improper in any one, much less a preacher." In another bizarre case, a man from New York moved to the town of Washington and became a Methodist preacher in that area; he wed a rich widow and was then found to be an imposter whose first wife was still living.[18]

The relationships between preachers and the young women in their congregations did occasionally result in marriages. Sophia B. Andrews joined the Methodist Church in 1850, and the following year a new preacher arrived. She wrote her cousin, "By the way this young minister Mr. Hays is one of the most interesting gentlemen I ever met. He is at once fine-looking, intelligent, pious and polished in his manners. I am afraid I shall fall in love with him. How unfortunate it would be if I should and not find the feeling reciprocated!" The charming young Sophia need not have worried, for her feelings were reciprocated. She and the Reverend Hays were happily married until his tragic death from yellow fever in 1856.[19]

Many Mississippi ministers "acquired for themselves plantations" by marrying planters' daughters, a phenomenon that was common enough to arouse public criticism and rumors. One Mississippi newspaper reported the marriage of a Methodist minister to a "young lady of fortune" and added, "There seems to exist a powerful attraction between divines of note and females of this class." A group of women speculated on why men entered the ministry; one said, "They want to marry! In proof of this, sir! they will preach around till they marry some rich man's daughter." Many preachers, including William Winans and John G. Jones, married into the ranks of slaveholding families. Perhaps the best example of a minister who married well was the Methodist reverend Charles K. Marshall of Vicksburg; he married the daughter of Newitt Vick, the founder of the city, and she brought her husband an estate valued at $102,000.[20]

Since early evangelicals were largely drawn from the plain folk, more prominent families often kept their distance and resisted any conversions. The attraction preachers showed for planters' daughters may have made fathers more reluctant to see their wives and daughters attend evangelical services. Sarah Humphreys, the daughter of wealthy parents, joined the

Methodist Church in 1821 at the age of nineteen. Her parents allowed her to attend services "[a]s part of her education, and as one means of introducing her into society . . . but it was by no means the wish of her father's household that she should enter the Church." When young Sarah joined the Methodist Church, she followed their strict code of behavior and dress, a code alien to her more affluent family and friends, who found her decision to give up "worldly amusements" and "gewgaws of dress" "an unexplained mystery."[21]

Although the churches did not ordain women or allow them to hold offices, many churches, especially Baptist and Methodist churches, allowed women to vote in church conferences. Most Baptist churches' Rules of Order included a statement along the following lines: "The government [of the church] is with the body of the church and is equally the right and privilege of each member thereof."[22] Women did not take these rights for granted and sometimes struggled to protect them. The Sarepta Baptist Church covenant of 1810 clearly stated, "The Sisters shall be entitled to all the privileges of the male members in the church." But five years later the church enacted the following amendment: "The subject of the sisters duty in the church considered we consider it their duty to learn of the Apostle [Paul] not to speak in the church nor usurp authority." Unfortunately, records do not reveal what provoked the change or the women's response to it. The reasoning was commonplace; a book on church governance written for southern Baptist churches argued that women should not vote because they were "subject to men" and because "women ought not *to speak in the churches*." Even so, the author acknowledged that women did vote in a minority of churches. In 1834 Sarepta once again considered the question of women's voting, and the church repealed the 1815 amendment with a resolution: "[T]he rule making it the duty of sisters not to speak in the church be reversed and read thus 'They shall be entitled to all the privileges of the male members in the church.' "[23]

Women's struggles to retain their rights and privileges reinforced the idea of sisterhood and led naturally to separate women's religious organizations. Mississippi women organized early in the state's history, as women did in other southern towns. In 1816 a group of ninety Protestant women in Natchez organized the Female Charitable Society to support a school and to care for needy orphans and widows. The women raised substantial funds annually, and they invested surplus funds in bank stocks. The women decided to build an orphanage and to maintain "complete control" over it; they were incorporated by the state legislature in 1819. In 1821 they opened the new orphanage and successfully maintained it by contributions from all Protestant groups in the city.[24]

The asylum received occasional grants from the state and later received the proceeds of a tax on billiard tables, but most revenue came from private sources. By the 1850s the women had on hand almost twenty thousand dollars with which to construct a new orphanage, and, while women across the South lost control of benevolent enterprises during that decade, the women in Natchez continued to operate the institution until after the Civil War. As one minister noted in 1855, "The most interesting fact connected with the Institution, is that, it was originally established and has always been conducted by the ladies of Natchez. It is strictly and emphatically their enterprise. . . . The Orphan Asylum has been handed down from mother to daughter through three generations of the females of Natchez."[25]

Women's religious groups also appeared in smaller towns and villages across the state. In 1820 a women's prayer meeting began in the nearby town of Washington. William Winans mentioned other similar Methodist organizations in the 1820s, and they were well established by the 1830s. Women's societies were among the largest donors to the state Methodist conference and to the Mississippi Baptist Convention.[26] Baptist women organized missionary societies after the Baptist Board of Foreign Missions sent a missionary, James A. Ranaldson of Massachusetts, to the Mississippi Territory in 1816. In 1822 Baptist women organized the Ladies Charitable Mission Society, an auxiliary to the Mississippi Baptist Missionary and Education Society. The society's constitution stated, "The Gospel . . . has laid our sex under a peculiar tribute of praise and gratitude." Membership was open to "[a]ny female who wishes to do good . . . by subscribing to the constitution, and paying annually in advance, in money, or in articles of clothing, or even in superfluous ornaments, to any amount within the compass of her circumstances, as the suitable expression of her degree of charity." Local groups sprang up across the state and actively raised funds. These fund-raising events became a regular part of the activities in towns and hamlets across the state. For example, the women of the Jackson Baptist Church planned a fair at city hall to raise funds to repair the church, an event that brought in an impressive $590. Such organizations played a vital role in church life. Baptists in Columbus organized their church in 1832; the minister and his wife, John and Pamelia Armstrong, "organized a Female Society almost immediately and it became one of the most vital and vigorous forces in that great historic church." Methodist women in Columbus "set themselves to work to purchase a parsonage—they were not very long in finding . . . a brick home surrounded with forest trees . . . . They are to pay $3500.00 for the house & lot—and have already raised a large portion of the money." The grateful minister had moved in within a couple of months. By the late 1830s the religious women of Columbus "maintained three Sunday Schools, three ladies' sewing societies, a Bible society, a foreign mission society, and a temperance society."[27]

Presbyterian women were important in the Natchez Female Charitable Society, and in 1829 Presbyterians in Port Gibson organized the Ladies Benevolent Society. Such organizations appeared in Presbyterian churches throughout the state during the antebellum period.[28] The Natchez Female Charitable Society was perhaps the most ambitious women's group, but women from all denominations helped furnish local churches, contributed sizeable amounts of money to their churches and missionary societies, and bought or built parsonages. Across Mississippi, churchwomen created a variety of organizations, and, while their contributions were often ignored in the local church records, the groups played a vital role both in the churches and in the lives of southern women. As Donald Mathews wrote, "[T]hese organizations would become, with the churches, the focal point of social activities for women in the South."[29]

The debate over the proper role of women in the churches and in society was played out in the rapidly expanding religious press, where articles for and about women were a regular feature. The press celebrated the so-called Cult of True Womanhood in terms that women across the country would have recognized. On the one hand, articles advised women to be good wives and mothers. A typical article advised women to "[e]ndeavor to make your husband's habitation alluring and delightful to him. Let it be to him a sanctuary. . . . [M]ake it a repose from his cares, a shelter from the world. . . . Let home be your empire—your world." Another emphasized the importance of "domestic love" and noted that it was in "the

unrestricted intercourse of the domestic circle where the heart must find
. . . real enjoyment." And yet another announced that "in no relation does
woman exercise so deep an influence . . . as in that of mother."[30]

The Cult of True Womanhood emphasized domestic virtues, but at
the same time other articles in the press argued for a more active role
for women. An article entitled "Womanhood and Work" proclaimed that
"[a]mong the changes that have taken place in society within the past century, not one is so significant as the wonderful activity of women in various
departments of intellectual and industrial life. . . . [T]hey are at work;
thanks to Providence for this bright era in the history of humanity." One
writer suggested that expanding opportunities for women was following
in the footsteps of Jesus, who made "male and female 'all one in Himself.' " Jesus sought to "emancipate them from human impositions, and
equalize them in Divine privileges" by making "the Marys apostles, even
to the apostles themselves." Another article in the Methodist press boasted
that "[o]ur church has been foremost in this country in urging and sustain-
ing . . . Female Education," but, the article continued, "Womanly activity
is largely lost to the Church, simply for the reason that there is not Church
appreciation of its value and excellence." The church should be in the
forefront of opening opportunities for women. The writer said, "If we
undertake to educate our women, let us also follow them out into life . . .
and see that they have a field for their energy." [31]

While much of the emphasis on female education in this period focused on fashionable, genteel accomplishments, these virtues of hospitality
were despised by evangelicals who supported a different form of higher
education for women. In 1818 the Methodist conference established the
Elizabeth Female Academy in Washington, Mississippi, at the urging of
local Methodist women who were responsible for its creation. The academy predates Emma Hart Willard's Troy Female Seminary in New York,
established in 1821, which is generally recognized as the first school in the
country to offer a secondary education to women. The academy had a
male superintendent, but a governess actually ran the institution and
taught the students. The bylaws required her to be "pious, learned, and of
grave and dignified deportment." The bylaws also called for three "respectable Matrons" to serve as patronesses; they were to visit and inspect
the school and report any problems to the all-male board of trustees. The

ambitious curriculum included chemistry, natural philosophy, botany, Latin, intellectual philosophy, mythology, and history.[32]

The school emphasized moral teachings rather than fashionable accomplishments. Students attended religious services regularly and observed a strict moral code. For example, students could not receive visitors, and they were required to dress simply, without "beads, jewelry, artificial flowers, curls, feathers, or any superfluous decoration." As one religious newspaper warned, "Woman is not placed in this world to eat the bread of idleness, and to receive the flatteries of others." Given the evangelical hostility to worldly amusements, the young women could not attend "balls, dancing parties, theatrical performances, or festive entertainments." As Donald Mathews pointed out, the evangelical ideal for women was an important part of their challenge to the society around them. "Evangelicals distinguished between themselves and the world by focusing on the differences between worldly and converted women," he wrote. Such a concern is clearly evident in the academy's rules against finery and worldly amusements. The academy was not intended as a finishing school for the daughters of the planter elite. Indeed, evangelicals delighted in ridiculing frivolous elite women, as in this 1852 poem entitled "The Modern Belle":

> Her feet are so very little,
> Her hands are so very white,
> Her jewels are so very heavy,
> And her head so very light;
> Her color is made of cosmetics,
> Though this she never will own,
> Her body's made mostly of cotton,
> Her heart is made wholly of stone.[33]

The academy's sponsors drew upon the emerging ideal of the Republican Wife as they designed the school and its curriculum; this republican ideology emphasized marriage as the most important familial relationship, with the bond between husband and wife having more significance than the one between parent and child. In this conception of the ideal family, where there were conjugal equals, women occupied a more central role not only in the family but in the larger society. Women served as the guardians of male virtue, and, through their beneficial influence within the family, women would ultimately reform the morals of the entire society. In fact, the very concept of virtue, a fundamental aspect of republican ideology, became increasingly feminized. In keeping with this ideology, the founders of the academy explained that the institution would confer "much benefit upon the state" by educating young women in the "principles of Liberty, Free government and obligations of patriotism."[34]

The academy operated for over twenty-five years, until the transfer of the state capital from Washington to Jackson led to its demise. The evangelical commitment to women's education continued, however, and by then these groups operated several other denominational schools for women. Evangelicals took pride in their support of female education; a speaker at the 1829 commencement at the Elizabeth Academy said, "Nothing reflects more honor upon the present age than the liberality displayed in the education of females." Mississippi women attempted to make the most of the sphere allotted to them and insisted on a greater commitment to women's education. Increasing educational opportunities and higher literacy rates for women meant that women became a part of a larger literate culture, and their importance within the churches gave them access to the expanding religious press, where views like those above could find their way into print.[35]

Evangelical men and women struggled with contradictory views of women's role in the church and in society. How successfully did women shoulder the responsibilities of evangelicalism? The question is impossible to answer with any certainty, but the records of church disciplinary proceedings are a source of information about how women behaved once in fellowship. All evangelical churches maintained a strict discipline and regularly tried members who violated the evangelical code. An examination of females' trials indicates that women found it much easier to conform to evangelical expectations than men. White women were charged 150 times in this sample, far fewer than the 593 charges against white men, despite the female majority in the typical evangelical church. In none of the churches surveyed here did the disciplinary actions against women approach their percentage of the membership. For example, Bethany Baptist Church had a majority of female members by 1843 (52.6 percent), yet cases against women accounted for only 15.3 percent, and even this figure is high compared to many other churches. In those churches where women voted they could influence the process, and their votes could be decisive. Often in such churches women also served on committees appointed to visit other women who faced charges in the church courts. In most churches, however, white men oversaw church discipline.

As these cases make clear, evangelicals had a different standard of behavior for women; theirs were the duties of wives and mothers. If these cases are any indication, women accepted that role with little difficulty. Most charges against Mississippi women were for minor offenses, and dancing accounted for over one-third of the charges (40.7 percent) against white women. Evangelicals feared that dancing would lead women into greater sin and temptation. In 1861, for example, the Presbyterian Synod of Mississippi condemned dancing and "all kindred amusements which are calculated to awaken thoughts and feelings inconsistent with the seventh commandment [Neither shalt thou commit adultery]."[36] Evangelicals believed women to be naturally more emotional, less capable of self-restraint than men. As one religious newspaper observed, "Women are naturally more warm hearted and enthusiastic than men, more easily excited, and give way to their feelings with less restraint."[37]

Another 21.3 percent of the charges are for unspecific allegations such as misconduct, disorder, nonfellowship, contempt, or immorality. Unfortunately, these cannot be identified with any certainty, though only the charge of immorality was usually applied to a serious offense, often of a sexual nature. The next most sizeable group, twenty-six cases (17.3 percent), charged women with joining another denomination. The same charge occurred only seven times (1.2 percent) in the male group. This discrepancy likely results from women who wed husbands from another denomination. Intoxication accounted for only five (3.3 percent) of the allegations against white women. The small number of allegations reflects the existing norm against female drinking.[38] These four categories of charges constitute 82.7 percent of the total.

In only a handful of cases were women charged with violating the strictures surrounding their roles as wives and mothers. The first general category, sex and family life, included fornication, illegitimate births, leaving husbands, adultery, bigamy, and unscriptural marriage. These accounted for 8.7 percent of the total allegations against white women, compared to 4.7 percent of the allegations against white males. A reference to actual numbers rather than percentages in the Mississippi sample shows seven charges of adultery against men compared to two charges against women, six allegations of bigamy against men and one against a woman, three charges of fornication against men and three against women, two allegations against men for leaving their wives, and three charges against women who left husbands. Of course, no man was charged with an illegitimate birth, while three women were. But, by the same token, women were not charged with spouse or child abuse, attempted rape, or family disputes, while nine such charges were made against men. Through the disciplinary process, evangelicals attempted to protect the institution of marriage and defend the family. Women and men who violated the sacred bonds found themselves standing before a church court.

In this sample of allegations against women, by far the most common charge against them involved a relatively minor offense—dancing. In contrast to earlier studies, the sample does not show discrimination against women in church conferences. If discrimination was at work, it operated against men who were disciplined and excluded at far higher rates than women. For example, an 1860 membership list from Academy Baptist Church showed that 6.7 percent of the white males had been excluded, but only 1.2 percent of the white women were so severely punished. Viewed another way, 28.6 percent of the twenty-one cases involved white males, but only 4.8 percent involved white females.

This evidence suggests that white women deeply internalized the evangelical ethic. Historian Elizabeth Fox-Genovese argued that "[r]eligion lay at the core of slaveholding women's identity. It provided their most important standard for personal excellence and legitimated their sense of self in relation to the other members of their society." Certainly the low number of disciplinary cases against women lends credence to her suggestion; white churchwomen more successfully shouldered the burdens of evangelicalism than white men. While the duties evangelicals imposed on white men sometimes conflicted with prevailing social norms, the separate and subordinate position of women in the churches reinforced their position in the larger society.[39]

Largely because of its celebration of the equality of all believers and the opportunities it offered to godly women, evangelicalism attracted large numbers of women from the start. In the early years, many female conversions took place over the objections of husbands and fathers, and clergymen encouraged the women's defiance. Evangelical doctrine, values, and practices inverted power structures and upset relations between sexes, races, and classes. White southern men often reacted violently to conversions among their wives, children, and slaves for a complex set of reasons that included the spiritual empowerment that conversions brought, the sense of moral superiority that converts felt over nonbelievers, and the branding by Methodists of male values and behaviors as sinful, which robbed men of their moral authority. Women and slaves were drawn to evangelicalism by the respect, the spiritual equality, and the substantive leadership opportunities that it offered. Only such powerful motivators could lure female converts to a religion so "ridiculed, feared, and harassed."[40] Though barred from the pulpits in evangelical churches, women prayed, prophesied, exhorted, and otherwise exercised their spiritual gifts. Clergymen and devout women often developed close relationships, but some ministers feared being upstaged by them. Threatened by a growing female majority and confronted by the desires of men to control their own households, preachers took steps to accommodate white men. Beginning about 1800, the clergymen began to rein in these women by limiting their public role in services and by stripping them of the right to vote in churches. They tailored their message on slavery to gain access to slaves scattered on plantations and restricted black preachers. Increasingly, ministers adopted a muscular, martial Christianity and embraced the code of honor. The infusion of an evangelical ethos throughout southern culture testified to their success.

No topic in southern religious history is more important or more contested than the role of women. The effort to reconstruct women's contributions to Christianity is an ongoing project fraught with difficulties, none more challenging than a historical legacy that has largely obscured women's involvement. For that reason feminist scholars have insisted that historians must apply a "hermeneutic of suspicion"[41] to a religious history that has omitted or downplayed the essential role of faithful women. Indeed, the scope of women's contributions to southern churches, the role religion played in women's lives, and the emergence of a women's culture closely tied to southern churches and religion are topics that remain either understudied or contested by scholars of southern religion and southern women.

With regard to the condition of slaves here . . . there is no country where they are better treated. . . . I observe what you say of the protection afforded by the laws of Virginia to slaves. . . . Legislators should be deeply versed in a knowledge of the human mind, and its various springs of action, who pretend to set rules, by law, between the authority of the governors and the duty of the governed. It matters not whether we speak of the despot and his subjects, or the master and his slaves. If you break in upon the authority of the one you place arms in the hands of the other, which sooner or later, will be directed against those whom they consider their oppressors. . . . Slavery can only be defended perhaps on the principle of expediency, yet where it exists, and where they so largely outnumber the whites, you must concede almost absolute power to the master. If this principle be not admitted the alternatives are, insurrection, with all its horrors, or emancipation with all its evils.

—WILLIAM DUNBAR[1]

4 "Until the Secret Thunder Bursts": Blacks, Slavery, and the Evangelical Movement, 1799–1860

Here is one of the most honest descriptions of slavery to be found from the pen of a southern slaveholder, one that clearly shows the iron fist beneath the velvet glove. As Dunbar makes clear, by 1800 antebellum southern society was firmly grounded in inequality and domination; no slave society could be otherwise. While evangelicals challenged some aspects of their society, ultimately they made no attempt to alter the asymmetrical relations of power either between masters and slaves or between men and women. As noted in the previous chapters, elements in their ideology were revolutionary, and blacks and women found a meaning in their faith that white men never intended.

The evangelicals had abandoned any meaningful attempt to abolish slavery before the movement came to Mississippi, if they had really ever made one, but in these early years their partnership with the institution continued to be troubled. They wrestled with the contradictions between their militant egalitarianism and the demands of a slave society in part because slaves forced them to do so. The degradation and enslavement of Africans and African Americans served as the ultimate basis of Mississippi's society, and the polarization of white society would be quickly healed on that basis. The depth and sincerity of the evangelical challenge to slavery continues to be one of the hotly debated issues among historians of the antebellum period. Evangelicals changed the lives of the slaves, and, at the same time, slaves changed evangelicalism. As historian W. E. B. Du Bois observed, "[T]he Methodists and Baptists of America owe much of their condition to the . . . influence of their millions of Negro converts."[2] Evangelicals preached equality in Christ, and blacks and women attempted, with some success, to force the white men who governed the churches to face the true meaning of their creed. As Dunbar suggested, however, they could go only so far. During the early nineteenth century the evangelical churches grew at phenomenal rates, and women and blacks played major roles in that growth. That dramatic expansion also brought changes, particularly in the evangelicals' aspirations and goals. At the same time, evangelicals abandoned the egalitarianism that made such broader participation possible.

One of the most controversial topics in the study of southern religion is assessment of the African religious heritage. A few historians, most notably Jon Butler, have argued that enslaved Africans lost their traditional systems of worship and their collective religious practices. He suggests that slaves in British North America suffered a "spiritual holocaust" and were largely unable to maintain their traditional African religious systems, even though some religious practices survived. Other scholars have traced African American religious practices back to their African roots. Historian Mechal Sobel focused on cultural interactions among yeoman whites and slaves in eighteenth-century Virginia and found a convergence of Anglo and African religious beliefs. Blacks, she contended, accepted most of the Christian eschatology, while white evangelicals embraced the trances and visions of African faith, their sense of a spirit journey, and belief in a reunion with ancestors after death.[3] Most scholars would agree with Sylvia Frey and Betty Wood, who argued that Africans sold into slavery represented "a variety of cultural forms: traditional religions, Africanized Christianity, and Africanized Islam." Africans could not re-create their traditional religious systems anywhere in the Americas, but "[w]hat they were able to do, and often very successfully, was to piece together new systems from the remnants of the old." A remarkable group of African religious leaders emerged throughout the South during the Great Awakening; their congregations served as the "citadels of African evangelism" and produced the first generation of black missionaries after the Revolution.[4]

For Frey and Wood, the major turning point for the Christianization of African Americans is the period from 1785 to 1830. Before 1785, Christianity affected only an "insignificant minority" of slaves, but after 1785 it began to make rapid inroads in the slave community so that, by 1815, Christianity was the "dominant religious influence among Afro-Atlantic peoples." In the South, that process was divided into two phases, a short but intense post-Revolutionary phase from 1785 to 1790 that was largely confined to Virginia, and a more widespread phase from 1800 to 1830 fueled by the Great Revival. The authors explore the biracial character of the Great Revival, which "decisively shaped black and white religious culture." While cultural interaction and exchange was an important feature of biracial worship, the larger trend was toward the creation of a distinctive Afro-cultural identity. Black Christians created their own moral universe, an "integrating theology" that incorporated blacks and whites and men and women. In their ritual and practice, black Christians emphasized a more expressive and participatory worship where music and ecstatic behavior expressed different religious expectations.[5]

Evidence from Mississippi supports their interpretation. Slaves made up a high percentage of the population in frontier Mississippi compared to other southern states, a statistic that helps explain the growing number of black evangelicals. In Mississippi the black population increased from almost 40 percent of the total population in 1800 to nearly 50 percent in 1830, and after 1840 the state had a black majority. Evangelicals sought to reach out to that large, unchurched population, but their ambivalent position on slavery made masters wary. Among Methodist minister Daniel De Vinne's many complaints against the pillared folk was that he could not "get them to feel rich enough to let their poor servants come to preaching." He often met with a dozen slaves, he complained, "when the sound of the horn might summons 250 and 300 to meeting. . . . These poor creatures I never see & some never hear the gospel." In 1818 a religious convention met in Washington, Mississippi, and called on slave owners to provide religious instruction to their slaves and to allow them to worship.

The convention resolved that "whereas that degraded portion of our population, the children of Africa, must be regarded as possessed of immortal
souls like ours, for whom as well as for us the blood of atonement has been
shed, and whose salvation, like our own, is only to be accomplished
through sanctification of the spirit . . . this Convention strongly recommends to all masters and employers of slaves, to see that they be initiated
into the principles of the Christian faith; . . . and by every practicable
means, to facilitate and encourage their attendance in the sanctuary from
Sabbath to Sabbath."[6]

Despite masters' qualms, many Mississippi slaves did convert to
Christianity, and they even organized their own independent "African"
churches as they did across the region in this period. Some of the largest
churches in early Mississippi were these independent African congregations. In 1818, for example, the members of Bogue Chitto Baptist Church
considered "[t]he Request of the Black Brethren to be constituted into a
church. . . . [T]he same is hearby [sic] granted. . . . The Constitution of
the Black Brethren to be on the first Lords Day in January next." It is
important to note here that blacks instigated the creation of this independent black church, and whites cooperated with them in that effort. While
it is impossible to know how many independent black churches existed,
the scattered references suggest that they were not uncommon. In 1820
the Pearl River Baptist Association's twenty-three member churches included an African church that sent black delegates to the association's
meetings. In 1825 the largest church in the Union Baptist Association was
an African church with 115 members, about one-fifth of the membership
of the entire association. At least one African church belonged to the Mississippi Baptist Association from 1810 to 1820. These African churches
provide evidence of a maturing African American Christianity; the formation of such churches suggests that Christianity was spreading rapidly
among the enslaved population, and it was spreading under black control.[7]

In the Mississippi territorial period and during early statehood, independent African churches attracted more black members than the biracial
churches. For example, of the fourteen members of Jerusalem Baptist
Church in 1822, only one was black. In 1824 Galilee Baptist Church had
a hundred and nine white members, but only ten blacks. In 1804 only
seventy-two blacks belonged to the Methodist churches in the territory.[8]

Of course, more blacks may have attended the biracial services than these figures would suggest, but the large membership figures available for independent black churches imply that blacks preferred to worship separately.

Clearly, these independent black churches also had black preachers, a remarkable group of religious leaders that W. E. B. Du Bois characterized as "the most unique personality developed by the Negro on American soil." Throughout the antebellum period, both blacks and whites worshiped under the ministry of black preachers.[9] These black preachers had a considerable impact on evangelicalism, and evidence from Mississippi supports Donald Mathews's observation that "whites as well as blacks recalled the power and authority of black preachers." The first black preacher in Mississippi on record was Joseph Willis, a free black and a licensed Baptist preacher, who began his ministry in the Natchez region in 1798. He moved to Louisiana in 1804, organized the first Baptist church in the state, and served as the first moderator of the Louisiana Baptist Association. "Brother Willis" continued to attend the meetings of the Mississippi Baptist Association.[10]

In the early decades of the evangelical movement, black preachers benefitted from the ideal of the equality of all believers and exercised a wide ministry among both blacks and whites, and some blacks carried on successful ministries even after the 1830s. In August 1845, William Winans "heard Isaac, a Mulatto slave, deliver a very interesting discourse. I have heard Presiding Elders who could not equal his performance." Isaac preached to biracial congregations; Winans wrote of a later service, "Isaac . . . addressed the coloured people (of whom there was a great crowd) much to the gratification of many of the white people who heard him." Former slave Jim Allen attended a "neighborhood church" with a biracial congregation where "[d]ere was a white preacher and sometimes a nigger preacher would sit in de pulpit wid him." A state Baptist newspaper memorialized Jack Hinton, a slave preacher, in an 1858 obituary. Hinton, a North Carolina native, came to Columbus in 1836 with his master. He was a member of the Baptist church there and was "recognized as a preacher to the blacks." He was considered "earnest and effective," and the whites knew that "his influence with the negroes was almost incredible, while with the white people he was esteemed and highly respected."[11]

Some black ministers like Hinton managed to walk a fine line that allowed them to carry on an open ministry, but the number of licensed black preachers apparently declined in the wake of what Donald Mathews refers to as the "white reaction" of the 1820s and 1830s. As whites began to show a greater interest in slaves' religious beliefs in the wake of the mission movement and as Denmark Vesey's conspiracy in South Carolina and Nat Turner's rebellion in Virginia demonstrated the revolutionary potential of black religious leaders, slave preachers faced growing suspicion from whites. After the late 1820s, black preachers increasingly suffered from discriminatory laws and harassment. In 1825 the Hopewell Baptist Church allowed "Br. John . . . to sing & pray and exhort among the people of his own color," but two years later the church imposed restrictions on John's ministry. In one instance he was charged with striking a fellow slave with a whip, and in 1829 the church ordered him to stop preaching because of "[s]undry reports against" him. The Bogue Chitto Baptist Church allowed "Bro. Jesse" to preach, and he became so popular that nearby Salem Baptist Church requested that he be allowed to preach to them. In 1827 he was cleared of an adultery charge but was dismissed from the church in 1828. In 1830 the New Hope Baptist Church resolved that the slave preacher Peter could "no longer exercise in publick, further than to sing, [and] pray amongst his own colour. . . ," and in 1832 he was charged with gambling. In 1832 the church allowed Cary to preach within the church, but two years later they questioned his gift and concluded that he was not called to the ministry. They allowed another slave, Jerry, to preach until 1839, when they determined that the state laws prohibited slaves from preaching "any where else but at home"; thereafter they stopped any slave member from preaching. In 1853 the Magnolia Baptist Church charged that a black "by the name of Jeffrey (Styling himself a Baptist minister) has . . . been preaching to the colored population of Port Gibson and vicinity, teaching strange doctrine." Whether or not Jeffrey's "strange doctrine" was revolutionary in nature is unclear, but whites were especially disturbed by slave preachers like Alfred Oates, who was charged for "holding Publick meetings and teaching the Collard People that it was not Right to obey there oners [sic]."[12]

An 1860 article in the Methodist press stated: "Negro preachers were formerly very common in the South, and many of them were very useful. We have listened with delight and profit to many a sermon from preachers as sable as ever came from Africa. Indeed, there are many of them yet, preaching more or less every sabbath. . . . Had there been no anti-slavery party, no free states, so called, no fanaticism, no abolition excitement, this state of things . . . would have increased and improved. But now it is on the decline. But few colored men are now allowed to preach. It cannot be otherwise, under the circumstances." As these cases suggest, white suspicion prevented most blacks from preaching to biracial congregations after 1830. In addition, Winans's observation that slave preachers could sometimes outshine even the most elevated white ministers may also explain whites' efforts to bar black preachers from pulpits. Whatever the motives, black preachers were increasingly forced underground, which encouraged the growth of the "invisible church" in the quarters where black preachers exerted great influence.[13]

The effect black preachers had on the slave community is, unfortunately, almost impossible to document in these early years, but seeing one of their number elevated to a position of high visibility and prestige must have had an impact on other slaves. Certainly black preachers were largely responsible for the growing number of black converts. Some slave preachers had direct ties to Africa. Laura Montgomery of Amite County recalled that slaves sometimes attended a biracial church, but they enjoyed their own services "when de black African would come over frum a neighbor's place to preach. . . ." Ann Drake of Pike county also worshiped under the ministry of an African preacher; she remembered that "[a] Big black African man done de preachin. Dat African wore long rings in his ears, but he culd preach." Jim Martin, also of Pike County, may have heard the same preacher; he recalled hearing "a sho nuff African . . . 'spound the gospel: he wus a old man."[14]

Religion was central to the lives of African American women in bondage like Laura Montgomery, who converted in large numbers. Enslaved physically, women discovered spiritual freedom and the ability to resist the dehumanizing force of the institution in religion. Through their faith, women found the strength to cope with the travails of slavery. Worship services helped unite the slave community, provided modes of resistance, and eased backbreaking labors. While the slave preacher is a well-known figure in plantation lore, the important role of slave women as religious leaders in their community has not been fully appreciated. Among themselves, and in meetings with men, women exhorted, prayed, taught, and sang, all significant ministerial roles. Women also helped preserve African elements in worship, most clearly in visionary experiences and other rituals and practices.

Almost every plantation had a slave preacher, but these men were not the only religious leaders in the quarters. For example, Henrietta Murray of Choctaw County recalled that her "grandma taught a Sunday School class on Sunday afternoons durin' slavery days an' taught us all we knowed. We didn't have any church but had prayer meetin' an' preachin' at our homes ever Sunday evenin'." Harriet Sanders of Oktibbeha County had the mother wit; she said, "De lawd keepin me here for a purpose, and lets me know what gwin happen. I believe if you serve God, he will show you in spirit all dat is gwine happin." Visionary experiences played an important part in the religious lives of enslaved women. Dora Jackson recalled that her mother "and some other women wus washing clothes down at a creek, when all at once dey look up at de sky, and dey see guns and swords streaking cross dey sky. Den all at once de guns stack up." This vision appeared shortly before the outbreak of the Civil War. Mark Oliver, a former slave in Coahoma County, remembered Aunt Sylvia, who "was so smart she foreknowed things before they took place." Renowned for her gift of prophecy, Aunt Sylvia conducted the religious meetings in the slave quarters. The slaves used the "children's house" as their "meeting place of prayer," and "Aunt Sylvia gave the lecture. She was a good thinker. Looked as if she knowed everything just from her mother wit. She was the only preacher we knowed anything about."[15]

Visionary experiences such as these are a crucial aspect of slave religion and an important link between African and European religious systems. Both European and African religious systems emphasized the importance of another world, a spiritual world, that could not be understood through the usual senses. The other world was inhabited by various beings and entities, including the spirits of the dead, who sometimes communicated with a few gifted individuals. This basic concept of spiritual revelation, then, provided a dynamic link between the two religious systems. Christianity was founded on revelations, such as those to Moses and the Hebrew prophets, and many Christians also accepted the validity of lesser revelations through dreams, prophetic events, divination, or actual contact with spirits. When Africans were exposed to Christianity, revelations played a central role in their conversion and provided African and African American converts with a source of spiritual authority beyond and above that of white clergymen, whose homiletics on black inferiority, for example, could be superseded through revelations. It was not necessary for Africans to replace their own cosmologies with a Christian one; rather, they received revelations in the African tradition that meshed with Christianity. The evangelical emphasis on the New Birth and on dramatic conversion experiences, their acknowledgment that God spoke to them through dreams, visions, and other forms of divination, accommodated African cosmology and the African emphasis on continuous revelation. This process would have been facilitated by the presence of African priests; perhaps the native African preachers that Mississippi slaves heard were such individuals.[16]

Given the importance of continuous revelation, worship was not limited to Sundays but rather permeated life in the quarters. Slaves lightened the heavy burdens of their labors through their faith. Laura Ford of Hinds County noted that "[w]e did all our real worshiping in de fiel's, out deir we could turn loose in our own way. We could sing, shout an' pray." Vinnie Busby observed that "de real times when we sho' nuf praised de Lord wuz in de fields. Dey tole tales an' praised de Lord an' sang de ole songs. . . ." These times of worship could be deeply moving, so much so that at least one slave woman "got religion between the plow-handles." Such services relieved the tedium of field work, and songs helped set the rhythm for gang labor. Harriet Miller said that when slaves "wus in de field at wurk de allus sung to keep time wid de hoe en dat wuld mek 'em work faster, en dey sung de ole time songs sich as 'On Jordan's Stormy Banks I Stand'. . . ." Along with the songs, "dy sho prayed to be sot free." Religion could be an important source of resistance in the quarters, a fact that explains why some masters tried to prevent worship among slaves. Nettie Rocket of Tate County recounted the story of an old slave woman who "was down over de tubs washin' one day an' got so full o' ligion she started prayin'." Her master forbade worship on his plantation, and he "come to find out de trouble an' threatened to whip her fo' disobeyin his orders." The woman was not intimidated; she replied, "You can whip me—you can kill dis body but you can't kill my soul." Her master scoffed, saying, "[Y]ou God damn fool you ain't got no sense no way," but he never again attempted to prevent her from praying. Masters might exact backbreaking labor from their slaves, but through religion slaves could transform even this aspect of their bondage into an act of resistance.[17]

Other masters had no qualms about slaves worshiping under white supervision, but tried to prevent slaves from meeting on their own. The strength of the "invisible institution" in the quarters indicates the slaves' ability to evade such control and forge a separate and vibrant African American culture. Victoria Randle Lawson observed that her "[m]aster didn't allow us to hab no of meetens if'n he knew it," but the slaves were so expert at evading the master that they "had meetin at night at one house and next night at a nudder." Clara C. Young of Monroe County looked back on the secret meetings as joyful times: "De mos' fun we hed was at our meetin's." She recalled that "[w]e hed dem mos' every Sunday. . . . De meetins last frum early in de mawnin' 'til late at night. . . ." The master did not object to meetings held during the day on Sunday, but he "thought if we stayed up ha'f de night we woulden' work so hard de next day, an dat was de truf."[18]

Both Lawson and Young recalled that slaves used wash pots to help conceal secret services. According to Lawson, "[W]e put a wash pot down in front of de meeten house so's de overseer couldn't hear us a singing and a prayin. Dis wash pot caught de sound." Young noted that "when dark cum de men fo'ks wud hang up a wash pot, bottom up'ards, in de little brush chu'ch house us hed, so's it'd catch de noise an de oberseer woulden' hear us singin' an shoutin'." Over and over again Mississippi slaves noted the use of pots in such clandestine services. Rachel Santee Reed recalled a different use of the pot for worship. Reed's mother "used to put us chulluns outside de cabin in de quarters and den she would shut de doors and shut de windows tight and sit a tub of water in middle of floor and kneel down and pray that de yolk of bondage be removed from de nigger's neck. All de niggers done dat, dey did. Ma allus said de sound of dey voices went down into the tub of water and de white folks couldn't hear dem prayin'."[19] In many West African cultures, pots had deep symbolic meaning, especially for women. Pots were associated with the womb, with fertility, with the cosmos itself. Water, too, had deep religious meaning, given its symbolism as a life force. In many African traditions, bodies of water were alive with gods.

The power of such enslaved women's prayers was commemorated in spirituals:

> My mother prayed in de wilderness,
> In de wilderness,
> In de wilderness.
> My mother prayed in de wilderness,
> An' then I'm a goin' home
> Then I'm a goin' home
> We will all make ready Lord,
> An' then I'm a goin' home.
> She plead her cause in de wilderness,
> In de wilderness,
> In de wilderness,
> She plead her cause in de wilderness,
> An' then I'm a goin' home.[20]

Perhaps the association of prayer with the wilderness in this spiritual harkens back to the importance of nature gods in African worship. In addition, like many spirituals, this one can also be read as a metaphor for freedom and a literal escape from bondage. Rachel Santee Reed's mother was not the only one to pray for the yoke of slavery to be lifted. Dora Franks recalled that "I started prayin' for freedom and all de rest of de women did de same thing."[21]

"You can whip me—you can kill dis body but you can't kill my soul." It is almost impossible to overestimate the transforming power of this belief in the enslaved women's lives. Through it, women denied any effort on their masters' part to lessen their humanity. Here lay the ultimate resistance to enslavement, an effective weapon to combat the most damaging effects of slavery on the human spirit. This simple statement ranks as one of the most defiant ever uttered by a slave woman; on the one hand it acknowledged the brutal reality of slavery as complete control over another person's body, but it robbed the master of any sense of control over the slave's soul. Masters who encouraged Christianity as a means of recon-

ciling slaves to bondage made a drastic error. Christianity may have enabled slaves to better endure slavery, but it kept the hope for freedom
bright.

The spread of Christianity among blacks also represents a maturing
African American society. Enslaved Africans came from a wide swath of
central Africa, from a variety of tribes, cultures, religious and language
groups. With the growth of a creole population, an African American culture emerged cemented in part by a growing Christian faith. While slaves
retained a great deal from their African heritage, "the specifics of African
religions . . . could not be transported intact to the American South."
Slaves drawn from various African cultures shared many basic beliefs, but
these beliefs lacked coherence. In order to survive, blacks had to find some
means of reconciling themselves to slavery and its demands. As historian
Mechal Sobel wrote, "The African/American was thus uniquely ready for
the Great Awakenings. First, coming from a living mystery faith in Africa,
he was prepared to participate in the Christian mystery. Second, because
of his noncoherent world view, he deeply yearned for new coherence and
a new sense of unity and purpose."[22]

Blacks enthusiastically joined the first evangelical services in the Mississippi Territory; for example, a black man and his wife were two of the
eight people who organized the first Methodist church in the territory in
1799. The vital role blacks played in the camp meetings and their impact
on forms of worship have already been discussed. By the 1820s, as the
number of interested blacks increased, evangelical ministers held separate
services for them.[23] In 1821 Winans "met the black Society" in Washington, Mississippi, "and baptized three of their children. . . ." Later the same
year at Washington he "met the blacks in love feast order" and observed
that "[m]any spoke well." Sometimes whites attended such services and
joined their black brethren in worship. In 1823 "we met the Blacks at the
M[eeting] House" in Woodville, "and held love feast. This was quite a
refreshing season. Many of these poor people appeared happier than kings
(unless the kings new [sic] the love of Jesus) and some whites that were
present were very happy also."[24] Obviously, blacks and whites found the
same message edifying and responded with the same emotional intensity.
Even the services aimed particularly at blacks were far more than simply
"slaves obey your masters"; such a sermon would not have created a "re-

freshing season" among either blacks or whites. White ministers sometimes found themselves competing for the attention of their black
congregants. Methodist John Jones was interrupted during a sermon by a
Campbellite preacher who stood up and asked the audience to go with
him into the woods where he would preach. Jones reported that "most of
the *negroes* from behind the house did go with him, and a few others."[25]

Slaves in the African American and biracial evangelical churches
gained powerful symbols of humanity and spiritual equality. White evangelicals recognized blacks as their spiritual brothers and sisters with souls
equal to their own, a recognition that shook the foundations of the slave
system. The emphasis on the equality of believers was even more significant, since evidence suggests that most slaves attended the same churches
as their masters.[26] While no full-blown ideology of slavery had developed
by the early 1800s, slavery had been justified because of the slaves' hea-
thenism, and English laws forbidding the enslavement of Christians prevented many masters from allowing slaves to be baptized in the early
colonial era. Other justifications for enslavement included a presumption
of racial inferiority, and even a denial that blacks had souls. Evangelicals,
however, ministered to blacks, admitted them to their congregations in
the same ways as whites, listened as blacks recounted their conversion experiences, baptized them in the same waters, extended to them the right
hand of fellowship (a symbolic rite welcoming new members into the spiritual community), often called them "Brother" or "Sister," performed
marriage ceremonies, and, perhaps most dramatically, licensed blacks to
preach. Blacks and whites worshiped together in the outdoor services, in
the small log churches, or in private homes opened for services. Perhaps
seated separately but still in proximity, blacks and whites interacted and
together shaped the character of worship services. The realities of slavery
were never completely removed, however, and white evangelicals insisted
that prospective slave members have their masters' written permission to
join the fellowship if their master was not a member.

For some evangelicals, biracial worship had a deep and lasting impact
on their lives. Because of their interactions in religious settings, blacks and
whites often saw one another in a new and different light. William Winans
remembered that while he had seen few blacks as a child, he had somehow
learned "to consider them as inferior race of human beings. . . ." His

opinion changed dramatically when he attended a love feast where a black man recounted his religious experience. The black man's "deep and ardent piety" greatly affected Winans, who saw the man's faith as "the highest attainment to which man can aspire. . . ." Winans wrote, "Many, very many instances have, since that time, assured me that . . . 'God's no respecter of persons,' colors, or conditions. Among the most deeply pious Christians who I have known, have been many black people who, ignorant in other matters, degraded in conditions—many of them *slaves*, were children of God by Faith, and heirs to the promise of life eternal through Christ Jesus." Devout Presbyterian John W. Hundley freed his slaves in his will in 1829 and left funds to a Presbyterian school in Jefferson County with a request to the school's trustees to admit blacks.[27]

Evangelicals conceived of the biracial religious community as a family of God, a concept reflected in their use of familial nomenclature. Ideally, secular distinctions disappeared once members joined the fellowship; in the words of St. Paul, "There is neither Jew nor Greek, there is neither bond nor free, there is neither male nor female: for ye are all one in Christ Jesus" (Gal. 3:28). The apostle, of course, expressed an ideal seldom if ever achieved in any Christian community, but the egalitarian spirit clearly existed in the frontier biracial churches. Bethlehem Baptist Church, like many others, demanded that "[t]he appellation of brother shall be used in the church by members in their address to each other." Blacks and whites were often (but not always) called "Brother" and "Sister" in evangelical churches. While the use of familial nomenclature does not imply equality, it does suggest that white evangelicals recognized that blacks had souls equal before God despite the badge of color and the bonds of servitude. The use of such terms of address may seem like a small thing, but in a hierarchical society forms of address were laden with meaning. Nonevangelical whites typically used only first names when speaking to blacks; it was a code that both races clearly understood. In such a context the use of "Brother" and "Sister" in biracial churches carried special significance and indicated a changed status.[28]

Another ritual, extending the right hand of fellowship, followed baptism in the Baptist churches. When a person joined the church, the members filed past, shook the new member's hand, and welcomed him or her into the Christian fellowship. The act was an important symbol of acceptance, a public declaration that this individual now belonged to the religious community. When "Adam a black brother" joined the Louisville Baptist Church, he "came forward and related to the church what the Lord had done for him, the church being satisfied, unanimously received him a member and extended to him the right hand of fellowship." In many churches, congregations extended the right hand of fellowship to both blacks and whites throughout the antebellum period. Here, again, this ritual violated a widely held taboo against public physical contact and was a recognition of blacks as equals. A handshake is not so simple when it would otherwise be withheld as a symbol of inequality.[29]

As more and more slaves joined the churches, many evangelicals in Mississippi condemned slavery. John G. Jones, a native Mississippian who later became a Methodist minister, confessed that "[p]revious to my embracing religion, I . . . thought it was right for us to have as many of them [slaves] as we could get, and took a pleasure in the government of them, even when I had to use some violence to keep them in subjection." After his conversion, however, Jones "began to look on slavery as a great moral evil. . . ." Many evangelicals apparently agreed with Jones; he wrote that before the late 1820s and 1830s "few professors of Christianity, either among the laity or clergy, thought of attempting the justification of African slavery . . . from Holy Scripture." Most people, according to Jones, assumed that slavery "was a great social, political, and moral evil, which, while it had to be endured for the present, ought as soon as possible to be removed." He suggests that most Mississippi Methodists in the opening decades of the nineteenth century, like their brethren in other parts of the South, favored the gradual emancipation of slaves. Alexander Talley, another Methodist minister, asked prophetically, "[H]as Heaven no blessing in store for this class of her creatures. Are we doomed to pass on until the secret thunder burst . . . [?]"[30]

The issue of slavery plagued the evangelicals. The first question printed in the Mississippi Baptist Association's 1808 minutes regarded slavery: "What steps would be most desirable to take with members of our society whose treatment of their slaves is unscriptural?" The association recommended that the churches "take notice of any improper treatment of their members toward their slaves and deal with them in brotherly love according to the rules of doctrine." A master charged with cruelty would be treated in the same fashion as any other offender. A committee would be appointed to investigate the charges; if they were valid, disciplinary action would be taken. Evangelicals occasionally charged, tried, and disciplined abusive masters. For example, in 1827 the members of Pisgah Presbyterian Church called William Thompson before the church conference after he "cruelly whipped a slave. . . ." The 1810 covenant of the Sarepta Baptist Church included the following: "We promise to treat our servants with humanity and not impose on them any thing cruel or unmerciful."[31]

Eleven years later the Mississippi Baptist Association published a lengthy address to masters and slaves in which the association clearly outlined the duties of both parties. A dutiful slave should "be industrious, honest, faithful, submissive and humble. . . ." The Baptists did not defend slavery as a positive good, nor did they enter into a biblical defense of the institution. They did state, however, that "under the dispensations of God you have been brought into a state of bondage, however dark, mysterious and unpleasant those dispensations may appear to you we have no doubt that they are founded in wisdom and goodness." The Baptists acknowledged that slaves had few pleasures in life and wrote that their "drudgeries and toil . . . ought to excite sympathy and compassion in the hearts of those who enjoy the fruits of their labor." They warned masters to "[l]et not Avarice . . . induce you to oppress your servant lest his groans, his sweat, and his blood ascent [sic] up to God as a witness against you."[32]

Evangelicals also publicly defended slaves' religious rights in 1822 when a new law code, known as Poindexter's Code, placed prohibitions on black worship.[33] Winans wrote that Poindexter's Code met with "general satisfaction" except for the restrictions it placed on slaves' right to worship among themselves and its requirement that black services be conducted by a white minister. Winans wrote that "[s]uch a wanton curtailment of the religious privileges of the Slaves . . . aroused very general and strong feelings of opposition in all Christian Communities in the State; and it was deemed proper that this opposition should be such as to bear in a manner most forcible with politicians."[34]

Many Baptists also opposed the code; both the Pearl River and Mississippi Baptist associations appointed committees to seek the repeal of the law. The passage of Poindexter's Code temporarily interfered with the activities of black preachers since it required that services be conducted by a white minister. In 1822, for example, the members of Zion Hill Baptist Church considered licensing Smart, a slave, to "exercise his gift" to preach but delayed their decision "in consequence of an Act passed in the Legislature." The state legislature heeded the message sent by the voters and revised the code along lines suggested by Winans. A revision of the code permitted blacks to preach, and in 1826 Zion Hill allowed Smart to "exercise his gift within the bounds of the church as far as the Lord may direct him." A year later the church allowed him to exercise his gift outside the church. The new law no longer prohibited black preachers or black meetings, but it required that services either "be conducted by a regularly ordained or licensed white minister, or attended by at least two discreet and respectable white persons, appointed by some regular church or religious society." The law made it necessary for African churches to have some sort of affiliation with a white organization. The battle over the code foreshadowed the future of independent black worship. Evangelicals had preserved limited religious freedom for blacks, but the revised code was simply a forerunner of further legal restrictions to come in the wake of Nat Turner's 1831 revolt, which demonstrated the revolutionary potential of independent black worship and a dynamic black religious leader.[35]

The new restrictions on independent black worship brought more blacks into biracial churches. In a circular letter written in 1829 the Mississippi Baptist Association agreed that the lack of religious instruction of slaves weighed heavily against them. "[T]here is a criminal neglect among us," they wrote. The Baptists stopped short of a biblical defense of slavery and reaffirmed the slaves' humanity: "An all wise God, in order to execute some of his unfathomable designs, has thought proper to permit a portion of the human family to be reduced to servitude." According to the Baptists, the slaves' condition was not an act of God: "Among us, those who are reduced to servitude are, also, *by the laws of the land*, made slaves. . . ." They hesitated to recognize the institution of slavery and wrote that despite the law "we shall only regard them in the light of servants. . . ." The Baptists condemned masters who abused slaves and described "men even in this, our own country, who look upon slaves with no more respect than upon a dumb beast. . . ." Holding firm to their egalitarian traditions, the Baptists wrote, "For, however sable their hue, and however degraded their condition in this life, they possess rational and immortal souls. . . ."[36]

Here the Baptists reaffirmed the acknowledged equality of men, but by 1829 churches had begun to provide separate accommodations for black worshipers rather than seating them in the rear of the sanctuary as had been common practice. In that year Salem Baptist Church attached a shed to the side of the church building for blacks. A high partition divided the races, but the raised pulpit allowed blacks to see the preacher. Other churches also explored ways to seat blacks separately.[37] According to Patrick H. Thompson, a black Baptist church historian who published in the late nineteenth century, there were three types of churches for blacks in antebellum Mississippi: first, separate black churches under the supervision of a white church; second, churches where blacks used the same building as whites, but at different times; and, finally, churches where slaves attended the same service as their masters but were segregated from whites. In Thompson's view, the third situation was the most common. Many churches provided separate accommodations for blacks partly as a result of growing black attendance. A Presbyterian minister in Natchez observed that "when the church was opened last March [1815] I observed no place was assigned to the blacks. The poor creatures were hanging about the doors, afraid to enter." In 1829 the Bethany Baptist Church Conference "[t]ook under consideration the situation of the Black people who attend preaching at this church. . . ." They appointed a committee of five white men "to devise a plan of building an addition to our Meeting house for their accommodation. . . ." Their plan was not recorded, but perhaps it resembled the arrangement at Mountain Creek Baptist Church, which had "an enclosure the whole length of one side with an opening through which the slaves could see and listen to the services."[38] In such churches, blacks and whites continued to hear the same sermon, but the physical separation of the races and the suggestion of black inferiority that accompanied it show a waning of the early churches' egalitarianism.

The overcrowding reported by churches throughout the state suggests that religious interest was spreading rapidly among slaves. A committee appointed to consider "the moral and religious improvement of colored population" in the Aberdeen Baptist Association reported in 1845 that "God is reviving his work among them; there is an increasing desire to hear the word preached; but it must be regretted that there is no provision for them at many of our churches. It is not uncommon to see them crowd about the doors, without seats or even shelter to shield them from the inclemency of the weather. Still on their part there is a manifest desire to hear the gospel." The committee pleaded with their fellow Christians: "Dear Brethren, can we not do something? Will we not make some special effort to advance the Redeemer's kingdom among those who toil and labor for us? We should build additions to our churches, and give them better opportunities of hearing the gospel." Association records indicate that churches responded to this plea, and black membership grew rapidly. The association records did not report black membership in 1845, but in 1848 only twelve of the thirty-three member churches reported any black members, and the total black membership was about 250. By 1861, however, twenty-two of the thirty-one churches reported black members, with a total of 655 black and 1,354 white members. Baptist associations across the state followed the same course; by the mid-1840s associations typically reported black membership separately and appointed special committees to consider the needs of black members.[39]

As black membership grew, a shed or gallery provided only a temporary solution to the problem of overcrowding. In 1839 the Mississippi Baptist Convention found "that some few of our Churches, and some of our Methodist friends, have adopted the plan of holding separate meetings for the blacks; and that such a course is generally attended with an increased interest among them. . . ."[40] Separate services for blacks became increasingly common across the state, the result of both a desire on the part of whites to physically separate blacks and a black preference for segregated services. This arrangement gave blacks an opportunity to exert some control over their services and allowed them more independence in institutional worship than at any time since Poindexter's Code had restricted black worship.

Separate worship services for blacks became increasingly common throughout the antebellum period. Whites occasionally consulted blacks before holding segregated services; for example, the white members of Clear Creek Baptist Church "met . . . to confer with the Black Brothers and Sisters . . . to make some Raingment [arrangement] for them. . . ." In 1854 the members of Concord Baptist Church thanked their pastor "for preaching especially to the blacks and request him to continue to do so and that Brethren be requested as many as can do so to be present during services to them." Blacks and whites often heard the same preacher at Clear Creek, as they did at such racially segregated services across the state, though occasionally a white lay speaker ministered to blacks. Typically, the white congregation met on Sunday morning, and the blacks congregated in the afternoon.[41]

Like many whites, blacks liked an emotional worship style and a congregational ministry; as more and more churches abandoned these traditional styles of worship, blacks preferred segregated services where they could exert more control. A frequent complaint from former slaves was that the formal, staid worship services typical of many evangelical churches by the late antebellum period did not appeal to them. Isom Weathersby reported that "[u]s went ter meetin' 'bout once a month to de white folks meetin' house, but us didn't jine in wid de services. The service wuz good bus us liked our own whar us could git in de spirit an' pray an' shout."[42] Perhaps, too, slaves—who preferred more emotionally demonstrative services—felt inhibited by the presence of whites and hence preferred separate worship.

Whites oversaw these separate black services, but the degree to which they exercised control varied. State law required that whites be present at such services, but that law was not always obeyed. Liberty Baptist Church appointed a group of seven white men "to attend said meetings and act as police." At Concord Baptist Church "Brethren be requested as many as can do so to be present during service to them." At the Aberdeen Baptist Church supervision seems to have been light—"[a]bout once a month members of the white church were appointed to attend the negro church meetings." According to Dr. J. M. Heard of West Point, blacks there attended both the morning service and a later segregated service; he wrote that "[t]he negroes all belonged to the same church with their owners, . . . and at 3 o'clock in the afternoon they had the whole church to themselves." At Mt. Helm Baptist Church in Jackson blacks worshiped in the basement; in fact, Prior Lee, a white lay preacher who worked among blacks, donated bricks to build a new church with the condition that blacks be allowed to use that part of the building. From 1835 to 1867 blacks used the building for a variety of services; according to Thompson, "Much of the early worship of this church was spent in prayer meetings. 'The Early Service Prayer Meeting' was one in which they spent their happiest moments, no white person being present to molest them or make them afraid."[43]

Thriving quasi-independent black churches like Mt. Helm sprang up in towns across the South, and in Mississippi black churches in Aberdeen, Natchez, Vicksburg, and other towns were among the largest congregations in the entire state. The black Baptist church in Aberdeen, for instance, was the largest in north Mississippi, with 437 members, and in 1847 the congregation built a church to seat 300 people. Black Baptists in Natchez technically belonged to the Wall Street Baptist Church, which in 1856 had 16 white members and 499 black members. The church reported in 1856 that the "[w]hite Church met but seldom; worship principally with other denominations. Colored Church worship together every Sabbath." Blacks worshiped in a separate building called Rose Hill Baptist Church, built with contributions from whites and blacks, and a free black man held the deed to the church property. While a few whites attended services to insure legality, blacks controlled their own affairs under the leadership of an unlicenced slave preacher named Randle Pollard.[44] An African Methodist Episcopal Church functioned in Vicksburg from 1846 to 1858, and in 1849 the Columbus Methodist Church appointed a committee to find a suitable building for the use of the black "society & congregation in connection with this church." One year later the Columbus Methodist reported "a considerable revival among the colored congregation."[45] These quasi-independent churches would play a major role in the development of black religious denominations in the postbellum period, but their activities were more restricted in the antebellum period. Confined to the state's towns, they could not reach most slaves who lived in rural areas. As important and visible as these churches were, and as crucial as they would later become, the majority of blacks worshiped either in segregated or biracial services.

Even in churches where blacks and whites attended the same service, discrimination against blacks became more common. For example, in early churches, and in some later ones, the ritual of extending the right hand of fellowship applied equally to both blacks and whites. Other churches, however, followed the practice described in a Baptist newspaper, whose editor wrote that the ritual was not a church ordinance, and it was not necessary to have black members extend their hands to a new white member. "As to the colored members," he wrote, "we would invite them as a body only when a colored member was to be received." He assumed that blacks would not perceive this as being discriminatory, though blacks understood and resented the implications of such unequal treatment. Churches appointed committees or gave the pastor the responsibility of extending the hand of fellowship to blacks.[46]

Unlike the right hand of fellowship, communion was a church ordinance, and here, too, discrimination became more common. The Methodists, Baptists, and Presbyterians held separate communion services for blacks in the 1820s and after. In 1849, for example, the church conference at the Louisville First Baptist Church decided that "[i]t would be best to Administer the sacrament [*sic*] of the Lords Supper to the Coloured Church separately and apart from the white portion of the church. . . ." In some cases, churches allowed blacks to administer communion; Academy Baptist Church, for example, resolved "that Daniel, a colored brother, be appointed to wait on the blacks on Communion occasions." The church records offer no explanation for the separate communion services, although at Louisville the change was suggested by the white layperson who ministered to the blacks. Whether the suggestion originated with the lay preacher or the black congregation is unclear.[47]

Churches frequently appointed special committees, usually composed of slaveholders, to oversee blacks' behavior, to receive black members into the church, and to hear their testimony in discipline cases. The creation of such committees marked a dramatic departure from past practice, in which such cases were handled in the same ways for whites and blacks. The forming of these committees had important implications for biracial worship and marked a further separation of the races. In 1854 Academy Baptist Church appointed a committee "to regulate the conduct of Blacks on Sabath [*sic*] of our church meeting. . . ." A similar committee at New Providence Baptist Church was "to have an over sight of the blacks & have them disperse after preaching." A committee at Bethany Baptist Church ordered blacks to leave the church grounds immediately after services and warned that "[i]f the said cullard [*sic*] people do not comply with the . . . Rules we do request that pateroles to . . . take them and chastise them according to law. . . ." Frank Hughes, an ex-slave in Clay County, remembered "patarollers" policing separate black services at biracial churches.[48]

The social aspect of religious services was important for both blacks and whites, especially in Mississippi with its widely dispersed population. Sunday services provided slaves from different plantations with a rare opportunity to gather together, yet whites attempted to deprive them of this opportunity, or closely supervise their activity, which inhibited the formation of a black community within the white-controlled churches.

Perhaps the most important corollary of separation and discrimination, one overlooked by whites, was an increase in black autonomy within the biracial churches. In 1845, for example, the Concord Baptist Church decided that, since blacks held separate services conducted by their white minister, they should also hold a separate church conference. They authorized their "[p]astor in connection with the white brethren present on such occasions, to hold conference, with the black members, for their special benefit, and that each couloured [sic] member be entitled to a vote in the reception, rejection & exclusion of those of their own coulour." Liberty Baptist Church appointed two slave men "as watchmen to report to this church any of our colored members who may become disorderly. Also to stimulate them to Christian duty." A Methodist circuit rider in the state observed that white supervision of separate black conferences was light. While the white minister usually chaired the meeting, the conference was actually conducted by the black secretary, who apparently wielded great influence. The secretary acted " 'as the presiding judge of their church trials' and was 'the umpire to whom is referred not only the minor difficulties of the church members, but of the colored people at large.' " Whether blacks in such positions were chosen by whites or elected by blacks is unclear, but the end result in either case was greater black autonomy. By either allowing or forcing blacks into separate congregations and by giving them control over their members, whites unwittingly helped pave the way for the postbellum racial division of the churches.[49]

Still, many blacks resented the churches' abandonment of the egalitarian tradition and the subsequent treatment of blacks as less than equal.[50] Mattie Dillworth, an ex-slave from Lafayette County, recalled that "befor' de surrender I had to sit on a back seat, but dere cum a time sho Lord when I cu'd sit rite spang on de fron' seat." Jake Dawkins of Monroe County said, "The only time I 'member going to a meetin' was when de marster took all de slaves over to de white folks church at New Hope and had a white preacher to preach to us. But Lawd, he never did much preachin'. His text was, 'Obey your master and mistress', and he never told us a word about savin' our souls from hell fire and damnation." Another former slave, Jack Jones of Oktibbeha County, recalled that, according to the white preacher, even heaven would be segregated: "He stated that the white preacher enjoined the Negro to be . . . good slaves. As a result they would go to the Negro Heaven, or kitchen heaven. Uncle Jack laughed and said that anyway the slave thought, they would get plenty to eat."[51]

Other slaves, however, recalled a more positive experience in the biracial churches, additional evidence that the egalitarian tradition continued in some churches throughout the antebellum period. In a Webster County church blacks "were allowed to go there and shout just like the white folks." Another ex-slave from Webster County said that "we was allus welcome" at the local church. George Washington Miller described a Presbyterian church that had "pews for the white and for the black, and often the leading negro deacon 'Uncle Dick' sat in the pulpit. Everybody liked him. I remember preacher Reed, whom I thought almost was God hisself." Westly Little of Smith County vividly recalled his conversion at a biracial antebellum church service: "We went to church at de white folks meetin' house. One Sunday when I wuz jes' a strip ob a boy de preacher preached on how man wuz made from de dust o' de earth an' would return to dust. I wuz converted at dat sermon."[52] Slaves like Westly Little did not hear a sermon different from the one whites heard, and the message was clearly more than simply "slaves, obey your masters." Henry Gibbs recalled that "[o]ur slaves all come to dis hard shell Baptist Church out dere at Church hill. In May, we'd have foot-washins. De women would wash each others feet, and men would wash each others feet." When asked what he thought about religion, the former slave replied, "God Almighty gave every boy [body?] de same spirit—the Spirit of God."[53] That emphasis on equality would remain deeply ingrained in black theology.

Even as they began to move toward greater distinctions based on race, evangelicals felt the impact of the radical vision that had motivated their early opposition to slavery. In the late 1820s evangelicals began to support the efforts of the American Colonization Society. Initially the society's purpose was the transportation of free blacks to Africa, a course supported by many Mississippians. Beginning in 1827 the Reverend William Winans successfully solicited funds on behalf of the society. In the same year, the Methodist annual conference endorsed the organization's efforts and asked preachers to take an offering for the society around July 4. The Methodists passed a similar resolution the following year and published their position in the *African Repository* and New York's *Christian Advocate and Journal*. By 1829 the society had collected almost a thousand dollars, much of it from or by evangelicals. Efforts to organize a state society in the fall of 1828 failed because slaves heard rumors about the society and believed that its purpose was to gain their emancipation, a misconception that frightened slave owners.[54]

The Mississippi Colonization Society was successfully organized in June 1831 at a Natchez meeting. Almost all the society's organizers were either members of the planter elite or evangelicals. For decades the two groups had eyed one another with suspicion and outright hostility, but the conversion of wealthy planters, the growing wealth of many evangelicals, and the influence exerted by prominent ministers had narrowed the gap between the two. The society's president, Stephen Duncan, was a successful planter and physician, president of the Bank of Mississippi, and one of the state's wealthiest men. Gerard C. Brandon, the state's governor, and Cowles Mead, former secretary of the Mississippi Territory, were also officers, as was Isaac R. Nicholson, Natchez lawyer, speaker of the state house of representatives and later member of the state supreme court.[55]

One-fifth of the society's officers were ministers. Among these was the Reverend John C. Burruss, Methodist minister and president of the Elizabeth Female Academy, described as "an elegant gentleman, a finished scholar, and an elegant preacher." Benjamin Drake, also an officer, was a prominent Methodist minister who succeeded Burruss as president of the academy. William Winans became one of the society's most tireless members. Edward McGehee of Wilkinson County, another officer, was an active lay leader in the Methodist Church who owned approximately one thousand slaves, making him one of the South's largest slaveholders. At least three of the officers were Presbyterian ministers: Zebulon Butler, who preached at Port Gibson, Jeremiah Chamberlain, who served as president of Oakland College, and Benjamin Chase. Several members of the Mississippi Colonization Society also served as officers of the American

Colonization Society; among them were Duncan, Winans, and Mc-Gehee.[56]

The society had as its purpose the transportation of free blacks out of the state to be colonized in Africa, but it soon turned its attention to freeing and transporting slaves. From its organization until around 1840 the society enjoyed great success in the state. During that period Mississippians donated approximately a hundred thousand dollars to the colonization movement. The Methodist conference appointed Winans to raise funds for the society in Mississippi and Alabama; he became one of the society's most visible and valuable supporters in the Southwest. No doubt Winans and other evangelicals helped turn the society's attention toward the freeing of slaves in keeping with their long-held belief in gradual emancipation. At least four local auxiliary societies were organized in southwestern Mississippi. Agents from the national society visited the state frequently, raised considerable sums of money, and assisted in organizing local societies. Evangelical churches allowed these representatives to deliver their addresses in the churches, and they also allowed the state and local societies to meet in their buildings.[57]

The state society was so successful that in the mid-1830s its leaders decided to establish a separate colony in Liberia for Mississippi blacks called "Mississippi in Africa." Approximately 570 blacks, the majority of whom were freed slaves, settled in the colony. Many of these slaves were freed by evangelicals. For example, the Methodist William Foster, who died in 1834, freed twenty-one of his slaves to be transported to Liberia, and Edward B. Randolph of Columbus, Mississippi, another Methodist, freed his slaves shortly after his conversion in 1834 and paid for their transportation to Africa.[58]

The society's success in the state was short-lived, and it faced growing difficulties in the late 1830s as the debate between northern abolitionists and southern slaveholders heated up. Robert J. Walker, United States senator from Mississippi, told his colleagues that "among the unfortunate consequences which had been produced in Mississippi, owing to the . . . Abolitionists was the unpopularity of the Colonization Society, which previously . . . had been extremely popular." Members of the slaveholding elite quickly abandoned the society, while evangelicals who remained friendly to the society found themselves branded as abolitionists. In the

1840s Winans faced such charges after he delivered a speech favoring colonization. In the face of such attacks Winans defended himself by embracing slavery, a life-saving tactic that many other evangelicals must have taken.[59]

Evangelicalism sometimes bridged the gulf separating black from white, master from slave. Egalitarianism was too much a part of southern evangelical ideology to be completely erased. Blacks and whites who worshiped in biracial services sometimes transcended the barriers of skin color and status. In 1836 the members of Clear Creek Baptist Church mourned the death of a fellow member: "Mary a Coloured Sister belonging to Mrs. Miner departed this life last March leaving behind the most cheering evidence both in her life & in her death that she has gone to the Socty [Society] of the Spirits of the just made perfect in heaven."[60] Clearly the white member who penned this tribute to Mary expected to meet her in that egalitarian society of the just, not in a separate "kitchen heaven."

Regarding the South in the post-Revolutionary years, historian Eugene Genovese wrote, "One generation might be able to oppose slavery and favor everything it made possible, but the next had to choose sides."[61] His quotation is applicable to the first generation of Mississippi evangelicals. In the early years of the movement in Mississippi the evangelicals remained ambivalent toward slavery, and some even advocated abolition. Their hostility toward the institution and their advocacy of egalitarianism encouraged black conversion; more and more slaves joined the churches, organized their own independent congregations, and entered the biracial churches when independent worship was no longer possible.

As the decade of the 1820s drew to a close, evangelicals continued to espouse egalitarianism and spiritual equality among all men, and many maintained their opposition to slavery, or at least wrestled with its larger implications, but in the late 1820s the seeds of compromise with slavery and racial separation, with its implicit statement of inequality, were sown. Support of the American Colonization Society marked the final attempt by white evangelicals to end slavery. As Genovese said, they had to choose sides, and tragically, they chose slavery.

Despite the diversity in the biracial religious experience in antebellum Mississippi, the broad pattern was one of moving from relative egalitarianism to segregation and discrimination. This overarching trend should not obscure the fact that many churches held to the traditional evangelical style of worship and to the traditional theology emphasizing their belief that all are one in Christ. In these settings, blacks and whites continued to worship together, to be baptized together, to shout and sing together, and to meet on a common ground where race could be temporarily transcended. Even the discriminatory practices of many churches held an unforeseen advantage for black Christians. For the first time since the early 1800s, blacks enjoyed the opportunity of worship with little or no white supervision. Blacks demanded and usually received a service in keeping with their theology. A few blacks gained leadership positions in the biracial churches, especially in churches with segregated services. Despite legal obstacles and white harassment, black preachers continued to minister to members of both races. Separate services were a valuable training ground and helped prepare blacks for postbellum religious independence. As John Boles observed, "In the churches black men and women found persuasive reason to live as morally responsible adults, discovered arenas for the practice of black leadership, and experienced a far greater degree of equality with the surrounding whites than anywhere else in southern society. No wonder the church was the dominant institutional force in the lives of so many black southerners throughout the antebellum period and into our own time."[62]

Men & women may adorn there [sic] *own persons with all the collours* [sic] *of a Rainbow. They may dance & Sing and ride up & down in their fine carriages but happiness is not theirs.*

—Rev. Thomas Jefferson Lowry[1]

This day was appointed by Gov. McRea as a day of thanksgiving. Our business men generally close doors, and observed the day with a good deal of solemnity, large congregation . . . in the M[ethodist] E[piscopal] Church. Heard bro. Hutchinson Meth[odist] preach— good sermon, . . . dealt largely in Roman history.

—Rev. Nathan J. Fox[2]

The house of God must be built—the parent and the child, the servant and his master, the rich and the poor, all, all are interested in the message sent from God, and all should find a place.

—W. Hamilton Watkins[3]

5

A Religion in Cotton Bales, 1830–1860

Such dramatic and durable growth and expansion took place during the years from the 1830s to the Civil War that people referred to that period as the "Flush Times." The state's population more than doubled from 1830 to 1840, and then nearly doubled once again from 1840 to 1850. By 1840 the state had become the second in the nation, after South Carolina, to have a black majority, as the plantation system expanded and the production of cotton soared. By the end of the 1830s Mississippi was the leading cotton producer in the South. Other victims of this system, along with slaves, were the Choctaws and Chickasaws, who were removed from the northern two-thirds of the state in the 1830s as the United States government appropriated their vast tribal lands. Emigrants rushed in to settle the millions of acres of cession lands; many were wealthy planters with their slaves, while others were small farmers from the piedmont regions of Virginia, Georgia, and the Carolinas with few or no slaves. Some of the richest cotton planters in the South lived in the state, but the majority of white farmers either did not own slaves or owned fewer than twenty. Estimates suggest that the planter

class—those who owned twenty or more slaves—made up about 20 percent of the white farm population, though the proportion of planters in
the population varied widely, and they were concentrated, of course, in
the plantation regions.[4]

Evangelicals were shocked by the mad scramble for riches, and a
writer in one religious periodical hoped that "Mississippi will not much
longer deposit her religion in Cotton Bales." Baptists in the state wrote,
"The tide of emigration, setting in with such rapidity upon our State, from
almost every direction, calls loudly upon us to increase our efforts. . . . A
population as heterogeneous and unsettled as is generally found in every
new country, possesses . . . the elements of civil discord and destruction. . . ."[5] As quickly as possible, evangelical missionaries arrived in the
cession lands, and other emigrants organized churches without outside
assistance. In 1821 the Carolina Conference of the Methodist Church sent
two preachers as missionaries to north Mississippi, and in 1832 the Mississippi conference began making appointments in the cession lands. Many
new settlers were evangelicals who yearned to be part of a religious community, who sought through evangelicalism a greater sense of stability and
a means of forging more personal ties in a newly settled land. Josiah Hinds,
who settled in Itawamba County in 1839, described his new home: "We
are among strangers now in a strange land. . . . We are almost in the
woods—one cabbin [sic] onley [sic] to shelter us and our little ones, and . . .
a few neighbors who are kind but ignorant, [and] no Churches erected
for the worship of God." For settlers like Hinds, religion provided the
foundation for building a community; he soon established class meetings
and helped organize a Methodist church and a temperance society.[6]

Revivals and camp meetings had subsided in southern Mississippi, but
the conditions that had fed the movement two decades earlier were present on this new frontier. Thousands of emigrants poured into a wilderness
environment where social structure was weak, communal bonds were almost nonexistent, and settlement was sparse. Revivals brought converts,
and the organization of churches proceeded at an impressive rate. For example, in 1830 there was not a single Baptist church in Choctaw County;
by 1834 the Choctaw Baptist Association had thirty-four member
churches, eighteen ministers, and one thousand members.[7]

This rapid growth was part of a larger national evangelical expansion during which evangelical membership, wealth, and influence grew at a remarkable rate. In 1780 there were only 6 Baptist associations in the entire United States, but by 1860 the number had increased to more than 500. In 1783 the Methodists had 1 conference and by 1843 had 32. In 1776 the Presbyterians had 9 regional presbyteries; by 1855 the Old School Presbyterians had 148 presbyteries and the New School had 108. Methodists had about 50 congregations in 1783 and about 20,000 in 1860; Baptist congregations numbered about 400 in 1780 and more than 12,000 in 1860. The number of Presbyterian congregations grew from about 500 in 1780 to 6,400 in 1860.[8]

The growth rate in Mississippi mirrored this dramatic national expansion. In 1818 the Methodist Church in the state had 2,235 members; by 1860 the number had increased to 61,000. The Baptist churches grew from about 5,000 members in 1835 to 41,482 by 1860. The Presbyterian Church, by far the smallest of the three, had only 634 members in 1830, a number that had increased to 7,136 by 1861. That growth came at a cost and brought changes to the churches that many evangelicals refused to accept. The doctrinal disputes and denominational splits that accompanied this expansion were not new to the evangelical movement. The Great Revival had spawned its share of controversy and divisions, but the move from sects to denominations brought a new round of divisions to the churches. As historian Jon Butler noted, the rise of denominational institutions brought a rise in denominational authority, a change that clashed with the concept of the equality of all believers. Authority within the churches and within these larger institutions was exercised from the top down rather than from the bottom up. The change marked an important stage in evangelical development. Evangelicals would no longer be a people set apart from the world, a despised sect who challenged the values of their society.[9]

Mississippi Baptists organized a state convention in 1822, but battles between Missionary and Anti-Missionary Baptists (also referred to as Hardshell or Primitive Baptists) destroyed it. The convention also faced a major challenge from the followers of Alexander Campbell, still nominally Baptist, who waged a bitter struggle against missionary societies and hierarchical ecclesiastical organizations. The Primitive Baptists and Campbellites regarded missionary societies as nonscriptural organizations created by northern and eastern ministers to spread their influence throughout the nation. The challenge posed by the Campbellites and other reform groups, the split over missions, and the debate over an educated ministry combined to destroy the Mississippi state convention in 1829, but it was reorganized in 1836, again on missionary principles and, once again, it led to divisions within the Baptist Church.[10]

The Missionary Baptists predominated in the towns and more prosperous regions of the state. They saw themselves as progressive, modern Christians whose calls for an educated ministry were well suited to the times. Anti-missionary churches and associations were generally located in rural areas outside the plantation regions; believing that all authority should be lodged in the local congregation, they held fast to their Calvinist faith, and many of them joined a new denomination—the Primitive Baptists. By 1839 enough churches had broken away to form the Primitive Baptist Association, and by the 1850s there were at least six Primitive associations. The Primitive Baptists blasted their Missionary Baptist brethren for straying from traditional Baptist theology by supporting the doctrine of General Atonement, which held that salvation was available to everyone—a doctrine that conflicted with the Calvinist doctrines of election and predestination. In addition, they protested missionary, tract, and temperance societies and even Sunday schools, because they found no foundation for these in scripture; they scoffed at theological schools and calls for an educated ministry.[11] In their first Circular Letter, they heaped ridicule on their opponents:

> Were it possible to see the apostles of our Lord in company with some of our modern Baptists . . . what a contrast would appear! The one you would see going afoot with a pair of sandals on his feet; the other mounted on a fine steed, with fine boots on his feet—the one with his fisher's coat on; the other the finest broadcloth—the one with rough hands, all exposed by reason of hard labor; the other with fair hands covered with gloves. . . . The one saying, silver and gold I have none—and at another time, thy money perish with thee; the other saying three or four thousand dollars more will be of great benefit in advancing the Redeemer's kingdom.[12]

Even after the Primitive Baptists withdrew, many of the issues that drove them away continued to plague the Missionary Baptists. The Landmark Movement, which arose in the 1850s, also divided Baptists over the fundamental tenets of their faith. A central issue for the Landmarkers, as for the Primitive Baptists, was their insistence that each Baptist church was "isolated and independent" and, like the early churches described in the New Testament, was "independent of all other bodies, civil or religious, and the highest and only source of ecclesiastical authority on earth. . . .This church acknowledges no body of men on earth, council, conference or assembly as its head, but Christ alone. . . ." The Landmarkers were also hostile to ministers' claims to supreme authority within the churches. James Robinson Graves, publisher of the *Tennessee Baptist* and the primary leader of the movement, railed against the idea that ministers had any administrative authority in Baptist churches.[13]

Unlike the Primitive Baptists, the Landmarkers did not oppose Baptist associations so long as they did not interfere with local church government, and they also supported Sunday schools and theological seminaries under their own control. Thus it was possible for Baptists to favor Landmark reforms without leading to the sort of schism that divided the Primitive and Missionary Baptists. That flexibility helps explain the broad support Landmarkers gained from organizations like the Mississippi Baptist Association, which endorsed the Landmark cause throughout the 1850s and 1860s.[14]

As an offshoot of the Church of England, the Methodist Episcopal Church began as a hierarchical institution, though it was affected by many of the same debates that shook the Baptist Church.[15] The Methodist Protestant Church launched a challenge against the Methodist Episcopal Church that closely mirrored the Primitive Baptist attack on the Missionary Baptists; here, too, the underlying issues were hierarchical church structure, the role of the laity, and the status of the clergy. The Methodist Protestant movement began at the 1827 annual conference held in Baltimore, Maryland, when several disaffected preachers and twenty-two laymen who wanted to decentralize authority and give more power to the laity were expelled from the conference. Three years later they founded the Methodist Protestant Church.[16] In Mississippi the Methodist Protestant Church was strongest in the southeastern Piney Woods counties and the counties recently carved from the cession lands. The first church was organized in Jasper County in 1829, and the first annual conference met in 1841. At the time of this conference the church reported seven circuits with five hundred four white members and seventy-five blacks, a tiny number compared to the tens of thousands in the Methodist Episcopal Church.[17]

In 1814 the Presbyterian minister James Smylie persuaded the Synod of Kentucky to create a separate presbytery for the Southwest, the Synod of Mississippi and South Alabama, which met for the first time in 1815, and twenty years later a separate Synod of Mississippi was created. The Presbyterians, the wealthiest and most socially prominent of the evangelicals, were apparently content with their church's structure. The only controversy surrounded the division on the national level between the conservative Old School and the more liberal New School Presbyterians. The theological debates between the two intensified in the 1830s as support for the abolition of slavery grew in the New School ranks, and the two split in the church schism of 1837, a separation that most southern synods endorsed unanimously or with a few dissenting votes. The Presbyterians actively promoted education in the state; ministers like Smylie operated schools, and the Presbytery supported institutions of higher learning, most notably Oakland College.[18]

Presbyterians had already fought their battles over ministerial education, the role of the laity, and church structure during the Great Revival. The Cumberland Presbyterian Church broke away in 1810 over these issues. They competed with the Presbyterians in Mississippi and became the fourth-largest denomination in the state. The Presbyterian Church was strongest in the southern part of the state, particularly in towns and plantation areas, while the Cumberland Presbyterians were more numerous in the northern part of the state, in rural and poorer areas.[19]

Progressive evangelicals attempted to improve their society and fight illiteracy through support for education, especially Sunday schools. Many ministers had operated private academies to supplement their meager salaries, but institutional efforts expanded after the 1830s. Presbyterians noted in 1831 that "there is an increasing attention to the education of the rising generation. The Great Head of the church has sealed his approbation of Sabbath School efforts." The Sunday schools multiplied rapidly, and by the 1850s they were well established throughout the state. Often several Protestant denominations worked together to organize Sunday schools. In

Jackson evangelicals organized the Union School, which met regularly in the basement of the Baptist Church, while in Port Gibson Methodists and Presbyterians conducted a joint "free" Sunday school as early as the late 1820s. In 1837 the Sunday school in the First Methodist Church in Columbus, for example, had a superintendent, eight male teachers, seven female teachers, sixty-four male scholars, sixty-one females, and a hundred five volumes in its library; by 1851 the school had grown to include a superintendent, an assistant superintendent, a secretary, a librarian, a treasurer, thirteen male teachers, eighteen female teachers, seventy-eight male scholars, eighty-eight females, and a library of one thousand volumes. Sunday school celebrations became major events in communities around the state; a celebration held at the Jackson fairgrounds in 1859 was attended by two thousand teachers and two thousand students from towns across central Mississippi.[20]

Some evangelicals established Sunday schools for slaves. A Baptist newspaper advised masters to bring slaves to Sabbath schools, using the familiar argument that "[o]ur servants would be better, more faithful and obedient. . . ." By 1846 Columbus Methodists were operating a "Coloured Sabbath School" which was "in a most prosperous state and could Sufficient attention be paid them, much good would be done." Before the 1830s, blacks in some parts of the South learned to read and write in Sunday schools, but in Mississippi, state law prohibited teaching slaves to read and write, and suspicious masters vehemently opposed such instruction. Through Sunday schools and private academies evangelicals came to dominate education in the South. In the private academies they often taught the planters' sons, while the Sunday schools gave them access to the children of the plain folk. By these means, evangelicals further spread their beliefs through southern society.[21]

Ministers and denominational associations also encouraged members to support the burgeoning number of religious newspapers and magazines. By participating in these activities, ministers helped diffuse religion through their culture and left their imprint on American culture. This religious press was largely in the hands of reform ministers who favored a departure from the old ways. The Baptists created the state's first religious newspaper, the *South-Western Religious Luminary*, established in Natchez in 1836. It championed the creation of the Mississippi Baptist Convention and a more educated ministry, encouraged Baptists to shift their interest from rural areas to towns, and urged them to minister to the rich, not just the poor. An 1837 article in a Natchez religious newspaper, for example, said that it was easy to preach to a poor man in a "mud-walled cottage," but called on Baptist preachers "to ascend the steps of the royal palace, and enter the princely mansion. . . ."[22]

As the evangelical denominations grew and prospered, many ministers sought higher status and recognition as professionals, an ambition that could be achieved only by separating themselves from the laity and elevating their position within the churches and society. The desire for professional status was especially strong among the graduates of the new seminaries, who saw themselves as part of a rapidly expanding professional society emerging across America during the 1830s. The issue was not simply one of greater respect for ministers or the maintenance of decorum in church services but involved a fundamentally new definition of the ministry and the role of the laity in worship. Ministers elevated the importance of the ministerial gift and discouraged lay members from exercising their gifts of prayer and exhortation in ways that competed with their own.[23]

Many evangelicals tried to hold fast to more traditional forms of worship as debate began between older, more rural, and poorer evangelicals and a younger, more affluent group who wanted to abandon the old ways. The growing wealth of the church and many of its members often conflicted with its egalitarianism, and many town churches became fashionable places. In 1837 a Methodist minister complained that the Presbyterians were completing "a fine church . . . and when it's done they will be likely to take some of our hearers—as a great many like fine things." In 1855 William Winans, who had once expelled women from the church for dressing in finery, lamented, "I found Georgiana Carter, who had, I believe, but six rings on her fingers besides considerable other jewelry. Such are many modern Methodists!" He would have fumed at the wealthy women who attended Rehobeth Methodist Church in Copiah County. Melissa Taliaferro, for instance, wore "a pale blue silk ruffled to the waist, very low neck and short sleeves, showing her plump white shoulders, and such a big hoop skirt she could hardly get in the church door. . . . [S]he always wore those 'party dresses' to church . . . with bare neck and arms." The rich and gay Taliaferro, Brown, and Hawkins women, dressed in their silks, Spanish mantillas, and New York fashions, stood in sharp contrast to the poor women in the church. Unlike these elite women who came to church in carriages, the plain folk walked. They were women like Miss Matthias and Mrs. Hogan, "who always walked and sat together." They "always wore black calico dresses and black sunbonnets. Tall and slim, their skirts hung strait down—no hoops. Their faces look very long and thin. . . . They never spoke and never smiled." By 1848 a Baptist newspaper was warning, "It is folly for persons to inveigh against dress and its seductions." In many towns, simple meeting houses were replaced by more elaborate and expensive structures. The Presbyterian church in Port Gibson, one of the state's best-known structures, with its steeple topped by a huge hand, index finger pointed heavenward, cost forty thousand dollars. Town ministers also expected to live in a style befitting their station; the Presbyterian manse in Natchez cost sixteen thousand dollars in 1838, while the Methodist minister resided in an elaborate home called the Parsonage, a gift from a Natchez millionaire who lived in one of the city's finest mansions, Rosalie. These costly town buildings stood in stark contrast to the simple, unadorned log or frame country churches.[24]

Many evangelicals, especially those in towns, began to espouse the virtues of hospitality the earlier evangelicals had once disdained, and agreed that their clergymen should be educated and genteel. For example, the Reverend Dr. Haden Leavel, a Methodist minister and physician who preached in Jackson and Vicksburg in the 1840s, was a Kentucky native, "blessed with a liberal education" and known for "his suavity of manners." A Methodist newspaper reported that there was "a growing tendency" in the Methodist Church "to accommodate the spirit of the age, by acknowledging that its ministry, is not exactly the thing for modern society." The Presbyterians, of course, had always placed a high value on an educated clergy, but in the 1830s the Methodists and Baptists also debated the issue, and their conferences and associations generally favored more strenuous qualifications for clergymen. In 1831 Benjamin Drake chaired a committee at the Methodist Annual Conference that recommended higher examination standards for ministers, and the Mississippi Methodist Conference contributed to the support of several seminaries. The Baptists established the Judson Institute in 1836 to educate ministers. One Baptist minister stated that "no man unless a Hebrew scholar, was qualified to occupy a

pulpit!" The increasing number of educated ministers in the state's towns
and the widening economic, social, and intellectual division between the
clergy and the laity was part of a general southern and national pattern.[25]

While some members of the planter elite went into the evangelical
churches, others either refused to do so or left the evangelical churches
for the Episcopal Church; parvenus like Jefferson Davis abandoned the
Baptist Church for the more aristocratic Episcopal Church. A few evangelical ministers, like Edward Fontaine and Adam Cloud, who had begun
their careers as Methodists, joined the Episcopal Church as well. The
Episcopal Diocese of Mississippi was established in 1826 with three parishes located in the plantation regions at Church Hill, Natchez, Port Gibson, and Woodville. Under the capable leadership of Bishop William
Mercer Green, who became the state's first resident bishop in 1849, the
Episcopal Church grew steadily, and by 1855 had thirty clergymen, thirty-
three parishes, and more than nine hundred members in the state. Given
the evangelical background of many of its members and ministers and the
climate in which it operated, it is hardly surprising that the Episcopal
Church in the South was strongly tinged with an evangelical spirit.[26]

As evangelicals moved up the socioeconomic ladder, many of the town
ministers became quite wealthy; indeed, as a group, town ministers across
the South were surprisingly prosperous. Historian E. Brooks Holifield, in
his survey of southern town ministers, found that their average wealth was
approximately four times that of the average American. Such affluence
made these ministers even more acceptable to wealthy congregations in
cotton towns like Natchez, Port Gibson, Columbus, and Vicksburg. In
Natchez, for example, the Presbyterian minister, Perry Chase, had an estate valued at sixty-five thousand dollars in 1860, and W. G. Millsaps, a
Methodist, held forty-five thousand dollars.[27]

A sharp debate began between these professionalized clergymen and
their less wealthy, socially inferior, and less educated brethren who questioned the value of an educated clergy. William Winans, who had only
two weeks of formal schooling, championed the country preachers' cause.
Though he was self-taught and spent much time in the saddle as he traveled his extensive circuits, no one doubted his intellectual abilities; a fellow
minister called him "one of the greatest minds on the continent. . . . He
was an intellectual giant." After his friend Benjamin Drake chaired the

committee that recommended higher qualification standards, Winans challenged Drake's conclusions: "[M]uch as we need polish, it seems to me we need *Stamina* more. I mean we need more of the spirit, the zeal, the industry, the devotion of the ministerial character more than we need intellectual culture." Winans heaped scorn on the educated ministers: "They have other refined and elevated tastes that must be accommodated. The churches where they condescend to hear the gospel must, if possible, be magnificent piles of Gothic architecture. The seats must be *pews*, to keep apart the elite and the vulgar, and must be carpeted and cushioned. The music must be the scientific performance of a well-trained choir, accompanied by the deep, solemn, awe-inspiring tones of the organ. Nothing less than all this can match the pretensions of such excelsior, Methodist-taught graduates." The country ministers maintained that God's call, not a seminary degree, determined who should preach the Gospel.[28]

Town ministers and country preachers criticized each other's preaching styles, and town and country congregations expressed their preferences. The town congregations favored a "smooth and harmonious" style free of "affectation" and "flourishes." The "heavenly tone," so popular with early evangelicals, fell out of favor. A dissatisfied member of a country church "heard the Rev. Capers *read* an essay of his on *Reason* & Religion" during which "a great many took short *naps*, & Some took tolerably long ones." Obviously, the Reverend Capers made no attempt to set his dozing congregation on fire with the Holy Spirit, nor did he expect lay involvement in the ministerial effort. A Presbyterian minister described a country preacher's sermon: "His manner of preaching was *Methodistical*, clapping . . . his hands stamping with his feet, and occasionally throwing in such expressions as 'God bless your soul' 'God love you' & c. characterized his discourse." Town ministers tried to escape the association of this preaching style with all Methodists and Baptists, while country preachers called on their city counterparts to remember their roots and put excitement back in their discourse.[29]

Rural congregations preferred men like Brother Huston, who preached in Sulphur Springs Baptist Church in Newton County. Described as "a plain man, above sixty years old, of limited education, who earned his living on the farm," Huston did not preach for money, but "for the glory of God and the salvation of sinners." Without formal education, "Greek and Hebrew were unknown tongues" to him, and "the writings of the Fathers, and the speculations of philosophers were closed books." Instead, he relied solely on scripture: "[T]he Bible was to him, the Book of books, the source of wisdom and power, the living word of a living God, written by the finger of the Almighty on the Rock Forever." His straightforward theology held that "sin and death came through man's first disobedience, that Jesus died to redeem him from that curse, and that those who believed on Him should not perish but have eternal life." It was this simple but powerful message that he conveyed to his listeners: "[T]hat was the theme of all his sermons . . . there was no theological dogma, no discussion of the mission of the church, . . . but 'good tidings' of great joy, —tidings of eternal life to those under the curse of eternal death." His vivid images of Moses and fiery serpents in the wilderness or the "mighty tragedy" of Jesus on the cross were followed by his earnest pleas for "men and women to come to Jesus for refuge, and live forever." His simple services, accompanied by Sacred Harp singing, attracted large crowds "from every direction for miles around."[30]

A cappella congregational singing played a vital role in early evangelical services such as this one in Newton County, but as part of the reduction in lay participation in services, many urban churches in the 1830s organized choirs rather than allowing congregational singing, and the role of singing in the church also became a heated issue. According to John G. Jones, "In many of the fashionable churches of the present day, all that the congregation hear during 'the service of song' is the mingled din of instrumental music and the screaming of human voices." The introduction of choirs and instruments had a far-reaching impact on the traditional evangelical folk music; lining out hymns and shape-note singing, for example, were impossible with choirs and musical accompaniment. Walter Edwin Tynes, later a Baptist preacher, recalled that "[t]he first organ introduced in church in this immediate section was denounced by one of the old preachers as a 'fiddle box,' and thus related to the demoralizing dance."[31] Jones clearly recognized that singing was an important gift and a powerful instrument of conversion. He wrote: "We have known persons awakened, converted, sanctified, and otherwise abundantly comforted and edified under these concluding songs. But, alas for the spirituality of the

Church, and . . . for the salvation of souls, this gushing, stirring, melting, and enrapturing method of singing . . . has been superseded by a new style, which . . . has but little—often none—of the spirit and power of our former 'service of song.' "[32]

In 1838 the Mississippi Methodist Conference resolved that "the introduction of instrumental music into public worship . . . and the conducting of the music in our churches by choirs . . . is injurious to the spirituality of singing, and is inconsistent with the directions of our Discipline." The Methodist Discipline devoted over half its directions to singing in worship, reflecting the importance attached to this form of ministry in the early church. Despite the 1838 resolution, the use of instrumental music and choirs continued to spread, and debate over the practice disrupted the annual conferences throughout the antebellum period and beyond.[33]

Many Methodist, Baptist, and Presbyterian churches gave up the intimate, lay-oriented services that had played such a vital role in the earlier decades of the century. Methodists abandoned class meetings and love feasts, two kinds of services in which lay participation and leadership were crucial and emotionally demonstrative worship common. One Methodist called on the annual conference to enforce the discipline and "do all you can to *revive* class meetings, for is it not the wheel within the wheel." Rather than enforcing the discipline and encouraging or requiring ministers to hold such services, the general conference in 1866 recognized the new situation and changed the rule making attendance at class meetings a test of membership. Missionary Baptist churches abandoned the intimate foot-washing ceremonies, and the Baptist press declared that the ceremony was not an ordinance of the church. By the 1840s the festal Presbyterian communion season was largely a memory.[34]

Often the opponents of religious modernization tied their opposition to the chase for wealth in the state and the growing disparities between rich and poor evangelicals. Primitive Baptists in Leake County, for example, criticized Missionary Baptists for "placing the gospel side by side with common merchandise, and placing the poor brother on an unequal footing with the rich hypocrite." An association of Primitive Baptists in Monroe County charged that their opponents "are running greedily after the things of this world," condemned "fairs whare [sic] toys and merchandise of various kinds are vended," and found "many unfair means . . . for the purpose of getting money." Harking back to the early church, they reported "no where do we hear of Paul or any other apostle Hiring himself out to preach the gospel for wages—for money." A writer in a Methodist newspaper blasted the love of filthy lucre: "One answer, and one alone, comes up to almost all the ills and desolations of human existence. . . . It rumbles out in the ruinous voice of the earthquake—in storm—in terror—in despair—the 'almighty dollar,' the 'dollar almighty.' "[35]

As town ministers led the churches in the quest for status and prestige, they sought to gain a higher professional status for themselves. Increasingly, ministers set themselves above the laity; they elevated the importance of the ministerial gift while depreciating gifts traditionally exercised by the laity. In more and more churches, the laity became spectators, and the enthusiastic services so common in the early churches were replaced by more sedate, less emotional ones. These professional clergymen saw themselves as the leaders of a movement that would strengthen the churches through a larger membership and an expanding network of auxiliary organizations. Obviously, many members approved of the changes in the churches, and the burdens of membership grew lighter as the shift to a clerical ministry put fewer demands on the laity. Churches often sought to assume a dominant posture in their communities; being a part of the largest or wealthiest church could be a source of great satisfaction for many members. A more formal service appealed to a more refined churchgoer, while others might be moved by a splendid interior and a practiced choir. The yearning for status, wealth, and influence impelled modernist evangelicals toward the acceptance of slavery and led them away from the egalitarianism of the early churches.

Few Mississippi evangelicals could be described as rabid abolitionists even before 1830, but as Methodist John G. Jones observed, most believed that slavery "was a great social, political, and moral evil, which, while it had to be endured for the present, ought as soon as possible to be removed." He wrote that "[o]ur conference was never what abolitionists call proslavery, but was perhaps universally in favor of a gradual and judiciously conducted emancipation." The belief that slavery was unjust represented a broad American consensus that grew out of the noblest ideals of the Revolutionary era. Those sentiments echoed in an 1818 ruling from the

Mississippi Supreme Court that stated, "Slavery is condemned by reason and the laws of nature."[36]

Up until the 1830s, gradualist emancipation schemes allowed most southerners, including the majority of evangelicals, to denounce slavery as an evil, shed crocodile tears over ever finding the proper time or method of abolishing it, and continue to buy, sell, and own slaves. Problems arose only when the northern abolitionists abandoned gradual or voluntary plans for emancipation, which many southerners also supported, to more radical schemes of immediate abolition. The debate began over the morality of slavery, and as such it was a religious debate before it became a political one. It was fueled largely by religious leaders on both sides of the Mason-Dixon Line, and it was no coincidence that religious institutions were torn apart long before political institutions suffered the same fate.[37]

John G. Jones's change of heart on the slavery issue illustrates the complexities many evangelicals faced. Jones grew up in a slaveholding family of yeoman farmers and, until his conversion, had no qualms about slavery. After his conversion, however, he advised friends not to buy slaves, distributed John Wesley's antislavery pamphlet, and offered to free his slaves, though they chose instead to be sold to a kindly master to avoid being transported out of the state as the law required. He wrote of "the curse of negro slavery" and described it as "a great evil." His attitude changed dramatically, however, after he began to read biblical defenses of slavery. In 1840, he wrote, "More mature experience and a more thorough examination of the whole subject has greatly modified my views of 'negro slavery.' "[38]

He was not alone; between 1830 and 1840 most southern evangelicals adopted a systematic, biblical proslavery ideology. Mississippians took an early lead in developing the biblical defense of slavery. In the late 1820s Presbyterian divine James Smylie began to defend slavery on biblical grounds. In his background and career, Smylie had much in common with his contemporary proslavery authors. Little is known of his early life, but as a young man he became a student at the Reverend David Caldwell's famous "Log College" in Guilford County, North Carolina, the alma mater of most southern Presbyterian ministers in the late eighteenth and early nineteenth centuries. Following his ordination in 1806, Smylie settled in the Mississippi Territory along with other family members and later purchased more than a thousand acres of land; he lived in high style on his plantation, called Myrtle Heath. He was one of the largest slave-holders in Amite County and a member of the South's planter aristoc-racy.[39]

Like other proslavery advocates, Smylie was not an obscure country parson but held a prominent position within his church and society. His Presbyterianism also put him in the mainstream, for more proslavery writ-ers came from that denomination than from any other. No doubt the high educational requirement for Presbyterian ministers helps explain their preponderance, as does their theology, since Calvinism was free of the Arminian doctrine of free salvation equally available to all believers. His background as an educator and slaveholder was also common for such authors.[40]

It was no coincidence that the defense of slavery began with a wealthy slaveowner who ministered to the state's most affluent denomination. His biblical defense of slavery initially set him apart from his fellow evangeli-cals, who found such a defense to be at odds with evangelical tradition. But while other ministers supported colonization or other schemes to end slavery, "Mr. Smylie sat down to a quiet, honest and critical examination of the Holy Bible," an exercise that convinced him "that the enslavement of the Hamitic race had been recognized as justifiable under every dispen-sation of the Church . . . that the holiest men . . . in the Bible had been connected with it, without censure, and that the relative duties of masters and servants were clearly defined in the New Testament Scriptures, which was demonstrative evidence that the relation was . . . compatible with Christianity."[41]

Smylie's reliance on the curse of Ham to help justify slavery reveals that he was engaged in more than a study of scripture; clearly he was also reading other proslavery tracts. For more than a thousand years, Christian, Moslem, and Jewish scholars had carefully honed a version of Noah's angry curse against Ham, the son who mocked his nakedness, which linked Ham's son Canaan, cursed to be a servant, with Africans. This malevolent interpretation grew out of the story of Noah and the flood and the idea that all humans after the deluge were descended from one of the three sons of Noah, either Shem, Japeth, or Ham. Over time, biblical scholars and theologians from many different religious traditions reinforced the idea that Africans were descended from the sons of Ham and therefore destined to live out their lives in enslavement and servitude. By the time southern Christians began to defend slavery in the 1830s, the curse of Ham was already an ancient and fully articulated construct, a malleable one especially popular with Protestant advocates of African bondage.[42] By combining this justification with other references to slavery or other forms of bondage from the Old and New Testament, proslavery ministers like Smylie erected what appeared to be an impressive biblical defense of slavery, and the only proslavery argument likely to carry any weight during the period was one with a powerful religious support.

In the late 1820s, Smylie composed a sermon on the subject that he chose to deliver not in one of the rural churches he pastored in his area, but at the elite Presbyterian Church in Port Gibson. Initially his sermon got a negative response, but he was a notoriously strong-willed man, convinced of his own opinions. In 1836 the Presbytery of Chillicothe, Ohio, a hotbed of abolitionism, sent an antislavery petition to the Presbytery of Mississippi. Smylie wrote a long response based on his sermon, but the Mississippi Presbytery was too disturbed by his radical ideas to accept it. Despite continued warnings from his colleagues, Smylie published the response as a pamphlet, but since no publisher would accept it he was forced to have it printed privately.[43]

The controversial nature of the pamphlet provoked more interest in it, and it "circulated generally through the country, and was the first . . . ever published in the Southwest on that side of the question." Abolitionists' attacks on the work also increased sales, and Smylie and New York abolitionist Gerrit Smith engaged in a fierce newspaper battle. Smylie "was covered with odium, and honored with a large amount of abuse from the abolitionists. . . ." The pamphlet circulated widely in the Southwest, and historian Walter Brownlow Posey believed that Smylie's work soon dominated religious thought on the question across the Deep South. Smylie wrote with satisfaction, "Contrary to my fears, my Methodist, Presbyterian, Episcopalian & Baptist brethren, (so far as I have heard) cordially approve of the doctrines of the pamphlet." The religious press reviewed the pamphlet in glowing terms. As one editor wrote, "The pamphlet, mentioned in our paper week before last, seems to have an almost unbounded popularity wherever it is read. . . . The South can do no less than take up Mr. Smylie's present edition without any delay."[44]

At the heart of Smylie's pamphlet is his emphasis on the household as the bedrock of southern society, the foundation on which all else rested.[45] For progressive clergymen like Smylie, the family represented the strongest link in a society's chain of governance. Free and equal white males presided over the household as they did over the larger republican society. One Presbyterian minister in the state wrote, "The true Scriptural idea of slavery . . . is that of a patriarchal relation." The master, he continued, "is essentially the head of the household in all relations—the head of his wife—the head over his children—and the head over his servants." Smylie warned that abolition would erode even the most fundamental relationships. "The licentiousness of the female character in France . . . ," he wrote, "is a true test of the effects of the Rights of Women, written by [William] Godwin, one of the High Priests of the abolition of marriage."[46]

The proslavery vision of society, then, subordinated women to the governance of white men as surely as it did slaves. So long as the evangelicals focused their attention on individual conversion, stressed the converts' relationship to God rather than to family, and preached the equality of all believers, it is hardly surprising that men often opposed the conversion of their wives and children as forcefully as they did the conversion of slaves. Just as evangelicals assured masters that conversion would make better slaves, they assured husbands that conversion would make wives more content with their subordinate position. Any criticisms of the subordinate relations within the family were intended not to threaten that subordination, but to perfect it. In 1859 a writer in a Baptist newspaper advocated the repeal of laws against teaching slaves to read. As he searched for a parallel to the slave experience, he drew on the status of women; an educated slave posed no greater danger than an educated wife, he argued. He admitted, however, that "[t]here are *things* that some folks call men, who regard women no more than slaves, and would have them do more work than favorite negroes, or horses." Evangelicals argued that religion and even limited education would make better slaves and "better wives." Christianity and religious training prepared women for their station in the household as wives and mothers.[47]

A proslavery stance, then, marked a repudiation of the enlightened

Revolutionary ideals of individual rights, liberty, and equality, and celebrated instead a vision of a modern, hierarchical slave society based on
mutual responsibilities and social cohesion. Proslavery writers and abolitionists engaged in a battle over the proper interpretation of the Revolutionary heritage. Southerners questioned whether natural rights as
expressed in the Declaration of Independence existed at all. William Winans denied that the rights Thomas Jefferson listed in the declaration were
inalienable, and, in any event, maintained that the enlightened author
himself did not "consider the slaves of the United States as *parties* to her
political Institutions, or *partakers* in her *political* rights."[48] Proslavery southerners repudiated the liberal legacy of the Revolution and cut the South
off from the national mainstream. Proslavery ideology set the South on a
course that led it ever further away from developments in the rest of the
nation. As the South adopted the proslavery argument, the nation became
increasingly a house divided. Abolitionists and proslavery clergymen
waged a battle over the nation's history and the proper interpretation of
its past, a battle with tremendous implications for the nation's future.

With an impressive display of exegesis, proslavery clergymen forged
links between religion, family, slavery, and society in a way that maximized
their influence within southern society. They became the chief defenders
of the South's most cherished institution and set themselves up as judges
over the entire paternal slave system. As one minister explained to slaveholders, "They [the slaves] are yours—wholly yours; and no one has, according to the teachings of Heaven, and the laws of men, any right to
interfere, in the smallest degree, with you or them, except myself." As
Smylie wrote, "The pulpit has, and must forever have, a prodigious influence. It is like the lever and the fulcrum, of the ancient Archemedes
[*sic*]—it is competent to move a world."[49]

One group of southern Christians remained completely unconvinced
by the biblical proslavery argument. Enslaved Christians held fast to their
belief that slavery violated the laws of God. Riley Moore, a former slave
in Montgomery County, believed that white ministers who preached the
biblical defense of slavery to slave congregations "ought to have been
hung fo' preachin' false doctrin'. They was no such thing in the Bible."
Charlie Moses, an ex-slave who was also a preacher, said, "When I gets ta'
thinkin' back on them days I feels like risin' out o' this heah' bed an'

tellin' everybody 'bout the harsh treatment us colored folks was given. My Marster was mean an' cruel an' I hates him, hates him. The God Almighty has condemned him to eternal fiah', of that I is certain."⁵⁰

Despite their proud boasts, proslavery ministers clearly did not move the entire world—but they reshaped their portion of it. Their view of southern society became linked in the minds of whites with the defense of slavery, and spread from prominent pulpits and through pamphlets and the religious and secular press. After the early 1830s, more and more white evangelicals adopted the biblical defense of slavery and defended the South from abolitionists' attacks. White evangelicals who refused to join the pro-slavery chorus generally left the state for the North or kept their opinions to themselves. While many white Mississippians had once believed slavery to be a moral, political, and social evil, proslavery sentiment based on bib-lical readings quickly became the new orthodoxy. One newspaper in 1838 urged its readers to shun their neighbors who believed slavery to be "*mor-ally, socially, and politically*, wrong. . . ." Should such people be tolerated, the editors warned, the South might as well "lower our colours and capitu-late to the Abolitionists at once. At this crisis we want no such men among us. The South should be purged of them."⁵¹

Southern clergymen were also willing to sacrifice national religious organizations on the altar of slavery when it became clear that their de-fense of the institution would deprive them of leadership positions within those organizations. As early as 1820 ministers at the Methodist General Conference engaged in bitter disputes over slavery. The conflict came to a head at the 1844 conference when the Methodist Church was torn asun-der, and southern ministers bolted to form the Methodist Episcopal Church, South. The division of the Methodist Church attracted the most attention, but the Baptist and Presbyterian churches also split along re-gional lines. In 1844 when the Baptist Triennial Convention's Board of the Home Mission Society, which was dominated by northerners, refused to appoint a slaveholding preacher as a missionary, southerners withdrew and created a Board of Domestic Missions under their own control. The separation was completed the following year when delegates from eight southern states and the District of Columbia met in Georgia and estab-lished the Southern Baptist Convention, a move endorsed by the Missis-sippi Baptist Association. Technically, the Presbyterian Church remained united until 1861, but their apparent national unity was possible only because of the 1838 division between the old and new schools that took most abolitionists out of the church. By 1845, then, the southern churches were firmly in the proslavery camp.[52]

Evangelicalism was affected by the political, social, and economic currents of the antebellum period and affected them in turn. The population explosion and the opening of new land gave evangelicals a field of labor that they quickly exploited, and churches often formed the nucleus of new communities. The period known as Flush Times proved to be a turning point for evangelicals. Many of them benefited from the rapid economic growth and found the prosperity they had sought on the frontier. That newfound wealth, and the growing dependence on slavery that accompanied it, led to dramatic changes in evangelical churches. By the 1830s evangelical modernists had shifted their emphasis away from the individual. They increasingly criticized the camp meetings and the emotional New Birth conversion experience; they abandoned class meetings, foot-washing ceremonies, and communion seasons; they gave up gender-segregated seating in favor of family pews; and they restricted the role of the laity in services.

The period from 1830 to 1860 saw a major shift in evangelical theology as progressives abandoned the traditional evangelical emphasis on the equality of believers and advocated instead a hierarchical, corporate view of the religious community, a change with tremendous implications for blacks and women. These clergymen and their supporters expanded evangelical influence not simply through individual conversion but through corporate bodies such as the various religious societies, schools, and colleges and through their vision of the household, perhaps their most common metaphor. While a few evangelicals continued their antislavery efforts, another current developed within their ranks, and they would be forced to choose sides on the slavery question. Many evangelicals remained ambivalent about slavery and criticized it openly until the mid-1830s, but after that time progressive ministers developed a biblical proslavery argument that completely dominated the region. Criticism of the institution was no longer tolerated as events outside the state, particularly the abolitionist movement, affected Mississippi churches.

Almighty God, who . . . watcheth over all things, and in whose hands is the disposal of all events, we look up to Thee for thy protection and blessing amidst the apparent and great dangers with which we are encompassed. Thou hast, in thy wisdom, permitted us to be threatened with the many evils of an unnatural and destructive war. Save us, we beseech Thee from the hands of our enemies.

—WILLIAM M. GREEN, BISHOP OF THE
EPISCOPAL DIOCESE OF MISSISSIPPI,
April 24, 1861[1]

6 The Chastening Rod: Religion in the Civil War and Reconstruction, 1861–1876

In January 1861 eighteen-year-old Lucy Irion looked forward with some trepidation to a fast-day service at the Presbyterian Church in Columbus. Despite her youth, she understood the depth of the nation's troubles. On January 4, 1861, she wrote, "The political state of the country has almost come to a crisis. Tomorrow is a fast day. I expect I will go to hear Mr. Lyon's sermon prepared for the occasion." The following day, she noted, "was appointed by President Buchanan as a day for fasting & prayer in behalf of the dreadful condition of our once glorious Union. We had no breakfast. . . . [W]e prepared for church, as Mr. Lyon was to preach a sermon. . . . Oh! 'twas splendid too. Had a large congregation & perfect attention. . . . Oh, our glorious country is falling, falling. All Wise, avert the evil which now seems inevitable." Perhaps the Reverend James H. Lyon contributed to Lucy's grim mood, for he was an ardent Unionist. In another fast-day sermon delivered in June 1861, he "devoted a long preliminary to this sermon in inveighing against letting down and prostituting the pulpit . . . which has been done to a most lamentable extent by nearly all the pulpits in the land. . . ."[2] Across Mississippi, evangelicals assembled on that solemn day to offer prayers in the time of crisis.

As some evangelicals saw more clearly than others, the outbreak of war in 1861 would bring drastic changes to their community. The orderly patriarchal slave society they had labored to create quickly unraveled under the strains of war. Evangelical ministers as a group did not lead the secession movement, but through their proslavery ideology, their own sectional divisions, and their vehement condemnations of northern abolitionists and politicians, they made their sympathies clear and contributed to southern sectionalism with all its tragic consequences. Some evangelical ministers like Lyon opposed secession and the war, but few of them made that opposition as public as he did; others gave their enthusiastic support. Across the state, people turned to their churches and their ministers to make sense of the tragedy that quickly engulfed them. Churches filled with women in mourning as thousands of Mississippians died on the battlefields. Federal raids and occupations disrupted services, and biracial churches lost black members who fled to freedom during the conflict.

Despite the horrors and disruptions of the war, or perhaps because of them, revivals broke out in many other churches, which drew large numbers of new black and white converts. The Confederate defeat and the abolition of slavery led to periods of soul-searching among many white evangelicals who had accepted the biblical defense of slavery and believed that God favored the South in the struggle. For blacks, the Civil War came as an answer to many generations' prayers for freedom, which may explain the growth of the black membership in many biracial churches during the war. In religious terms, the most dramatic consequence of the Confederate defeat, one that marks the sharpest break between religious life in the antebellum South and in the postbellum South, was the division of the churches along racial lines. In some cases, the division took place even before the war ended, in others, after Robert E. Lee's surrender, and in still others only after many years of painful readjustment.

In the late 1850s and early 1860s, evangelical voices joined a growing, strident chorus. One evangelical preacher recalled the period before 1861 as one of "fierce and bitter political prejudices and fiery speeches of impassioned orators which had been multiplying and growing in heat for more than a generation, until the climax was reached in secession. . . ." While few evangelical ministers openly advocated secession before 1861, their impassioned defense of slavery and attacks on abolitionists increased sectional tensions. A Baptist newspaper article criticized "the fanatics of the North" and defended slavery "because of our honest conviction that it is socially, politically and morally right." Ministers like William Winans, a Pennsylvania native himself, called abolitionists "*fanatics—lunatics*" and praised the South's "chivalric notions in regard to foreign interference in domestic concerns. . . ." As secession loomed on the horizon, the Reverend Thomas W. Caskey of Jackson's Christian Church, for example, toured the state to "talk the people out of the Union," and, once the deed was done, state Baptist, Methodist, and Presbyterian denominational bodies endorsed secession. After the war began, many ministers joined the army or served as chaplains. For example, twenty-six Methodists became chaplains, five worked as missionaries, and twenty-two others joined the army.[3]

As the Confederate government attempted to create and nurture a sense of nationalism, the support of the evangelical churches became vital. More blatantly than at any time since the end of the colonial period, a national government attempted to exploit religion for its own ends. Religion proved to be the means of linking the move for independence to a higher moral quest, the defense of the South's divinely ordained civilization. The Confederate government sought the blessings of religion by proclaiming public fast days, which churches observed. In June 1861 Robert B. Alexander, a slaveowner in north Mississippi, "went to church [and] heard Rev. See preach or rather give a war Talk & a very good one at that. . . ." In 1862 he wrote, "To day we fasted, Negroes & all we went to Church heard Rev See deliver a fine lecture on the war . . . ," though we are left to wonder what prayers those slaves may have lifted up during the fast-day service. President Davis proclaimed nine fast days, and "Congress, state legislatures, and denominational bodies designated so many more that a strict compliance with all might have saved enough food to feed Lee's hungry army." Compliance was not always strict, and one group of well-meaning Mississippi churchwomen celebrated a fast day with a church fair and a supper, but for most church members these were solemn occasions. Many religious southerners saw evidence of God's approbation in the Confederate victories at Manassas, the Seven Days, Chancellorsville, and Chickamauga, all of which followed fast days. A woman in Crawfordsville, Mississippi, expressed her faith in the observations when she asked the state government to proclaim yet another fast day: "From a thorough search of God's word I find no denial of peace to nations that humble themselves before God. Another fast day is absolutely necessary for the good of the land." The events served the Confederate government as propaganda tools, an especially powerful one given the high visibility of many preachers and importance of church life for many southerners.[4]

Southern women responded to the demands of war by organizing aid societies, producing articles for soldiers, and working in hospitals. Churchwomen in Carthage, Mississippi, organized their Ladies' Soldiers Aid Society in February 1862. A model of efficient organization, its officers, all women, included a president, approximately twelve vice presidents scattered across the county, a secretary, a treasurer, and five managers. These women also worked in a local hospital, despite the fact that some men "seemed vexed at them for their ministering to the wants of the soldiers." As the war actually came to Mississippi, the work intensified. In 1862 James Lyon referred to Columbus as "one great hospital"; all public buildings, including churches, were used as hospitals. Lyon noted that women, including his wife, "took an unusual interest in the hospital." The Roman Catholic Sisters of Mercy closed their school in Vicksburg and became traveling nurses who worked in hospitals in Mississippi Springs, Jackson, and Oxford. Women staffed the five hospitals set up in Holly Springs in 1862. One nurse, Cordelia Lewis Scales, reported, "You cant cross a street or turn a corner, but what . . . you see wounded or sick soldiers." The Scales home operated as one of the hospitals, and Cordelia Scales labored to care for the needy. The pace was so hectic that she wrote, "For five days I did not take my clothes off." Another Mississippi nurse, Sophia Hays, described the terrible mortality rates in these hospitals, the sufferings of the patients, and the courage it required to stay at her post. She wrote in May 1862, "Each day several passed away to their last home. I stood by the bedside of many of them. . . . Oh how my heart ached to hear them in their moments of delirium vainly calling for mother, sister or aunt."[5] Such scenes were horrible reminders of the good death so many evangelicals had craved in the antebellum period when they could have died surrounded by loved ones. If evangelicals before the war had exhibited a macabre fascination with death and dying, the bloodletting of the Civil War satiated that need, and the glowing descriptions of deathbed scenes and romantic images of dying disappeared from the records.

Confederate women turned to the church for support in such trying times, and, as more and more men left for the battlefields, the female majority in churches increased. Federal raids or occupations often made regular services impossible, much to the consternation of faithful women. Lettie Vick Downs, who lived near Vicksburg, lamented in 1863 that she had been unable to attend church during the past year due to the war, and she longed for the day when she could worship in church once again. Another woman wrote that "[t]he church is gradually filling up with black dresses and mourning veils." After her brother died in November 1863, she became one of those women in black. Devastated by her loss, she wrote, "It seems as though . . . my heart became flint. I am almost afraid to love too dearly anyone now." After another brother gave his life for the cause, she cried, "Oh God! when shall retribution commence? How long, O Lord, how long. It is not Christian to have such a heart."[6]

The records of Academy Baptist Church for November 1864 provide a typical example of the disruptive effects of the war: "Owing to the existence of the war and our exposed condition and the many raids of the Federal army we have had no regular preaching & no conference since Nov. 1862." Many churches went without preaching services for months and many others virtually suspended business. In 1864 the Methodists in the Port Gibson conference reported that "the church is scattered & wasted to a great extent by the war. . . . Sunday School is still kept up though frequently interrupted by the Yanks capturing Teachers & other causes." The Reverend Samuel Agnew, a Presbyterian minister in north Mississippi, left a vivid account of the difficulties he encountered during the period. In 1862 he wrote, "The pickets now occupy the Church and feed their horses in the Church-yard. They use some of the benches for troughs." In 1864 the church building was used to house the sick, and Agnew wrote that "[t]he stench of the dead is very unpleasant." He saw one shallow grave of a Union soldier with a hand emerging from the grave. After Union troops captured Jackson, "A Yankee chaplin preached in the [Presbyterian] church, after which the church was desecrated by the soldiers. Carpets and hymn books were stolen (furniture burned in the streets)."[7]

As Union troops moved in and as the Confederacy slowly crumbled, the African American community saw the hand of God at work in answer to their prayers for freedom. As former slave Dora Brewer recalled, when slaves "got sense enuf to pray for freedom den de war come." Another former slave, Dora Franks, said, "I started prayin' for freedom and all de rest of de women did de same thing. De war started pretty soon after dat and all de men folks went off ad left de plantation for de women and de niggers to run." With many men away at war and with Federal troops moving through the state, many slaves simply ignored their owners or escaped to freedom. The Reverend Samuel Agnew found the slaves belonging to his family openly hostile and unwilling to obey orders. He said of one slave, "She does not conceal her thoughts but plainly manifests her opinions." Many of the Agnew slaves escaped, and those that remained "have got so 'high' that they would not obey my orders." Mrs. Alfred Ingraham encountered the same situation on her family's plantation near Vicksburg: "The men are far more respectful and obliging than the women; the latter refuse to come and work one and all." With Federal troops nearby, the Ingrahams, like other "masters," could neither keep their slaves on the plantation nor exact obedience from those who chose to remain. Slavery disintegrated across the South as "power shifted from the 'big house' to the slave cabins."[8] Churches tried to shore up the institution, and disciplinary actions against slaves rose dramatically during the war as thousands of slaves ran away to join the Union armies. Line Creek Baptist Church, for example, charged runaway slave members with "rebellion against the laws of the land" and appointed a committee "to keep blacks under subjection by the church." Running away was by far the most common allegation against black men in evangelical churches during the war years, and about 30 percent of the charges were against black women, who also fled in large numbers. Several churches appointed committees to determine the number of blacks who had left, and often excluded many runaways at once.[9]

While many blacks rejoiced at the opportunity to escape to freedom, many whites despaired as Confederate reversals mounted, and especially after the telling defeat at Vicksburg. The Reverend Walter E. Tynes described "a great revolt in public sentiment" that swept the state in 1863 with the fall of Vicksburg and General Lee's conclusive defeat at Gettysburg. He wrote that these disasters "all forced overwhelming conviction that the cause was a failure, and that further bloodshed was useless. Added to this was the passage of a law by the Confederate Government conscripting all men between certain ages, excepting only a few, but especially every man who owned as many as twenty Negroes. This law provoked much criticism and the charge that it was a 'rich man's war and a poor man's fight.' Many men both in the army and out lost all enthusiasm for the cause. Then it was also learned that President Davis and Vice-President Alexander H. Stephens had disagreed about the conduct of the war. . . . It was a time of general demoralization, beyond description."[10] That demoralization became evident among evangelical ministers and congregations.

Many ministers found it more and more difficult to preach fast-day sermons in the face of looming defeat. In Columbus the Reverend Lyon found himself trapped into delivering a fast-day sermon since the Baptist minister was away and the Methodist minister cleverly "plead indisposition." Lyon, who had opposed secession from the start, castigated his flock: "I had no comfort to give the people—no flattery for them or their rulers—their *sins*, their violations of God's law had brought the sword upon the land—and the only hope was in repentance. . . . Three gentlemen . . . left the house, in away [*sic*] that showed that they were offended—but I could not change my tone. My text was the 1st verse of the 58 chapter of Isaiah" ["Cry aloud, spare not, lift up thy voice like a trumpet, and shew my people their transgressions, and the house of Jacob their sins"]. The fast-day sermons changed from the uplifting "war talks" at the war's outset to jeremiads in which ministers blamed Confederate defeats on a sinful people. Ever since the early national period evangelicals had linked virtue with national success, an idea that offered cold comfort in a time of defeat.[11]

Most evangelicals agreed with Lyon that failure resulted from sin and that repentance offered the only hope. When the congregation of College Hill Presbyterian Church met in 1863, they issued this eloquent statement of their sorrows:

> Resolved that those present deem it their duty to place on
> record for the benefit and information of posterity some facts

as history which will show the dealings of God with us as a
church and congregation. . . . We would first note that a large
number of members at the first call of our country enlisted in
her cause for whose preservation, safety, and spiritual welfare
many sincere and fervent prayers have been offered up to Almighty God. . . .Some of these loved ones have . . . fallen on
the field of battle bravely standing up in the defense of their
country. . . . A melancholy gloom overhangs our beloved community. . . . The hearts of many of our members as they weekly
enter the sanctuary are bowed in sorrow. . . . But acknowledge
the hand of a sovereign God in these sore afflictions and sub-
missively kiss the chastening rod and say thy will be done, O
Lord.

The community was spared the ravages of war until late in 1862 when
thirty thousand Federal troops moved into the area. They occupied the
church, took food, animals, and other goods, burned some homes, and
encouraged slaves to leave their masters. The Presbyterians estimated
their loss at two hundred thousand dollars.

Such is a mere outline of the heavy calamity which God in
his providence has seen fit to inflict upon our community. To
say that there were good reasons for this . . . is saying what the
Bible and the providence of God in all past ages has taught the
nations of the earth. . . . [T]he sin for which punishment is
inflicted in this life is brought to our knowledge by the penalty
inflicted upon us. Thus our sin . . . is not honoring God to the
full extent of our duty. . . . Then it is our duty . . . to humble
ourselves, repent in the dust, plead for his mercy, his grace, and
the light of his Holy Spirit to enable us henceforth to devote
ourselves, our powers of body and faculties of mind, our call-
ings and property to the service of the church and benefit of
the world.[12]

Many evangelicals, like the Presbyterians at Church Hill, internalized
the message of the jeremiads; clearly southerners had been tested and
found wanting. Out of that gloomy sense of despair grew a conviction that
only greater faith could turn the tide once again in favor of the Confederacy. As one woman wrote in 1863, "[W]e will come out of the furnace
doubly purified for the good work & fight that God has given us to do For

to the people of the Confederacy is given the sublime mission of maintaining the supremacy of our Father in Heaven."[13] Such sentiments helped fuel a widespread revival movement among Mississippi evangelicals.

In 1863 a series of revivals broke out across the state. Ministers from various denominations held successful revivals in Starkville that continued for several weeks and brought scores of new converts. The Strong River Baptist Association rejoiced "that we have been blessed with a larger accession to our churches than in any previous year since our organization. The number added to our churches by baptism . . . being 320." That figure compared to 79 members added by baptism in 1861. The Aberdeen Baptist Association in north Mississippi reported that "some of the churches of our Association have been blessed with precious revivals of religion; . . . abroad we hear of extensive revivals, and from the army the revival news is glorious." A religious newspaper observed that "the period of the war was remarkable for extensive revivals of religion throughout the armies and States of the South."[14]

The strict evangelical moral code demanded "order" and "duty" from members of both races, and churches attempted to maintain social stability. As one historian wrote, during a war only the church could "exercise a direct and guiding influence on the conduct of the individual citizen." Churches attempted to control some of the worst abuses resulting from the war. One Baptist association, for example, issued a warning against the evil of extortion in 1863. "[O]ur country, in its present distressed condition, is thronged with those who Extort not only from the rich, but who wring from the indigent the means of subsistence to the last dollar. We cannot expect the favor of God in our struggle for independence as long as we indulge in known sin." Extortion was evidence of materialism and greed, sins that undercut republican virtue and endangered the entire war effort.[15]

Biracial churches continued to hold separate services for blacks whenever possible, but the war virtually destroyed the mission to the slaves. Henry P. Lewis, Methodist missionary to slaves at the Cayuga Colored Mission, wrote, "Slaveholders were afraid to have their slaves preached to. One good man . . . wanted me to remain on the work and preach to his negroes. But after consulting with my presiding elder and prominent men of the work it was thought best not to attempt to organize. . . ." During the war many of the missions were abandoned completely. Most of the missions quickly collapsed, a result of the shortage of ministers, Federal occupation of the large mission areas along the Mississippi River, lack of funds, and the escape of many slaves from the plantations.[16]

The end of the war in 1865 brought a sense of relief to many evangelicals who shared the sentiments of the Reverend Tynes and his neighbors: "[W]e were all grieved and brokenhearted over the loss of so many thousands of our brave young men, yet there was a feeling of great relief that the cruel war was over." With that relief came a period of soul-searching for many white evangelicals who feared "that we are a 'God-forsaken' people. . . . [T]he religion of the country has been weighed in the balances, and found wanting." When the members of Unity Presbyterian Church assembled in July 1865 they acknowledged that "much of this church is in a cold & luke warm state forgetful alike of its duties to itself, the world & to God whom it professes to love & worship."[17]

Some evangelicals believed that God had brought defeat on them as punishment for the evils of slavery. The Reverend James Lyon wrote that slave owners "vilely abused" slavery and used it "only for selfish and sordid purposes, regardless of the natural rights of the slave. . . ." He listed thirteen fallacies expressed by the demagogues he held responsible for the war, one of which was, "Slavery is *right*—our cause is righteous and a righteous God is bound to guarantee our ultimate success, & c & c." When the Baptist Committee on the Colored Population met in 1866, they mourned "that our time, and talents, and wealth, (when we had it) had not been more sacredly devoted to the advancement of human happiness, and the promotion of the Redeemer's Kingdom" among their slaves.[18]

In a similar vein, Episcopal minister Edward Fontaine told his congregation in 1865:

> We of the South have committed sins for which we are receiving the chastisement of this war; and for which we should humbly repent and pray for our pardon. Among these sins we may enumerate that avarice and ostentation which pervaded all classes of the educated, & wealthy slave-holders. . . . But few plantations were adorned with churches for the slaves, and furnished with salaried ministers to teach them their duty to God

and their masters. . . . If the same amount of money expended in paying 'severe overseers,' in useless & ostentatious ornaments . . . had been devoted to building churches, paying missionaries, and providing pious and talented teachers for our slaves, I do not think this war would have visited the South with all it's [sic] unspeakable horrors.[19]

When ministers embraced the biblical defense of slavery in the 1830s, they warned masters that divine sanction of the institution depended upon a proper exercise of duty. Now they held slaveowners responsible for the terrible destruction brought about by the war. The churches were destitute, and the faithful mourned what one group of Baptists described as "the desolations of Zion." Church buildings had been burned and desecrated, thousands of members lay dead, ministers were few, congregations were scattered, and the association of evangelicals with a failed cause planted seeds of doubt in many minds.[20]

And yet defeat did not necessarily mean that white southerners were no longer God's chosen people; instead, defeat laid the groundwork for a further expansion of evangelicalism in the postbellum South. Rather than turning against religion, whites flocked to the churches as their world collapsed, and ministers proclaimed that the South would ultimately benefit from its suffering, that it would be tried by fire, and they reassured their listeners that God worked from a master plan unfathomable but no less just. Evangelical churches benefitted from postbellum revivals. For whites, the revivals grew out of their profound sense of loss and disillusionment, and the perception that their social, cultural, and economic lives had been overturned. From across the state came reports of great revivals at the war's end.[21]

Former slaves saw in the Confederate defeat an answer to their prayers, and they did not look to a Lost Cause but to a victorious one. They demonstrated their gratitude to God by joining the churches in increasing numbers. Of all the momentous changes of the tumultuous Reconstruction period, none was more far-reaching for black and white Christians than the separation of the churches along racial lines, part of a broader black movement for individual and community autonomy. During the Reconstruction period, the biracial worship that had characterized southern evangelicalism for a century came to an end. Sometimes the change occurred quickly and bitterly, but often the separations came gradually and with surprising goodwill. Along with the family and schools, the churches served as a bedrock of the black community. These churches did not spring up as if by magic, but rather grew directly out of the antebellum biracial churches. Generally, either blacks were forced out of the biracial churches by whites who refused to recognize the new realities of the post-war period, or blacks and whites cooperated to set up the independent churches that blacks wanted.[22]

Blacks moved quickly either to establish religious equality in the biracial churches or to leave them for independent black churches. A. T. Morgan, a northerner who leased a Mississippi Delta plantation immediately after the war, wrote that "a movement had been for some months under way among the freed people, looking to their separation from the 'white folks' churches, where their position has always been a servile one, and that the white folks had been making very strenuous exertions indeed to prevent such a result. They were not willing, of course, to receive their former slaves into full Christian fellowship, nor were they willing to tear down the railing in their place of worship which marked the arbitrary line that the master-class had drawn between white and black worshiper."[23]

The case of Bethany Presbyterian Church demonstrates that many whites preferred to have blacks leave the biracial churches rather than recognize blacks as equal members of the church. When members of Bethany Presbyterian Church organized a subscription drive to build a new church, black members enthusiastically joined the effort and pledged more than a hundred dollars. Samuel Agnew, the preacher at Bethany, wrote, "Blacks are taking hold of the new church with the right spirit, I am glad to see such an interest taken in the church. . . . [T]he Blacks will give the church enterprise a better life than I hoped for." Later that year, however, the white building committee refused "to receive the negro subscription for the Church" after a heated discussion. As a result, the black members left the church, and their names were stricken from its rolls. Blacks at Bethany, like former slaves across the South, tested their newfound freedom and sought a more equal footing in society, an attempt that many whites resented and angrily repulsed.[24]

While the former slaves at Bethany tried to work within the biracial church, other blacks left the biracial churches and created their own institutions without white assistance. In 1866, for example, New Providence Baptist Church appointed a committee to visit the "colored brethren who have absented themselves from the church for mos. [months] past." In 1864 Jerusalem Baptist Church had sixty-five black members, but all of them were gone by 1866. As former slave and postbellum preacher Charles Moore recalled, "I didn't spec' nothin outten freedom septin' peace an' happiness an' the right to go my way as I please. An' that is the way the Almighty wants it."[25]

In other churches, biracial congregations divided amicably, and whites assisted blacks in organizing their own churches. The members of Bethesda Baptist Church agreed in 1867 to allow blacks to hold a separate revival meeting, and later in the same year, "The colored members signified a desire to withdraw from the church to organize an independent church and asked permission for the use of the church house one sabbath each month and Saturday before if necessary." The church granted their request with the provision that blacks pay for any damages to the church, that they not schedule services to conflict with white services, and that they assist in maintaining the baptismal pool. Similarly, blacks continued to be a part of Academy Baptist Church after the war, but they met separately and had a black preacher. In 1869 the church called a conference "for the purpose of organizing the colored people of Academy into a separate church by a unanimous request from them." Though organized as a separate church, the blacks used the Academy church building until the 1870s. In 1867 the members of Magnolia Baptist Church met and the following business transpired: "On motion before the white members present it was Resolved that all the colored members of this church have the privilege of formally withdrawing from this Church to unite with the church about to be constituted." Blacks used the church building until December 1871, when the whites withdrew that privilege. In Liberty Baptist Church whites agreed to allow blacks to choose their own minister and use the meeting house one Sunday in each month. In 1867 the church licensed Jerry Blow, a black preacher, and later that year the old slave gallery was removed. Blacks used the building until 1872.[26]

This gradual separation of blacks and whites prevailed in the state's biracial churches. In 1870 the Salem Baptist Association in Jasper County recommended that where black members "are of sufficient numbers as to form churches and can procure preaching, and wish to form churches of their own, that they should be dismissed in order and assisted in doing so, but where they wish to remain with us as heretofore and are orderly, we think they should be allowed to do so." In 1872 the association suggested that separate churches should be organized. Black membership in the Salem association's churches declined from 206 in 1865 to 122 in 1870. As late as 1872, 81 blacks continued to worship in biracial churches in the association. Blacks continued to appear in the records of Fellowship Baptist Church as late as 1876.[27] As Methodists in the Mississippi conference acknowledged, "It must be evident to the most casual observer that the old plan of involuntary provision for them [blacks] will not answer. They feel that it is not of their own choice, and hence, . . . they set up for themselves." The conference resolved to "encourage and help the colored people to build churches." The Methodist General Conference set up a separate Colored Conference in 1867.[28]

In the biracial churches blacks had never been completely free of white supervision, and important elements of black Christianity as practiced in the "invisible church" in the quarters seldom intruded into these institutional settings. Once blacks began to form their own congregations, however, a dramatic and significant merger between the institutional church and the invisible church took place. Many white evangelicals watched the process with dismay, and the merger of folk and institutional worship set black evangelical churches apart from white churches of the same denominations in terms of ritual and practice.

The most far-reaching social change in the postbellum South involved the status of the newly freed slaves, and emancipation struck terror into the hearts of many whites. African Americans' desire for autonomy conflicted with a white determination to maintain racial supremacy and control black labor. The planters' desperate need for labor gave blacks bargaining power in the immediate postwar period, and churches were often a part of the bargain. Planters sometimes agreed to assist blacks in building churches (which often doubled as schools) in order to secure laborers. A. T. Morgan found that "[t]he freed people had long been anxious to have a church of their own, but did not feel able to pay the cost of such a one as they desired." He constructed a twelve-hundred-dollar building to serve as a church and school in a successful effort to compete for labor. Such schools were virtually extensions of the black churches; Morgan wrote, "The pastor, a very light colored man, who had been a slave . . . and all officers of the church, were present either as scholars or teachers." Some planters attempted to control black worship on plantations by hiring the white or black preacher of their choice, or by including provisions in their labor contracts limiting religious worship to particular times and places, but these efforts failed.[29]

Churches were the centers of the black community, and they served as schools, as meeting places for political gatherings, and as centers of black resistance to oppression. One black association required ministers to "instruct their congregations to get pass books, and keep their own accounts straight with all men; then when they come to settle their accounts with the merchants, they will know how much they owe." Another black association pledged that "we, as an association, will ever pray for the success of that great party known as the Republican Party, that gave us our freedom." According to A. T. Morgan, "The Sabbath-school on the hill, in the little church we helped to build, was to me a sanctuary, our Yankee stronghold, one of God's fortresses."[30]

African American preachers, often among the best educated and most respected men in their communities, played a central role in Reconstruction politics. The most prominent example of the preacher-politician in the state was Hiram Revels, the first African American to serve in the United States Senate, but he was hardly alone. Of sixteen blacks elected to the state's 1868 constitutional convention, six were ministers. Black preachers also made up more than 40 percent of black Union League organizers in the state whose occupations can be identified. A Jackson newspaper charged that "[c]ertain colored clergymen, residing in this city, are said to be agents of these Leagues, under pay, and thus while pretending to teach the gospel, they, in fact, get their flocks together under the pretense of religious service, and then administer to their deluded victims the unlawful, irreverent, irreligious and blasphemous oaths of the Loyal League." Political activism made the churches targets of violence. During a serious riot in the town of Meridian in 1871, for example, at least thirty blacks died and a black church was burned. The black Mt. Olivet Baptist

Association demanded that "it is the moral duty of the City of Meridian to replace that [Baptist] house."[31]

Despite the violence and attempts at intimidation, African Americans refused to relinquish control of their religious life to southern whites or to northern missionaries. Blacks desperately wanted schools and recognized that they could learn from northern teachers, but the church was a different matter. Northern whites, like most southern whites, had little appreciation for the complexities of African American religious beliefs and insisted that blacks desperately needed reform in their religious practices. Northern agencies like the American Missionary Association (AMA) moved into Mississippi as early as 1863, when they organized religious meetings and schools in the contraband camps. At first, the missionaries were favorably impressed with the freed people's deep religiosity; as one white missionary wrote from Natchez, "*[M]ost of them are a praying people,*" and another had high praise for black preachers: "[W]e find examples of talent, faith and zeal among some of their preachers that would edify any christian pulpit[.]"[32]

Blacks flocked to AMA Sunday schools and prayer meetings, but the northerners' attempts to establish Congregational churches among them failed completely. One AMA official recognized that such attempts were not likely to succeed "as the people now belong . . . to the churches (Baptist & Methodist) already in existence." Southern whites greatly feared northern influence on black religious life; as one Baptist association warned, "We conceive that there is great danger of this work passing out of our hands into the hands of men and institutions antagonistic to the interests and welfare of our beloved South." But southern blacks had no intention of losing their religious autonomy to southern or northern whites. Even efforts by northern black denominations such as the African Methodist Episcopal Church met with only limited success, since their missionaries often demanded an educated ministry and had little respect for the emotional services southern blacks preferred.[33]

Religious practices formerly hidden in the "invisible church" became a vital part of postbellum institutional worship. Though some of these practices originated in the Great Revival, others clearly reflected African religious traditions. Among the beliefs and practices with African roots were visionary conversion experiences, or "travelin'." One missionary in

Columbus reported, "A 'revival' is in progress in the colored M.E. Chh. and three of my scholars have 'come thro' as they say, having been three days & nights in an unconscious state and after 'coming thro' telling *wonderful tales* of *visions* & c. . . . There are two colored chhs. in this city One a large M[ethodist].E[piscopal]. Ch[urc]h. . . . Their services are of the most frantic nature, the pastor often gets the 'power' & jumps & throws himself (physically) in his pulpit."[34]

Another AMA teacher, Maria Waterbury, recorded many similar examples during her stay in the state. In 1872, for instance, she attended a baptism service where twenty-four blacks were baptized in the Tombigbee River. She noted that a thousand people of both races crowded the river banks. Before the baptisms, converts participated in a service in the "African church," where they related their "experiences." She wrote, "An old man said, 'I started travelin', an' went on, an' on, 'til I cum to ole hell, an' I see de devil, an asked him ef I might plow dar. He said I might, an' I plowed tu furrows on de firey mane o' hell. Den I seed an ole woman wid her hair all burnt off. Den I seed a pair o' balances, an' was weighed in 'em an' was light as a feather. Ef I'de a knowed God wus sich a sweet God, I'de prayed my knees tu de bone.' "

Over and over again the converts related similar visionary experiences.[35] Waterbury also recorded one of the rare accounts of the ring shout in the state:

> It usually began when the preaching was nearly done. Aunt Chloe, or Dinah, would get blest, and seemed to be unable to contain the blessing, and would spring to her feet, and begin shaking hands with the nearest one to her, and in a moment the example would be contagious, and two-thirds of the congregation would rise to their feet, each shaking hands with some other, the men on one side of the church, women on the other; and soon all would swing into the center of the church, in front of the pulpit, and shouts of some would rend the air, while those who could sing, would sing as though their life depended on their making a noise, all the time swaying their bodies up and down and circling among each other, shaking hands, and moving feet as if keeping time to the music. The preacher would come down out of the pulpit, and stand ready for the hand shaking. All would seem either solemn, or joyous,

and perhaps after twenty minutes of such exercise, the pastor would lift his hand, when instantly the noise would cease, while he pronounced the benediction, and the worshipers would pass out of the church. . . . One of the scholars, who had participated in the dance, . . . said "That's what is called the Heavenly Dance." The songs usual on the occasion were

> I wonder Lord will I ever get to heaven
> To walk them golden streets.

or,

> I'm just at the fountain, Lord,
> That never runs dry.[36]

This Afro-Baptist service had much in common with the early evangelical services and with those in Primitive Baptist churches, but other elements of theology and ritual were fundamentally different from that of the white or biracial churches and represent the survival of African religious traditions.

Within a few years of the war's end, black Baptists began organizing their own associations, patterned closely after the white associations. In 1868 blacks organized the Jackson Missionary Baptist Association and the First Baptist Antioch Association; by 1876 more than twenty-five black associations existed in the state.[37] Records from the Mt. Olivet Baptist Association organized in Macon in 1869 demonstrate the process at work. In July 1869 delegates from fourteen black Baptist churches across northeastern Mississippi assembled in Macon to organize the Mt. Olivet association. Delegates at this first meeting requested the assistance of two local white ministers. The assembly approved Articles of Faith and Rules of Decorum borrowed directly from white Baptist associations, and they appointed corresponding messengers "to the Choctaw and other Associations of white Missionary Baptists within our territorial limits." By 1871 the association included thirty-nine churches, and fifteen others applied for admission. An important issue for the associations was the proper qualifications for ministers, and they called for higher educational requirements for preachers. The association appointed a committee on education, which reported that "[t]he subject of education is one of great moment, of

intrinsic value, and indispensable to all branches of science and professions. . . . [T]he Gospel Minister has need to be a living, walking library,
nay more; a living, walking Encyclopedia." Similarly, the black First Saints
Baptist Association resolved "never to ordain a minister who cannot read
the Scriptures." Such calls for an educated ministry were a regular feature
of black Baptist associations throughout the Reconstruction period.[38]

Associations supported higher educational requirements for ministers
and urged their member churches to abandon the elements of African
American worship that differed from traditional biracial practices; in 1872
one black church leader recommended "that our ministers discourage the
practice of moaning, shouting, and jumping in churches. . . . We, then, as
the true church, must fight against barbarism, superstition, conjuration."
Associations proclaimed that "it is necessary for us to quit these old customs."[39]

Even though these associations accepted white assistance and condemned certain aspects of slave religion, they were not under white control, as their outspoken support of the Republican Party demonstrates.
Many blacks found in their faith a sense of moral worth and saw in the end
of slavery evidence that they were God's chosen people. As one minister
reviewed recent history in a sermon before a statewide black Baptist convention, he said that before the war whites had been taught "to believe
that they were the peculiar and favored work of God's hand, and that the
poor African race was born to be their slaves. That made them believe that
a negro had no rights that a white man was bound to respect. But we praise
God. . . . [W]e find in the face of all that heathenish teaching, that slavery
is dead; as such we all ought to be engaged together in building up the old
waste places. . . . [I]f one people will oppress the other, God, ere long, will
throw confusion in their midst." Here, indeed, was a powerful message
for a newly freed people, one that blended a faith in a just God with a
realistic assessment of their oppressors, one that recalled an African heritage and held out the magnanimous offer of interracial cooperation. The
black Baptists were remarkably successful in their efforts, and by 1873 the
statewide General Missionary Baptist Association of Mississippi included
327 churches with 29,524 members.[40]

Women enjoyed a prominent role in the new black churches. Unlike
white or biracial churches, at least some black Baptist churches created the

office of "deaconess" for female members, though unfortunately the duties of the office are unclear. Just as white women joined benevolent societies, black women in the postbellum period taught in schools, participated in community charitable organizations, and collected money for church causes. Black churchwomen were especially active in raising money for educational activities. In 1878 the president of a black Baptist organization observed, "Our new field of labor that we opened for the sisters, is doing very well for a new thing. . . . [T]here are a great many good sisters in our churches, who have never had the opportunity to work for the education of their own sex. But we are organizing the 'Five Sisters' at Natchez."[41]

Through hard work, perseverance, and mutual assistance, black men and women worked to create their own independent religious institutions. They benefited from their biracial religious experience and drew on it when they wrote their own covenants and rules of decorum, set up their church structures, and organized their associations. At the same time, they drew upon their African past and the powerful religious traditions handed down from one generation to the next during more than two centuries of enslavement. They melded these traditions and experiences to create a vibrant and enduring faith that served as the bedrock of the African American community.

The Civil War brought dramatic changes to the biracial churches and accelerated a trend toward racial separation that had begun in the antebellum period. During Reconstruction, blacks created their own religious institutions and forged an identity and religious life suited to their needs as free people. The creation of black churches must be considered one of the most lasting and important achievements of the formerly enslaved African Americans, and the churches were the first and the largest institutions under black control. Although biracial worship continued in many churches during the period, the refusal of whites to recognize blacks as equal members and the blacks' desire for autonomy led to racial separation, an event that permanently altered the southern religious landscape.

Have the evil days diverted us from the work of God, have they weakened our faith or slackened our hands? It should be just the other way. Redeeming the times, because *the days are evil, is the reasoning of the inspired penman.*

—NEW ORLEANS *CHRISTIAN ADVOCATE*, January 4, 1877

7 "Redeeming the Times": From Reconstruction to Reform

As the quotation from the *Christian Advocate* suggests, many leading ministers in the period following Reconstruction called upon their congregations to look beyond the promise of individual salvation to the hope of transforming society. At virtually the same time, northern theologians called on Christians to bring the social order into harmony with the teaching of Jesus Christ by reforming the abuses associated with industrial capitalism. Though debate has long raged among historians of southern religion on the existence of a Social Gospel movement in the region, it seems clear that Mississippi Christians embraced many of the humanitarian and political reforms characteristic of the Social Gospel in the North. In surprising ways, ministers embraced the idea that the redeeming power of God worked through individuals to transform society. In the South in particular, applying the teachings of Jesus to society was often a dangerous exercise, and, at a time when race relations were at their worst, the churches offered practically the only voice of moderation. On the surface, the religious life in the state followed familiar patterns as the mainline denominations furthered their hold on the region, but below the surface, and scarcely noticed at the time, new fundamentalists and Pentecostal sects were emerging among poor blacks and whites. Though tiny in relation to the mainline denominations, these groups were the source of enormous creative and spiritual energy. When these poor Christians thought of redemption, they still looked toward the salvation of individuals and the maintenance of a community of believers. For members of the major denominations, however, redemption of the society, often through the agency of the state, became a focus of increasing concern.

On Sunday morning, June 30, 1897, the Reverend Robert E. Lee Craig took the pulpit at St. Andrew's Episcopal Church in Jackson and delivered a sermon that sent shock waves through the congregation and the entire state. His subject was temperance, a popular cause among many reform-minded church members in Mississippi, but not at St. Andrew's, where the members of the vestry and their followers had "been for years the citadel of the saloon power in that city." Wealthy, worldly, and socially prominent members of the vestry "furnished the brain, the social influence, and respectability which gave the saloon its chief backing."[1] Reverend Craig had discovered that six of nine vestrymen had signed a petition in favor of a local option election to reopen saloons in Hinds County, and he demanded in his sermon that they either withdraw their names from that petition or resign from the vestry. The outraged vestrymen met and adopted a series of resolutions condemning Craig's action and charging that he had exceeded his authority. When Craig entered the pulpit the following Sabbath, he stunned the congregation by resigning his office, an act that was reported in newspapers across the state and beyond. Church members urged the young minister to reconsider and persuaded him to call a congregational meeting for a vote on the vestry's resolutions. At that July 4 meeting the church members voted 110 to 27 in support of their rector. Temperance advocates heralded the vote as a great victory; one of the state's leading newspapers exulted that the event marked "the final downfall of the whiskey power in the Capital City," and the New York Sun considered the "Great Temperance Victory" at St. Andrew's front-page news.[2]

The temperance movement was one of the most powerful reform movements of the age; the effort to curb the consumption of alcohol began in the antebellum period and gathered steam after the Civil War, when a wide coalition of religious Americans from conservative fundamentalists to liberal Social Gospelers joined forces to stamp out "America's darkest crime."[3] Once the trials and tribulations of the Reconstruction era were over, prohibition became a "Burning Question" in Mississippi, with evangelicals on the front lines.[4]

By the 1880s prohibition rallies were being held across the state, and religious men and women rallied to the cause. Prominent evangelists, including the noted Methodist tent revivalist Sam Jones, helped lead the charge and railed against the evils of drink. A resident of Aberdeen noted in 1890 that Jones was "tearing the town to pieces" with "[h]is attack on saloons, gamblers and other vices. . . . He attacked everything in plain language . . . as boldly as John the Baptist attacked Herod." One Panola County resident noted with disgust in 1887 that his county would vote in favor of prohibition due to the efforts of "[a]ll the cussed old Methodist preachers."[5] Baptists were no less diligent; almost every Baptist association had a temperance committee, and the superintendent of the state's Anti-Saloon League, T. J. Bailey, was a leading Baptist minister. Women, too, joined in the fight, and in November 1882 Frances E. Willard, president of the Women's Christian Temperance Union, visited Corinth, where she organized the state's first WCTU chapter. Influential ministers welcomed such efforts from women, still the majority of church members; Bishop Charles B. Galloway of the Methodist Episcopal Church, South, a native Mississippian and a tireless supporter of temperance, told women to emulate "the mighty uprising of the Western women armed with prayer and Christian song, for the overthrow of intemperance."[6]

Thousands of Mississippi women heeded the call, and one of the WCTU's most active officers, Belle Kearney, was a Mississippian. Daughter of a wealthy slaveholder in Madison County, Kearney was born on her father's plantation in 1864. The Confederacy's defeat left her family's fortune in tatters, and, like many former slave owners, Kearney's father could not cope with the realities of the New South. For a few years they continued to live extravagantly and mortgaged the plantation to pay for their lifestyle. Neither of her parents "knew how to work, nor how to manage so as to make a dollar, nor how to keep it after it was gained." Within a few years, all but the house and four hundred acres of land was lost to foreclosure, "the last dollar was spent and the last servant dismissed." At the age of nine, Kearney took over the cooking and housework for her large family.[7]

Given the family's strained finances, Belle's education was sporadic. For a time her family provided free room and board to a woman who taught the children, but that luxury was soon replaced by the local public school. She attended a private academy for two years, until her father could no longer afford the tuition of five dollars a month. An eager and intelligent young woman, Belle was humiliated and crushed by southern conventions that made it impossible for her to continue her education or to work to support herself and pay for her own schooling. As she put it, "Of all unhappy sights, the most pitiable is that of a human life, rich in possibilities and strong with divine yearnings for better things than it has known, atrophying in the prison house of blind and palsied custom." Belle chafed at the "unnatural code of the manorial leisure of other days," a code that had "vanished with slavery," though it took several years for southerners to fully appreciate that fact. She rebelled inwardly as she returned to the drudgery of the plantation, an existence she despised so much that she "died to God and to humanity."[8]

Although Belle had converted at a revival at the age of twelve and followed her devout mother into the Methodist Church, she came to "despise Christianity and sneered at every profession of trust in a Supreme Being." Her home was a regular stopping place for Methodist ministers, and her mother spent several hours a day poring over the scriptures and religious commentaries, but she felt nothing but "intense disgust." In desperation, she "swallowed her pride" and took in sewing for local black women in an effort to earn a few dollars of her own. She used her hard-earned money to escape from the plantation for a regular round of balls and parties in Oxford, Jackson, and Canton, where she stayed with relatives, but her frivolous lifestyle led her to "a desperate fight" with her soul. Out of that soul-searching, she became determined to find some employment for herself despite her family's objections. At the age of nineteen she took a position as a schoolteacher, first in private academies but then in the public schools, where she earned a higher salary.[9]

Gradually, Kearney adopted more radical views about women's rights, views even her parents came to share. Once a wage earner herself, for example, she became convinced that women should have the right to vote. She rejoiced at the growing number of southern women employed in the public schools and in the expanding educational opportunities for women in state-supported industrial and normal schools. Gradually, too, she began to read the scriptures and to search for a sense of inner peace. Eventually, her quest was successful, and her careful study of the New Testament led to a spiritual reawakening; she rejoiced, "*I had found Jesus Christ.*" Her faith deepened her conviction that she was destined for some special mission. For her, as for many other intelligent and ambitious southern women, the "Women's Christian Temperance Union was the golden key that unlocked the prison doors of pent-up possibilities." The WCTU opened up important avenues for female leadership, public involvement, and political participation.[10]

In 1889, Frances E. Willard, the determined and capable leader of the National Women's Christian Temperance Union, spoke in Jackson. This was Willard's seventh visit to the state and her most visible since 1882, when she had addressed the state legislature. An "immense audience" attended her lecture, including Kearney, who shared Willard's vision "of the glad day when not one woman only, but women of all lands shall have entered into the *human* heritage—as man's equal in society, church and state." A Methodist minister, Dr. W. C. Black, who was a friend of Kearney's, brought her to the attention of Mrs. Mary E. Ervin, leader of the Mississippi WCTU, who recruited Kearney to lead organization efforts in the state. She accepted the position and rejoiced that "[t]he call of God had come. . . . My mission was found. . . . *I closed the door to all the world but God,*—AND WROTE MY SPEECHES."[11]

Kearney was extremely successful at her work and used her connections with churches and ministers to further the prohibition cause. She first identified potential towns for organization and wrote local ministers, asking them to open their churches and allow collections to be taken to defray expenses. If this strategy failed, she wrote local churchwomen, who undertook the necessary arrangements for her public lectures. Her speeches revolved around the WCTU's goals to "carry the philosophy of Jesus Christ into politics, to make a practical application of the laws of God to those of men; to cause morality to become the rock-bed of our national life and brotherhood the ozone of its atmosphere; to advance the welfare of women; to defend the childhood of the world, and to protect the home." WCTU members worked among the poor of both races, pushed for political reforms, established Sunday schools, and raised funds to carry out foreign missions. Kearney worked with great success in the state until 1895, when the international society recognized her skills and appointed her "round-the-world missionary."[12]

The prohibition campaign was a stunning success; by the time the Reverend Craig delivered his stinging sermon, all but five of Mississippi's seventy-five counties had outlawed the sale of liquor. In 1908 the legislature passed a statewide prohibition law, and the prohibition advocates in the state then worked in support of the Eighteenth Amendment to the Constitution. Mississippi became the first state to ratify the amendment in January 1918, and it was adopted in 1919. Even with the passage of the amendment, the prohibitionists remained vigilant; groups like the WCTU and the Anti-Saloon League continued their work, Baptist associations still had their temperance committees, and representatives from temperance organizations were frequent speakers at meetings of women's religious groups. The Methodist Woman's Missionary Society appointed a legislative committee that attended sessions of the legislature when prohibition bills were discussed and even attended city and county court sessions when prohibition cases were tried. Their concern was well-founded, because prohibition proved to be unenforceable, and the Eighteenth Amendment was repealed in 1933. The state was the last to legalize the sale of alcohol; not until 1966 did it revert to its local option law, and the fight continued at the county level (and, indeed, continues to this day). In 1947, for example, the Christian Citizens League met in Hinds County to seek strict enforcement of prohibition laws, and, after a statewide rally in 1948, the group spread to counties across the state.[13]

Prohibition marked not only a greater degree of political activism on the part of women in the state but also a greater degree of national cooperation as Mississippians joined in the country's crusade. Bishop Galloway emphasized the importance of cooperation between the North and the South; in an 1899 speech he told a northern audience, "[T]o-day I am glad that there is a star on our flag that answers to the name of Mississippi. . . . [O]ur sons were among the bravest of the brave in the islands of Cuba and the Philippines. They are fighting there to-day for that flag that waves—and may it ever wave—over our reunited land. . . . Let citizens of every color, race, politics and creed unite in the effort against the saloon." Kearney, who took pride in being a slaveholder's daughter, agreed with Galloway and expressed her own "profound thankfulness that the Civil War ended as it did; that fraternity was restored; that no longer was there a North and a South but an undivided country; a united purpose, under one flag, to work out our sublime destiny—the development for the world of principles of self-government."[14] She may have espoused those principles for the rest of the world, but did not suggest full self-government for Mississippi and its disenfranchised African American population.

Not all Mississippians would have gone so far as to give thanks that the Civil War ended as it did, though many did share Kearney's belief that the South had contributions to make to the nation's "sublime destiny." Indeed, an integral part of the redemption of the South in the years following Reconstruction revolved around the memory of the Lost Cause and the way in which white southerners interpreted that defeat and its implications for their future. The memory and interpretation of the Lost Cause were largely in the hands of postwar Confederate memorial organizations, especially the United Confederate Veterans (UCV) and the United Daughters of the Confederacy (UDC). These groups sponsored the ceremonies and rituals that shaped white southern attitudes toward defeat.

Perhaps the most surprising thing about these organizations and the intense interest among white southerners for the memorial events and other activities they sponsored is that the groups didn't form until the late 1880s, a generation after the war's end. Historians have grappled with the implications of this timing for southern history. The Lost Cause movement has been interpreted as a genuine "civil religion" for the South, a complex system of religious belief with its own "symbols, myth, ritual, theology, and organization, all directed toward meeting the profound concerns of postwar Southerners." Other scholars have rejected the notion that the Lost Cause represents a genuine civil religion, given that it had a limited number of adherents and only a transitory cultural importance that declined sharply in the twentieth century. To these scholars, the Lost Cause helped unify southern whites, particularly veterans and members of the middle class, during a period of rapid social change. Through the

UDC, women played a vital role in the religion of the Lost Cause. One of its members lauded the "moral grandeur of an organization of women, banded together to be the vindicators of the earth's noblest heroes, the men of the Confederacy." Such reassurance must have been important at a time when women like Kearney were promoting a revolution in the status of women.[15]

In a variety of ways, then, adherents of the Lost Cause attempted to ease the transition from the Old South to the New, to ensure that such a transformation did not come at the cost of their traditional southern virtues. The Lost Cause did not perpetuate sectionalism or fan the flames of racial animosity. Like Bishop Galloway, who has been identified as "the best-known Lost Cause paternalist," proponents favored segregation, but condemned many aspects of the emerging Jim Crow system. The main focus was not on race, but rather on explaining defeat and extolling southern and Confederate virtues to a white audience caught up in rapid social and economic change. Richmond served as the Mecca of the religion of the Lost Cause, but Mississippi did have one of the greatest Confederate heros in Jefferson Davis, who had lived much of his life in the state and spent his later years on the Gulf Coast. Indeed, organizations like the UDC were largely responsible for raising Davis's popularity to a position that rivaled even Robert E. Lee's. Given his unpopularity during the war, Davis welcomed his own redemption and played the role prescribed for him. In a speech before the Southern Historical Society in New Orleans in the 1880s he said, "[O]ur cause was so just, so sacred, that, had I known all that has come to pass, had I known what was to be inflicted upon me, all that my country was to endure, I would do it all over again. . . . If there be anything that justifies human war, it is defense of country, of family, of constitutional rights." Clearly, it was important for southerners to believe that four years of bloody warfare and tens of thousands of lives had not been lost in vain and that these virtues still had a place in contemporary southern, and even national, life. The organ of the United Confederate Veterans explained that "[i]t is our duty to keep the memory of our heroes green. Yet they belong not to us alone; they belong to the whole country; they belong to America."[16]

This sense of national reconciliation combined with an expanding economy and growing participation in the country's popular culture contributed to a growing sense of nationalism, a spirit encouraged by the Spanish-American War and World War I, both of which southerners supported with enthusiasm. The Mississippi Methodist Conference in 1917 declared that "this is not simply a war 'to make the world safe for democracy,' but a struggle to save even the semblance of a Christian civilization." As the representative of thousands of "patriotic Christian people" they urged Mississippians to "fight in this just cause unto death. . . ." Lost Cause ministers like the Right Reverend Theodore DuBose Bratton, Episcopal bishop of Mississippi, celebrated the "Christian South" and affirmed that "[s]hould this great body of Anglo-Americans ever cease to be Christian or become less Christian than it is, the effect upon our entire nation would be disastrous beyond the power of thought to conceive."[17] (Note the bishop's use of the term "Anglo-Americans" in his definition of the Christian South.) At last, the virtues of the Lost Cause could serve a victorious one.

As Mississippians joined the crusade to save Christian civilization and reentered the national mainstream, they fostered reforms undertaken by their northern counterparts. Prohibition is one example of the national spirit of reform that animated the late nineteenth and early twentieth centuries, and, while historians have focused their attention on northern reform movements, particularly those in northern cities, southern religious groups also moved forward on a wide variety of reforms. One major effort undertaken by several groups was the improvement of health care in the state. In 1900, for example, the Vicksburg chapter of the United Daughters of the Confederacy raised a thousand dollars to build a hospital annex intended to serve needy veterans, an ambitious project made possible through a two-thousand-dollar grant from the state legislature. The Baptists became the first denomination in the state to enter the health care field when they acquired a small hospital in Jackson in 1911. They immediately began to expand it and launched a hundred-thousand-dollar building program. A new three-story, fifty-bed hospital opened in 1914, and it was enlarged to a hundred twenty-six beds in 1922. Though small, the hospital served over forty thousand patients in its first twenty years of operation and provided approximately fifteen thousand dollars in charity work each year.[18]

Another religious group active in the health care field was the King's

Daughters, an interdenominational women's charitable society first organized in New York in 1886. The King's Daughters opened their first hospital in Meridian in 1913, and by the 1930s they were operating nine hospitals in the state. In 1930 the Mississippi order had the highest expenditures of any state (over six hundred thousand dollars), as well as more hospitals and more societies (forty). Chapters without hospitals sometimes maintained wards in local institutions or paid for operations.[19]

Major denominations in the state also operated orphanages as a part of their domestic missions program, a concern that dated back to 1816, when the religious women of Natchez opened the state's first orphanage. The establishment of orphanages became a part of the social reform movement of the late nineteenth century when the Baptists opened their institution in a rented cottage in Jackson in 1897. The cottage soon proved to be too small, and within a few years the orphanage relocated to a larger complex of buildings, including a school that opened in 1900. In 1914–15 the orphanage was the site of an experiment directed by the United States Public Health Service to find a cure for pellagra, which affected one hundred thirty children in the home in 1914 and was a major health scourge throughout the South. The experiment led to the discovery that the disease was caused by dietary deficiencies, particularly the cornbread-and-molasses diet common at the orphanage and across the region. The Baptist orphanage provided care to over twelve hundred children during its first twenty-five years in operation.[20]

As the discussion of prohibition and health care indicates, women were at the forefront of the reform movements. Mississippi ministers like Bishop Galloway called on women to lead the state forward; he declared that "the peculiar condition of the South calls upon her women to resuscitate her faded life and rebuild her fallen greatness. . . . The mission of southern womanhood . . . is the social, moral, and as a consequence, political regeneration of the South."[21] It was a high calling, but one that women tackled with enthusiasm in the period after Reconstruction. Of course, women's organizations were not new, but at last they received recognition from the larger denominational bodies and were able to work more closely together and to control their own resources.

In 1875 the Mississippi Baptist Convention first recognized women's organizations; its members recommended that women's societies be established in all churches, and they appointed a committee on women's work. In 1876 only fifteen societies were reported in the state's Baptist churches. The Southern Baptist Convention went further in 1878 by appointing a central committee of women in each southern state to promote female missionary societies; such efforts were successful, and by 1885 the number of societies in the state had grown to one hundred twelve. Methodist women entered the mission field in 1878 when the general conference met in Atlanta, Georgia, and established the Woman's Foreign Missionary Society, with twenty-three women from across the South appointed to lead the group. Even though "at first some shrank from taking office, or appearing in a public way," the movement soon gained momentum, and a stream of Mississippi women became foreign missionaries. Most of them went to China, but others labored in Japan, Korea, Mexico, Brazil and Africa.[22]

A clearer understanding of the importance of women's work to a church can be gained from examining women's efforts in the First Presbyterian Church of Oxford. The women of the church had a ladies auxiliary during the antebellum period, but their contributions to the church often went unrecorded, and even their financial contributions were turned over to the male leaders and disappeared into the general collection rather than being recorded separately. The auxiliary lapsed during the Civil War, though the women were active in caring for the sick and wounded soldiers who crowded the town. In 1868 about thirty women reorganized the Ladies Aid Society to carry out "home and foreign mission work." They raised hundreds of dollars annually by sewing dresses, gowns, bonnets, aprons, and quilts and by hosting suppers or other forms of entertainment; they donated money to foreign missionaries, purchased an organ for the Indian Mission, and gave to the denominational fund as well.

The old frame church was in constant need of repair, and the women supported the construction of a new church, a project that met with considerable opposition from the men. One of the most forceful advocates of a new building was Mrs. Jane Rascoe, the leader of the women's group, a woman of "character and clearness of vision." Her nemesis was Colonel H. A. Barr, an elder of the church since 1852 and a man of "strong, vigorous and dominating character." Barr was deeply religious and dedicated to his beloved church; indeed, it was said that "[h]e loved the kingdom of

God as the apple of his eye. . . . [H]e thought the Presbyterian church just about comprised the vineyard of the Lord; that the Southern Presbyterian church was the favorite corner of the vineyard and that in that corner God delighted most of all in the special vine that was the Oxford church!" His zeal was so great that some members came to resent his influence, none more so than Mrs. Rascoe.

Colonel Barr blocked the construction of a new building, and the women, like "docile wives and dutiful daughters," outwardly accepted defeat and spent three hundred dollars repairing and plastering the old structure, funded most of the cost of a new roof, and gave another eight hundred dollars toward the construction of a manse. Behind that cooperative facade the women laid plans for a new building; with the idea of being "wise as serpents and harmless as doves," they put most of their funds in long-term bank accounts so that it was "beyond the grasp of those in 'high authority,' " or, in other words, out of the men's reach. When the idea of building a new church came up in 1880, the women were ready to pledge a thousand dollars toward that goal. With that sum in hand, the men agreed, and a new church was erected; the women proudly claimed that "it was laid on a foundation of pies and cakes." They also purchased the carpet, pulpit furniture, chandeliers, and lamps, and fenced the church and manse for a total contribution of $2,340. Mrs. Rascoe also wanted an organ in the new church, which Colonel Barr opposed. Once again the women outfoxed the colonel by paying most of the cost. The outraged Colonel Barr, "who had hitherto led the singing, never sang a note in church again except when the organist was absent!"

The Oxford women also supported domestic and foreign missions through adult, young ladies, and children's missionary societies. Mrs. Rascoe held the meetings of the adult group in her home and conducted the children's society until her tragic death in the 1898 yellow fever epidemic. The adult meetings consisted of prayers and presentations from members on such topics as "The Jews," "Nations Without Missionaries," and "Evangelizing Africa by the Negro—Will He Go?" Over the years the women raised hundreds of dollars for mission work, honored Mrs. Rascoe by establishing a cot in the Elizabeth Blake Hospital in China in her name, made clothes and gave money to the Palmer Orphanage, and in 1918 created a war work committee to support World War I. In 1900 the church built a "negro mission school" that the women helped support; in 1915 they appointed a committee to discuss "the local work among the negroes," and beginning in 1919 they regularly sent a delegate to the Colored Women's Conference. By the 1920s over a hundred women belonged to the society, and they raised more than one thousand dollars annually.[23] The story of the Oxford women could be replicated hundreds of times in describing women's groups across the state.

As the Oxford example suggests, by 1920 women were moving beyond their traditional focus on missions and buildings toward a broader concept of their domestic mission work, one that focused increasingly on race relations. Mrs. L. W. Alford, president of the Methodist Women's Department of Missions in the state in the 1920s, wrote, "For the missionary program to go forward there must be a change of attitudes. God is the father of all people, red, brown, yellow, black and white. Our superiority complex in regard to ourselves and our nation must be taken off the pedestal. . . . With the Christianizing of our attitudes will come the fellowship of nations and the brotherhood of races." By 1928 interracial committees functioned in the Methodist women's groups, and by 1930 women held statewide interracial meetings. Increasingly, the church's committees on Christian social relations focused on racial issues and on the sorts of reform movements usually associated with the earlier Social Gospel movement in northern cities. As Katherine A. Wilson, state superintendent of Christian Social Relations from 1938 to 1940, reported, "The first hurdle was to get across the fact that 'social' did not mean parties, but the conditions of society."[24]

The Methodist commitment to better race relations began in the late nineteenth century as Jim Crow laws and the new state constitution of 1890 increased discrimination and worsened race relations. Perhaps the most outspoken critic of the state's new racial policies was Bishop Galloway, who was hailed as "A Fearless Bishop" for tackling this thorny issue head-on. In the 1890s, for example, in a typical sermon, he said, "There is no disguising the fact that there is great unrest and growing discontent among the negroes of the South. They feel friendless and almost helpless. The lynchings that disgrace our civilization, the persistent efforts to deprive the negro of the rights of citizenship, the advocacy by some politicians of limiting the school advantages provided for them, and the widening gulf of separation between the younger generation of both races, has produced a measure of despair." He railed against rabidly racist politicians like James K. Vardaman, the "White Chief," who played the race card to win elections. Galloway noted that blacks furnished "an easy and exciting issue" for such demagogues. "It requires but little ability to excite the fears and inflame the prejudices of a people," he observed with disdain. Bishop Galloway was tireless in his condemnation of lynching, both in the pulpit and in print, and the Methodist press soon took up the crusade. When Galloway died in 1909, black ministers in Jackson sent flowers and requested that black citizens be allowed to follow the body of their "distinguished friend" to the cemetery.[25]

Another prominent and outspoken advocate of racial justice in the state was the Right Reverend Theodore DuBose Bratton, Episcopal bishop of Mississippi, who published an important monograph on the subject in 1922. Bratton asked, "What, then, is the Negro's status in American political life? . . . Is it true democracy that would leave half of a population . . . unrepresented, all the way from the State Legislature to policemen of a negro ward in town? . . . Our forefathers fought for liberty to bestow it on all when the time came that the humblest members were prepared to assume its responsibilities. A later generation fought for Democracy—that crowning and pervading principle of liberty. . . . Shall the Church of God be wise enough, and devoted enough, and fearless enough, to lead the people of God to realize what has been purchased with blood and consecrated by sacrifice?" Bratton went on to defend blacks' rights to equal justice: "He asks, and he has the right which God gives to His people to ask, that, as a free man, he be treated as a man; that, as justice is the right of life, he be accorded it; that, as a citizen, he be granted the rights of citizenship—the equal right of life, liberty and the pursuit of happiness; that laws governing citizenship be applied with equal justice to Negroes and to Whites."[26]

These were brave words, indeed, for any Mississippian to utter. Bratton's call for whites to treat blacks as men carried a special force at a time when radical racists and social Darwinists questioned blacks' very humanity. For example, white Baptists complained in 1903 that "[t]here is now a dangerous book in circulation among our people. . . . [M]any professed Christians, who know more about the North Pole than they do about the Bible, find time to read this book, '*The Negro a Beast*,' and talk about the poor negro as being some kind of a brute without a name." Such books were common—and popular—in the early years of the new century.[27] Bratton worked diligently in the cause, and was one of the founders of the Mississippi Council on Interracial Cooperation, established by "outstanding Negro and white people interested in creating better race relations." Many other ministers, black and white, joined Bratton in the council; its purpose was to "educate the public to an awareness of conditions which result in injustice to many citizens. . . . [I]t seeks to be governed by the teachings and spirit of Jesus."[28]

The areas of concern that Galloway identified—racism, lynching, education, and civil rights—would be taken up by Methodist women. Mrs. J. Morgan Stevens, superintendent of Christian Social Relations, echoed Galloway's sentiments in her 1931 address to the committee's annual meeting: "The work in race relations is emerging from the dense fog of prejudice and inhibitions that has smothered it ever since the Civil War. We are beginning to realize that God had laid right at our doors one of the largest projects in nation building that had ever confronted a people." In their efforts to improve education for blacks, Methodist women in 1930 worked with the Colored Methodist Episcopal Church to establish summer leadership training schools for black women at Mississippi Industrial College in Holly Springs to serve north Mississippi and one at Jackson College to serve the southern part of the state. Women's auxiliaries across the state paid the expenses for black women to attend. In 1940 the state accepted Jackson College as a training school for black teachers, a direct outgrowth of the summer program. The women also began a program to visit black schools in 1931, and they conducted a survey that revealed the discrimination in the distribution of state school funds. They lobbied the legislature to extend the school year for blacks, to raise salaries for black teachers, and to build better schools for blacks. Some local auxiliaries assisted black teachers and parents in organizing parent-teacher associations and other clubs.[29]

Presbyterian women undertook similar efforts to promote education and cooperation in the 1940s. Interracial committees were created in each Presbyterial Women's Auxiliary. They offered scholarships for black students to Stillman Institute, taught Bible classes in black schools, and sponsored local one-day Christian conferences of Negro women, as well as the Annual Christian Conference of Negro Women at Jackson College. In the 1930s and 1940s Mrs. C. C. Alford was in charge of the "Negro Work," which was reported to be "growing each year." After the auxiliary's annual meeting in 1945 many of the women "attended a meeting in the Negro Baptist church, which was held under the direction of Mrs. J. B. Robinson, chairman of the Committee on Interracial Work. . . ."[30]

The women also cooperated with black women's societies. The white interdenominational Federated Missionary Societies of Jackson, for example, worked closely with black missionary societies in 1931. White societies "adopted" a black church and cosponsored a daily vacation Bible school for black children taught by members of both races. Whites also assisted black women in organizing Sunday schools and other auxiliaries. In some cases, black women were invited to speak to white auxiliary meetings. Mrs. Eurie M. Weston, superintendent of the Methodist Christian Social Relations Committee in 1936, reported that "[o]ther services varying from instructions in the first principles of sanitation, running the entire gamut of physical and education needs, and ending with a spiritual joint observance of the World Day of Prayer, prove that interracial cooperation is no longer a thing of theory only, but one of the realities of every day Christian living."[31]

In 1937, the Reverend A. L. Holland, minister of the black Central Methodist Church in Jackson, spoke before the Woman's Missionary Society of Galloway Memorial Methodist Church and described the serious problems confronting the black community in the area: delinquency and crime were on the rise; there were no playgrounds for black youths, no meeting places for clubs or other groups. The women, with support from the men's and women's Bible classes, agreed to assist Holland in opening a black community center by paying half the operating expenses. Within a short time, the Central Methodist Church had mortgaged its property to raise funds to purchase a house which served as the Bethlehem Center. It quickly became a bustling hub of activity, as adult sewing classes, Scout troops, kindergartens, and other projects operated there. By the 1940s an average of 2,450 people attended activities there each month.[32]

Methodist women took another major step in January 1931 when they organized the Mississippi Association of Women for the Prevention of

Lynching (MAWPL). Even before this association's creation the Legislative Committee of the Woman's Missionary Society had urged state law enforcement officials to prevent lynchings. Members of the MAWPL launched an educational campaign in high schools and colleges that reached thousands of students, and they used the missionary societies to spread their message to every county in the state. In addition, their articles appeared in the state press, and sheriffs in each county received quarterly letters lobbying for greater preventive measures. Their antilynching crusade received the official endorsement of the Mississippi Methodist Annual Conference in 1936.[33]

Despite the outspoken efforts of brave leaders like Bratton and Galloway and of the Methodist women, most white Mississippians, including church members, were determined to maintain the color line through terror, intimidation, and violence whenever necessary. That determination limited what preachers outside prominent pulpits could say, even if they were so inclined. One white Mississippian acknowledged that "[t]he only ways to keep the pro-lynching element in the church is to say nothing which would tend to make them uncomfortable as church members." Indeed, whites made some lynchings sound more like church socials than the brutal attacks they actually were. Mississippi native and African American antilynching crusader Ida B. Wells put the matter more directly: "American Christians are too busy saving the souls of white Christians from burning in hell-fire to save the lives of black ones from present burning in fires kindled by white Christians."[34]

As laudable as these efforts to improve race relations were, they remained flawed by racism and paternalism, and their impact on society was limited. But in the Jim Crow South, theirs were virtually the only voices of moderation and cooperation, however imperfect they might have been. For these men and women, the call for racial understanding grew directly out of their faith; perhaps Bishop Galloway said it best when he told one of his critics, "I am simply pleading for the ethics of the Man of Galilee to be applied in our dealing with the negro race."[35] It was a deceptively simple response, one that would rise up to challenge Mississippians in the years ahead. There is no question that these seeds of racial justice often fell on stony ground, but when the movement for racial equality took root and grew in the years after World War II, the groundwork done in this period came to fruition.

For most Mississippians, the period from the end of Reconstruction to World War I was one of consolidation and constancy in their religious life; it was a time of expansion, but along familiar lines. For the mainline denominations, those three decades were a time of dramatic growth, not only in membership but also in wealth and prestige. Ministers railed against "a growing love for luxuries, comforts and leisure" among Mississippians, made possible by higher living standards and an improving economy. In fact, southerners' per capita income rose faster than the national average from 1900 to 1920. The economic growth helps to account for a church-building boom that began in about 1903. The value of church property in the state jumped by 150 percent from 1900 to 1912, an increase that reflects the construction not only of more expensive churches but also of more parsonages.[36]

In important ways, the major denominations expanded their field of vision beyond the salvation of souls to a larger concept of a social mission, one that led them to embark on a wide range of reform and charitable initiatives, though always within the accepted paternalistic racial boundaries that few religious groups challenged directly. Here, as in the entire history of evangelical churches, the role of women cannot be overemphasized. Through their work they were drawn closer to their northern brethren and sisters, and the greater intimacy and sense of shared goals served to dilute some of the provincialism that had long characterized southern religious life. In terms of race relations the major denominations were at the forefront of a southern liberal paternalism that is easily and justifiably condemned as conservative and racist but must also be considered in the context of the period. At a time when race relations were at a nadir and when lynchings reached record numbers, their paternalism, flawed as it was, provided practically the only white criticism and resistance to the worsening racial climate.

We are with the new tide. We stand at the crossroads. We watch each new procession. The hot wires carrying urgent appeals. Print compels us. Voices are speaking. Men are moving! And we shall be with them.

—RICHARD WRIGHT[1]

8 Standing at the Crossroads: From World War I to World War II

For the most part, the period from World War I to the end of World War II was one of expansion, growth, and maturation for Mississippi churches. The end of World War I and continued economic advancement brought dramatic social changes to the state, changes that challenged religious folk. The 1920s also ushered in what one minister called the "Age of Indiscretion." He wrote that in the wake of World War I "a psychological cyclone struck the earth and has been followed, not so much by reconstruction and readjustments, as by the rotting of the wreckage. . . ."[2] To some extent, the events between the world wars did seem like cyclones. The state's economic system, grounded in plantation agriculture and sharecropping and tenancy, was revolutionized. That system had helped buttress the system of white supremacy, which would also be shaken to its very foundations during these years. For many white Mississippians in particular, the decline of these institutions must have seemed like a rotting of wreckage, and religious fundamentalism was one response to the rapid social changes. But these years were not marked simply by decline and decay. By far the most impressive religious development in the state was the remarkable growth of the black churches, particularly the black Baptists.

In 1936 black Baptists were the largest denomination in the state; with 322,362 members they had over twice the number of members claimed by the white Southern Baptists, their nearest competitor, who had 150,000 members. Indeed, black Baptists composed more than 40 percent of the total church membership in the entire state. When the Civil War ended in 1865 black church membership was divided roughly evenly between Methodists and Baptists, but by 1936 only 60,803 blacks belonged to the three major black Methodist denominations. While black Baptist membership expanded more than 25 percent from 1906 to 1936, membership in the African Methodist Episcopal Church (AME Church) fell by about 36 percent during the same period, and membership in the Colored Methodist Episcopal Church (CME Church) remained stagnant.[3] One problem confronting black Methodists was their dependence on an educated ministry; given the few black colleges and seminaries and the poverty of the black community, it was especially difficult to train ministers.

The autobiography of John J. Morant, a black minister in the AME Church, reveals the hardships that confronted black Methodist ministers in the state. Morant was born about 1875 near Vicksburg and from an early age felt called to preach; he recalled that "[e]ven as a small child I felt a love for the Divine Being, and at the age of five I was a children's preacher, holding meetings under an improvised brush shelter. . . ." He was converted at age eight while picking cotton and delivered his first sermon at the age of fourteen after his minister, the Reverend H. C. Bruce, recognized his gift. He became a protégé of the Reverend Bruce, and in 1889 he was admitted into the north Mississippi conference. His first appointment was to Corinth, where he arrived with five cents in his pocket. He worked hard there and built up "a good church."[4]

After two years he was transferred to a black settlement named Cob Switch, near Columbus, which was also called "Hell's Half Acre." There he faced great hardships: "The church building was a common shack, the offering was one dollar and ten cents. The members were poor and semi-slaves. Black molasses and cornbread was the common meal." He was desperately unhappy there and soon moved to West Point, where he made forty converts and enjoyed more success; still he yearned to leave the "hills," which the ministers called "starvation," and return to the Delta. He preached in the Delta for several years but wanted an education. He successfully petitioned his conference for a scholarship to Wilberforce University in Ohio, though his petition was almost refused when he said that he did not want to be the sort of preacher who "harangued the people with his fingers in his ears, spitting, sweating, and stumping." He was rebuked for criticizing "the old fathers," but won his scholarship.[5]

He studied at Wilberforce for five years and did well enough to be chosen to deliver one of the graduation orations; he said, in part, "Right cannot fail; justice, though asleep a long time, will never die. And though the mills of justice grind slowly they grind exceedingly fine." He returned to Mississippi and conducted successful ministries at churches in Brookhaven, Greenwood, Greenville, and other towns. Apparently he continued to preach and write about justice and the eventual triumph of right over might, enough so that his "writing was considered inflammatory." At one point he was forced to leave Greenwood to save his own life from a lynch mob after "big newspaper headlines inflamed many people to utter violent threats."[6]

In 1905 he took the pulpit at Bethel Church in Vicksburg, "the mother of African Methodism in Mississippi." He added one hundred new members in two years and in 1912 led in the construction of a new twelve-thousand-dollar church, one of many such building campaigns he conducted as minister. His success there finally brought him a measure of stability; he was the first AME pastor to remain in one place for as long as seven years. He became presiding elder of the Vicksburg District and eventually moved into education himself by serving as dean of the L. W. Lampton Theological Seminary after World War II.[7] Morant's story offers a few clues as to the difficulties the Methodists faced. Clearly, it required great sacrifice and determination to gain an education and enter the ministry. It is also clear that after making such sacrifices men were not eager to labor among desperately poor, uneducated people who had little use for an educated minister and probably preferred one of the "old fathers" that Morant so disdained.

African American novelist Richard Wright, born on a plantation near Natchez in 1908, offers a rare glimpse into the worship services of black churches in the 1920s in his remarkable autobiography *Black Boy*. He describes attending a Methodist church with his mother:

> In the black Protestant church I entered a new world: prim, brown, puritanical girls who taught in the public schools; black college students who tried to conceal their plantation origin; black boys and girls emerging self-consciously from adolescence; wobbly-bosomed black and yellow church matrons; black janitors and porters who sang proudly in the choir; subdued redcaps and carpenters who served as deacons; meek, blank-eyed black and yellow washerwomen who shouted and moaned and danced when hymns were sung; jovial, potbellied black bishops; skinny old maids who were constantly giving rallies to raise money; snobbery, clannishness, gossip, intrigue, petty class rivalry, and conspicuous displays of cheap clothing. . . . I liked it and I did not like it.

Unlike the Seventh-Day Adventist Church he sometimes attended with his devout grandmother, this was the church of the middle class—schoolteachers, college students, porters, and carpenters were the leaders here. Even as a young teenager he was aware of the "snobbery" and "petty class rivalry" among its members, probably because he was not of the middle class himself. When his classmates pressed him to join the church, they assured him that "this is a new day. . . .We don't holler and moan in church no more. Come to church and be a member of the community." At least some members of the congregation shared Morant's desire to leave the traditional forms of ecstatic worship behind. There was a strong emphasis on the idea of community; again, he was pressured "to become a member of a responsible community church."[8]

This emphasis on the concept of a "responsible community church" suggests that these Methodists, like their white counterparts, were moving away from the traditional focus on the salvation of individuals to a broader, corporate concept of their mission. It was this spirit that encouraged the churchwomen to raise funds and to join with white women in their social work, or that led the members of Central Methodist to mortgage their property to open a community center. And while Morant offers no specific information about his controversial writings, his background and the fact that he was almost lynched suggest that his concerns were much like those of Bishop Galloway—racism, lynching, education, and civil rights. Wright also hints at another feature of these churches: from elders to ministers to presiding elders to bishops, these churches and the larger denominational structures were hierarchical and patriarchal in their governance.

The opponents of denominationalism and those who favored ecstatic worship services and a strict gospel discipline found themselves less and less content in the mainline churches. Increasingly, traditionalist members of both races looked to newly emerging fundamentalist churches to meet their spiritual needs. Religious census figures show this process at work during the early decades of the twentieth century, though it is likely that the membership figures for these churches were consistently underreported, given their small size, their own aversion to such trappings of denominationalism, and their unconventional locations in storefronts or private homes. Nevertheless, the census takers found 777 members of the Seventh-Day Adventist Church in Mississippi in 1936, up from 380 in 1906; 1,178 members of the Assemblies of God, a group that had not been reported in 1906 or 1916; 3,740 members of the Church of Christ, Holiness, up from 96 in 1906; and 4,030 members of the various congregations of Church of God, none of which had been reported in 1906.[9]

One of these emerging denominations, the Church of Christ, Holiness, originated in Jackson in 1896 under the dynamic leadership of the Reverend Charles P. Jones, pastor of the Mt. Helm Baptist Church, Jackson's oldest black church. Jones's departure from Baptist doctrine had begun a few years before his arrival in Mississippi from Alabama. As he explained it:

> I found myself in need of a deeper experience of grace, a larger power. As I asked God for this grace He demanded that I let Him sanctify me; which I did. For as He demanded of me, I fasted and prayed three days and nights. He then sanctified me sweetly in His love. New visions of Christ, of God, of truth, were given me. The earnestness of the Spirit was mine. I was sealed unto the day of Redemption. The blessing of God rested upon me—all on the merits of Jesus. For in myself I felt more unworthy and undone than ever. It was the nearness, the eminence, the reality of the presence of God that exalted my spirit and filled me with joy, the joy of the Holy Ghost.[10]

At the heart of Jones's experience was the idea of sanctification, which was central to the Holiness movement. The concept of sanctification or a "second blessing" has deep roots in Christianity, and John Wesley brought the doctrine to the forefront with his emphasis on a postconversion second work of grace. An emphasis on sanctification refocused attention on individual conversion experiences and carried with it a strict moral code, at a time when the major denominations were moving toward a more corporate view of the religious community and away from their role as moral courts. Indeed, one white Baptist minister mourned that, by the early twentieth century, "there is no sin nor crime . . . which one may not commit and still remain a member of the church," and the once-common practice of church discipline had largely vanished in the major denominations. When Jones began to preach about his experience, particularly about the doctrine of sanctification and healing, and demanded that the members of Mt. Helm follow his rigorous guidelines, which included giving up smoking, dancing, card playing, and drinking, opposition arose against him. A "Committee of 100" requested that he resign, and, when he refused, they successfully sought a court order forcing him to give up the pulpit.[11]

He and a group of followers established a new congregation that met for a time in a store building. Soon, however, they bought a lot and built a new church located just one block from Mt. Helm. Jones took his message to Vicksburg where several other ministers "received the gift of the Holy Ghost" and established churches of their own. As the membership grew, a church school was established in 1900. He also set up a printing press that published a magazine called *Truth* and his own booklets and hymns. Soon Church of Christ, Holiness congregations spread to other states, and it became the largest of the Holiness churches. In 1918 Jones left his thriving church in Jackson to found a successful church in Los Angeles.[12]

Once again Wright offers insights into the services of one of the most dynamic of these fundamentalist groups, the Seventh-Day Adventists. The power and poetry of the dramatic services he attended with his grandmother were firmly etched in his memory:

> The elders of her church expounded a gospel clogged with images of vast lakes of eternal fire, of seas vanishing, of valleys

of dry bones, of the sun burning to ashes, of the moon turning to blood, of stars falling to the earth, of a wooden staff being transformed into a serpent, of voices speaking out of clouds, of men walking upon water, of God riding whirlwinds, of water changing into wine, of the dead rising and living, of the blind seeing, of the lame walking; a salvation that teemed with fantastic beasts having multiple heads and horns and eyes and feet; sermons of statues possessing heads of gold, shoulders of silver, legs of brass, and feet of clay; a cosmic tale that began before time and ended with the clouds of the sky rolling away at the Second Coming of Christ; chronicles that concluded with Armageddon; dramas thronged with all the billions of human beings who had ever lived or died as God judged the quick and the dead.[13]

For dispossessed members of both races, here was a God of awesome power and a faith of deep mystery.

It was also a demanding faith; among its services was an "all-night ritualistic prayer meeting" that Wright reluctantly attended with his relatives. He despised the long ordeal, but could not remain completely insensitive to the emotional energy released there:

> During the passionate prayers and the chanted hymns I would sit squirming on a bench . . . listening indifferently to the theme of cosmic annihilation, loving the hymns for their sensual caress. . . . Many of the religious symbols appealed to my sensibilities and I responded to the dramatic vision of life held by the church, feeling that to live day by day with death as one's sole thought was to be so compassionately sensitive toward all life as to view all men as slowly dying, and the trembling sense of fate that welled up, sweet and melancholy, from the hymns blended with the sense of fate that I had already caught from life.[14]

Once again, Wright identified central elements of the faith. Groups like the Adventists are often labeled "fatalistic," as if their awareness of human mortality led only to complacency with life's lot, no matter how unfortunate or unjust. But as Wright points out, such a sensibility could also engender a sense of compassion, and closely linked to the awareness of death was the judgement that followed.

Adventist missionaries first arrived in Mississippi in 1895 on board their steamboat, named the *Morning Star*. They began their work at Vicksburg and soon raised the suspicions of local whites as blacks began to convert. In general, whites showed little concern about black religious life, but the Adventists believed that the Sabbath fell on Saturday, not Sunday, and refused to work on the holy day. Even some black Baptists in Vicksburg adopted Saturday as the Sabbath, which resulted in a meeting between the missionaries and black ministers. Some blacks "have given up their jobs rather than work on Saturday," and whites feared that "the labor question may be seriously affected" by what they termed a "religious fad." Many people's attitudes changed four years later when a severe flood struck the Yazoo River. The Adventists steered the *Morning Star* into the swollen waters and distributed food, clothing, and supplies to victims. From their first church at Vicksburg, the movement spread to members of both races. By 1918 they were holding an annual statewide tent revival meeting in Jackson.[15]

Another Pentecostal group, the Assemblies of God, held their first services at Magnolia Springs Holiness Campground in the fall of 1899. This meeting became an annual event that drew participants from several states. Like the other Pentecostal groups, the Assemblies of God grew through Bible schools, healing crusades, and itinerant evangelists. By 1909 they were operating the School of the Prophets in Hattiesburg, which trained preachers and sent them out across the state. They welcomed women preachers, and the School of the Prophets was open to them. The women dressed modestly, often in white, and wore no jewelry. A Meridian newspaper described one of these evangelists, Maria B. Woodworth-Elter, as "easily among the most interesting and captivating evangelists . . . a woman of great faith . . . sweet spirited, firm and business-like."[16] By 1929 half of the church's newly licensed ministers in the state were women, probably at least 25 percent of the total number of ministers in the field.[17]

Their worship services, frequently held under brush arbors, harkened back to the early days of the evangelical movement. Characterized by shouting and singing, by emotional love feasts and foot-washing ceremonies, these biracial revival services borrowed directly from the early evangelical traditions. The very language used to describe the meetings echoed that of a century before. At the 1915 meeting at the Magnolia campground, for example, "[T]he fire fell with sin-destroying power. Thirty-five were saved and sixteen joined the church." At a 1919 meeting in Pierce, "The saints rejoiced, shouted, talked in tongues, danced, and prophesied."[18] Converts reportedly "took their singing and shouting to the fields and blessed God, instead of cussed, when the plow cut a root which smacked him on the shin. Even a man's mules could tell if his master's religion was sincere. . . ."[19] In 1925 the Assemblies reported sixteen churches in the state and twenty-seven by 1936. Most black converts went into the Church of God in Christ which had at least ninety churches in the state by 1936.[20]

The fundamentalist churches like the Assemblies of God were the most dynamic religious institutions in the South, and, as was true of the evangelical churches of a century before, their emphasis on the equality of believers, their encouragement of emotionally demonstrative worship, and their willingness to allow experimentation and innovation in ritual and practice led to a remarkable outpouring of spiritualism and creativity. Like the evangelicals of the Great Revival, the fundamentalists wrought a revolution in religious music that carried over into popular music as well. The emerging black Pentecostal denominations transformed congregational singing into a new form known as gospel music, marked by "driving rhythms and percussive instrumental accompaniment." Mainline denominations moved away from congregational singing to the use of practiced choirs and elevated the sermon to make it the high point of worship services, but Pentecostals "used congregational singing as a way of achieving climatic experiences of spiritual transcendence."[21]

Congressman Mike Espy memorialized Mississippi's place in gospel music on the floor of the U.S. House of Representatives in 1990; he said, "[I]f not the 'Birthplace of Gospel Music,' Mississippi most certainly is one of the places where Gospel chose to deliver many of her offsprings."[22] Mississippi natives like Willie Mae Ford Smith, known as "Mother Smith," pioneered modern gospel music in cooperation with Thomas A. Dorsey in the 1920s and 1930s. Dorsey, a native of Georgia, first won fame as a blues musician but abandoned popular music to promote gospel. Mother Smith, a native of Rolling Fork, left the state at the age of twelve, carrying her blues-influenced gospel style from the Delta to St. Louis. She began working with Dorsey's National Convention of Gospel Choirs and

Choruses in the early 1930s and became director of the convention's solo-ist bureau. Her soaring contralto and vocal arrangements influenced a generation of gospel performers including Mahalia Jackson. She won wide acclaim as a performer at the Newport Jazz Festival, as a star of the 1981 documentary *Say Amen, Somebody* and as a recipient of a National Heritage Award from the National Endowment for the Arts in 1988. Another Mis-sissippian, Theodore R. Frye, also worked with Dorsey and played an im-portant role in the evolution of gospel music. Born in Fayette in 1899, Frye studied music and piano and served as director of a church choir before his move to Chicago in 1927. Drawing on his roots, he became known as a singer who could "move a house" with his emotional style.[23] With Dorsey, he was a cofounder of the National Convention of Gospel Choirs and Choruses in 1932.

One of the most popular gospel groups in Chicago was the Five Blind Boys of Mississippi. The group was organized by Archie Brownlee, who attended the Piney Woods Country Life School in Rankin County, Mis-sissippi. Inspired in part by the success of the Fisk Jubilee Quartet, Brown-lee organized the Cotton Blossom Singers from among his classmates. The group became locally successful and earned enough money to pay their tuition. In 1944 they moved to Chicago and changed their name to the Original Five Blind Boys of Mississippi; after touring successfully for several years they began recording in the early 1950s and had a series of hits over the following decade.

Along with Chicago, Detroit was a mecca for Mississippi blacks, and they made the Motor City another center for gospel music. Black Pente-costal congregations appeared in Detroit in the mid-twenties, and Dorsey established a chapter of the gospel convention there in the 1930s. In 1942 Anna Broy Crockett, then in her mid-twenties, arrived in the city from Lexington, Mississippi, and began organizing gospel choirs, but the "major force"[24] behind gospel in Detroit was the Reverend C. L. Franklin, born in Indianola, the birthplace of B. B. King. He dropped out of school in the tenth grade and was a migrant farm worker before becoming a preacher at the age of seventeen. He was the pastor of churches in Green-ville and Clarksdale before moving north. From his pulpit at the Bethle-hem Baptist Church in Detroit he became a tireless promoter of gospel and a famous singer and gospel preacher. He recorded more than sixty sermons, delivered in the emotional style blending song and the spoken word common to black preachers in Mississippi for generations. His daughter, Aretha, learned from her father and carried aspects of his form into her own legendary style.

The Pentecostals and other black fundamentalists had created a cultural force that their small churches could not contain, and gospel soon merged with other kinds of music such as work songs and field hollers to form the blues. While the hard-drinking, hard-living blues might seem far removed from religion, scholars have found that "the blues actually coexisted quite peacefully with organized religion and appeared even to complement it on occasion." B. B. King explored the links between the blues and religious music in the Delta: "I think what really got me into the music more than anything else was that my uncle's brother-in-law was a sanctified preacher, and he played guitar in the church. I think that's what did it more than anything else. . . . I really liked the sound of a guitar in the church." In fact, King felt powerfully drawn to gospel music: "I first wanted to be a gospel singer. . . . That's really what I wanted to be. I didn't want to be a blues singer."[25]

When asked to explain why the blues were born in Mississippi he said, "I think that in Mississippi you had this combination of believers and non-believers, I mean church-goers and others. . . . I don't think I really mean they don't believe in God, but a lot of them didn't go the way of the church, but they had the church training. . . . By having the church training, you still have that same feeling that church people, so to speak, have." King, like many other blues performers, might play at a club on Saturday night and church on Sunday morning. He recalled, "I enjoyed going to church, I enjoyed being a part of the church, . . . but I enjoyed also going and dancing on Saturday nights. . . . I was accepted in the church, and I was also accepted on the corner." King's experience was by no means exceptional among the state's great bluesmen; others, including Charley Patton, John Lee Hooker, and Muddy Waters, had a similar religious upbringing, and some blues performers moved from the pulpit to the nightclub at various times in their lives. King's observation about the shared "church feeling" among Mississippi blacks supports historian Edward Ayers's assertion that "[t]he blues and the church spoke in a common

Afro-American vernacular, lowering the boundary between secular and religious music."[26]

The boundary between secular and religious music also blurred in white Pentecostal and fundamentalist churches, where a similar process of musical innovation occurred in white gospel music. Like black gospel, white gospel developed out of traditional musical forms, particularly the shape-note style, popular in parts of rural Mississippi since the early nineteenth century, "but it drew much of its dynamism and much of its personnel from the Holiness-Pentecostal movement of the late nineteenth and early twentieth centuries." In 1911 a group of singers met at the community schoolhouse in Dancy, located in the clay hills of north-central Mississippi, and organized the Webster County Singing Convention. Webster County was a center of the shape-note tradition; indeed, the all-day singing convention was introduced by the sacred harp singers, but this was a gospel convention. A major departure from the shape-note tradition was that gospel singers used musical instruments, and, like those in the black holiness churches, white dissidents allowed a variety of musical instruments in their services.[27]

The spread of white gospel was encouraged by the efforts of major southern music publishing companies, including the Stamps-Baxter Company of Texas and the A. J. Showalter Company of Georgia, both of which were active in Mississippi. These companies trained singers who fanned out across the South to teach music schools and sell songbooks; in addition, they sent out their own quartets to tour the region and to record their songs.[28]

White gospel music quickly became big business, and by the end of the 1920s gospel quartets were popular on records and on radio. Ever since the colonial period, evangelicals have been quick to employ the latest technologies to spread their message. By the 1920s they still maintained their impressive publishing houses, and new fundamentalist denominations quickly established their own publishing companies and magazines, but they also exploited the recording industry. Almost every Mississippi family that could afford one owned a Victrola—often it was their most prized possession—and white gospel recordings were the first aimed at a southern audience.[29]

Radio also played a major role in popularizing the gospel sound, and evangelicals of every stripe were quick to realize the potential of the new technology. The first commercial radio station in the state went into operation in 1924, and religious programming was an important part of the schedule. The third licensee in the state was Howard S. Williams, a lay evangelist from Hattiesburg. His license carried the unusual stipulation that his portable station was to be relocated every two weeks as he took his tent revival from one location to another. Williams, a native of Alabama, began his career as a journalist and worked as a correspondent for the *Jackson Daily News*. In 1922 he was assigned to cover a tent revival conducted by Gypsy Smith, but his assignment led to a dramatic conversion experience. He quit his job, sold his stock in the newspaper, bought a tent and two pianos, and spent the rest of his life preaching the gospel. When he died in 1960, he had preached in more than twenty states, held three hundred forty-two revivals, and converted some forty thousand people. The mainline denominations also saw the potential of radio. The First Presbyterian Church of Meridian, for example, received a license to operate a radio station in 1925; by 1931 the Laurel station had remote lines to the Presbyterian, Baptist, and Methodist churches. Radio stations routinely carried Sunday services, and some, like the Hattiesburg station, had a daily "Chapel Time." These early stations often carried a mix of music, from classical to country to gospel, and a variety of spoken productions, from comedy dialogues to sermons.[30]

Perhaps the most graphic example of the tensions between modernism and traditionalism in the 1920s is the evolution controversy best dramatized by the Scopes trial held in Dayton, Tennessee, in 1925. The trial pitted William Jennings Bryan, a former presidential candidate and cabinet officer turned antievolution crusader, against Clarence Darrow, the most famous trial lawyer of the day and an avowed agnostic, who defended schoolteacher John Scopes on behalf of the American Civil Liberties Union. One of the most widely reported events of the decade, the trial resulted in Scopes's conviction but also provided critics of the South with powerful ammunition in their portrayal of the region as a religious backwater. Many people outside the South saw the trial as the last gasp of fundamentalism and believed that antievolution had been ridiculed into oblivion. In fact, however, Scopes's conviction encouraged opponents of the teaching of evolution in the South. According to one small-town newspaper in Mississippi, the lesson from Dayton was that Christian people should not "pay men to teach their children false doctrines, which if believed generally would overthrow all the institutions of this country and would turn back the civilization of this world . . . destroy the Bible and rift America and American institutions." The state government rallied to prevent such a catastrophe. The Mississippi legislature rejected an antievolution bill in 1925, but the state superintendent of schools responded by banning the teaching of evolution in the state's classrooms. State representative L. Walter Evans, a minister in the Church of God, saw the popularity of the ban and introduced a bill to prohibit the teaching of evolution in 1926. One of the bill's champions was Mississippi Baptist evangelist Thomas T. Martin, author of a 1923 antievolution diatribe entitled *Hell and the High Schools: Christ or Evolution, Which?* Martin aimed his harshest criticism at the educational elite, "a lot of high brows supported by your taxes," and called on parents to take control of their children's education.[31]

Martin lobbied strenuously for the Evans bill and was invited to address a joint session of the legislature. He answered the charge that if the state passed such a bill it would open itself up to the sort of ridicule in the national press that had been visited on Tennessee with the following question: "Shall the legislature of Mississippi . . . barter the faith of the children of Mississippi in God's word and the Savior for the fulsome praise of a paganized press?"[32] Despite a negative recommendation from the house education committee, the bill passed by a vote of seventy-six to thirty-two. The senate education committee also gave the bill a negative vote, but the senate passed the bill by twenty-nine to sixteen votes. When the bill reached the desk of Governor Henry L. Whitfield, the chancellor of the University of Mississippi, Alfred Hume, urged him to veto it, but little other opposition to the bill manifested itself, and the governor signed it into law in March 1926. The ACLU offered to represent any teacher willing to challenge the bill in the courts, but no one came forward. While the national press was quick to declare the demise of fundamentalism in the wake of the Scopes trial, events in Mississippi indicate that, as was so often the case, the South was different. Though fundamentalism retreated from the national stage, the movement continued to grow in the South.

Fundamentalism did not disappear after Scopes so much as it was overshadowed by other concerns as the nation fell into the depths of the

Great Depression. The prosperity of the 1920s proved to be illusory. Cotton prices fell after 1920, and even before the Great Depression gripped the nation, the southern economy had fallen so rapidly that almost all the relative income gains made up to 1920 were lost by 1930.[33] Across the state most churches saw membership drop drastically. All the major white Protestant churches suffered major losses; the Methodist Episcopal Church, South, declined from 134,573 members in 1926 to 107,245 in 1936, membership in the Southern Baptist Church fell from 211,370 to 150,000, and the Presbyterian Church went from 22,999 to 18,445 members. The Negro Baptist grew from 226,989 members in 1926 to 322,362 in 1936, but the AME Church dropped from 22,439 to 19,592 members, and the AME Zion fell from 18,361 to 13,687 members. Aside from black Baptists, the only churches showing major gains were the fundamentalist and Pentecostal churches and the Roman Catholic Church.

An examination of one church's response to the crisis of the Great Depression can illustrate how churches confronted the catastrophe. In 1930 Calvary Baptist Church in Jackson appointed a five-man committee to present a plan to cut expenses. The church had grown rapidly over the last decade, and had a membership of sixteen hundred. They recommended a moderate plan that eliminated salaries for members of the choir, reduced some payments to church funds, got rid of one telephone, and urged the "strictest economy" in electricity and water use. But as church collections fell, more draconian cuts were necessary. The church slashed other salaries and purchased no Sunday school literature. As hard times hit, "Many members lost their jobs and went back to their original homes or left Jackson seeking work elsewhere."[34]

Churches like Calvary Baptist had to try to keep their revenues up without driving away unemployed members who could no longer afford to contribute. An announcement in a 1933 church bulletin read, *"To the Unemployed*—Let us make it plain again that we are not looking to you for financial support now. . . . You are always welcome at Calvary—So, above everything, let us have your presence and prayers. . . . Let no announcement from the platform trouble you." The church attempted to meet the needs of unemployed members by setting up a commissary where merchants donated groceries and clothing for those in need.[35] Despite their best efforts, the churches' resources were not sufficient to relieve the distress that gripped the state as the depression wore on.

Perhaps the most ambitious attempt made by religious groups to confront the hardships of the depression was the Delta Cooperative Farm located in Bolivar County. The farm was the brainchild of some of the nation's most prominent reformers and theologians, foremost among them Reinhold Niebuhr, arguably the most influential American theologian of this century. No group in America was hit harder by the depression than southern tenants and sharecroppers. One group of scholars writing in the 1930s summed up the situation in the following grim terms: "Although adding a billion dollars annually to the wealth of the world, the cotton farmers themselves are the most impoverished and backward of any large group in America. . . . The status of tenancy demands complete dependence; it requires no education and demands no initiative. The landlord keeps the records and determines the earnings. He controls the courts, the agencies of law enforcement and . . . can effectively thwart any efforts at organization. . . ."[36] Estimates placed the number of sharecroppers in the South at eight million—five million whites and three million blacks. In Mississippi 72 percent of all farmers were tenants or croppers, most of whom lived in abject poverty exacerbated by high rates of illiteracy, poor diet, and devastating diseases. The average farm consisted of only sixty-two acres of land, with twenty-six acres in cultivation. The average value of all farm machinery was $11.01, and the average value of all livestock was $24.54 "or the value of a single scrawny cow."[37] The crop lien system led to a cycle of debt and poverty from which few croppers ever escaped.

New Deal farm programs did little to address the needs of the poorest of the poor and in fact often exacerbated their problems. Federal programs were typically designed and administered by the white planters, who were their chief beneficiaries. Landlords often cheated croppers and tenants out of government farm payments or forced them off the land to evade their obligations. In 1934 a group of black and white sharecroppers in Arkansas organized the Southern Tenant Farmers' Union, which quickly grew to over twenty-five thousand members in several southern states. Landlords responded to the union's efforts with a "reign of terror"; union meetings were banned and broken up, and members were arrested and jailed on trumped-up charges, evicted from their homes, removed from relief rolls, beaten, mobbed, and even murdered.

The union members' desperate struggle came to the attention of some of America's most dedicated social activists, including Dr. Sherwood Eddy, Norman Thomas, and Niebuhr. Eddy and a group of men interested in the union movement visited Arkansas, where they faced threats, intimidation, and arrest. Shocked and outraged by what they saw, the men left Arkansas determined to take action on the croppers' behalf. The men wanted to find a way to help the sharecroppers help themselves and settled on a plan to buy a tract of land on which to establish a cooperative farm, which they envisioned as the first in a chain of such projects to be established across the South. With borrowed funds they bought a two-thousand-acre cotton plantation in the Mississippi Delta and created a board of trustees, including Eddy and Niebuhr, to hold the property and oversee the project. The only prominent Mississippi religious leader to serve on the board was the outspoken Right Reverend Theodore DuBose Bratton, Episcopal Bishop of Mississippi. They chose Sam H. Franklin, a Tennessee native and former missionary to Japan, as director of the farm. When international tensions forced Franklin out of the Far East, "he felt he must identify himself with the deepest need in his own land . . . among the sharecroppers in his own portion of the South." Thirty families lived on the farm, eighteen black and twelve white.[38]

The cooperative was founded on the belief in "realistic religion as a social dynamic," which meant "the return of Christianity to its prophetic mission of identification with the dispossessed, of bearing witness of the judgment of God in history upon the injustices of the existing economic and political order, and of aiding men to enter into the possibilities of a more abundant life with which God has endowed His creation." Another of the cooperative's "foundation principles"[39] was interracial justice, though the group was also "determined that the Delta Cooperative should not be destroyed by coming into open conflict with local segregation laws and customs."[40] For example, a state law of 1930 prohibited the teaching of "social equality" in any school in the state. In order to avoid conflict, the cooperative's housing and schools were segregated, but all meetings and services, such as the clinic, the cooperative store, and the credit union, were open to everyone. Along with planting cotton, the cooperative purchased a sawmill and in the first year sold a cotton crop worth twelve thousand dollars and lumber worth five thousand dollars.

Not surprisingly, local landowners and their allies, including members of the clergy, eyed the cooperative with suspicion. Reinhold Niebuhr and other leaders met with a group of local ministers who "called us in to express their apprehensions about the interracial policy of the Delta Co-operative Farm and to suggest in veiled terms that this represented 'Yankee' interference with the customs of the south." The leaders of the cooperative assured the ministers that "the farm would not unnecessarily challenge the prejudices of the south . . . ," but Niebuhr wrote that "[a] group of ministers of the gospel, defending the unchristian *mores* of their community, is always a slightly pathetic sight." Niebuhr was moved by the simple faith he saw among the croppers, but complained that despite their faith "they are religiously disinherited." Clergymen like those he met had no interest in the farmers' plight:

> The organized church as such does not serve them. It is as middle class in the south as anywhere else. On the countryside it serves the planters and the merchants of the village. The sharecroppers are served by lay preachers, who develop spontaneously without religious training. Their theological notions are crude but their close relations to their people drives them into socially significant actions which the more intelligent church leaders might well envy. . . . Lay preachers have been in the forefront of the movement for the organization of both agrarian and industrial laborers in the south. . . . They express the religious protest against social injustice in terms reminiscent of the classical examples of this protest. They know their Bible. . . . Thus the Southern Tenant Farmers Union has a "Ceremony of the Land" in which the choicest biblical passages are recited in their meetings to give religious sanction to the cry "Land to the Landless."[41]

Despite opposition, the cooperative survived and prospered, and another venture, called Providence Cooperative Farm, was established in Holmes County.

The two cooperative farms survived for over twenty years but fell victim to the rising tide of racism that followed the Supreme Court's 1954

Felders Campground. Beginning in the early 1800s, camp meetings helped spread evangelicalism on the Mississippi frontier. Camp meetings became a regular feature of religious life in the state and were usually held in the late summer when crops were laid by. This campground in southwestern Mississippi has been used since those early days.

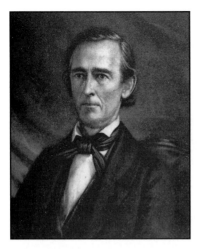

Benjamin M. Drake (1800–1860).
Itinerant and revivalist, Drake held
appointments at Claiborne, Washington, and Vicksburg. Noted for his
fine personal appearance and polished manners, he was seen as the
ideal minister for important urban
churches.

William Winans (1788–1857). A Pennsylvania native, Winans volunteered as
a pioneer itinerant in 1810 and lived
in Amite County. He served as a trustee
of Elizabeth Female Academy and Cen-
tenary College. Winans drafted a resolution condemning abolitionism and it was
adopted by the General Conference of
1836. He also served on the committee
that drafted the Plan of Separation for
the division of the Methodist Church in
1844.

William Mercer Green (1798–1887).
The first Bishop of the Protestant
Episcopal Diocese of Mississippi,
Green served from 1850–1883. He
was also an educator and one of the
founders of the University of the
South in Sewanee, Tennessee.

Church Hill Chapel (mid-1800s). The Episcopal Church in Mississippi was concentrated in the plantation districts and in urban areas where its religious views appealed to the state's planter and commercial elite. The elegant and costly churches reflected the wealth and refinement of their members.

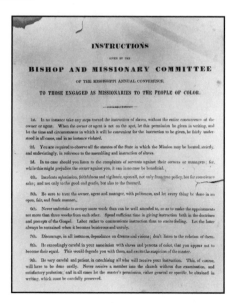

Mississippi Methodists launched their mission to the slaves in the 1830s and reached out to slaveowners in their instructions to missionaries.

Constructed in 1860, the handsome First Methodist Church in Columbus reflected the wealth of the Lowndes County cotton town and was home to a large biracial congregation.

Toxish Baptist Church (Pontotoc County) is representative of the simple churches that dotted the Mississippi countryside from the antebellum period well into the twentieth century. Many of them remain in use today. Note the separate entrances for men and women.

The interior of the Toxish Baptist Church exemplifies the simplicity of early Mississippi churches. Men often sat on the right, women on the left, and blacks in the rear.

The congregation at Carrollton Methodist Church dressed in their Sunday best for this late-nineteenth century photograph. Notice the female majority, typical of churches in the state.

Methodist Bishop Charles B. Galloway (1849–1909). Known as the "Fighting Bishop" for his strong stands against lynching and other social ills of the late nineteenth century and a Lost Cause paternalist, he took a liberal position on racial issues and women's rights.

Belle Kearney (1863–1939). The daughter of a Mississippi slaveholder, Kearney became a nationally and internationally recognized organizer for the Women's Christian Temperance Union after her religious conversion motivated her to enter reform efforts. A representative of the "New Women" of the South, she was the first woman senator in the Mississippi legislature.

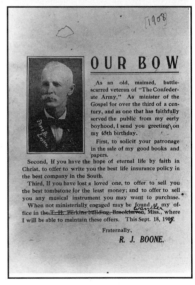

The enterprising R. J. Boone combined preaching the gospel with the Religion of the Lost Cause and sold life insurance, tombstones, and musical instruments.

First Baptist Church, Greenwood (early twentieth century). Imposing urban churches like this one indicated the changing values and wealth of evangelicals in the state. A comparison with Toxish also shows the widening gulf between urban and rural congregations.

Often regarded as extremely conservative, evangelicals were quick to adapt the latest technology to their efforts to spread the Word. This men's Sunday school group in Jackson used a train called "The Flying Squadron" to "Go Tell the Story."

Traveling evangelists like Sam Jones filled tent meetings and large meeting halls in the late-nineteenth century.

These rare photographs of Holiness church services were taken by Eudora Welty in the 1930s. *Eudora Welty Collection — Mississippi Department of Archives and History*

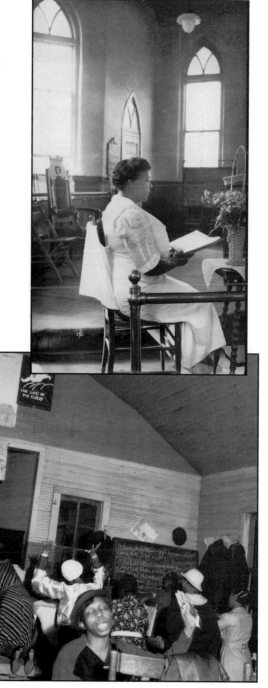

SECOND ANNUAL

Tri-Racial Good Will Festival

Carthage, Mississippi, High School Football Field

Thursday, October 27, 1949 2:00 P. M.

The Rev. Dwyn M. Mounger of the Carthage Presbyterian Church presiding

Program:

The National Anthem: The Carthage High School Band

Invocation

Singing by Negro Schools of Leake County: Sponsored by Jeans Agent Mildred Rushing and Home Demonstration Agent Mabel Jefferson.

Remarks: Superintendent C. R. Murphy, Harmony Vocational High School.

Indian Ball Game (Stick Ball): Arranged by the Indian Council in cooperation with the Carthage Rotary Club. Mr. Grover Parks is the narrator.

Address: The Honorable William Zimmerman, Jr., Associate Commissioner of Indian Affairs of the Department of The Interior, Washington, D. C.

Free Will Offering: Toward Expenses

Piano Solos By Robert Lee Whittington

Indian Ball Game: Second Half.

Address: By Joe Chitto, Chief of the Choctaw Council. The address will be given first in English and then in the Choctaw language.

Benediction

Indian Basket Show: Arts and Crafts and auction sale of Indian baskets and art work, 4:00-5:00 P. M. (Arranged by the Carthage Twentieth Century Club and Indian Officials.)

Intermission: Supper served to Indian Ball Players and Dancers, 6:00-7:00 P. M. (Supper underwritten by the Carthage Rotary Club.)

All-Indian Hillbilly Band: The Pearl River Jubilee Boys, 6:00-7:00 P. M.

Choctaw Native Dances: Including: Snake, Duck, Sun, War, Stomp, and other dances. (Planned by Indian Council and Carthage Culture Club.)

This program is made possible by the cooperative efforts of all three races in the area, Indian officials and teachers and the Civic Clubs of Carthage. We appreciate the work of the following Choctaw officials and teachers: Supt. A. H. McMullen of the Indian Agency, Mr. J. A. Jarrell, Mr. J. D. Langford, Mr. Paul Vance, and Miss Oda Jarrell. In addition to the Clubs mentioned above we are indebted to: The Carthage Lions Club for the field, drink stands, goal posts, ushers, etc.; The Carthage Business and Professional Women's Club for local advertising and programs; The Rotary Club for outside publicity; and the Twentieth Century Club for finances.

We are indebted to the Army and Air Force Recruiting Service for the use of the public address system so necessary to the program.

We especially appreciate the efforts of Mr. W. N. Morton in supervising the preparation of supper for the Indians participating in the program.

The afternoon program will be broadcast over station WJXN of Jackson, Mississippi.

"Nerve us incessantly with affirmations. Do not bark against the bad, but chant the beauties of the good." —Emerson.

CAMP MEETING

of the

United Pentecostal Church

MISSISSIPPI DISTRICT
ON THE CAMPUS OF THE

Pentecostal Bible Institute

TUPELO, MISSISSIPPI

AUGUST 7th   through 11th

Rev. V. A. Guidroz
SPECIAL SPEAKER

WEDNESDAY — YOUNG PEOPLE'S DAY

THURSDAY — SUNDAY SCHOOL & BIBLE SCHOOL DAY

FRIDAY — MISSIONARY DAY
HOME & FOREIGN

MEALS and BED.............$1.00 per day
Special rates for children under twelve.
A limited number of private rooms available at additional cost.

BRING YOUR BEDDING AND TOILET ARTICLES

FIRST SERVICE . . . . . 1:30 p.m. MONDAY, AUGUST 7
LAST SERVICE . . . . . 7:30 p.m. FRIDAY, AUGUST 11

FOUR SERVICES DAILY:
7:30 a.m. - Prayer Meeting
8:30 a.m. - Breakfast
10:00 a.m. - Worship and Preaching
12:00 noon - Recess
1:00 p.m. - Worship and Teaching
3:00 p.m. - Dinner
7:30 p.m. - Evening Service - Rev. V. A. Guidroz, Speaker

FOR INFORMATION AND RESERVATIONS, WRITE TO

REV. M. H. HANSFORD, District Supt.
611 15th Avenue, Laurel, Mississippi

ABOVE: The "cooperative efforts of all three races" to mount this 1949 Tri-Racial Good Will Festival in Carthage is evidence of the all-too-brief period of promise for improved race relations following World War II.

Pentecostalism grew rapidly in Mississippi after World War II through camp meetings like the one advertised here. Drawing on historic camp-meeting traditions, the Pentecostal meetings rivaled early nineteenth-century meetings in their emotional intensity.

The campus of Belhaven College in Jackson. Belhaven, one of several denominational colleges in Mississippi, was first chartered as a privately owned institution. It was donated to the Presbyterian Church in 1910 and serves as the flagship Presbyterian college in the state with an enrollment of over 1,000 students in the 2000–2001 academic year.

From 1942 to 1967, the Temple Beth Isreal congregation worshiped in this building. Mississippi was once home to thriving Jewish communities in towns such as Natchez, Port Gibson, and others where Jewish merchants played an important role in the state's commercial life.

Moss-draped grave site in Biloxi Cemetery on the Mississippi Gulf Coast

The Blessing of the Fleet. This ceremony, performed by the Biloxi Diocese's Bishop, reflects the importance of fishing and fishing boats in the lives of Gulf Coast residents.

These angels appeared in a Jackson Christmas pageant, a common feature of twentieth-century church life.

A black congregation gathers outside a cinder-block church near Philadelphia.

An unidentified preacher near Philadelphia continues the dramatic preaching style handed down from early enslaved preachers in Mississippi.

ruling to desegregate public schools in *Brown v. Board of Education of To-peka, Kansas*. The Citizens' Council, organized by middle-class Mississippians to combat the order and preserve segregation, launched an investigation into the cooperative farms. Over one thousand people attended a mass meeting of the council in Holmes County, where they heard testimony that black and white children swam together on the farms, that the cooperative's physician received communist literature with his shipments of medical supplies from the North, and that biracial business meetings were held. The council approved a resolution condemning the cooperative and recommending that the leaders leave the county. For several months the leaders held out, but in the face of threats and intimidation they eventually abandoned their utopian experiment. But parts of the dream survived: the buildings served as a community center for the former residents who continued to live nearby, and the clinic, credit union, and cooperative store remained open. But for H. L. Mitchell, the founder of the Southern Tenant Farmers' Union, the cooperative farms had a larger significance; he wrote, "The project . . . paved the way for the ultimate abolition of segregation. If it had not been for patterns of interracial activity established by people like us in the 1930s, the civil rights leaders would have found the going even harder in the 1960s, when they too laid their lives on the line."[42] However noble such experiments were, and however successful they might have been for the scores of families involved, the cooperative movement could not pull the sharecroppers out of poverty.

In the late 1930s anthropologist Hortense Powdermaker conducted a cultural study of the small Delta town of Indianola, which she called "Cottonville." The place and its people were almost as exotic to her as the Stone Age people in New Guinea whom she had studied previously. She provided a richly detailed portrait of the black and white communities at the end of the Great Depression, and as an anthropologist she was especially interested in religious life. She found that religion shaped the world-view of both blacks and whites but in very different ways. The town was strictly segregated by race, and most whites were native-born members of the middle class. Among whites, she found that "[f]or the majority of the older and middle-aged, the church is an axis about which much of their life revolves." Whites belonged to either the Baptist, Methodist, Presbyterian, Episcopalian, or Catholic churches, and held a "[f]undamentalist type of belief with its absolute conceptions of right and wrong, heaven and hell, sin and virtue." In such a homogeneous system, "Doubt and skepticism are reduced to a minimum" since "all questions fall back upon the assurance that in the beginning the Lord created heaven and earth . . . including the presence of evil and the relative positions of the white and black races." Only a "small minority take their Christianity so seriously that it tinges their racial attitudes."[43]

For most whites, social life also revolved around the churches. Older and middle-aged whites took part in Sunday worship services and adult Sunday school classes, prayer meetings on Wednesday nights, Ladies' Missionary Society meetings on Tuesdays, choir rehearsals on Fridays, and frequent church socials. Younger whites attended church, though less often than their elders, and their social life revolved around parties, movies, and other secular activities. Drinking, smoking, and extramarital sexual relations were common among them. Greatly influenced by popular culture and outside influences, young whites had "increasing contact with the outside world." Powdermaker also found that young people had a somewhat weaker attachment to the segregationist creed and a more casual view of race relations. Members of the younger generation "neither like nor hate nor fear the Negroes so intensely as do their elders."[44]

Religion also lay at the center of black community life; indeed, Powdermaker wrote, "The Negro church is the one institution where the colored people of the community are in full control." There were six black churches in town: an African Methodist Episcopal church, a Methodist Episcopal church, First and Second Baptist churches, a Christian church, and a Church of God in Christ. Only the Methodist Episcopal church held services every Sunday, though Sunday school classes met each week. Again, much of the community's social life revolved around the churches and their women's missionary society meetings, choir practices, and fundraising "socials." Church members had "little or no feeling of denominational difference," and members frequently attended services and fundraisers in other churches. Only the members of the Church of God in Christ, dismissed as "Holy Rollers" by others, held aloof from a fifth-Sunday interdenominational Sunday school service. Churches drew members from all social classes, except for the Church of God in Christ, whose members came from the lower middle class.[45]

While most churches drew members from all classes, participation in church activities and membership were closely tied to social rank. Most members of the tiny black upper class belonged to a church, and about half of them held important positions as deacons or elders. They frowned on the emotional displays common to members of the middle and lower classes in church services. Members of the upper middle class made up the majority of members and provided most of the leadership. Members of the lower middle class generally belonged to a church, but were less regular in their attendance, held fewer offices, and were less active in women's societies. Lower-class blacks sometimes attended services, especially revivals and social functions, but were less likely to join. As in the white churches, women made up the majority of members, and in the black churches women largely controlled church finances. The preachers themselves usually came from the lower middle class.[46]

While the black churches had much in common with their white counterparts, striking differences appeared in the conduct of services, individual participation in services, and ideology. Services in the black churches usually opened with prayers from members of the congregation, then singing from a choir, followed by the sermon. Both the prayers and sermon were often chanted, as they were in early evangelical services. These emotional sermons frequently produced an equally emotional response in the congregation; indeed, the level of that response was the measure of a successful sermon. Shouting was common, as were more dramatic physical exercises. In one Baptist Church, for example, the preacher's voice "booms and breaks" as he chanted "of sins and the glories of heaven." As his sermon rose to its fever pitch, "A large woman in a front pew begins to shout. She screams, waves her arms, throws herself about. Three women . . . try to hold her down, but she breaks loose and hurls herself onto another bench. Men jump up and hold her. She relaxes suddenly and becomes unconscious." More prayers, a collection, and singing followed until the service ended two hours after it began.[47] Such services were typical of all denominations, and clearly preserved many features common to all evangelicals in the early nineteenth century.

In their sermons, ministers often told their listeners that they might be poor in material things, but they were rich if they had faith in God and were offered a bright prospect of future rewards in heaven. That message has been criticized as upholding the status quo and replacing action with some pie-in-the-sky dreams, but the sermons brought "real solace" to the hardworking women and men in the pews. In more significant ways, the black ministers' message departed from that of their white counterparts, especially in maintaining that "[b]enevolent mercy rather than stern justice is the chief attribute of the Negro's God." White ministers were more likely to preach about a vengeful God and the terrible punishments that awaited sinners, while black ministers portrayed "with equal vividness the joys that await the godly. . . . The accent has shifted from hell to heaven, from retribution to forgiveness, from fear to hope."[48]

The most consistent message in black churches was "the great emphasis placed upon the Christian virtue of brotherly love." Over and over again in sermons and Sunday school lessons, preachers and teachers urged black worshipers to love their neighbors of both races and "vanquish bitterness within their hearts." In one Sunday school class, for example, "The teacher talks about the hatred to the colored people for the unjust Whites. A tale is told of a man who worked all season for a white planter and then was cheated out of half his earnings. 'Is it possible for us not to hate him?' asks the teacher. A young woman answers: 'Yes, but it is possible, but hard.' There is a sympathetic laugh from all."[49]

The teacher then expressed pity for whites, whose sins would surely be punished, and warned that "[i]f we hate them . . . we poison ourselves." She told her students of Mahatma Gandhi, his heroic struggle in India, and "the great power he has won through sincerity and love." A lengthy class discussion followed. The teacher concluded, " 'The race situation is getting better in Mississippi. . . . Why? Because the younger generation of white men and women are coming to see that the old ways of treating the Negro are not Christ's way.' . . . Whites will become more Christlike, she assures her class, and concludes by repeating again that they must drive out hatred for the Whites and substitute love."[50]

In a similar vein, Chalmers Archer, Jr., remembered attending a Baptist church near the Delta town of Tchula in the same period. He had vivid recollections of emotional services and delicious food. He recalled church suppers as "happy and fun-filled affairs," but he also acknowledged that "there was serious talk afterward. There was talk about the injustices all over."[51] Two decades before Martin Luther King, Jr., set foot in Montgomery, a generation before he brought his message to Mississippi, blacks were already being schooled in the message of nonviolence and racial justice. In this context, the enthusiastic response to his message on the part of local people across the state seems far more understandable; those seeds had already been sown.

As this example suggests, blacks' attitudes toward whites varied considerably, especially according to age. Partly as a result of lessons like the one quoted above, the attitudes young people had were different from those of older people, and attitudes were continuing to change rapidly. In the 1930s, the members of the oldest generation in the community had been born either before, during, or immediately after the Civil War. By and large, members of this generation were less educated than their juniors and more likely to acknowledge white supremacy.

Members of the next generation, middle-aged blacks, were less dependent on whites, had less contact with them, and were more educated. Thanks to newspapers, movies, and radios, they were far more aware of the broader world. "They have heard about the ideal of democracy which says that all men are equal; they have been introduced to the idea of the Melting Pot; they have become identified with American institutions, and celebrate the Fourth of July as their own holiday." They had seen blacks succeed in businesses and professions once deemed the province of whites only. Such sentiments merged with religious belief to give these blacks a view far different from that of the previous generation. As one forty-year-old black woman asked, "Didn't the Lord make us all? The Whites have the power and all the advantages now, but they ain't no different from the colored folks. They're all alike." Over and over again, "The same question is repeated . . . in tones ranging from despair to fury: 'Didn't the Lord make us all? Then how can we be so different.' "[52]

Finally, among the younger generation, the children of middle-aged blacks, resentment against segregation and discrimination was "keen and outspoken." They shared with their parents a belief in equality, but "[t]hey differ in not possessing or wanting to possess the tact and diplomacy of their elders." For them, such maneuvers amounted to an admission of white superiority and wounded their self-esteem. They preferred to avoid contact with whites whenever possible. Though they were still in a minority, "It is their attitude that is spreading and the more passive one that is on the wane, as . . . ideas of what is due the individual citizen penetrate ever more deeply into the Negro group."[53]

The keen-eyed anthropologist recognized that the younger whites had less faith in religion, less confidence in the system of segregation and discrimination, less allegiance to the values of their elders, and less tendency to rely on their parents' wisdom than previous generations. Younger blacks, too, felt less confidence in the wisdom of the previous generation, rejecting the role their parents had played toward whites, but, unlike the whites, "beneath his present confusion and discouragement he does have a new belief in his race, his own potentialities, the possibility of eventual amelioration, for which few young Whites in the community have an equivalent. Above all, he has, in the sense of a cause which must be served, a potential integrating force, capable of being mobilized by some new formulation of values and aims and some new leadership in which he could have confidence."[54] Though Powdermaker could not foresee the future course of their cause and the powerful force that would motivate them, she recognized far more clearly than Mississippi whites that blacks would not accept their condition for much longer.

Many Mississippians, especially religious women, also recognized that the state had to improve race relations. Growing out of the Social Gospel movement, the largely middle-class reform movement that arose in the late nineteenth century and emphasized the redemption of the social order rather than the salvation of individual souls, the current movement was made up of churchwomen; they took the lead in all areas of reform, including race relations. One such woman was Mary Wharton, whose example illustrates how women came to advocate improved race relations. For over thirty years, Mary Wharton labored in the all-white First Presbyterian Church of Port Gibson. She served as choir director, organist, pianist, and Sunday school and Bible class teacher and was praised as "a giant in the classroom."[55] At the time of her death in 1954, she had spent thirteen years teaching an adult Bible class, and her many volumes of carefully prepared lessons reveal the effort she put into her work. She also held prominent positions in statewide women's groups; for example, she served as chair of home missions and as chair of stewardship in the Mississippi Presbytery. She was born in 1889 to deeply religious parents; her father served as organist and elder in the First Presbyterian Church and her mother was noted for her piety. Following in her father's footsteps, she began the study of music at the age of four, and, by the time she was eight years old, she was playing the organ for Sunday school. A talented musician, she studied at the Chicago Musical College, played with the Chicago Symphony, and taught music at Queen's College in North Carolina and at Belhaven College in Jackson, Mississippi. Miss Wharton, who never married, dedicated her life to her teaching, her church, and her community.

Mary Wharton's family background, her education, and her profession placed her in the ranks of the state's elite. Like many religious women of her class, she promoted the concerns of the Social Gospel movement, particularly in the areas of prohibition, child labor, education, and race relations.[56] Wharton's concerns included broader questions of social and racial justice. In one lesson she related the story of Thomas Carlyle, who had surveyed the London slums and said bitterly, "God does nothing." Miss Wharton insisted that God calls Christians to do his work, and she lamented that, despite the fact that there were 680 million Christians in the world, "We have failed to *find & give* the solution to the problem of international relations or to deal . . . with the *great social evils*. . . ."[57] As she surveyed the nation's "deadly enemies" for her class she identified broken homes, low moral standards, intemperance, "cruel injustice," and racial intolerance as America's chief social ills.[58]

A survey of the lessons she taught over her thirty-year tenure reveals that racial justice was a consistent theme for her. In one characteristic lesson she told her students that "[r]acial intolerance is ruled out as far as [the] teachings of Christ are concerned. . . . A man truly converted to Christ is not an improved man but a transformed man. . . . Every nation is bettered for having in its blood stream the vigor of dif[ferent] races. . . . We the people are all God's children and we need each other."[59]

In a lesson entitled "The Christian and the Race Problem" she plainly informed her class that "[w]e have a race problem because one race feels superior to another." In her view, "There is no doubt that [the] solution of [the] race problem rests with *Christians* because we have [the] *right spirit* for *meeting* the *issue*. . . . We have to free ourselves from . . . prejudice . . . [and] treat [the] race problem as [a] *human problem*. . . . We value our liberty [and] opportunity & must make them for others." She condemned

an education system that spent "12.00 per year per child" for the education of black children and "100.00 for white." She warned her listeners
that "[t]he situation *is a grave one*. . . . Christ must have a *breaking heart* as
he views [the] hatred and ill will some of us have towards various races."[60]

The international crises of the 1930s and 1940s caused Miss Wharton
great distress, and she equated imperialism and racism abroad with the
situation in her native state. She said, "It is a strange thing that for the
simple reason that one is born a Jew, another a German, one an Italian,
another Ethiopian, one is white, another black, people should treat other
people as inferior . . . because of the inferiority that exist [*sic*] only in an
inferior mind."[61] Her views on racial justice, grounded simply but firmly
in the most basic tenets of her faith, were hardly exceptional for religious
white women of her status. Like many "conservative liberals" in the
South, Wharton made general pleas for racial justice and equality that
were restrained and tempered; there is no evidence, for example, that she
criticized segregation.[62]

To some extent, change was already in the air in the 1930s as New
Deal programs upset the one-crop agricultural system and government
relief lessened dependence on white landowners. Of course, blacks suffered serious discrimination in the New Deal programs, but they benefited,
too, as federal dollars boosted the state's economy and as farm income rose
by 134 percent during the 1930s.[63] Greater changes were on the horizon,
however, as World War II brought a revolution to the state. The war gave
a new impetus to blacks' demands for equal justice and further confirmed
the beliefs held so firmly by the younger generation.

The changes wrought by New Deal programs and World War II
transformed Mississippi. New Deal agricultural policies designed to re-
duce acreage also reduced the number of tenants and sharecroppers. New
Deal relief programs, though deeply flawed in their implementation,
nonetheless helped free many blacks from the grip of landlords and merchants. With the outbreak of war, thousands of young men left the fields
for military service, and thousands of other men and women left rural
areas for jobs in towns. Coastal shipbuilders and other military contractors
scattered across the state created a high demand for labor, and, by 1941,
ten thousand people worked in defense plants. In the Delta, for example,
the rural farm population declined by 19 percent during the 1940s, and

the overall black population fell by 10 percent. Across the state the number of black croppers fell by twenty thousand during the war, and the number of white croppers declined by eighty-five hundred. On the one hand, New Deal agricultural policies and high wartime prices benefited landowners and enabled them to further mechanize their enterprises, but the decline of the sharecropping system had larger "racial and political as well as economic implications."[64]

In 1941 Richard Wright sensed the changes that were in the air: "The seasons of the plantation no longer dictate the lives of many of us: hundreds of thousands of us are moving into the sphere of conscious history. We are with the new tide. We stand at the crossroads. We watch each new procession. The hot wires carrying urgent appeals. Print compels us. Voices are speaking. Men are moving! And we shall be with them."[65]

World War II was the great epic struggle of the twentieth century; seldom have the forces of good and evil been thrown in such high relief, and the Allies were quick to wrap themselves in the mantle of righteousness. But the horrors of Adolf Hitler's racial policies raised serious questions about the system of segregation and discrimination that kept millions of American blacks in subjection. That contradiction was not lost on black Mississippians. Perhaps black veterans were the one group most aware of the gulf separating America's high-minded wartime rhetoric and its shameful realities. Jodie Saffold, a black farmer in Holmes County, recalled that "[a]fter World War II, there was lots of people that been to war, blacks that had been to war and had been segregated. But they saw they could die for their country and everything else, and they come back to Mississippi. . . . They were a lot less willing to be treated like second-class citizens, like a DOG." Robert Cooper Howard, a veteran from Holmes County, reported that the "only thang I was wantin' was *equal justice*, just like everybody else. An' why is it that I go to the army, served in Uncle Sam's army three years and four months, then come back and be treated as if I hadn't went? And I figure that if I can go int' Uncle Sam's army to try an' fight for America, I can come back and be counted as an American. Not as somebody that's throwed aside."[66]

As white ministers motivated Mississippians to continue the struggle against the Axis powers, they also drew upon a vision of justice, brotherhood, and democracy that ran counter to the Jim Crow system. The Methodist bishop, Marvin A. Franklin, for example, gave a sermon entitled "Hitler's Paganism and the Principles of the Kingdom of Christ." The German dictator based his Third Reich on four ideas: "(a). The Superman; (b). The Super-Race; (3). the Super State; and (4). The Super Morality and Religion." Franklin counterpoised these to the "four basic truths as fundamental" to Christ's Kingdom: "(1.) God is our Father—Not of the favored few, but of all men, the last and the least as well; (2.) All men are brothers—with a common Father it follows that all men are truly brothers; (3.) Each individual soul is priceless; his rights, privileges, responsibilities must not be denied; (4.) The only redemptive, preserving, uniting, and saving force in the world is love." The bishop saw the United Nations as the best hope for "a world in which men can stand straight and have the feel of freedom."[67]

Bishop Franklin called for a new postwar world founded on righteousness and "[j]ustice for all people," a world where eight million sharecroppers would earn more than $250 per year, where ten million people would not live in illiteracy, and where millions would not live in poverty or suffer unemployment. He observed ruefully that the South headed the list on most of these social ills and warned that a society based on the brotherhood of man would not allow one group to degrade or exploit another. In another wartime sermon he said, "Special privileges for the few, enslavement for the multitude is not fair or right. . . . No race, or class, or people must be exploited."[68]

Bishop Franklin did not limit his call for justice to the relative security of the pulpit or the religious press. In a 1949 article in the *Jackson Daily News* entitled "Negro Race Deserves Fair Fighting Chance," he called for better education and better housing for blacks, and, on a more controversial note, he wrote, "The Negro should be given an increasing opportunity to make his contribution as a citizen of the community in which he lives." He welcomed the "rising tide of better understanding" between the races and proclaimed that "[b]igotry has waned, [and] prejudice has decreased. . . ." He praised the long Methodist tradition in the quest for better race relations, particularly the efforts of Bishop Charles B. Galloway and of churchwomen who "have been in the forefront."[69]

Franklin's sentiments were echoed by a prominent group of black and white Mississippians who in 1948 called on "Christian people . . . to develop a positive, constructive and aggressive program throughout our state for a co-operative and harmonious effort in behalf of negro education and culture, and in making provision for the negro to participate normally in the practice of his citizenship. . . ." Headed by the Reverend H. Brent Schaeffer, a white Lutheran minister in Jackson and chairman of the state branch of the Southern Regional Council, an Atlanta-based organization dedicated to bettering race relations, the group included such prominent whites as the Catholic bishop, Joseph B. Brunini, newspaper editor Hodding Carter, and a number of black and white ministers from all major denominations. These men encouraged the appointment of two state commissions, each with biracial membership: one to make recommendations to improve black education and another "to formulate a program of relationships in the civic body. . . ."[70]

It might appear that black and white southerners came through the trials and tribulations of the Great Depression and World War II with a common vision of what the postwar South should be like—a vision based on brotherhood, racial equality, and economic justice—but postwar events would prove to be more conflicted. The stance of these religious and civic leaders is even more significant when placed in a larger context. President Harry Truman's support of black civil rights outraged many southern Democrats, including Mississippi's governor, Fielding Wright, who helped create the Dixiecrat movement. In 1948 Wright and five thousand state Democrats met in Jackson and attacked Truman's civil rights agenda. A short time later he organized a meeting representing nine southern state Democratic parties who threatened to leave the party unless the national convention adopted a firm states' rights plank. When the national convention enacted a civil rights plank instead, the entire Mississippi delegation bolted the convention. The Dixiecrats nominated South Carolinian Strom Thurmond as their presidential candidate and Fielding Wright as vice president, a ticket that won 90 percent of the Democratic vote in the state in the 1948 election.

The war had barely ended when trouble appeared on the religious horizon. In 1946 Methodist congregations in the state began to complain that church literature was too liberal. The board of stewards of the Millsaps Memorial Methodist Church in Jackson called on the church to investigate articles in church publications that advocated "social equality among races" and others that were "communistic in their teachings." The men's Bible class at Galloway Methodist Church, with a membership of over 150, passed a similar resolution. John W. Satterfield, class teacher, said, "We feel that these types of articles are foreign to what church literature should contain." Without a single dissenting vote, the First Methodist Church of Canton resolved that church literature "is Communistic in trend and in direct contradiction to the traditions and principles held by the vast majority of Southern Methodists." Ministers tried to play down the concerns over literature; the Reverend J. W. Leggett of the Capitol Street Methodist Church said, "The resolutions and the newspapers are making a mountain out of a molehill." In fact, however, the debate over literature was a harbinger of things to come. Satterfield, for example, was an extremely prominent man in the capital city—a past president of the American Bar Association who would become a major player in the Citizens' Council and a close advisor to segregationist governor Ross Barnett.[71]

It was clear that the Great Depression and World War II had ushered in changes beyond anything southerners could have imagined. During these years, the sharecropping system that provided the backbone of the state's economy was undermined by federal agricultural and relief programs and by wartime prosperity that created employment opportunities off the farms. World War II also called into question the doctrine of white supremacy, and the less economically dependent blacks were on whites the more able they were to challenge the system. Black churches, which had grown steadily since World War I, gave their members important experience in community organization and a theology that directly challenged white supremacy. In less obvious ways the period also saw the emergence of dynamic new forces in southern religious life. Of central importance in this regard is the birth of the fundamentalist-Pentecostal movement that has been characterized as the "Third Force in Christendom." Few people could have predicted from these churches' humble beginnings among lower-class blacks and whites that they would grow into powerful social movements in the postwar period, but such has been the history of Christianity from the earliest times.

*Oh, it is good for children of one family to dwell together in unity!
And why should it not be so? Are we not children of the same father.
. . . Must our sojourn in this vale of tears be embittered by strife
and bad feeling?*

—BISHOP JOHN J. M. CHANCHE[1]

Jews are highly assimilated in Mississippi. . . . We blended."

—HILARY CHIZ, JACKSON, MISSISSIPPI

*[P]eople in Mississippi don't worry about what religion you are any-
more—as long as you are religious.*

—BILL ALLAIN, FORMER GOVERNOR
OF MISSISSIPPI[2]

9 Outsider Religious Groups in Mississippi

Given the dominance of evangelical Protestants among religious folk in Mississippi, which is pronounced enough to give the appearance of religious homogeneity, it is easy to overlook smaller religious groups in the state. But there has been some degree of religious diversity in Mississippi, representing important traditions that should not be ignored in any comprehensive study of the state's religious life. Historian David Edwin Harrell, Jr., suggested that religious groups outside the southern mainstream are significant because, given their distinctive theological foundations, they represent important currents in the region's intellectual life. In addition, he pointed out, these diverse religious movements created culturally distinct southerners. The degree to which the members of such groups were in fact culturally distinct from their neighbors raises challenging questions about the nature of these movements and their role in Mississippi society, for, while Harrell is correct in observing that members of religious denominations outside the Protestant mainstream differ from other religious adherents on major issues including marriage, children, and alcohol consumption, for example, it is also true that members of these "outsider" groups actually used that position to invent their own "southernness."[3]

Of the many outsider groups in the state, the Roman Catholic Church was by far the largest, oldest, and best established. Under both French and Spanish rule, the Catholic Church was the established church in the colony, but with the withdrawal of the Spanish in 1798 the position of the church changed radically. In January 1798 Bishop Penalver ordered Father Francis Lennan to evacuate from the Natchez District and to take with him all church furnishings and sacred vessels. The bishop went so far as to suggest that the church building be removed, but Father Lennan insisted that it should be left to the remaining Catholics in the town. When Spanish officials and residents departed, only a tiny remnant remained to carry on the faith. By the end of the eighteenth century Governor Winthrop Sargent could find only a dozen Catholic families in Natchez. The handful of Catholics in the Natchez District included a few men of wealth and position, such as planter and former Spanish official Stephen Minor, Colonel Daniel Clark, Captain William Vousdan, Brian Bruin, and others. These men and their compatriots petitioned Bishop Carroll to send a priest to the neglected region, but, given the shortage of priests available to him, Carroll had difficulty finding any long-term solution. Still, the congregation struggled to survive on the irregular visits of priests from other areas; they regained possession of the Natchez church that had been taken by the United States government as part of the lands owned by the Spanish government, and in 1807 they were incorporated by the state. They leased the church building to the city for the price of one peppercorn annually, and reserved the right to hold occasional services there, but by 1815 visiting Presbyterian missionaries to Natchez found only "an old Roman Chapel, almost in ruins."[4]

Just when it seemed certain that the Catholic Church had completely collapsed, Don Manuel Garcia de Texada, a wealthy and long-time member, left the sum of fifteen hundred dollars to the congregation on the condition that they formally organize within two years. In 1818 the church was reincorporated, and in 1819 the trustees found a pastor. For the next decade the congregation struggled as priests came and went until December 28, 1832, when tragedy struck and fire destroyed the old Spanish chapel. Again the church languished for years without a permanent pastor, but in July 1837 Pope Gregory XVI established a new diocese of Natchez, and two years later Bishop John J. M. Chanche arrived to take up his duties. The bishop found about six hundred Catholics in the Natchez area, but not a single church in the entire state. Only two priests currently resided in the diocese, one in Natchez and one in Vicksburg. The new bishop set out immediately to construct an impressive cathedral which he expected to "give the needed stimulus to the whole mission" and "attract the Protestants to our ceremonies."[5] In a city so caught up in conspicuous displays of wealth and opulence, the bishop may well have felt compelled to give his church a place of high distinction, but when the first ceremony was held in the new building on Christmas Day in 1843 it was little more than a shell, and the congregation struggled for decades, often at the threat of sale by auction, to pay for the structure. When Bishop James O. van de Velde arrived on the scene in 1853 he described the building as "a spacious barn—no plaster, no window panes, no pews."[6]

As Velde reviewed his diocese, he estimated that ten thousand Catholics resided in the state, but ministering to that number was difficult, since they were widely scattered across the state's farms and plantations and since only thirteen priests labored in the field. Few places were large enough to support a resident priest, and a scant eleven churches had been built across the state. In addition, the Natchez church supported an orphanage for girls with seventy residents and a girl's school with forty students, both under the direction of the Daughters of St. Vincent of Paul. Another boarding school for young ladies operated in Sulphur Springs under the care of the Sisters of St. Joseph had nearly fifty students, and the same house operated a girl's day school in Bay St. Louis with a similar enrollment.

Velde explained to the foreign missionary society that they could not appreciate the conditions he labored under without fully understanding the implications of working in a state with a black majority; indeed, he informed the society that "[t]hese poor Negroes form in some respects my chief anxiety."[7] Bishop Chanche had made the conversion of blacks a high priority. When he first arrived in Natchez, he had found only two black Catholics in the town, and mourned that the blacks had "thus far . . . been entirely abandoned." In the early 1840s he instituted religious classes for blacks with about two hundred in attendance. The bishop sought to interest a religious order in working among slaves on the plantations, but he found no takers; he lamented, "The mission of the Negroes is still very important and weighs heavily on my heart."[8] For Bishop van de Velde, too, blacks represented a vast field of labor, but one with great obstacles; he wrote, "The Negroes must be attended in great measure on the plantation, because . . . in our case there are so few churches, and, even where there is a church, the Negroes of four or five plantations would fill it up and leave no room for the whites. . . . The priests, then, must go to the plantations. . . ."[9]

Of course, blacks had probably never been entirely absent from the Catholic Church in Natchez or on the Gulf Coast. The history of the Pomet and Girodeau families of Natchez strongly suggests that blacks were active church members. Leonard Pomet, a free man of color, served as a parish trustee in the late eighteenth or early nineteenth century. His daughter, Felicite Pomet Girodeau, was a mainstay of the Natchez church. Her husband, Gabriel Girodeau, worked as a jeweler and also served as a trustee, as did his brother, Antonio Girodeau. Soon widowed, Felicite Girodeau devoted herself to her church; her home often housed visiting clergy, and her parlor served as the chapel when Natchez was without a church building. She sponsored thirty-two baptisms between 1836 and 1860 for individuals of various racial and ethnic backgrounds, and witnessed many marriages. When she died in 1862, "the whole congregation and many citizens" attended her funeral.[10]

The role of the Pomet and Girodeau families hints at the complexities that confronted the Catholic Church as racial, caste, and ethnic divisions created layers of difficulty, and suggests that in early Natchez, as in New Orleans, free people of color in general and colored Creoles in particular occupied a middle ground between whites and slaves inside the church. Colored Creoles generally adopted the social values of the whites, as did Madame Girodeau, herself the owner of several slaves. Unlike New Orleans, however, Natchez did not have a colored Creole community large enough support the rich cultural and associative life that existed among them in the Crescent City, nor was there a substantial white Creole community with which colored Creoles could ally. As the Natchez church shifted from one dominated by whites of French and Spanish descent to one dominated by native-born whites, the church increasingly reflected the racial and social values of its membership. If Catholics in general can be characterized as outsiders in southern and American society, this status is even more true of black Catholics in the South. Historian Randall M. Miller succinctly summed up their situation: "Negro Catholics had to work out their religious identities in a social environment that was often hostile to them, in a cultural environment that was not wholly responsible to or shared by them, and in an institutional church environment that could never be controlled by them."[11]

The degree to which the Catholic Church endorsed the social, racial, and political beliefs of the dominant culture can be seen in Bishop William Henry Elder's support of the Confederate cause. The bishop, a Maryland native, was not an open advocate of secession, but, once the state took that step, he wrote, "Our Confederacy is formed. Let us do all we can for its preservation and prosperity. We had a grand celebration on Washington's birthday. . . . It was to celebrate the formation of our Confederacy, and provisional Govt., in which I heartily rejoice. . . ."[12] That rejoicing was soon replaced by a more somber mood as the realities of a long and bloody war cast a pall over the state. The cathedral opened every day from 4:00 p.m. to sunset for prayer as casualties mounted within the congregation. The bishop visited hospitals and battlefields, ministered to the sick and the dying, and took the tragic news of death to family members. Catholic schools closed when the sisters became nurses in hospitals and camps. In 1862 Natchez fell to the Union Navy, and by the following year thousands of former slaves crowded the contraband camps in the occupied town, food was scarce, and inflation had devastated the economy. The bishop and his priests regularly visited the overcrowded, disease-ridden camps, attended the sick, and offered instruction in the faith; his efforts resulted in numerous conversions and baptisms, with the bishop personally baptizing over five hundred black men, women, and children.

Bishop Elder became a hero of the Confederate cause in 1864 when Union general James M. Tuttle ordered that prayers be said in all churches for the president of the United States and for the Union army. Elder refused to obey the order and appealed to Secretary of War Edwin M. Stanton and to President Abraham Lincoln to reverse the order. Despite Lincoln's instructions to the contrary, the Union officials ordered Elder to comply, and, when he refused, the officials ordered that he be expelled from the Union lines, that the cathedral be closed, and that the bishop be arrested. For seventeen days he was held under house arrest in Vidalia, Louisiana, across the river from Natchez. Though he suffered no harm, the bishop was compared to St. Peter in chains, a suffering martyr to the cause, "the fearless soldier of the South. . . ."[13]

Still centered in Natchez, the church suffered along with the town in the period following the Civil War, when the once-wealthy and opulent city lost 25 percent of its population and its plantation economy was in shambles. Still considered a missionary field, the church depended heavily on funds from Catholic missionary societies, especially the Propagation de la Foi Society headquartered in Lyon, France. The St. Mary's orphanage for boys and girls was filled to overflowing, and only rations from the federal government saved the children from distress. Sister Mary Thomas described the situation there in a plea to Major General O. O. Howard, director of the Freedman's Bureau, in an 1868 letter: "Our household contains from 120 to 126 . . . girls alone without the boys, who are over sixty more. . . . In other times when affairs and prospects were more flourishing our asylums were freely supplied with liberality by generous benefactors. All are changed now. Some have died. Others who were rich then have become poor." In the face of such difficulties the ladies of Natchez came to the support of the orphanage by sponsoring an annual fair, which brought in several thousand dollars annually.[14]

Education was another important part of the Catholic Church's program in Natchez. Attempts to establish Catholic schools in the antebellum period foundered, but in 1862 Bishop William Henry Elder authorized the purchase of a lot across from the cathedral as the site for a school for boys which opened under the charge of the Christian Brothers in 1865. In 1867 the Sisters of Charity opened St. Joseph's School for Girls, but at a cost of five dollars per month, the school was too expensive for many church members, and a free school continued to operate in St. Mary's Orphan Asylum. St. Joseph's offered training in "[a]ll English branches, including Botany, Chemistry, Book-Keeping, Algebra and all kinds of Plain and Fancy Needle Work. . . . French and Music form extra charges"; it was a curriculum typical of southern schools for girls.[15]

Education was a vital part of the Catholic Church's missionary work among African Americans. In 1866 the church opened a school for African

American children in the basement of the cathedral, and the following
year established the Society of the Holy Family of Colored Persons, a
benevolent society to assist the poor. In 1867 Bishop Elder observed that
the African American population was "well disposed to listen and to believe. But they are easily turned away." The church organized separate
catechism classes and occasional separate worship services for blacks. Of
all the benefits the Catholic Church could offer blacks, education was the
most attractive to them; the bishop noted that they "are anxious to have
their children acquire learning." In keeping with the rising tide of segregation, the bishop wrote that such schools should be separated by race. For
many years the school struggled along with a handful of students, but in
1886 the Sisters of Charity assumed responsibility for the newly named
St. Francis School, and the number of students rose dramatically from
about twenty to sixty-five students.[16]

The St. Francis School was the precursor of a separate parish for African American Catholics in Natchez. Before the Third Plenary Council,
which assembled in Baltimore in 1885, no separate parishes existed for
black and white Catholics, but this council approved separate parishes as
a means of making black converts. Their decision also recognized the
growing separation between the races during the Jim Crow era and made
it possible for southern Catholics, in particular, to draw the color line. In
1888 the Natchez *Democrat* observed that "[i]t can scarcely be thought
that Southern people can be brought to agree to this Northern view of
social equality in church polity," a view that Natchez Catholics obviously
shared. Bishop Thomas Heslin, who occupied his post in Natchez in 1889,
took an immediate interest in the school and in African American Catholics. Perhaps the large number of black Catholics in New Orleans, where
Heslin had lived for many years before moving to Natchez, made the new
bishop more aware of the possibilities for expansion among them. Heslin
purchased a lot, built a schoolhouse, and remodeled an existing structure
to serve as a convent. In addition, he called Father Anthony N. Peters
to take charge of the new school and to work exclusively among African
Americans. Peters's devotion to his cause was further evidenced by his
donation of a thousand dollars toward the work among blacks. Heslin
stated that he preferred to keep the parish united and to add a gallery to
the cathedral for extra sitting room (whether or not he envisioned the

gallery as seating for blacks is unclear), but he had been convinced that the best hope of making converts among blacks was to give them their own church. He believed that blacks viewed the cathedral as "a church for Whites" and that they would prefer "a church that they could call exclusively their own." The bishop probably saw similar examples all around him as blacks left biracial Protestant churches in Natchez and created their own institutions.[17]

The school prospered, and African Americans showed much interest in the young church, but it was inconveniently located away from the center of town. In order to raise funds for the purchase of a lot and the construction of a brick church and school, Father Peters embarked on an ambitious fund-raising tour of northern cities in 1892. After nearly a year spent in making appeals from northern pulpits, Peters returned with sufficient funds to erect a new school and church. In 1893 black Catholics voted on whether or not to leave the cathedral or form a separate parish. Of the twenty people who attended the meeting, eleven favored separation and eight opposed it. The vote broke largely along generational lines; older members who had a long association with the cathedral opposed the move, while younger people who had attended the school and its church favored the break. The completion of the handsome new Church of the Holy Family with the funds raised by Father Peters swayed many of those who had formerly opposed the division, and the organization of a "good choir" at Holy Family drew still others. In the end, the new parish drew a "large and flourishing congregation."[18]

Heslin encouraged missionary work among African Americans across the state in racially segregated churches and schools. The Catholic Church enjoyed its greatest success among African Americans along the Gulf Coast, where the church had a long history. When Father Joseph Wise took up his duties in Pascagoula in 1873, he wrote, "[T]he Negro population seems to be generally Catholic, and I intend to give a good deal of my time to them."[19] When Bishop Heslin arrived in the state in 1889, there was not a single separate black church, but by the time of his death in 1911 churches had been established in Natchez, Pascagoula, Pass Christian, Vicksburg, Jackson, and Meridian, each with a church school. Bishop Heslin's successor, Bishop John Edward Gunn, showed a similar interest in the welfare of black Catholics, and with his encouragement additional missions were established at Greenville, Biloxi, Sulphur Springs, and DeLisle.

The Catholic Church's growing commitment to missionary work among African Americans led to the establishment of St. Augustine's Seminary for the training of future African American priests. The Reverend Aloysius Heick, superior of the Southern Missions of the Society of the Divine Word, first proposed a seminary for African Americans to Bishop Gunn in 1920. The bishop, long committed to work among blacks, responded enthusiastically, "I approve of the idea of a religious community of Colored priests. . . . Such a community would . . . be a blessing for the entire work. I would give them missions and I would give them faculties and a welcome to the work among their own people."[20] The preparatory college opened at Greenville in 1920 but in 1923 transferred to Bay St. Louis on the Gulf Coast, where the black Catholic community was strongest. Until 1927 the school offered a six-year preparatory program consisting of four years of secondary schooling and two years of college-level work. For those continuing after that, the school offered a three-year course of philosophy and a four-year program in theology. By 1936–37 the school had enrolled forty-eight students; between 1920 and 1937 a total of two hundred fifteen students studied at St. Augustine's, and forty-one graduated. While the establishment of St. Augustine's marked an improvement over the racial exclusion that had once barred African Americans from the priesthood, it also grew out of the system of segregation that kept African Americans in an inherently inferior position. In 1923 Pope Pius XI gave his nod of approval to the transfer of St. Augustine's to Bay St. Louis and to the training of a segregated clergy; he wrote, "Does it not indeed follow, from the very nature of the Church as a Divine Institution, that every tribe or people should have priests who are one with it in race and character, in habit of thought and temperament? . . . [I]t is indispensable that priests of the same race shall make it their lives' task to lead these people to the Christian Faith and to a higher cultural level."[21]

The Catholic Church also took an active interest in the plight of the Choctaw Indians who lived in Neshoba County. A remnant of a once proud, prosperous people, the Choctaws eked out a meager existence by hunting and fishing or farming small patches of land, almost all of which was owned by whites. When Bishop Francis Janssens traveled through the county on a missionary tour in 1883, he was struck by their plight and determined to send a missionary among them. On a trip to his native Holland, Bishop Janssens visited with the Reverend B. J. Bekkers, who pastored to a fashionable church there. Once acquainted with the conditions in Neshoba County, Bekkers volunteered to devote his life to that work. Bekkers arrived in Neshoba County in 1883; his initial labors were met with skepticism and indifference by the Choctaws, but Bekkers decided to buy a tract of land using funds donated in Holland and divide the land among Choctaws. The availability of land soon attracted the chief and other important men of the tribe, who moved to the new settlement with their families. Bekkers opened a school in 1884, staffed by the Sisters of Mercy after 1885. The mission's success surprised even Bishop Janssens, who later visited the mission and wrote, "The Indian mission of Holy Rosary is succeeding beyond expectations. Nearly 200 Indians were in church during my visit."[22] By 1900 the mission had a membership of 690 Native Americans and 108 whites, with three Carmelite fathers and three lay brothers working among them.

In 1903 the United States government encouraged the Native Americans to move to Oklahoma, and the Carmelite fathers accompanied those who chose to leave the state for the West. The remaining Choctaws, scattered throughout surrounding counties, were encouraged to move to the mission lands, where a school reopened with the help of sisters from various religious orders. The missionary work has continued there to the present day.

While native-born whites predominated in most congregations across the state, the church also served to integrate immigrants into Mississippi society. Although the population of the state was overwhelmingly native-born, pockets of Catholic immigrants could be found scattered around. When seafood packing houses opened in Biloxi in the 1880s, they attracted many European immigrants, including a community of about a hundred Austrian families from the Dalmatian coast, and later the companies recruited Acadian workers from Louisiana. Together these settlers formed a strong nucleus for a Catholic church in Biloxi, where "Poles, Bohemians, French, Austrians and Americans of the old stock had to be drawn together to work in harmony. . . ."[23] A Men's Aid Society helped bring representatives of these various ethnic groups together, and a festive blessing of the fishing fleet of about four hundred boats—their owners' pride and joy—served as another unifying ritual.

Similarly, large numbers of Italian farmers moved into parts of the Mississippi Delta in the early 1900s, as more and more African Americans joined the Great Migration to northern industrial cities. The Italians were regarded as ideal tenants and capable farmers, and their numbers grew. Prominent planter LeRoy Percy encouraged Italian immigration and initially regarded Italians as "industrious, peaceable . . . healthy, hearty and virtuous," but he and other planters grew disillusioned as the Italians became more assertive and protested harsh working conditions and dishonest labor practices. The church was the bedrock of the immigrant community and the center of their protests; Percy fumed that "[w]ithout the Priest, they are without a leader."[24] Some planters attempted to place the Italians in the same racial category as blacks, contrasted "Italians" and "whites," and in one case barred Italian children from a white school, but the segregated Catholic Church clearly placed the Italians among whites, not blacks, thereby giving additional support to the immigrants in their contest with the white planters and making them less vulnerable than blacks to discriminatory practices. Even though planters grew disillusioned with Italian laborers, the immigrants carved out a home for themselves. By the 1930s, for instance, the Cleveland parish, in the heart of the Delta, had a Catholic population of over a thousand people, 80 percent of Italian descent.

Another community of European Catholic farmers was founded at Seneca, located midway between Meridian and New Orleans, when in 1910 the Schwierjohn brothers purchased eight thousand acres of land from the Hinton Brothers Lumber Company and divided it into forty-acre plots which were sold to fourteen German Catholic families from Illinois. The immigrants agreed to pay two dollars extra for every acre they purchased as a contribution to a church building fund. By 1913 a church was finished and a priest appointed to the flock.

The Natchez congregation also had large numbers of foreign immigrants from Ireland, Holland, Belgium, Germany, France, Austria, and Canada, who lent a cosmopolitan air to the congregation. The church was well integrated into the Natchez community, and Protestants frequently attended worship services; in addition, about 40 percent of marriages at

St. Mary's in the 1880s included a non-Catholic partner. Special church functions drew large numbers of non-Catholic observers. One such event was the feast of Corpus Christi, which the congregation adopted as a special obligation of thanksgiving during the Civil War, and an annual religious ceremony at the city cemetery when non-Catholics joined the faithful in decorating family graves. St. Mary's joined other churches in keeping the Confederate memory alive; Catholics celebrated Confederate Memorial Day with a special mass, and in 1888 the Confederate Memorial Association began work on a monument located on a hill directly behind the cathedral. When the monument was unveiled in 1890 Bishop Thomas Helsin was chosen to bless the imposing granite and marble structure. Natchez further celebrated its antebellum past with a pilgrimage tour of its majestic mansions beginning in 1931. Organized by a group of socially prominent women, the successful event won praise from Bishop Richard O. Gerow, who emphasized that Catholics shared in the city's glorious past; he wrote Mrs. J. Balfour Miller, chief organizer, that the pilgrimage "served to show the people in other parts of the country what a wonderful history we have. It has shown, too, the culture of our people of this community."[25] Within a few years St. Mary's was a regular stop on the pilgrimage tour.

The Catholic orphanages also attracted the support of non-Catholics; in the 1880s, for example, the Natchez Elks Club raised over twelve hundred dollars and divided it equally among the two Catholic orphanages and the local Protestant home. Catholic women set out across the state every year on fund-raising drives that brought in several thousand dollars annually. By 1925 the city was holding a United Orphan Drive, which expanded in the 1940s to become a Community Chest drive to support a wide array of local charities. While the Catholic Church was initially somewhat skeptical of this ecumenical effort, they soon joined in with enthusiasm, Bishop Gerow serving as president of the drive in 1945.

The active missionary work and immigration brought about a rapid growth in the Catholic Church in the late nineteenth and early twentieth centuries. From 1888 to 1924 the number of Catholics doubled, to over thirty-one thousand in one hundred forty-nine churches and chapels, and the number of schools expanded to thirty-four. Despite their close adherence to southern mores, Catholics did face some prejudice and persecution, fueled in part by the second Ku Klux Klan and the strong nativistic currents abroad in the first decades of the twentieth century. In 1914 and 1916 the Mississippi legislature considered two anti-Catholic measures; one proposed to ban white teachers from black schools, which would have forced the church to close its black parochial schools, and the second proposed a convent inspection law. Strong opposition from the church and from its related lay organizations like the Knights of Columbus defeated both measures. During World War I some anti-Catholic sentiment surfaced, and Father L. Meister, a German-born priest serving at Aberdeen, was briefly arrested as a spy, but Bishop John Gunn allayed such fears by his strong and vocal support of the war effort. At a Liberty Loan rally held in Natchez, eight to ten thousand people heard the bishop deliver a stinging rebuke of Germany in the keynote address. While the Catholic Church had joined other local churches in preserving the memory of the Confederate past, World War I marked a symbolic reunification with the rest of the nation. At a 1918 victory mass the bishop echoed President Woodrow Wilson's idealistic vision for the postwar world and America's place in it: "America must see that the peace that follows the armistice of today be so strong, so Christ-like, so American that from pole to pole may resound the new democracy of the rights of man and the rights of God."[26] So great were the bishop's labors during the war that one Protestant commentator observed that "Bishop Gunn has done more to inspire and conserve the true principles of American loyalty to the flag and respect for law and order than any other man in the state of Mississippi."[27]

The spirit of nativism further increased after the war, and, despite Bishop Gunn's reputation for patriotism, the Ku Klux Klan continued to inflame anti-Catholic prejudice. In 1921 Bishop Gunn deplored "the very existence of such a bigoted society in Natchez," which he condemned as "both a disgrace as well as a menace." In 1923 the Knights of Columbus held a statewide convention in Natchez that the Klan marked by burning a large cross on the bluffs. The efforts of the Klan did not garner widespread public support, however, and many residents of Natchez apparently shared the bishop's hostile opinion of "that atmosphere of hate, suspicion, and bigotry" the Klan created.[28] The Klan's failure to ignite anti-Catholic prejudice is a testament both to the prevalence of racial prejudice as the most popular Klan issue in the South and to the success of the Catholic

Church's long tradition of acquiescence in the state's racial mores. When instructions from Rome encouraged southern Catholics to expand their efforts among blacks in 1935, the bishops of the Province of New Orleans, which included Mississippi, unanimously opposed "mixed schools" and agreed that the "social question . . . should be permitted to work out itself. . . ." The bishops asserted that "[t]he issue cannot be forced, especially in the South, where years of tradition and state laws constitute serious embarrassments and obstacles."[29]

Catholics were once again summoned to defend their country following the Japanese attack on Pearl Harbor. In the wake of the surprise attack, Bishop Gerow told the faithful that "[o]ur liberty, our way of life, our institutions—all that we hold dear—are threatened. In this sad hour, upon each and everyone devolves a sacred, solemn duty to rally under the leadership of our president in the defense of our flag and all that it represents."[30] In a similar vein, Timothy P. Galvin, a leader of the Knights of Columbus, told a meeting of that body that "[w]e are fighting to uphold the doctrine that all men are created equal in the sight of God."[31] Large military bases in the state brought an influx of Catholic military families, and Catholic social organizations threw themselves into the war effort by raising funds, collecting scrap metal and clothing, encouraging the purchase of war bonds, and undertaking other patriotic endeavors. Almost five thousand Mississippi Catholics served in the armed forces, one of every nine church members. When Germany surrendered on May 7, 1945, the bells of St. Mary's pealed in victory, and Bishop Gerow declared that "there must be founded a new world order, based upon justice, and right and mutual international cooperation."[32] No one could foresee in 1945 just how great the changes in the postwar world would be or how the demands for justice and righteousness would be ringing out in Mississippi more loudly, perhaps, than anywhere else in the world.

Just as Natchez served as the focal point of Catholic life in Mississippi for much of its history, the city also functioned as the nucleus of a thriving Jewish community. The first record of Jewish settlers in Natchez dates to the Spanish period, but it was not until the 1840s that an identifiable Jewish community emerged. Jewish peddlers, most of German or Alsatian origin, soon played an important role in the local economy. Carrying seventy-five pound packs, the peddlers traveled to isolated farms and plantations selling and bartering supplies and delivering mail. The peddlers soon parlayed their modest profits into retail stores located "under-the-hill." Jews purchased land for a cemetery, and in 1843 a congregation officially organized under the name Hevrah Kedusha ("burial society"). Similar groups of Jewish peddlers and merchants organized congregations in Port Gibson and Natchez in the antebellum period.

These Jewish communities expanded considerably after the Civil War. The war ravaged the state's economy, and the dramatic economic changes it brought in its wake, particularly the sharecropping system and the debt peonage that accompanied it, gave merchants a more important role in the postwar economic system, thereby opening up more opportunities for Jewish merchants in the state's economic life. Extension of credit to farm-ers and sharecroppers gave merchants control over the cotton crop and transformed merchants into suppliers and cotton agents for black and white farmers in their debt. In Natchez the number of Jewish merchants rose from twelve in 1858 to eighteen in 1866 to twenty-eight in 1877. By 1877 Jews owned over half of the dry goods stores and cotton buying houses in the city but made up only about 5 percent of the town's popula-tion. From the end of the Civil War well into the twentieth century, Jews operated about one-third of the businesses in Natchez.

The increasing economic power exercised by the town's Jewish resi-dents was reflected in social and political terms as well. In 1867 the Jewish congregation purchased a lot located in the center of town for their tem-ple. The cornerstone was laid in January 1870 in a ceremony conducted by Rabbi Isaac Mayer Wise, founder of Hebrew Union College in Cincin-nati, Ohio, the intellectual center of Reform Judaism in America. Wise's Reform movement sought to fuse Judaism and Americanism, to create an "American Judaism, free, progressive, enlightened, united and respected," a goal that meshed perfectly with the needs of the upwardly mobile, suc-cessful, and well-integrated Jewish community in Natchez.[33] Conflict emerged in the congregation between more conservative, older, orthodox members and the members who supported the Reform movement, but in 1871, under the leadership of Samuel Ullman, owner of a dry goods and cotton buying business, the congregation formally adopted the Reform service, which was shorter, simpler, and closer to Protestant services, with its sermons and hymns; changed its name to B'nai Israel; purchased an organ; and formed a choir and a Sunday school. The Reform service also allowed women a greater involvement in worship and gave them the opportunity to organize the same sorts of religious societies that played such an important role in Protestant churches in the South. The Hebrew Ladies Aid Association played an active part in the temple's work. In 1869, for example, the association offered an impressive $3,575 to the congregation to be used in constructing the new temple. In 1874 Temple B'nai Israel became a charter member of the Union of American Hebrew Congregations, Wise's Reform organization, and the new temple was formally dedicated in a March 1872 service led by Dr. Max Lilienthal, a noted scholar at Hebrew Union College.

The Jews of Natchez played an active role in the city's civic life. For example, Isaac Lowenberg served two terms as mayor beginning in 1873, and S. B. Laub held the same office from 1928 to 1936; Cassius L. Tillman served as sheriff in the 1880s, and thirteen Jews served as city aldermen. In addition, Jews were active in a variety of important business and social organizations, including the Natchez Board of Trade and the Natchez Cotton and Merchants' Exchange, the Masons, the Odd Fellows, the Prentiss Club, and the Knights of Pythias. Jews also built their own downtown social club, the Standard Club. Jewish women were active in the Natchez Garden Club and the Natchez Pilgrimage from their inceptions; the club and the pilgrimage, of course, stood at the pinnacle of Natchez social life. Mrs. Emma Marx was a founding member of the garden club, and Miss Jane Wexler was crowned Confederate Pageant Queen in 1935. When the temple went up in flames in 1903, the members of the Jefferson Street Methodist Church offered the Jewish congregation the use of the church until a new temple was constructed, an offer that the members of B'ani Israel accepted until the temple opened in 1905. Membership in the temple reached its high point in 1906 with 140 members; in that same year the state had 19 Jewish congregations with 746 members. The Natchez community, like others along the river, went into decline in 1908 when the boll weevil first devastated the state's cotton crop. The Jewish merchants and cotton buyers, heavily dependent on the cotton market and holding large debts tied to failed crops, suffered serious setbacks as the tiny pests destroyed up to half the crop annually.

The same economic opportunities that brought Jewish merchants to

Natchez took them to the other major ports along the Mississippi and into the Delta, especially to Port Gibson, Vicksburg, and Greenville, which also had thriving Reform Jewish communities composed of wealthy merchants. In 1892 the Jews of Port Gibson built one of the region's most distinctive temples, Gemiluth Chassed Synagogue, a brick structure of Greek Byzantine design with stained glass windows, topped by a distinctive Moorish dome. It served as the center of a community "that was at once discreetly separate and distinctly Southern."[34] While the Jewish congregations along the river declined after the early 1900s, the Beth Israel congregation in Jackson grew along with the capital city. The congregation built a synagogue in 1867, but it was destroyed by fire in 1874. The new temple, an impressive Gothic structure dedicated in 1875, served "as the religious meeting house of some of Jackson's most prominent citizens."[35] That building served the growing community until 1940 when construction of a new temple began.

Mississippi's Jewish and Catholic communities were small non-Protestant islands in the great sea of evangelical Protestantism in the state, but both groups found means of using their faith to more fully integrate themselves into the regional culture, and both succeeded, to a surprising degree, in avoiding the sort of prejudice and hostility that confronted members of their faiths in other parts of the country. Other religious groups, however, took a very different course, elaborating on rather than masking their differences from the prevailing culture. These groups invented an identity based on cultural separatism, even exaggerating their opposition in an effort to assign value to struggle, to build group cohesion, and to give their members greater self-confidence. The best example of such a movement in the state is the Church of Jesus Christ of Latter-day Saints, or the Mormons.

Mormon activity in the state began in the 1840s when converts appeared in north Mississippi. In 1845 members of the group appeared in Fulton, where they "marched up . . . convicted, converted and baptized nine proselytes to their faith." The local newspaper fumed that "[t]hey are still lumbering away as bold as wharf rats, while at work, but look as meek as half drowned mice, when in skeptical company. . . . We had hoped that we should not have to record an instance . . . of this foolery in Mississippi."[36] Widely ridiculed and persecuted in their home state, Mississippi

Mormons played a significant role in the denomination's history and legend. In 1843 John Brown and H. W. Church left Alabama, where they had served as missionaries, and entered Monroe County. There they found a Mormon branch centered around the family of John Crosby, prosperous owner of a fourteen-hundred-acre plantation and twenty-six slaves; his wife and six children formed the nucleus of the Mormon converts. John Brown married Crosby's daughter Elizabeth and set out to convert the rest of the family and the slaves. Brown and various members of the Crosby clan visited Nauvoo, Illinois, the site of Joseph Smith's Mormon city, but Smith's murder and the furor surrounding it put an end to their plan to move there. Brigham Young, the new Mormon leader, laid plans for a remarkable removal of the faithful from Nauvoo to the Utah territory. He sent Brown and the Crosbys back to Mississippi in 1846 to gather the Saints there and prepare to relocate. In April 1846 Brown led a caravan of sixty Mormon converts, including a few slaves, from Mississippi to Pueblo, Colorado, where they spent the winter. Brown and five other Mississippians, including three slaves, joined the Pioneer Band, who blazed the trail that the other Saints followed to Utah. Soon the Pueblo group joined them, making the Mississippians among the earliest immigrants to Utah. Brown returned to Mississippi and gathered the remaining converts, including his immediate family, who set out in three stages during February and March 1848. The group consisted of thirty whites and twenty-four slaves. With the emigration of this early group of converts, Mormonism apparently lapsed until the late nineteenth century.

In 1898 two Mormon elders, Frank Gardine and Marion Caldwell, arrived in Yazoo County. Like all Mormon missionaries, these two were fiercely polemical. "Clothed with the Priesthood, and with a burning testimony of the divinity of their work, they went about proclaiming the story of the restoration of the Gospel."[37] The two apparently met with some success and made many converts, but when forty elders in the state met for a district conference, the meeting was broken up by an angry mob of a hundred seventy-five men. According to church lore, the elders were driven from the county and "[f]or years no Elders of Zion entered therein."[38] In fact, by 1906 the Mormons outnumbered Jews in Mississippi, with one thousand eighteen adherents. But despite their aggressive evangelizing, the Mormons grew very slowly in the state. By 1967 their numbers had increased to slightly over five thousand, with about five hundred conversions annually.

The three groups discussed here—Catholics, Jews, and Mormons—do not account for all the non-Protestant religious groups in post–Civil War Mississippi; indeed, religious groups as varied as the Amish, Greek Orthodox, First Church of Christ Scientist, and others could be added to the list, but the three chronicled here represent the largest of the non-Protestant groups. In addition, the various strategies adopted by these religious "outsiders" in an overwhelmingly evangelical Protestant setting are illustrative of the ways in which such groups have survived and prospered. These religious Mississippians were regarded by many of their contemporaries, and sometimes by themselves, as "outsiders," people whose beliefs set them apart from the dominant culture. An examination of the Catholics and Jews in the state suggests, however, that both these groups used their religion to overcome outsider status. By conforming to the region's mores, particularly to its racial codes, most members of these religious groups were able to integrate themselves into the white mainstream. In this binary society, where racial prejudice overwhelmed all other areas of discrimination, most Jews and Catholics were accepted so long as they conformed on this compelling issue. Black Catholics, on the other hand, were a minority within a minority, though by their very existence they facilitated the definition of white Catholics as good southerners who offered no challenge to segregation or racial inequality. In some respects the Mormons offered a different strategy for growth and survival in the state. While Jews and Catholics downplayed their differences and sought to fully integrate themselves into the prevailing society, the Mormons sought persecution as a means of self-definition. It should be observed, however, that the Mormons did not challenge Jim Crow; it was not until 1978 that men of all races, though not women, were given the opportunity to enter the church's priesthood. In the end, all outsider religious movements have both adapted to and adopted the prevailing culture of the state.

In the final analysis the problem of race is not a political but a moral issue. . . . [T]he problem of race is America's greatest moral dilemma.

—MARTIN LUTHER KING, JR.[1]

IO "A Search for Life's Meanings": Religion and Civil Rights

For Dr. King and for many of his contemporaries of both races, the civil rights movement was first and foremost a moral and religious movement. A Sunday school teacher in the state entitled one of his lessons on racial issues "A Search for Life's Meanings." In Mississippi and across the South, people of both races turned to their churches and to their God as they searched for life's meanings. Religious leaders like Dr. King played important roles in the movement, churches served as centers of organizational activity, civil rights activists and segregationists alike appealed to scripture, and personal faith animated activists on both sides of the issue. In considering the links between the civil rights movement and religion it is important to distinguish between church people and churches as institutions. Even in the black community, many ministers and churches were reluctant to embrace the movement, and, while most national denominational bodies of white churches officially condemned segregation, local churches and their ministers and members often took a different position. As he surveyed the diversity of religious opinion on the great moral issue of the twentieth century, Dr. King wrote, "The church has a schism in its own soul that it must close."[2]

Dr. King was not the only person to reflect on the divided soul of southern religious bodies. In his landmark study of the civil rights era entitled *Mississippi: The Closed Society*, University of Mississippi historian James W. Silver wrote that "the closed society of Mississippi imposes on all its people acceptance of and obedience to an official orthodoxy." He outlined the chief tenets of the "segregation creed," which assumed "the sanction of the Bible and Christianity. . . ." And yet he observed that "almost every congregation in the state was composed of individuals who ranged from liberal to racist."[3] Given the title of his book, such an observation is a rather surprising one, and it raises significant questions about white southerners' religious life in the civil rights era. How does one reconcile that range of opinion on the vital question of race with a closed society? How did such diametrically opposed views arise within churches in the first place? How did these groups respond to the civil rights movement? In order to explore such questions we must look beyond the pulpit to the lay members and to lay organizations.

Many blacks in the years after World War II—determined to be counted as Americans—challenged Mississippi's Jim Crow system and attempted to register to vote. Many of these individuals were propelled into the civil rights movement by their religious beliefs. Among those courageous men was the Reverend L. T. Smith, born in rural Hinds County in 1902. As a youth, he was struck by the inequalities in education between the races and resented attending school in the local black church while whites had a separate school building. As a young man he moved to Jackson and worked as a postal carrier. At the same time, he completed high school and entered the Baptist ministry. He joined the Jackson branch of the National Association for the Advancement of Colored People (NAACP), which was first organized in the 1920s but became important only after World War II. Smith tried for years to register to vote, only to be stymied by the state's "understanding" clause, which required him to interpret a part of the state constitution to the satisfaction of the registrar. Only after using his daily breaks at work to pester the county clerk was he allowed to register. Through the determination of men like Smith and the work of the NAACP, the number of registered black voters in the state rose from an estimated seven thousand in 1948 to twenty thousand by 1952—a remarkable achievement, but still less than 6 percent of eligible black voters. Smith's struggle for equality was tied directly to his faith; he said, "Christ said, 'Love ye one another.' He didn't say—'White, you love white. Black, you love black.' But we are all God's children and the 'ye' would include us all." Another important leader in the NAACP was the Reverend William A. Bender, chaplain at Tougaloo College, who served as the first fieldworker in the state.[4]

With the help of men like Smith and Bender, the NAACP made modest gains in the early 1950s, and, with the support of white moderates, there was a growing consensus that black demands, especially for better schools, deserved to be addressed. A number of cases challenging segregation in public schools had begun to work their way up to the Supreme Court, and these legal challenges encouraged many southern states, including Mississippi, to consider equalizing separate systems, but, in a special session held in November 1953 to consider the education budget, the state house of representatives passed a bill requiring that the public schools be closed if the court ordered desegregation. Though rejected by the senate, the bill gave evidence that the state would take a hard-line stance against any court-ordered desegregation plan.

On Monday, May 17, 1954, the Supreme Court handed down its momentous decision against segregated schools in the *Brown* case. The day was reviled as "Black Monday" by white supremacists, and the decision sent shock waves through the state. Florence Mars, a white resident of Philadelphia, Mississippi, wrote that "[t]he war began with the Supreme Court decision of 1954. That decision burst upon a society already greatly changed from the one of my childhood, and one which would continue to change after the decision."[5] Initially stunned by the decision, white segregationists quickly rallied to oppose the order by any means at their disposal, including violence and murder, while the decision spurred blacks to push harder for equality.

Despite the example of ministers like Smith and Bender, not all black preachers supported the civil rights movement, particularly in the early years. A handful of black preachers were actually in the pay of whites. In the Mississippi Delta, for example, the influential Delta Council, an organization of leading white planters, financially supported a black newspaper edited by the Reverend H. H. Humes, who wrote editorials urging sharecroppers to stay on the plantations and accept their second-class political status. He also spied on post offices to learn which black sharecroppers received union information. Humes was one of the most prominent black ministers in the state and president of the General Missionary Baptist Convention, with four hundred thousand members.[6]

Few black preachers were such traitors to the cause, but many of them took a cautious attitude toward the emerging civil rights movement. Most black preachers were only part-time ministers; like most blacks, they worked for whites and were economically dependent on white employers. Others, fearful for their own lives and the security of their church buildings, refused to allow civil rights workers into the churches. As one civil rights worker in Holmes County recalled, "We got turned down a lot of times from the black minister. . . . He mostly was afraid because they [whites] whooped a few of 'em and bombed a few churches. The preacher didn't want his church burned down, and them old members was right along in his corner." Civil rights worker Anne Moody, a Centreville native, reported that hostile whites drove one black preacher out of town after he merely mentioned the NAACP in a sermon. Black preachers were easy targets for angry whites, who often took aim at them when civil rights agitation began, and many older church members, schooled in the ways of white violence and intimidation, also held back.[7]

There were exceptions to the rule. Courageous men like the Reverend J. J. Russell of Holmes County "stuck in there from start to finish." He faced serious threats; one of his churches was burned and another vandalized. He became such a liability that some churches refused to let him preach in their pulpits, so he held services in his home. Deeply committed to nonviolence, he described it as "*a sword that cuts without wounding. It's a sword that moves through cities and make people anew and leave buildings standin' and not burned down.*" The Reverend Aaron Johnson of Greenwood, army veteran and pastor of the First Christian Church, began his civil rights activity when he joined the NAACP in the mid-1950s and worked in voter registration. When the movement began in earnest, he opened the doors of his church as a meeting place, bailed activists out of jail, hid them from the authorities, and manned the picket lines himself. White employers threatened church members, local law enforcement officials circled the church on Sunday mornings and followed him wherever he went, attendance dropped, and his salary fell to seventeen dollars per week. Financial support from the denominational headquarters in Indianapolis enabled him to survive. Johnson recalled that "[a]t mass meetings, people would say 'We're behind you, Rev.' He used to wonder how far behind they were."[8]

The absence of black ministers from positions of leadership and the reluctance of many churches to endorse the movement in its early years should not lead to the assumption that religion played no role in the movement. As one history of the period emphasized, "[R]eligion infused the Movement from the outset." Activists worked through the church networks and used churches as meeting places for civil rights meetings and freedom schools; perhaps most important, the activists themselves drew their inspiration, courage, and dedication to the movement from their faith and from the sermons, prayers, and songs that pervaded every gathering.[9]

A glimpse at the career of Anne Moody as a civil rights activist can help underscore the importance of religion and religious networks. Moody grew up in the Baptist Church in Centreville and played piano for Sunday school and for other church activities. She joined the NAACP as a student at Tougaloo College in the early 1960s and soon became involved with the Student Nonviolent Coordinating Committee (SNCC) and its voter registration drive in the Delta. She and the other canvassers focused their efforts on the churches. She recalled, "On Sundays we usually went to Negro churches to speak. We were split into groups according to our religious affiliation. We were supposed to know how to reach those with the same faith as ourselves." They encountered resistance from some ministers and church members, who asked them not to return to their churches, but, in other cases, deacons and members put enough pressure on ministers and reluctant members to open churches.[10]

One organizer reported that he went to the black churches because they were "at the center of the community . . . 'the church belongs to the folks.' " Given the important role black women played in their churches, it seems natural that they would provide the same leadership in the civil rights movement. In the view of one historian of the period, women's leadership "derived from their roles as community workers and church leaders." So vital were women to the organizing efforts in the Delta that one worker referred to the movement there as "a woman's war." When asked about the prevalence of black women among the workers, one activist explained that "[t]he same types of women were the backbone of the Black churches. Women in the rural South have a long tradition of being doers." Of all those women "doers" none was more important than Fannie Lou Hamer of Ruleville. Historian John Dittmer wrote, "More than any other individual, Mrs. Hamer had come to symbolize the black struggle in Mississippi." She earned that degree of respect through her hard work in the face of adversity, her bravery, her eloquence, and the power of her songs. She attributed her success to her faith, saying, "Christ was a revolutionary person, out there where it was happening. That's what God is all about, and that's where I get my strength." She joined the Strangers Home Baptist Church at the age of twelve, regularly attended church, and knew the Bible so well that she could quote it better than many ministers. Growing out of a tradition stretching back to slave spirituals, protest songs inspired the movement, gave it energy and force, imbued it with power. Hamer's rich singing voice was a powerful weapon for freedom, and none who heard it ever forgot it, though capturing its essence in words was, and is, a more difficult undertaking. Harry Belafonte, the noted actor who sang along with her on occasion, said, "I can't describe her voice—as a voice. I have got to always talk about Fannie Lou Hamer singing and the *power* of her voice because there was a mission behind it and in it." Mrs. Hamer said, "Singing . . . is one of the main things that can keep us going. . . . It brings out the soul."[11]

Mrs. Hamer heaped scorn and abuse on black preachers who would not join the movement; she berated them as "chicken-eating preachers . . . selling out for the big Cadillacs." Women like her helped shame more and more preachers into joining the movement; as their congregations became increasingly active, the preachers climbed on board. By 1963 SNCC and the NAACP had organized boycotts of white businesses, sit-ins at lunch counters, and pray-ins on the post office steps in Jackson. By this time, black churches and ministers were at the center of these activities; in May 1963 black ministers and businessmen formed the Citizens Committee for Human Rights to organize protests. Mass rallies took place at black churches, and a delegation of black ministers presented a list of demands to the city's mayor. Efforts in the capital city culminated with the tragic assassination of Medgar Evers, who had been NAACP field secretary since 1954. After leaving a meeting at New Jerusalem Baptist Church on the night of June 11, 1963, Evers was shot in the back as he got out of his car in his driveway by a sniper later identified as Byron De La Beckwith. Anne Moody, just released from jail for her protests, attended the funeral, one of the largest ever seen in the city. She wrote, "This was the first time I had ever seen so many Negroes together. . . . Maybe Medgar's death had really brought them to the Movement. . . ." Instead, the assassination resulted in a period of confusion and fear. "Every Negro leader and organization in Jackson received threats," Moody recalled. "The ministers, in particular, didn't want to be next. . . ."[12]

Meanwhile, boycotts, registration drives, and other forms of protest were under way across the state. The Council of Federated Organizations (COFO) records reveal both the importance of churches and religious activity to the movement and the level of violence people faced. Organized in 1961 by representatives of the NAACP, SNCC, and other civil rights groups, COFO served as an umbrella group to coordinate activities around the state. A sample of depositions from June and July 1964 shows waves of violence and intimidation across the state. On June 16 in Philadelphia at the Mt. Zion Baptist Church: "Fire starts soon after Negro mass meeting adjourns. Three Negroes beaten by whites. This was freedom school site." On June 21 in Brandon: "Molotov cocktail explodes in basement of Sweet Rest Church of Christ Holiness." Four days later Williams Chapel in Ruleville was firebombed, and on June 26 the Church of Holy Ghost was set on fire "after local white pastor speaks to Negro Bible class (Fifth firebombing in 10 days)." On July 6 the McCraven Hill Missionary Baptist Church in Jackson was damaged by a kerosene fire, while in Raleigh Methodist and Baptist churches burned to the ground. On July 11, the Browning Pleasant Plain Missionary Baptist Church was torched after whites tried to buy it and blacks refused to sell. One day later Jerusalem Baptist Church and Bethel Methodist Church burned to the ground in Natchez. By 1964, forty-one black churches had gone up in flames.[13] The burning and bombing of black churches constitutes perhaps the most intensive and sustained attack on religious institutions in the twentieth century.

As the civil rights campaign intensified, whites divided over the issue, and that division was most obvious in the state's religious communities. In the wake of the *Brown* decision, regional and national denominational bodies including the Southern Baptist Convention, the Methodist Council of Bishops, and the Southern Presbyterian General Assembly took positions in favor of desegregation, a stance that provoked a backlash from their members. State Presbyterian leaders were quick to criticize their denominational body for its prointegration resolution. Governor Hugh White, a Presbyterian elder who built a dormitory for girls at Belhaven College, the state's Presbyterian college, vowed that "if the Supreme Court decision is observed in my church I will be forced to find some other place to worship." Dr. G. T. Gillespie, Sr., president emeritus of Belhaven, joined White in condemning the pro-*Brown* resolution. Baptist leaders also denounced the Southern Baptist Convention resolution as a violation of the separation of church and state. Like antebellum ministers who had attempted to wash their hands of the slavery issue by proclaiming that it was a purely political matter, Baptist leaders like Dr. Douglas Hudgins of the First Baptist Church in Jackson and future governor Ross Barnett, a deacon in that church, saw the question of public school integration as a political one. Methodist churches across the state passed resolutions condemning their council of bishops. The First Methodist Church of Lexington "disavows said stand and repudiates any suggestion that this church is bound by their stand." The First Methodist Church of Clarksdale condemned the bishops for meddling in politics and announced that it was "irrevocably opposed to integration of the negro and white races in the public schools and in the Methodist Churches of Mississippi." Integration, they warned, would "promote social equality, which in the annals of History had led almost without exception to miscegenation of the white and negro races."[14]

Mississippi's campaign of massive resistance to court-ordered desegregation quickly moved into high gear. Spearheaded by the Citizens' Council, which had been organized by Robert B. Patterson, a plantation manager in Indianola and member of the Methodist Church, the campaign turned into a juggernaut that threatened to sweep away all voices of reason and moderation. With its middle-class leadership and aura of respectability, the council grew rapidly and within a few months had more than twenty-five thousand members in the state. It relied on economic reprisals and social pressure and loudly proclaimed that it did not advocate violence, a stance that led journalist Hodding Carter, Jr., to call it the "uptown Klan." Support from the ultraconservative Hederman family, owners of the *Jackson Daily News* and the Jackson *Clarion-Ledger*, the state's largest dailies, gave the council unprecedented media access and allowed them to print and distribute more than eight million pieces of propaganda by 1958. Support from Ross Barnett, who became governor in 1960, made the council virtually an arm of the state government (or vice versa), and, through the State Sovereignty Commission, a quasi-secret state agency created in 1956 to safeguard segregation, the council received hundreds of thousands of dollars in state funds.[15]

The council quickly targeted moderate ministers; as one council publication put it, *"The Preacher is our most deadly enemy."* To combat the moderate views expressed by national denominational bodies and by many Mississippi ministers, the council enlisted the support of prominent segregationist ministers like the Reverend Gillespie, whose pamphlet entitled *A Christian View of Segregation* was widely distributed by the council. In their efforts to defend segregation through Scripture, Christian segregationists like Gillespie returned to the curse of Ham, one of the most enduring misinterpretations of the Bible. James Smylie, Mississippi's first apostle of slavery, had employed this same mischievous alleged curse over a century before in his popular defense of that institution. Seeing its reappearance so late in the twentieth century in defense of yet another form of racial discrimination is jarring. This complex and willful misreading of Scripture may appear pedantic, but historian Benjamin Braude calls it "one of the standard justifications for the degradation and enslavement of the African black in both South Africa and the American South." The Citizens' Council literature routinely used the curse of Ham in such publications as "Is Segregation Unchristian?" Indeed, the curse was so widely employed by segregationists that the General Board of Education of the Methodist Church published a two-page refutation for quick distribution. The Methodist document, written in the form of a dialogue, reviewed the many contradictions within the curse and concluded that "there is nothing to prove that Negroes are the result of God's curse and a race divinely ordained to servitude."[16]

The council targeted religious racial moderates across the state, especially at white colleges. Will Campbell, an outspoken Methodist minister, became director of religious life at the University of Mississippi in 1954. In 1956 he attempted to promote discussion of racial justice on campus by inviting speakers he knew to be sympathetic to the cause, including Episcopal minister Alvin Kershaw of Ohio, to speak at Religious Emphasis Week. When segregationists learned that Kershaw had contributed to the NAACP, the college administration forced Campbell to cancel the appearance. Six other speakers withdrew from the event, and the chairman of the sociology department and Campbell resigned in protest. The tempest spilled over to Mississippi State, where the Reverend Duncan Gray, Jr., an Episcopal priest and son of the state's Episcopal bishop, told a student group meeting in a Starkville church that "segregation is incompatible with the Christian faith." Gray was scheduled to speak the following week during the college's Religious Emphasis Week, but was forced to withdraw as newspapers spread his remarks. Again, several other speakers canceled their appearances in protest, but the college administration bowed to the segregationists.

At Millsaps College, the state's most moderate institution and one where interracial meetings had been held since 1948, the pattern was repeated when the college scheduled a forum on race relations in 1958. Ernst Borinski, a refugee from Nazi Germany and a sociologist at Tougaloo, helped organize the integrated events. Speaking at Millsaps, he said, "[R]acial segregation violates Christian premises," a statement that the council used to inflame public opinion. Once again a reluctant administration folded to public pressure, and the college's board of trustees issued a formal declaration upholding segregation. In the words of Hodding Carter, Jr., "[T]he undertaker who is president of the Jackson Citizens Council is prepared to embalm and bury the remains of academic freedom in Mississippi."[17] Unfortunately, the funeral would have attracted very few mourners.

White Baptists were the most vocal clerical supporters of the Citizens' Council and defenders of the racial status quo. Mississippi College, the premier Baptist institution in the state, served as the segregationist citadel. The college's president, Dr. D. M. Nelson, wrote a segregationist tract, printed and distributed by the Citizens' Council, which stated in part that the purpose of integration was "to mongrelize the two dominant races of the South." He vowed "to protect the fair sons and daughters of the purest strain of the Caucasian race" from the threat posed by integration, which was "based upon Karl Marx's doctrine of internationalism . . . the obliteration of all national and racial distinctions and the final amalgamation of all races."[18]

Dr. W. M. Caskey, a faculty member at the college, was also a frequent speaker at Citizens' Council meetings. In a characteristic statement of his views, he said, "We . . . believe with Governor Barnett, that our Southern segregation way is the Christian way. We are not racists. We advocate no violence. . . . But, we believe that this Bible teaches that Thou wast the original segregationists. . . ."[19] Caskey wrote that, after a speech to a Citizens' Council rally in Franklin County, "[M]y desk has been flooded with mail—all favorable. It's from folks in all walks. It includes deacons, Sun. School teachers, etc."[20]

One of those Sunday school teachers was Archibald Stimson Coody IV, a staunch segregationist. An examination of his career as a Sunday school teacher in Jackson's prominent First Christian Church reveals the remarkable depth of supremacist activity in religious settings and how far apart lay members and their ministers and denominational leaders could be. Born on a poor farm in Yazoo County in 1883, Coody attended a one-room schoolhouse for a few months of the year and earned a reputation as being "smart in his books." A loan from a well-to-do relative allowed him to attend Atlanta Pharmacy College, and after his graduation in 1905 he operated a drugstore and was secretary of the state pharmaceutical association for fourteen years. He served as mayor of Lucedale, Mississippi, in 1915, his only political venture. In 1916 he was admitted to the bar and moved to Jackson, where he found employment in the state tax commission; from 1918 to 1954 he was secretary of the commission. He was closely associated with many prominent politicians, including James K. Vardaman and Theodore Bilbo, and served as a speechwriter and advisor for Bilbo. He was a member of the First Christian Church in Jackson, an important church located a stone's throw from the state capitol building. He was an elder in the church for decades and taught a men's Bible class there from the 1920s to the 1950s, a class named the Coody Men's Class in his honor. His personal life was troubled; his wife suffered from a serious mental illness and was institutionalized in the state mental hospital. His only son described his father as someone who "has had his share of troubles. He had no education given to him. . . . He twice lost all his savings. . . . He is a man who had read and studied, and had been lonely because he had no one in his household to do likewise. . . . He has never had a home like other men."[21]

Racial issues were an obsession for A. S. Coody, who surpassed even Vardaman and Bilbo in his racist views. While Christianity led many believers to celebrate the brotherhood of mankind, Coody espoused a different interpretation of Scripture. Like proslavery ministers in the Old South, Coody believed that God had created the races and intended for them to remain distinct. He wrote, "God made white, black, red and yellow. . . . But God did not endow all races in the same way nor to the same extent." He maintained that "[t]he Creator made them as they are, and the wise man accepts the work of the Maker."[22]

Virtually every one of his Sunday school lessons returned to the issue of race, and most of them are shocking racist diatribes against blacks and Jews. In a typical lesson entitled "A Search for Life's Meanings," Coody informed his class that the races "are *not* equal" physically, mentally, or morally. He praised the superiority of European cultures and warned that "*[c]ivilizations or cultures* decay from within." The federal government, misled by the "*Cult of Equality*," had instituted policies that were "in reality, destroying the best element. Taxing workers . . . for [the] lazy and immoral."[23]

In Coody's view, southern white Christians confronted a vast international conspiracy. Communism was the chief enemy, with allies including the president, the Supreme Court, the NAACP, the National Council of Churches, and the United Nations. Communists "aim to destroy us. Me! You! Your children." Their methods included "mongrelization," "immigration," "Debt, Income Tax, Inheritance Tax, [and] Inflation." What he called "[t]heir War on [the] South" was led by President Harry Truman, who favored civil rights and integration, and by President Dwight D. Eisenhower, who also favored civil rights and "appointed Bitter South Haters," most notably Earl Warren, chief justice of the Supreme Court. To combat such a vast and powerful array of enemies, Coody advised that "[t]he first defense is Unity, Our Agency is [the] Citizen's [*sic*]Council."[24]

He was also a member of the Ku Klux Klan and noted with pride that he "openly defended the aims of Hitler to my Sunday School class."[25] On occasion, he advocated the use of violence. In 1956, for example, he wrote his son, "People are getting hot as a six shooter over this race question. . . . The mulatto coons are a little afraid of Mississippi. . . .We badly need a few shootings, to get the issue stirred. The hotter it gets, the more will people take sides, and as the Northern Negroes and Jews attack the South, the white people will come to our side."[26] He noted that some people said that "a Christian cannot make, or *AID* war," but he disagreed. "When can citizens defy [the] state?" he asked. In a just cause. Southerners should defy Earl Warren just as George Washington defied the British, even at the risk of their lives. The self-styled "Lone Eagle," Coody pledged to fight for "Land and Race."[27]

It should be noted that at the same time Coody was delivering his racist diatribes in Sunday school, Dr. Bert R. Johnson, the minister of the First Christian Church, was giving sermons calling on his congregation to "avoid those hates, animosities, racial prejudices, and the narrow provincialism that separate the human race into klans [note the spelling], tribes, warring groups, and seek to attain the unity of mankind that eventuates in the brotherhood of man."[28] Historian Samuel S. Hill, Jr., aptly described men's Bible classes in the South as "spectacularly large and cult-like, being built around the personality of a veteran teacher. . . . [T]hese classes tend to operate independently of the church which quarters them." In Hill's view, such classes served as bulwarks of southern orthodoxy, powerful reinforcers of the regional and religious status quo. Given the sentiments expressed by the Reverend Johnson, the First Christian Church would seem to be a perfect example of the mixed congregation that Silver described.

It would be easy, and comforting, to dismiss Coody as a crank and a crackpot even within his church, but his popularity and long tenure as a teacher belie such a conclusion. In fact, his ideas had a wide currency beyond the church classroom. He published a pamphlet entitled *The Race Question* outlining his racial views. Senator Theodore Bilbo wrote Coody to praise the work and ordered copies to circulate to his friends in the Senate. Bilbo added, "I believe if we will continue to propagandize the American people with the slogan of a physical separation of the races as the only solution of the race trouble that when all this 'hell breaks loose' we can get some real cooperation on the part of the public leaders of both North and South to a resettlement of the negro in Africa. It may be that we will have to kill half of them before the other half will be willing to seek a new country in Africa."[29] Albert Jones, director of the State Sovereignty Commission, also wrote Coody a letter of support and ordered five hundred copies of the pamphlet for distribution. Other letters arrived from D. M. Nelson, president of Mississippi College; United States Representative John Bell Williams; Walter Sillers, speaker of the state house of representatives; and scores of individuals from across the state and around the nation. The Ku Klux Klan presented him with a certificate of appreciation and a certificate of merit for his efforts. In 1961 he organized the Magnolia Heritage Society with prominent politicians, businessmen, newspaper editors, and others to resist integration.[30]

As Coody suggested, large numbers of laypeople deeply resented the moderate position taken by many ministers and denominational assemblies; his position may have been extreme, but many of his views were not. Laypeople organized to oppose their more moderate denominational leaders; groups such as the Mississippi Presbyterian Laymen's Association, the Association of Christian Conservatives, and the Mississippi Association of Methodist Ministers and Laymen (MAMML) organized religious opposition and often worked in concert with the Citizens' Councils.[31]

The MAMML, often referred to as the "Citizens' Council of the Methodist Church," began in the mid-1950s through the sponsorship of the Circuit Riders, Inc., an Ohio-based group organized in 1951 to fight communism and socialism in the church but also deeply involved in the fight against integration across the South. Southern states including Georgia and Louisiana employed Myers G. Lowman, the executive secretary of the Circuit Riders, as an "investigator," and the North Mississippi Conference of the Methodist Church criticized Governor Ross Barnett for sponsoring Lowman's visit to the state through the State Sovereignty Commission. One liberal Methodist who heard Lowman called his speech "the grandest indictment of everyone who had ever raised a finger for the extension of civil rights. . . ."[32]

With the encouragement of the Citizens' Council, the state government attempted to prevent the integration of state churches through legislation. In 1956 the senate considered a bill to require integrated churches to pay property taxes. The bill was denounced as an attack on the Catholic Church, which maintained the state's only integrated churches, and although it passed without an opposing vote in the senate, it was not enacted. The MAMML and the Citizens' Council were responsible for the Church Property Bill enacted by the state legislature in 1960. The bill made it possible for two-thirds of the adult members of a local church to take church property out of the control of the denomination through the chancery courts. Though the bill did not mention Methodists in particular, the debate made it clear that they were the target. One representative even proposed an amendment to abolish the Methodist Church in the state. Hodding Carter III wrote, "During the last regular session of the legislature in 1960, that body acted as little more than a rubber stamp for bills which had Council endorsement."[33]

The Citizens' Council waged a bitter and vituperative campaign against religious moderates who favored integration. A few headlines from *The Citizens' Council* will illustrate the point: "Does Church Favor Mongrelization?," "Southern Churches Balk at 'Social Gospel' Propaganda," "Are Some Church Leaders Betraying Their Country?," "Methodists Patriots Expose Pinks." Special council bulletins carried the message even further. One flyer read, " 'WAKE UP! Or be awakened by the squalls of a mulatto grandchild' ON WHICH SIDE ARE THE PREACHERS? . . . They have called upon the people to submit to the mongrelizers. . . . These men . . . come with sugar-coated words, in flowing robes and inverted collars, wearing crazy titles, such as Doctor of Divinity, Bishop, Rector, etc., urging people . . . to surrender everything their ancestors fought for . . . only to gratify the lust of African savages, Communists and judges. . . ." At the local level, county councils sent letters to all members questioning the position of preachers and upholding segregation as Christian. Through their friends in Washington, D.C., like Representative John Bell Williams, the council even solicited information on liberal ministers from the House Committee on Un-American Activities.[34]

Attacked by right-wing segregationists for being too liberal and almost equally denounced by their coreligionists outside the region for being too conservative, white religious leaders across the state were virtually paralyzed. White women were among the first to speak out in support of integration. Even as racial tensions rose to a fever pitch following the Supreme Court's *Brown* decision, Methodist women refused to retreat from their position on racial equality. In 1952 the Methodist Women's Division of Christian Service adopted the remarkably liberal "Charter of Racial Policies," which specifically advocated integration. The document received scant attention until after the *Brown* decision, when some delegates attempted to nullify the charter; one local chapter hired a lawyer to fight it, and members of the Citizens' Council threatened delegates. Despite such pressure and a flood of negative publicity, the overwhelming majority of delegates voted to retain the charter in their 1955 meeting. A few local societies withdrew from the conference, Klan members burned crosses on the lawns of Methodist women, and letters of condemnation and obscene telephone calls poured in. The women stood firm, however, and in 1962 again revised and strengthened the charter.[35]

There were also many cases of individual bravery, but it took some time, and waves of violence, murder, and disorder, before the churches as institutions began to make their voices heard over the segregationists' howls of protest. The deadly riot that broke out on the Ole Miss campus in September 1962 led a Methodist editor to ask, "Who really is to blame?" His soul-searching response was:

> We in the church are to blame because we allowed such a force of hate to build up in our state. We have known for eight years that there were pressure groups who boasted that if the people did not conform and cooperate with them, they would use social, political and economic pressures. In the name of patriotism, the groups thrived until they had control of our social, political and law-making forces. . . . Yes, the church is partly responsible. . . . Because we were not more vocal and outspoken; because we were not true to our Christian Convictions. . . . By choosing to do nothing, we have permitted political pressure groups to chart our course and have allowed the voice of moderation and goodwill to be completely ignored.[36]

Such sentiments spurred Methodist ministers to further action. In January 1963, twenty-eight "of the younger ministers" in the Mississippi conference issued a public statement upholding freedom of the pulpit, affirming their faith in the brotherhood of all mankind, condemning discrimination on the basis of race, and supporting public schools as "essential to the preservation and development of our true democracy."[37] As a storm of controversy broke over their heads, twenty-three other ministers voted "enthusiastically" to endorse the statement, while their bishop refused to be quoted and maintained silence. The lay leader of the Mississippi conference praised the "worthwhile" statement, and the associate lay leader also endorsed it and criticized "a climate of 'fear and hatred,' created by pressure groups, [that] has kept many Mississippians silent on the race issue." In a statement to the Associated Press that appeared on the front page of the *Clarion-Ledger*, Dr. W. B. Selah, longtime minister of Galloway Methodist Church, the state's largest Methodist church, made a strong and eloquent statement that read in part: "[W]e must seek for all men, black and white, the same justice, the same rights, and the same opportunities that we seek for ourselves. Nothing less than this is Christian love. To discriminate against a man because of his color . . . is contrary to the will of God. Forced segregation is wrong. . . . [T]here can be no color bar in a Christian church. . . . Race prejudice is a denial of Christian brotherhood."[38]

Segregationists inside and outside the Methodist Church reacted swiftly against the young ministers who had issued the statement and against Dr. Selah. Within a week, Dr. Selah was hospitalized with a bleeding ulcer, and, despite a vote of confidence from Galloway's official board, he soon resigned. The MAMML called public meetings to "restore conservative Methodist control" over the churches. Most of the young ministers were driven out of the state, as were many others who supported their stance. Between 1959 and 1964, seventy-nine ministers transferred out of the Mississippi conference. Such victories greatly encouraged the MAMML. These events took place in a climate of terror exemplified by acts of violence and destruction of black churches across the state. White Baptists took the lead in creating the Committee of Concern, supported by "virtually every denomination in Mississippi," that helped rebuild fifty-four churches.[39]

The spirit of hate abroad in the land found full expression in the aftermath of the tragic assassination of President John F. Kennedy in November 1963. White children were a chilling barometer of the level of hatred the president's moderate position on civil rights had earned him in Mississippi. One child said, "I bet my father did it." Others played a game in which they sang, "Bang. Bang. I killed Kennedy." High school students burst into spontaneous applause when the news of the assassination was announced over the speaker systems. An editorial in the Jackson *Free Press*, a small black newspaper, summed up the significance of the young people's reactions: "Too young to wear false mourning clothes, too young to feign what they did not feel, these children reflected the precise political atmosphere our state has so carefully taught." White adults were no more willing to don false mourning clothes. State legislators laughed at the news, and the phones rang incessantly at the Citizens' Council offices, where most of the callers said, "It was God's way of solving the civil rights crisis." The black community was plunged into "deep grief" over the president's death, the murder of Medgar Evers, and the death of four girls in the September 1963 church bombing in Birmingham. Houses in the black community were usually brightly lit during the Christmas season, but in 1963 the streets were eerily dark. Jackson's mayor tried to encourage the Christmas spirit by setting up a contest for the best Christmas decorations in the black community. He tried to enlist black ministers in the effort, "but they all refused to have anything to do with it and the project fell flat."[40]

As violence escalated, leaders of outsider religious groups in the state found themselves in an especially vulnerable position. Rabbi Charles Mantinband of Hattiesburg led a long, courageous fight for social justice during his sixteen years in the state. He was an active member of the board of the Southern Regional Council and the Mississippi Council on Human Relations, and the Citizens' Council targeted him in 1958. While he was away on a trip, the council warned the temple to remove their "mischief-making rabbi" or face the consequences. The congregation stood firm, but years of such pressure took their toll on him. In 1962 he wrote, "Life can be very placid and gracious in this part of the country—if one runs with the herd. . . . [T]here is a conspiracy of silence in respectable middle-class society. Sensitive souls, with vision and the courage of the Hebrew prophets, are drowned out." For years, he survived by resorting to " 'chochma,' that shrewd combination of wisdom and subtle humor," but by 1963 even that was clearly failing him. He wrote, "I suspect we are lacking in courage and in true spirituality. Some of us are very lonely." A few months later he left the state.[41]

Jews in Jackson faced even greater danger. Both the Klan and the Americans for the Preservation of the White Race (APWR) targeted Jews, and the APWR set up a booth at the state fair in Jackson that sold anti-Semitic literature. The KKK's Imperial Wizard in the state, Sam Holloway Bowers, Jr., of Laurel, loudly proclaimed the group to be a "Christian militant" organization and emphasized anti-Semitism. Bowers, Beckwith, and other far-right segregationists in the state were disciples of Dr. Wesley Swift, a California minister whose taped and published sermons introduced them to the Christian Identity Movement, which taught that both blacks and Jews were literally born of Satan. Bowers ordered a series of attacks in Jackson, including the bombing of Temple Beth Israel and another at the home of Dr. Perry Nussbaum, the temple's rabbi. On September 18, 1967, Temple Beth Israel was partially damaged by a bomb placed in a recessed doorway. Following the blast, the Jackson Clergy Alliance, established two months before with sixty members representing ten denominations, organized a "walk of penance." The alliance president, the Reverend Thomas Tiller, said that the walk grew out of a belief that "by default, we may have contributed to a climate of opinion which gives rise to terrorism. What concerns us, and others like us, is that we may not have been zealous enough in protecting our God-given freedoms." Despite several thousand dollars in reward money, the case was not solved, and another attack came two months later. Dr. Nussbaum and his wife, who were asleep at the time, barely escaped injury in a "terrific" dynamite blast that blew out the front of their home and shook much of North Jackson. Nussbaum urged Christian clergy to preach a message of peace for Thanksgiving, but concluded that there was "apparently no end of viciousness in sight." As if to fulfill that sentiment, Bowers ordered an attack on Meridian's Temple Beth Israel in May 1968. By this time, reward money had piled up and the Federal Bureau of Investigation had become involved. When Klan terrorists planned an attack on the home of Meyer Davidson, a prominent Jewish community leader in Meridian, local Klan members informed on them in return for cash, and the two terrorists were thwarted in a dramatic shootout outside Davidson's home. One bomber was killed in the gun battle, and the other was captured and convicted for a string of attacks.[42]

The Catholic Church, the largest outsider denomination in the state, also came under attack from right-wing segregationists. As early as 1956 the state legislature considered laws aimed at integrated Catholic churches, but the Catholic Church's role in the civil rights movement was more complex than their integrated congregations might suggest. When Father Tom Fry, a California clergyman, visited the state at the height of the civil rights movement, he was told that Bishop Richard O. Gerow had been publicly silent on the race question for thirty-six years. While the state legislature railed against integrated Catholic churches, Father Fry found that "[a]ll Negro Catholics are served by order priests, so the diocesan clergy are protected from pastoral experience with Negro frustrations and emotions." When seminarians from the University of Notre Dame planned to come to Mississippi during the 1964 Freedom Summer, the bishop ordered them to stay away, and he sent six other priests back to Oklahoma City after they spent a week with student workers in the freedom project.[43]

At the local level, however, Catholic churches could be far more aggressive in the fight for civil rights. Nowhere was this Catholic activism more clearly illustrated than in Greenwood. Located in the heart of the Delta, Greenwood was the center of the cotton trade and state headquarters of the Citizens' Council. With the help of the Reverend Aaron Johnson, SNCC began a registration campaign in 1962. When county supervisors attempted to cut a surplus commodity program that helped feed thousands of poor blacks, interest in the movement grew. Arson and violence against blacks drew widespread support, and Leflore County became a center of activity in the state. Black celebrities like Dick Gregory put in appearances, and the Kennedy administration began to take notice. Agents from the Federal Bureau of Investigation arrived on the scene, and the Justice Department filed a lawsuit against the city.[44]

Black optimism over federal involvement was short-lived, however, as Mississippi politicians in Washington urged the Justice Department to back off, and the federal agency reached a compromise with the city that left blacks little better off than before. Blacks launched a series of economic boycotts that had limited success, but by 1967 national attention

had shifted elsewhere, and the movement struggled to stay alive. At that
point Father Nathaniel Machesky, a white Franciscan priest in the parish
of St. Francis of Assisi in Greenwood, joined the effort. Father Machesky,
the Reverend William Wallace of the Colored Methodist Episcopal
Church, and the Reverend M. J. Black of the African Methodist Episcopal
Church spearheaded another boycott. The newly named Greenwood
Movement was administered from the offices of the St. Francis Center,
and nuns from the center joined the picket lines. A Klan leaflet described
the center as "a hot bed of integration and agitation. It could and should
be removed from the local scene. . . .Good Roman Catholics must . . . get
their house in order . . . before some one else does it for them." Segregationists fired shotgun blasts into the St. Francis Center and firebombed it.
In 1966 Father Machesky bailed Stokely Carmichael out of jail. After his
release, Carmichael gave an angry speech in which he first used his "black
power" slogan. Not surprisingly, 130 white Catholics in Greenwood
signed a petition asking that Machesky never be allowed to set foot in the
white Catholic Church. The Klan warned local blacks, "If any of you
should allow your selves to become intoxicated with this revolutionary
brew, rest assured, you will be promptly sobered up with massive doses of
BLACK POWDER, already in the hands of white, Christian patriots."[45]

Under Bishop Gerow's successor, Bishop Joseph Brunini, the Catholic
Church became more outspoken on racial issues. In April 1968 the Senate
of Priests of the Diocese of Natchez-Jackson issued a public letter addressed to Governor John Bell Williams calling on him to create a special
commission on race. Their letter was a stinging rebuke to the governor:
"In our State . . . our political and religious leadership has been, for the
most part, no more than an appeal for the repression of violence. This, by
the testimony of its results, cannot and will not substitute for the visionary
and positive leadership that is desperately needed." The priests proclaimed that "[r]acism contradicts the democratic and religious principles
of human equality and poses at the present time a serious threat to both of
these concepts." Brunini moved ahead with plans to desegregate Catholic
schools and in 1968 created a special committee on social justice and social
peace. Brunini wrote that segregation was "an affront to the informed
conscience," and warned that Catholic schools would "not offer a refuge
from integration." He called for an ecumenical effort from all denomina-

tions and all races to help achieve social justice and end racial discrimination.[46]

Of the various ecumenical organizations involved in the civil rights movement, none was more controversial in the state than the National Council of Churches (NCC) and its Commission on Religion and Race. The NCC had been organized in 1950 to represent more than thirty Protestant denominations, and McCarthyite witch hunters quickly targeted it as a communist-front organization, with prosegregation groups like the MAMML and the Circuit Riders eagerly spreading that propaganda. The NCC "caused screams of rage" in the state when it began training summer civil rights workers at its school in Ohio and investigating civil rights abuses. In 1963, for example, the NCC investigated the arrest of fifty-seven blacks in Greenwood who had been involved in a voter registration drive. When the church they met in was teargassed, the blacks appealed to the local sheriff, who arrested them for "breaching the peace." The NCC bailed the blacks out of jail. The organization also sent scores of clergymen into the state during Freedom Summer and helped defend them when they were arrested.[47]

The NCC's biggest and most controversial effort in the state was the Delta Ministry, which one writer referred to as "the most controversial mission project ever launched in this nation. . . ." The NCC established the ministry in 1964 as "the instrument to focus the concern and mobilize the resources of the churches in a ministry of service, reconciliation, and social reconstruction to the persons and society of the delta area." Headquartered in Greenville, the agency soon opened other offices in Hattiesburg and McComb. The Delta Ministry was met with skepticism and hostility from almost every side. Given the NCC's equivocal stance on black activism and the white leadership of the ministry, COFO leaders eyed them with suspicion. Needless to say, segregationists were openly hostile. The Delta Council's executive vice president, B. F. Smith, a Methodist layman, was outraged when the ministry labeled the Delta a "dreadful cancer in the midst of the nation" when, in his view, "We have had good race relations in the Delta. . . ." Even Hodding Carter, Jr., was hostile, and in a stinging editorial referred to the ministry leaders as "inept, inefficient revolutionaries."[48]

The ministry put white ministers on the hot seat, particularly those whose denominations were members of the NCC. Many white ministers expressed qualified support for the effort. The Reverend John D. Humphrey, a Methodist, agreed to serve on the Delta Ministry Commission. Though he knew that the ministry would be controversial, he said that he had "[f]or many years, . . . felt the need for a more effective ministry whereby the church would deal effectively with the problems related to human dignity and human need in what has been described as a 'closed society.' " He believed that the agency "could serve as a bridge between the races and conflicting social views, while at the same time serving the human needs of the Negro." The Methodist hierarchy took the same position, but, in their early discussions with ministry officials, it quickly became clear that the two sides were far apart. The Reverend Art Thomas, who had worked in the Freedom Summer campaign, was the first director. In an early meeting with Methodist officials he "stated to us frankly that the Delta Ministry staff had no intention of being in the middle reaching out to both sides." The Mississippi Methodist officials criticized the ministry for "putting all white Southerners in the same category—Ku Kluxers, right wingers, and dedicated Christian workers were all being lumped together" and bristled at their "attitude of condemnation and self-righteousness." The Methodists were somewhat encouraged when Thomas "admitted to us that they had a real problem with their association with COFO. He indirectly admitted that they were unhappy with the relationship and were seeking ways to break it."[49]

One sympathetic visitor reported that, after eighteen months, the Ministry "is ministering—and quite effectively in many respects—to the needs of thousands of poverty-stricken Negroes. But its failure as an agent of reconciliation between the white and Negro communities has often obscured its achievements." One ministry worker said, "The Lord knows, we've tried to open communications with the white community" and cited several failed attempts at meetings or joint projects. Another reported that "[w]e tried at first to get the cooperation of the white community, but we failed. . . . So we've had to move along without them because our first responsibility is to the Mississippi poor people." White ministers in the community, however, echoed the sentiments of a Presbyterian minister who said, "I've never been contacted by those Delta Ministry folks." In a staff report to NCC headquarters, the ministry officials reported that "[a] major difficulty, now facing the Delta Ministry, is not the action of the usual troublemakers, but the attitudes and practices of the so-called white moderates. These leaders, some of whom are known nationally for courageous stands against terror and murder [here read Hodding Carter, Jr.] . . . have not moved forward as fast as the rest of Mississippi. Many of them . . . find it hard to understand methods of working with Negroes that go beyond brotherhood week lectures. . . ." Methodist leaders in the state responded by expressing their "vigorous disapproval" of the ministry to the Methodist Church's board of missions in New York and by attempting to stop a $130,000 allocation from their denomination.[50]

In its first year and a half of operation, the ministry had an impressive list of achievements that included assisting thousands of blacks to register to vote; conducting citizenship classes; establishing several federally funded antipoverty programs, including Operation Head Start, which served nearly six thousand children; distributing tons of food and clothing to more than ten thousand poor families; and supporting strikes and other activities aimed at job discrimination. But the ministry was continually frustrated in its attempt to serve as a means of racial reconciliation. The ministry's goals committee reported that "the Ministry is forced to walk the tight-rope which history has stretched across the chasm between the races. . . . Christians, knowing the reality of original sin, should not be surprised when rational persuasion proves to be inadequate to convince the possessors of power that they are using their power unjustly. . . . Must it not be said that much of the white criticism of a Ministry that has concentrated on work with the dispossessed is in fact a rejection of a ministry . . . which challenges them to question the structures of prejudice in which they too are prisoners?"[51]

Attempts to integrate previously all-white churches also challenged whites to confront the structure of prejudice that had existed since Reconstruction. Conflicts within white churches intensified when blacks attempted to integrate churches in Jackson as an outgrowth of an ecumenical workshop held at Tougaloo College sponsored by the World Council of Churches. Groups of white and black students tried to attend worship services at several Jackson churches. They were admitted to Lutheran and Episcopal churches but turned away at Presbyterian and Methodist churches, particularly at Galloway Methodist Church, where a handful of white church members joined forces with the students. A Galloway Sunday school class invited a black student to speak to them, but church ushers met the black student, who was accompanied by a white church member, in the church foyer and refused them admission. The confrontation resulted in the arrest of four people, including the church member; at least ten other students and ministers were arrested in the city in October 1963 alone. Dr. W. B. Selah, Galloway's moderate minister, recommended that blacks be allowed to worship, but the church board overruled him, a defeat that contributed to his resignation. By March 1964 the number of arrests had increased to more than thirty. The Reverend Robert Raines, who visited Galloway from Philadelphia, Pennsylvania, found that "the congregation is deeply divided over the fact that their doors are closed to Negroes. . . . This is a matter of terrible anguish for the minority in the church who believe that Christ's church must be open to all people."[52]

One distressed editorialist in the *Mississippi Methodist Advocate* asked, "Why the Methodist Church?" The writer wondered why the Jackson police only made arrests outside Methodist churches. Some churches of other denominations violated state law by allowing blacks to enter, others turned them away, but no arrests followed in either case. The *Mississippi Register*, a Roman Catholic paper, warned that "the police power of the city is overstepping its bounds to an alarming degree," and linked arrests to the Citizens' Council's hostility to Methodism. "Is it mere coincidence," the paper asked, that arrests "followed the White Citizens [*sic*] Council's declared intention to save the churches . . . ?" Mayor Allen Thompson had left the decision to integrate in the hands of the local churches. As the number of visits escalated, however, Methodists charged that Thompson changed his policy under pressure from segregationists. One of the most shocking incidents occurred on Easter Sunday 1964, when two Methodist bishops, one of them black, were barred from entering Galloway, and on the same day seven white ministers and two blacks were arrested at Central Methodist Church. Despite the arrests, the students and their supporters persisted, Sunday after Sunday, year after year. Finally, in January 1966 the board at Galloway voted to admit all persons regardless of race. By that time, local policemen were under injunction and more reluctant to make arrests, and the board found they could not find a minister of the "desired stature" without making the change.[53]

Despite these signs of change, the violence was by no means over. During 1966 and 1967 moderate whites in the Jackson area faced several bombing attacks. One of those bombings was aimed at Dr. Nussbaum. Two other attacks targeted members of an interdenominational Christian renewal group; one of them was Bob Kochtitzky, a Galloway member. Members of a Galloway Sunday school class took out an advertisement expressing their support; they said that he had provoked the attack because "[h]e had kept the integrity of Christian Witness . . . in a society not yet willing to hear such witness. He had taken seriously the convictions that were imparted to him by the teachings of the church. He had dared to go beyond the respectable acquiescence of the polite forms of Christianity that so often characterize the poor witness of most of us." Their sentiments were echoed by the Reverend Warren Hamby, Galloway's minister, in a widely reported statement condemning the bombing. Few Mississippians could condone violence on such a scale, and the Klan's reign of terror came to an end. Its membership fell from about six thousand in 1965 to fewer than five hundred in the wake of the violence. Most observers agreed that by 1967 the mood in the state had shifted, and Mississippi was moving "with understandable anguish into authentic social revolution."[54]

That anguish was nowhere more clearly revealed than in the state's churches. Churches of almost every denomination, black and white, served as battlefields where liberals and conservatives, moderates and extremists fought one another in the state's greatest moral struggle of the twentieth century. In most respects, churches as institutions, whether black or white, failed to exert courageous leadership on civil rights until forced by their members or compelled by events to do so. That some individual members, ministers, and even churches stood on the front lines of freedom cannot be denied, but their bravery only cast the failures of their fellow Christians in sharper relief. The moral struggle went far beyond the churches, however, and the significance of religious belief for integrationists and segregationists cannot be overestimated. Here, in this domain of individual faith, we confront the truly remarkable range of interpretation regarding the most basic tenets of the Christian faith, even in a region so renowned for its religious conformity. Black integrationists and white segregationists alike reached far back into the Christian past as they sought theological support for their beliefs. Out of this dialectic, an overarching consensus emerged among the state's majority, one that rejected once and for all the pernicious curse of Ham and recognized blacks and whites as equal in the sight of God, one that linked the democratic and religious principles of equality. That is not to suggest that Mississippians solved the problems of racism—indeed, that dilemma proved much more enduring—but, nonetheless, the changes of the 1960s were far-reaching and lasting and were cause for some measure of optimism. A Presbyterian writer traveled through the Delta in 1966 and "talked with leaders in the white community, with businessmen, plantation owners, with militant young Negroes and 'Uncle Toms,' with preachers, educators, sales clerks, waitresses, and workers in the National Council of Churches' Delta Ministry. And out of it all came a twisted picture of hate and heartbreak, prejudice and pathos, change and confusion—but hope."[55]

Mississippians, like most Americans, have realized that the virtue, moral fiber and faith on which our country was born are the very remedies we need to keep it alive.

—KIRK FORDICE, FORMER GOVERNOR
OF MISSISSIPPI[1]

We want the homosexuals, the abortion people, the porno kings and the prostitutes to know that they are not welcome in this city. We don't want to become another San Francisco.

—REVEREND MIKE WELLS, MISSISSIPPI
MORAL MAJORITY[2]

Somebody told me the times is hard. "How are we gonna make it?" they ask. "Reagan is making it tough for us; can't get no bread, no money, no jobs. . . ."

—REVEREND T. B. MOORE,
TUNICA, MISSISSIPPI[3]

II Modernists and Traditionalists since the 1970s

As Mississippi enters the twenty-first century, its present and future continue to be bound to its past. The state remains a part of the Bible Belt, and, if recent trends are any indication, the state is becoming more religious, not less. Historian Charles Wilson remarked that "[e]ven though we've seen many changes in the past 30 years—in politics, race relations, the economy—religion shows great continuity."⁴ Statistics show the remarkable increase in church membership over the past several decades. A 1989 poll found that Jackson had more Bible readers than any other place in the country. A Gallup report found that Bible readers were more likely to be fifty or older, Protestant, have a high school education, have a household income under fifteen thousand dollars, and be black.⁵ While demographics may help explain the religious fervor in the state, other forces are clearly also at work. Wilson's observation that the state has faced dramatic changes since the 1960s while religion has grown ever stronger offers one clue in explaining the power of faith in the state, especially when the growth of fundamentalism is taken into account.

Like the rest of the nation, Mississippi has been shaken

by the dramatic "culture wars" that have defined national politics and religion in recent decades. The early 1980s saw the emergence of the twentieth century's second fundamentalist controversy marked by sharp conflict between liberal and moderate Christians on the one hand and conservative and fundamentalist Christians on the other over a group of issues loosely called "family values." Abortion replaced prohibition as the dominant political issue, while the enemies of evolution sought equal time for the teaching of creationism in public schools.[6] Given the predominance of conservatives in Mississippi's religious life, it may seem surprising that culture wars have affected the state at all. In many cases, religious leaders in the state seem to be preaching to the choir when they assail their liberal opponents.

The current conflict between liberal and conservative elements is only the most recent episode in an old story in American Protestantism in which such conflicts have played an elemental role in defining denominational and regional difference. Evangelicals on the Mississippi frontier defined themselves in opposition to elite culture and won a mass following among the common folk of both races; proslavery advocates linked Christianity with the South's most cherished institutions, defended the region against northern attacks, and won a dominant position in southern society; the ministers of the Lost Cause turned defeat into moral victory and led southern churches to an even more dominant position in the region's social and cultural life. Southerners have a long history of seeing themselves as a minority surrounded by a hostile culture, a strategy so successful that it has become a part of the religious culture of the region. Perhaps more than anything else, that strategy has prevented the southern evangelical majority from falling prey to complacency, as often happens to geographically concentrated religious groups.[7]

In January 1970 the Mississippi legislature debated a bill to repeal the state's antievolution law—the only law in the country prohibiting the teaching of evolution in public schools. Despite a 1968 Supreme Court ruling that struck down a similar law in Arkansas, the Mississippi legislators were in a stubborn mood after the high court's rulings on desegregation. Many lawmakers saw the antievolution bill as yet another symbol of traditional values under attack from a liberal court. As one representative said during debate, "Let's hold the line as a Christian state. . . . This is another attempt to chip away at religion."[8] The vote to repeal the measure failed by a wide majority. It was left up to the Mississippi Supreme Court to invalidate the law later that year.

It is highly symbolic that the decade of the 1970s opened with a debate over the teaching of evolution in public schools. Harking back as it did to the famous "monkey trial" that pitted the forces of religious conservatism against modern science, the debate was a harbinger of things to come. The most striking development in American religion since 1970 has been the dramatic rise of Christian conservatism. Though the movement is national in scope, it speaks with a decidedly southern accent. Once again, the historic conflict between religious modernists and traditionalists has reemerged with the rise of the New Christian Right (NCR) as a powerful regional and national force, and Mississippi has provided influential leaders and numerous foot soldiers for the conservative cause. As historian Samuel S. Hill observed, "The emergence of the New Christian Right on the southern scene . . . indicates discontinuity as well as continuity relative to the South's past."[9] The NCR's attachment to "traditional values," particularly those surrounding questions of family and gender such as opposition to abortion, homosexuality, pornography, and the Equal Rights Amendment, has strong appeal to religious traditionalists in the state. Of these issues, the antiabortion position and the condemnation of homosexuality mark a departure from the past. While many religious folk in the state would no doubt have condemned abortion and homosexuality all along, these were not issues of public debate. On the other hand, issues once prominent among religious traditionalists such as prohibition and racial ethics are not part of the NCR's agenda. Another feature of the new religious right that sets it apart from previous movements is that it largely operates outside the religious establishment in the state. The movement draws its strength primarily from members of independent churches and from conservative elements within the mainline denominations, and it is led by a relatively small group of conservative preachers and politicians allied to the right wing of the Republican Party.

The rapid expansion of conservative evangelicalism in the state can be observed through statistics on church membership. A 1971 survey found that 51.1 percent of the state's population worshiped in 4,382 churches comprising 27 denominations. The largest of these denominations was by far the Southern Baptists, with about 679,000 adherents, or 30.7 percent of the state's total population. The United Methodists were a distant second, with about 214,000 adherents, or 9.7 percent of the population. The Catholic Church, with about 83,000 adherents (3.7 percent), and the Presbyterian Church, with about 44,000 adherents (2 percent), rounded out the top four.[10] The same survey conducted in 1990 reveals striking changes. First, the survey found that 70.2 percent of the state's population worshiped in 5,433 churches divided into 51 denominations. This startling increase can be attributed in large measure to the growth of conservative groups not even mentioned in the 1971 survey. With over 869,000 adherents (33.8 percent of the total population), the Southern Baptists continued to dominate the religious landscape; the United Methodists remained virtually stagnant with over 240,000 adherents (9.9 percent); the Catholic Church showed a modest growth with over 94,000 adherents (3.7 percent), while the Presbyterian Church showed a sharp decline to 19,000 adherents (.8 percent). The survey found the largest increase among black Baptists and conservative groups like the Church of Christ, Pentecostal churches such as the Church of God Prophecy and Pentecostal Church of God, and conservative groups like the Seventh-Day Adventists.[11]

Of all the issues associated with the rise of the Christian right, none has been more volatile than the fight over abortion. While most churches have taken an official position on the question, the antiabortion movement is led in large part by extradenominational groups such as Capitol Connection, a Jackson-based antiabortion group, and the radical Christian Action Group founded by Roy McMillan, the state's most famous, or infamous, antiabortion extremist. McMillan is widely linked to national antiabortion extremists including Paul Hill, who murdered Dr. John Bayard Britton outside a Pensacola, Florida, abortion clinic in 1994. In 1994 McMillan estimated that he had spent seven thousand hours protesting outside abortion clinics confronting pregnant women attempting to enter the buildings. According to McMillan, his opposition to abortion grows out of his own experience; as he tells it, "I was abandoned in a shoe box at birth, naked, in the middle of the night, in the middle of winter, on the doorstep of a church in Alexandria, La.," a highly romanticized tale disputed by his adoptive mother in Kosciusko where he spent his childhood.[12]

McMillan is joined in his crusade by his wife, Dr. Beverly McMillan, who opened the first abortion clinic in Jackson in 1974 in the wake of the landmark *Roe v. Wade* case. Dr. McMillan, who had treated scores of women who suffered from incomplete or botched illegal abortions, saw the case as a humane one, and when several Jackson social workers and clergymen asked her to staff the first clinic, she agreed. Once in practice, however, she became increasingly disillusioned with abortion, resigned from the clinic in 1978, and began making antiabortion speeches in local churches. She met her future husband in one of those churches and credits him with changing the way she practices medicine; he convinced her, for example, to stop prescribing birth control of any kind for unmarried women. As a result of her husband's efforts, she often provides free treatment and support to women who decide against abortion. McMillan's Christian Action Group has a mailing list of five thousand names and brings in about a thousand dollars a month in contributions.

The groundwork laid by Roy McMillan encouraged Operation Rescue to make Jackson one of its seven targeted cities across the country in its highly controversial 1993 campaign. In addition, local groups including representatives of over sixty churches held Life Chain demonstrations in Jackson that drew over two thousand protestors who lined up hand-in-hand along a major Jackson thoroughfare. Roy McMillan also spearheaded a campaign to have the state legislature require parental permission for women under the age of eighteen to have an abortion. Such a bill passed with the support of "a crowd of Baptists, Presbyterians, Methodists and Catholics. . . ."[13] The abortion controversy has divided church members. In 1990, for example, Methodist bishop Robert C. Morgan issued a statement that read in part, "In continuity with past Christian teaching, we recognize tragic conflicts of life . . . that may justify abortion, and in such cases support the legal option of abortion under proper medical attention."[14] His statement not only provoked opposition from members of the Methodist Church but led to a prayer vigil organized by Roy McMillan and the Christian Action Group outside the Jackson church headquarters.

Of all the leaders of the NCR in Mississippi, none has garnered more national attention than the Reverend Donald E. Wildmon of Tupelo. The watchdog of network television and the bane of the National Endowment for the Arts, Wildmon is the founder of the National Federation for Decency, which became the American Family Association in 1987. Wildmon grew up in Ripley, where he attended the First United Methodist Church, played football, ran track, and earned a sash full of Boy Scout medals. When he was nine his ambition was to become a missionary to Africa, and by age nineteen he felt a call to the ministry. After rather poor academic performances at Mississippi State University and Millsaps College, he entered the divinity school at Emory University, where he completed the three-year program in two years with solid grades. After his ordination as a Methodist minister he founded the Lee Acres United Methodist Church in Tupelo, and eight years later moved to the First United Methodist Church in Southaven, where he felt his call to a new mission. According to Wildmon, his crusade began in 1978 as he sat watching television with his family; after finding only scenes of adultery, profanity, and violence, he switched off the set, determined to take action. He resigned as pastor of the First United Methodist Church in Southaven and embarked on what appeared to be a quixotic campaign against the network giants. In the spring of 1978 he announced his first boycott, aimed at Sears, which canceled its advertisements on two of the three shows he targeted (the three were *Three's Company*, *Charlie's Angels*, and *All in the Family*).

Following that success Wildmon joined forces with Jerry Falwell, leader of the Moral Majority, to found a new organization called the Coalition for Better Television (CBT), which soon claimed a membership of three million, though that figure was widely disputed, as one-third of the organizations listed as sponsors denied any connection with the group. Again, he scored a major victory when Procter & Gamble withdrew advertising from fifty shows targeted by the group. Despite its success and high visibility, the CBT folded only a year after its organization, when Falwell and Wildmon disagreed over tactics. Wildmon continued his campaign through a new group called Christian Leaders for Responsible Television (CLEAR-TV). For almost a decade he fought such corporate giants as Holiday Inn for showing R-rated movies in hotel rooms and MCA-Universal for releasing Martin Scorsese's *The Last Temptation of Christ*, a campaign that resulted in national picket lines and a huge influx of cash. After another campaign, Southland Corporation, owner of 7-Eleven stores, agreed to remove *Penthouse* and *Playboy* magazines from stores. He attacked Pepsi for a Madonna music video that showed burning crosses. In one of his most widely reported successes, CBS agreed to cut a few seconds from a Mighty Mouse cartoon that Wildmon maintained showed the cartoon rodent sniffing cocaine. By 1990 his highly visible and often successful tactics brought in over five million dollars annually in contributions.

But his victories against corporate America pale beside his most recent campaign against the National Endowment for the Arts. In 1989 a supporter sent Wildmon a newspaper clipping about an art exhibit, funded in part by the NEA, which included works by Andres Serrano. Among the works on display was the now-famous photograph showing a crucifix submerged in Serrano's urine. Wildmon sent copies of the photograph to every member of Congress and then threw his national organization into the fray by encouraging a massive letter-writing campaign that sent out over a million anti-NEA letters. The campaign quickly turned into a "cultural bonfire for the religious right" and drew national attention as congressmen including Senator Alfonse D'Amato of New York and Senator Jesse Helms of North Carolina and public figures including television evangelist Pat Robertson and Oliver North joined in.[15] Supporters of the beleaguered agency such as actress Jessica Tandy and the cellist Yo-Yo Ma appeared before congressional budget reauthorization hearings to plead for continued funding. NEA chairman John E. Frohnmayer, an elder in the Presbyterian Church, attempted to defend the agency by observing that such controversial grants misrepresented the majority of funded projects, but these statements only sent Wildmon in search of other "offensive" grants, including one for the San Francisco Gay and Lesbian Film Festival and a poster showing Jesse Helms nailed to a cross. His campaign kicked off one of the most dramatic political battles of recent memory, and resulted in sharp cuts to the NEA budget.

Despite his dramatic success at the national level, his impact in the state has been more limited. In Tupelo—widely regarded as a progressive, expanding city—Wildmon "elicits great yawns of indifference from many locals," while others fear that his national reputation sends an inaccurate view of the city that could impede its growth and drive away outside investment.[16] The North Mississippi United Methodist Annual Conference refused to endorse a resolution of support for the Coalition for Better Television, and in a 1980 campaign for a seat in the state house of representatives he came in third in a four-man race, with only one thousand votes. Despite his defeat, Wildmon maintained that his campaign did "raise some issues that are major issues in the nation right now."[17]

Wildmon's attack on the NEA for funding homosexual artists and homoerotic art is a case of his agenda merging with a broader NCR agenda that opposes homosexuality. A report that gays in Jackson wanted to organize a Metropolitan Community Church brought a swift response from the state's Moral Majority. A letter from Michael L. Wells, president of the state organization and pastor of Mountainview Baptist Church in Jackson, announced, "HOMOSEXUALS READY TO INVADE JACK-SON!!!" Judging from the tenor of the letter, the city had not faced so great a threat since the Union Army had invaded over a century before. "I know one thing," Wells wrote. "I don't want Jackson to become another San Francisco or Houston. . . . We must alert God-fearing Mississippians statewide about those that would destroy the moral standards of our beloved state and country. . . . I think you know well enough that I will tell it like it is. Whether it be on the dangers of homosexuality, pornography, or the infamous Planned Parenthood, *I will speak the whole truth*."[18] Plans went ahead for the Metropolitan Community Church, though Wells continued to use the issue in letters and speeches and encouraged greater policing of gay districts and the passage of state sodomy laws. Some religious groups attempted to counter such hostility. Integrity Mississippi, a homosexual Episcopal group recognized by the church, expressed "profound alarm and concern" over the Moral Majority's position and criticized the planned media campaign against the Metropolitan Community Church as a violation of religious freedom.[19] In Natchez St. Mary's Catholic Church sponsored a program called "Homosexuality and Us" intended "to help people talk about the . . . reestablishment of relationships . . . providing support and making people see that you love unconditionally."

The controversy over the Metropolitan Community Church paled beside the national furor over the creation of Camp Sister Spirit by Brenda and Wanda Henson on the Mississippi Gulf Coast in 1993. The lesbian couple envisioned turning their 120-acre parcel into a feminist educational and cultural retreat center, but their sexual orientation brought an outcry from local fundamentalists, harassment, and national publicity. Wanda Henson drew on her own faith to defend their goal: "Fundamentalists do not have a right to force their religious understandings on us. Our own religion, Unitarian Universalism, honors our lesbian love and our being loved. For us, being refugees is not an option."[20] The Hensons are still targeted for criticism by conservative groups, but continue their efforts.

The Moral Majority claimed chapters in thirty counties, though its refusal to release membership figures makes its support difficult to gauge. The organization also hired a lobbyist to carry its agenda to the state legislature and claimed to have killed bills requiring compulsory school attendance, which they said interfered with the family and threatened Christian schools, and licensing for Christian children's homes that were exempt from state health and safety regulations. The group also strongly supported an antipornography bill signed into law in 1983.

The Moral Majority was not the only religious body to lobby the legislature. In 1982 Dr. Paul Jones, executive director of the Mississippi Baptist Convention's Christian Action Committee, became a registered lobbyist. The step was part of an effort to address "moral, ethical and social problems that affect the citizens of Mississippi."[21] His appointment signaled a dramatic departure for Southern Baptists who had long defended complete separation of church and state, and also indicated the growing influence of conservatives within the Baptist ranks. As early as 1978 John Baker, associate director of the Baptist Joint Committee on Public Affairs, told the state convention that "[t]he church belongs in politics up to its eyebrows."[22]

By 1984 conservative Baptists were holding independent meetings at the state convention and strongly criticizing the denominational establishment. The sort of major split that divided the denomination's Southern Baptist Convention was averted by lay leader Charles Pickering, a prominent state politician, and by others who saw that conservatives were put on important committees and given a voice in organizing the convention. Tensions continued to fester, however, and the growing alienation between the conservatives and their mainline opponents could not be kept completely out of the state. In 1988 the Reverend John Thomason, pastor of the Northminster Baptist Church in Jackson, was elected president of the twenty-five-thousand-member Southern Baptist Alliance, composed of moderates opposed to conservative control of the Southern Baptist Convention. While Thomason maintained that the alliance was not the nucleus for a new moderate denomination, a Biloxi congregation led by the Reverend Bill Jenkins became the first in the nation aligned with the Southern Baptist Alliance but not with the Southern Baptist Convention. The division also surfaced in 1994 when the board of trustees of Mississippi College, the flagship school for the state's Baptists, amended the school's charter to prevent the Mississippi Baptist Convention from controlling the board. The trustees voted to enlarge the board and to select the majority of members themselves. Board chairman Harry Vickery said that the board took the action to "ensure that Mississippi College can remain true to its Baptist heritage and tradition of serving all Mississippi Baptists and their churches by distancing the college from denominational politics."[23]

Increasingly, grassroots supporters of the NCR took an interest in the political process. In 1980 Dr. William Keller, a Laurel optometrist, led five hundred Mississippians to Washington, D.C., to attend a "Washington for Jesus" rally. Keller said, "We are concerned about the drift of society as a whole away from the Christian principles this country was founded on. We are opposed to humanism, to this whole anti-God trend that if it feels good, do it." He carried a petition signed by two thousand voters that read in part, "[W]e determine to become more knowledgeable concerning the candidates and issues using our votes thereby." Frances Gilmore, state women's coordinator, said that the group came to the nation's Capitol at an hour of grim national crisis evidenced by schools that taught sex without morality, a federal welfare system that encouraged able-bodied people not to work, the threat of the Equal Rights Amendment, and a judiciary that opposed school prayer. She said, "[W]e're still God-fearing, God forbid we should ever be subject to the wilds of urban living."[24]

Recently, more sophisticated public policy organizations including the Mississippi Family Council (MFC) have entered the political fray. The MFC's goal is "to rebuild respect for the family in our society and to assist government policy-makers in assessing the impact of their actions on the families of Mississippi." The group focuses its attention on a variety of conservative issues including welfare reform, family tax relief, education reforms such as home schooling and school vouchers, parental rights, crime prevention, and opposition to same-sex marriages. The MFC made opposition to same-sex marriages a major legislative initiative in 1996, and

Kirk Fordice, who was then governor, issued an executive order banning same-sex marriages in the state. With members of the MFC by his side, the governor called gay marriages "an absurdity" and pledged to "preserve and protect the special status of marriage." Following the passage of a ban by the state legislature, Fordice signed a prohibition into law. "For too long in this freedom-loving land, cultural subversives have engaged in trench warfare on traditional family values," he announced. A few of the governor's critics observed that he was recovering from an automobile accident suffered while returning from a meeting with an unidentified woman out of state, the beginning of an escalating scandal, widely reported in the national media, that raised serious questions about his dedication to family values.[25]

One of the issues dividing modernists and traditionalists is the role of women in the church and in society. Mississippi Baptists debated the status of women in their 1984 state convention, and a resolution was proposed that said women could not be ordained as ministers or pastors, but that resolution was a nonbinding one, leaving the decision up to individual churches. In that same year, the nationwide Southern Baptist Convention adopted a resolution reminding women that Eve was the first to sin and that they should therefore remain silent in the churches and be submissive to men. John Thomason, leader of the Baptist moderates, has been a forceful advocate for the ordination of women. Drawing on a very different interpretation of Scripture, Thomason argued that the Bible was written in a patriarchal culture but that Jesus accepted the ministry of women. He expressed his belief that "on the basis of Scripture . . . God is gender blind. . . . The church today is on the horns of a dilemma. It wants to take the Bible seriously, but the Bible does not speak with a single voice."[26] The state's first female Southern Baptist ministers were Marian Young Talley and Ida M. Allen, both black women, ordained at the biracial North Jackson Baptist Church in 1991. These women struggled against the sort of theology that denied women ordination, Talley saying that she had once shared that belief: "I was once there too. . . . I've been in the Baptist church all my life, and like others I was taught that women just did not preach." The Reverend Bill Patrick, the black minister who ordained the women, said, "How can I question what God calls [them] to do?"[27]

The Reverend Amzie Cotton, a black preacher who brought his

Greater True Vine Holiness Baptist Church into the Mississippi Baptist Convention in 1984, also endorsed the ordination of women. When he left the pulpit at Greater True Vine to assume a position as bishop in the United Congress of Churches, his wife, Mary Cotton, replaced him. He established the Amzie Cotton School of Ministry to train and license women ministers, and observed, "I believe God gave me this ministry to help his women. . . . Women have been laboring in the gospel for a long time. It is hypocritical to say that God did not call women to the ministry."[28]

The issue also divided the Episcopal Church when Bishop Duncan Gray, veteran of the civil rights movement of the 1960s, commissioned a statewide study of women in the priesthood in 1975. The Reverend Colton Smith spoke for supporters of the ordination of women when he argued that "[a] priest at the altar represents all humanity—not just the male half of it. . . . The image of God is both male and female. . . ." The Reverend Norvel Yerger argued against women in the priesthood in terms the NCR would have found familiar, saying, "It simply does not fit in the same way it would be unappropriate [*sic*] to ask John Wayne to be in a movie in the role of Racquel Welch. . . . The sexual drama of creation will have been abandoned. . . . The husband has authority over his wife just as Christ had authority over the church."[29]

When the General Convention of the Episcopal Church approved the ordination of women at its 1976 meeting, a group of Mississippi priests vehemently opposed the move and organized the Churchmen for Apostolic Faith and Order (CAFO) to express their concerns. Again, CAFO represented their opposition to the move in terms strikingly similar to those of the evangelical right. The Reverend Thomas H. Waggener outlined the CAFO position in an address before the 150th Annual Council of the Diocese of Mississippi in January 1977:

> As we see it, a bare majority of the Delegates to General convention did not merely buy women's ordination, but they bought a package deal. . . . [W]hat is the package[?] . . . We have seen three deranged and irresponsible bishops illegally ordaining a group of women. . . . [P]riesthood is a sacrifice. . . . [I]t most certainly is not a bunch of self-centered, crazy women talking about their rights. . . . Will this parade of lunatic bish-

ops, perverse priests, and bizarre women never end! . . . We have the spectacle of the lesbian ordination of Ms. Barrett. . . . We have had an Episcopal priest preside at what was alleged to be the marriage of two men. . . . We have the delightful spectacle of an Episcopal priest preside at the 7th marriage of Elizabeth Taylor. . . . We see the refusal of the Church to condemn abortion as a means of birth control. . . . We are against women ordination, but the main thing we are against is the overthrow of the Bible as a standard of Christian faith and morals.[30]

A conscience clause allows bishops to refuse to ordain women priests, a course adopted by John M. Allin of Mississippi, who became presiding bishop in 1974.[31]

The rise of fundamentalism has also posed problems for the Catholic Church in the state. On the one hand, the Catholic Church shares part of the NCR agenda, opposition to abortion being the most striking example. Catholics cooperated with the NCR to push for restrictions on abortion by the state legislature, and in Natchez, for example, St. Mary's served as the meeting place for the Natchez Right to Life organization that reached out to conservative Christians in other denominations. But despite some common goals, the Catholic Church has been less comfortable with other aspects of the NCR platform. The Reverend Bill Cullen of St. Richard Catholic Church in Jackson outlined his fears about the rising tide of religious conservatism: "Fundamentalism, largely through TV evangelists, is coming to affect how we regard progress, human rights, just a widespread influence across the board. It's dangerous to mix a dogmatic religious approach to something that's a cultural or social problem. Fundamentalists are anti-feminists, pro-military and would do away with welfare. They want to enforce their code on everyone."[32]

Cullen's charge that fundamentalists were antifeminists was accurate, as earlier examples have demonstrated, but perhaps the Catholic Church was not in the best position to cast stones at that sensitive issue. In 1986 about a hundred Catholic women met at St. Richard, Cullen's own church, to express their frustrations over their status within the church. Arlene Rosner Barwick, who chaired the meeting, reported that "[w]omen want to be in decision-making positions, they want to be considered as thinking entities. . . . They represent more than 50 percent of the church and they want their voices heard. They don't want just celibate men making policy." The church's stance on abortion and birth control also came under fire; Barwick summed up the women's position by saying, "Women want the word on their own bodies."[33]

Of all the issues promoted by the NCR, perhaps none has been more heated than prayer in public schools, and here again Mississippi has been at the center of controversy. The 1993 case involving Bishop Knox, principal of Wingfield High School in south Jackson, garnered national headlines and provoked massive rallies in the state. The uproar began after students voted by a margin of 490 to 96 to have a prayer read over the school's public address system every morning. Deputy superintendent John Sanders told Knox not to allow the reading of a prayer over the public address system, but Knox permitted Kim Fails, the student body president, to do so. Following that act, Knox was fired by the superintendent, Ben Canada. The dismissal provoked an outpouring of support for Knox from across the state. About three hundred students walked out of classes at Tupelo High School to pray and sing hymns as a sign of support, and similar walkouts and rallies took place at Hattiesburg, Magee, Forest Hill, and other schools around the state. A statewide rally held a few weeks later drew over five thousand people to the state capitol. The Reverend Donald Wildmon provided Knox with legal counsel through his American Family Association Law Center.

Black ministers also organized their own rally at the state capitol in support of school prayer (Knox is African American). Reverend Hosea Hines, pastor of the five-hundred-member College Hill Baptist Church near the campus of Jackson State University, declared that "America needs revival. . . . America is suffering spiritually. We realize everybody has rights, but we have rights, too." Bea Branch, president-elect of the state National Association for the Advancement of Colored People (NAACP) said that the debate over prayer in public schools would bring closer cooperation between blacks and whites. "You are seeing the beginning of a new era in Mississippi," she optimistically announced.[34] The conservative Republican governor, Kirk Fordice, echoed her sentiments. He contrasted the biracial support for prayer in public schools with the divisions that had existed between the races thirty years before; he pointed out that black and white Mississippians were "joining hands, walking out and marching forward, together, for a common belief that is slowly sweeping America. That common belief is that there is a direct correlation between the systematic degradation of traditional, religious values and our country's eversicker social soul. . . . This national movement has begun in Mississippi centering around the issue of school prayer—but it is so much bigger than just prayer. . . . Mississippians, like most Americans, have realized that the virtue, moral fiber and faith on which our country was born are the very remedies we need to keep it alive."[35]

The state once again made national headlines over the issue of prayer in public schools when United States district court judge Neal Biggers ruled in 1996 that student-led intercom prayers and Bible history classes conducted at the North Pontotoc Attendance Center were unconstitutional. The judge did allow students to meet before school for prayer and Bible study provided that these were student-initiated and student-led and that parents signed a consent form. He also accepted a curriculum for an ancient Middle East history class, which had won approval from the Mississippi Department of Education. The court ordered that in such a course students must have readings from sources other than the Bible and must be exposed to historical analysis, and that religious doctrine must not be a part of the course. He also left the door open for the school district to hire Bible teachers with funds raised by an alliance of community churches so long as teachers were not hired based on their own religious beliefs. Supporters of school prayer, without a trace of irony, posted red, white, and blue signs bearing the slogan "Religious Freedom" in front of houses and businesses in town and emblazoned the message on T-shirts and bumper stickers. Lisa Herdahl, the Pontotoc County mother of six who had filed suit in 1994, argued that parents had the sole right to control the religious education of their children, an argument that Judge Biggers accepted.

Clearly, school prayer was one issue that brought black and white evangelicals together, but could the NCR's conservative religious agenda really provide a common ground for black and white Mississippians? Like Catholics, African American evangelicals have an uneasy relationship with the NCR. While many blacks agree with some NCR positions such as support for school prayer and opposition to abortion, the right-wing political agenda endorsed by the NCR makes any close cooperation difficult if not impossible.

Beginning in the late 1960s and 1970s, blacks and whites in the state made concerted efforts to cooperate across the racial divide. The proposed merger of the Methodist Church and the Evangelical United Brethren Church in the late 1960s brought racial tensions to the surface, since the merger included a plan to break down the Methodist Church's racial structure. The church was divided into six jurisdictions; five were regional, but the sixth was made up of all black Methodist churches in the country. Under the new scheme, black churches would join formerly segregated conferences if both the church and conference approved. In 1967 Methodist conferences across the country voted on the proposal. The north Mississippi conference rejected the elimination of the all-black central jurisdiction by a vote of 170 to 123; according to one delegate, the plan was "the first step toward integration in Mississippi." Delegates to the south Mississippi conference, however, gave the plan their overwhelming endorsement with a vote of 271 to 15. As one leader in the south conference pointed out, if this voluntary plan were rejected, a proposal less palatable to white southern Methodists might be the result. Combined with strong support in other parts of the South and across the country, the merger plan went forward, and the United Methodist Church was created in 1968. The national church's reputation for liberalism on racial issues continued to cause problems in the state. For example, in 1983 many white Mississippi Methodists protested national Methodist support of the United League of Holmes County, a black activist organization, and both conferences in the state passed resolutions calling on the church to stop that support. The national church responded with a plan to give local congregations more control over which non-Methodist organizations received funding. On a brighter note, black district superintendents have served successfully over white churches. The Reverend Bill Watkins, a white minister, chose to serve the predominantly black Vicksburg Wesley United Methodist Church in the 1990s because, he said, "If we are to make it in this country, we have to come together as one people."[36]

Black and white Baptists took early steps toward greater cooperation. With 640,000 white Baptists and 400,000 black Baptists in the state, numbers that dwarfed their nearest competitors, biracial cooperation held out the promise of considerable influence. As Early Kelly, secretary of the Mississippi Baptist Convention (MBC) said, "If blacks and whites join together in a united Christian front, Baptists can control the moral and religious climate of this state."[37] In 1975 Baptists created the Cooperative Ministries Program to sponsor joint efforts. Richard Brogan, director of the program, outlined a theological basis for such cooperation that reverberated with the egalitarian spirit of the early evangelicals, a theology that emphasized the unity of the human family, the universality of God's love, and the redemptive power of faith. Brogan said, "I dream that this department will be able to construct the bridge called TRUST between these major denominations in Mississippi. As I see it, 300 years of history have broken down almost every redemptive communication between these communities. National and Southern Baptists have substituted a painted smile and a cold handshake for the realities of a kindred spirit."[38]

Four years later Brogan saw signs of progress, saying that "we have moved far beyond surface progress, and we are recognizing each other's strengths and weaknesses. . . . [W]e are all realizing more and more . . . that America is a mosaic of different races and cultures, and lifestyles, rather than a melting pot to blend them all together."[39] One of the most ambitious efforts at biracial cooperation was the "Good News Mississippi" campaign launched by black and white Baptists in the state in 1979. The effort was coordinated by a biracial committee with representatives from the white Southern Baptist Convention and from most of the nine black national Baptist conventions in the state. The first major event of the campaign was a statewide rally of 312 black and white Baptist women. As the women met in small groups, they found common ground; Martha Nelson, wife of a Southern Baptist preacher, reported that "[d]escribing ourselves in terms of our families, our work and our participation in church and denomination life, I was reminded how very much we have in common. . . . As we shared something of our spiritual pilgrimage, I found the list of what we have in common growing lengthy indeed."[40] A statewide rally held in Jackson in March 1979 kicked off a month of simultaneous revivals in black and white Baptist churches across the state.

In a more controversial move, the MBC has offered financial assistance to new black congregations that affiliate with the overwhelmingly white group. By 1990 twelve black churches scattered across the state, from Gulfport and Biloxi on the Gulf Coast to McComb and Picayune in the south to Clarksdale and Greenville in the Delta and to Tupelo in the north, had joined the Southern Baptist Convention. Through the Cooperative Missions Department of the MBC, Brogan has supplied trailers as meeting places for new churches at a cost of fifty thousand dollars each. The trailers were provided for two to three years, after which time the MBC provided funds to purchase property and construct a permanent house of worship. The Reverend Amzie Cotton, whose support of women preachers was noted earlier, was among the first black preachers to affiliate with the MBC. Cotton, like other blacks who affiliated with the MBC, also maintained affiliations with predominately black denominations. Given his plan to start a congress of Holiness Baptist churches, Cotton's position within the MBC was suspect; the Hinds-Madison Baptist Association reported that Cotton had not filed the annual reports required of member churches, though Cotton maintained that "[n]o one can run me out of what God put me in."[41] The Reverend David Matthews, president of the black General Baptist State Convention of Mississippi, bristled at the financial inducements offered by the MBC, assistance that the financially strapped black conventions simply could not match. For Matthews, the financial assistance only allowed congregations and young ministers to avoid the hard lessons of building a new church from the ground up. "I had no one to give me funds for a church," he said. "I got where I am by years of sacrifices and commitment to the cause. Everything was not handed to me on a silver platter."[42]

Genuine biracial worship has been less successful and, indeed, has seldom been a goal of either black or white Baptists. When the Cooperative Ministries Program began in 1975, both black and white ministers emphasized that biracial worship was not one of their aims. "[W]hite Baptist ministers don't want blacks flocking to their churches. The pastors say black culture and flavor would be lost in the dominant white congregations. And Southern Baptists say they no longer have the ministers and personnel to staff black churches."[43] The state's only biracial Southern Baptist church, the North Jackson Baptist Church, has struggled to survive. Located in a neighborhood in transition, the church once had four hundred white members and prohibited blacks from entering the church, but as the surrounding neighborhood shifted from white to black, the membership dropped, and the congregation decided to work toward integration. But with only thirty members, the church struggled to repay a ninety-five-thousand-dollar interest-free loan provided by the Hinds-Madison Baptist Association. The Reverend J. W. Bristol, director of missions for the association, predicted that the church would not succeed as a biracial congregation and would eventually be all black.

One of the state's most prominent spokesmen for racial cooperation was John Perkins, founder of the Voice of Calvary Ministries, and "widely regarded as evangelical Christianity's foremost advocate of racial reconciliation, as well as a pioneer in blending social action with spreading the Gospel."[44] Perkins, a native of New Hebron, Mississippi, grew up poor and left school sometime between the third and fifth grades. After a local law enforcement officer shot and killed his older brother, a veteran of World War II, in the summer of 1946 under dubious circumstances, Perkins vowed to leave the state and never return. He moved to California a year later, married, and prospered, but after his conversion in 1957 he heard a call to return to his native state. He and his family moved to Mendenhall, where they began working with children, organized a Head Start program for Simpson County, and held Bible classes under a large tent. He also confronted the problems of substandard housing, inadequate health care, poor nutrition, and lack of educational and employment opportunities through an organization he founded in 1964 called Voice of Calvary Ministries (VOC). Perkins quickly realized that prayer was not enough: "Our oppression was a political oppression. . . . You could pray all day and they wouldn't move. Within a democratic society, we would have to participate in that society to make changes."[45] Actively involved in the civil rights movement, Perkins was one of three VOC leaders jailed after a civil rights march in Mendenhall February 7, 1970. Perkins and others were brutally beaten after their arrest, an experience that transformed him: "I began to see . . . what hate could do. It had turned . . . [the officers] into less than human beings. They had been told that just being white had meaning, but . . . in order to feel a sense of worth, they had to brutalize us. . . . I made a covenant with the Lord, that if He would allow me to come out of that jail alive, I would try to preach a Gospel that would confront whites and blacks equally calling them to Jesus Christ that would burn through race and culture and make us one. . . ."[46] The VOC in

Mendenhall quickly grew to include a thrift store, a health center operated by a New York City physician, a cooperative auto garage, a preschool program, adult literacy programs, Bible classes, a community gymnasium, and the Simpson County Housing Cooperative, which had built ten duplexes by 1980.

When Reagan budget cuts forced the Mendenhall office of the Central Mississippi Legal Services to close, the VOC kept it open as the Community Law Office. Staffed by Chicago native Suzanne Griggins and by Jesse Griffin, a native of nearby D'Lo who had participated in VOC programs as a youth, the office handles cases involving food stamps, Social Security disability payments, and other poverty law cases. Griggins and Griffin also conduct "Poor People's Law School" in interested churches in the county, where the two spend five nights lecturing on criminal, consumer, and land law. More broadly, the office has filed suit to reopen a 1971 desegregation case in Simpson County and is also working on a proposal to require county aldermen to be elected by wards rather than at large, a change that would give representation to the county's 37 percent black population.

The VOC moved its headquarters in 1973 to Jackson, where it has continued to grow and prosper. A centerpiece of the VOC program is Thriftco, a thrift-store cooperative, where one-third of the profits are returned to co-op members (memberships cost five dollars), one third is returned as dividends to investors, and the remaining one third is devoted to funding VOC community projects. The VOC is also involved in neighborhood revitalization projects in Jackson's depressed inner city. For instance, the VOC purchased a building that was in use as a bar and was a center of drug dealing and criminal activity in a run-down area known as "the flats." The building was renovated as a community center that will serve as the site for Good News Christian Club meetings, family and financial counseling services, educational workshops, and other standard VOC outreach services. The center served as the hub for a broader revitalization effort; the VOC also purchased over twenty dilapidated houses in the area, which will be restored and sold to low-income residents. About six hundred volunteers work for VOC every year, and its annual budget now exceeds one million dollars.

The VOC even attracted the attention of Pat Robertson, who person-

ally visited Jackson to inaugurate a "Heads Up" literacy program in cooperation with VOC. A VOC official explained that "CBN [Robertson's TV
ministry] is offering us a low-budget way to get an accelerated, comprehensive literacy program. They've underwritten the program and are
helping us get it started. We see that it could help a lot of people."[47] Many
people expressed their surprise that VOC would make common cause with
Robertson, but the VOC was careful to make a public disclaimer that
"Voice of Calvary does not endorse all of Pat Robertson's political
stands. . . ."[48]

In 1980 Perkins received an award from the Mississippi Religious
Leadership Conference, an honor he shared with Governor William Winter. He also was given an honorary degree by Wheaton College in Illinois,
the highly regarded evangelical college where he frequently spoke to ap-
preciative audiences. Perkins's dramatic conversion to Christianity manifested itself in a newfound ability to "think creatively and develop means
of helping the poor community." His untimely death in 1998 at the age
of forty-three was a tragic loss for the state. Wayne Gordon, cofounder
with Perkins of the Christian Community Development Association, cred-
ited Perkins with forging "the most dynamic, deepest, strongest black-
white relationship in the country—there's none like it." As part of a long
tradition of self-help in the black community born out of an ethic of mutu-
ality forged under slavery, the VOC is an inspiring example of grassroots
organization, empowerment, and social outreach, and Perkins's "call to a
radical grace among the races" may hold out Mississippi's best hope for
true racial reconciliation.[49]

Founded by Bishop Luke Edwards of the Christ Temple Pentecostal
Church in Meridian, the VOC, Reach, Inc., is a remarkable network of
self-help enterprises. Edwards recalls a Sunday morning when he looked
out over his congregation of two hundred people and realized that probably 95 percent of them were on public assistance: "They were waiting for
someone to deliver them, instead of delivering themselves. Some of them
were second-generation welfare families. Their minds had been pro-
grammed to handouts." Edwards believed, however, that these seemingly
impoverished blacks actually possessed considerable economic power that
could be harnessed to transform them into producers rather than consum-
ers. Like Perkins, Edwards had clearly been gifted with the ability to think

creatively. He set up an informal grocery store at the church, won approval
from state authorities to accept food stamps, contracted with local whole-
salers to purchase goods on credit, and then sold the goods in the cooperative at heavily discounted prices. Within a few months, the cooperative
had enough capital to purchase a supermarket. Reach members sold pea-
nuts and candy apples on the streets of Meridian to raise additional funds
that were used to buy two fast-food outlets, farmland, and farm equipment
sold at foreclosure. Continuing to work on a cooperative basis, the company pooled assets and labor and reinvested virtually all the profits into
new businesses. Within a few years the company had expanded its holdings
into a twenty-million-dollar empire that included three family restaurants,
a steel fabricating plant, two auto-parts stores, two garages, a used-car
dealership, a frozen-food packaging plant, a restaurant-equipment supply
firm, a theater, almost half the stock in the First Commerce Bank of Jackson, two meat-processing plants that supply the company restaurants, and
fifteen farms totaling over four thousand acres, including one of the
South's most successful hog-raising farms, which provide meat for the
processing plants.

Such economic success has not come without controversy and criticism. At the center of Reach, Inc., lies Holyland, a cooperative, communal
village of 250 people a short distance across the Alabama line. Based on
Edwards's vision of an Israeli kibbutz, the community is governed by strict
Pentecostal rules and hard work. Adults work twelve-to-eighteen-hour
days on the cooperative farms and earn no salary; food, clothing, and housing are provided by the cooperative, and any profits are funneled back into
Reach, Inc., for investment. Local white business owners and farmers who
compete with Reach have accused Edwards of operating a cult, and in
1990 the Alabama Department of Industrial Relations cited Holyland
Farms with 129 violations of child labor laws. Edwards, who grew up as
the son of a sharecropper in Florence, Alabama, and understood the value
of a day's work, agreed to comply with child labor laws but vowed to teach
children "the value of workfare, not welfare."[50]

Edwards lives modestly in a twenty-foot trailer home and is not likely
to be compared to the Reverend Sun Myung Moon or Jim Jones. In 1991
a former secretary and her husband won a $650,000 settlement against
Edwards for allegedly committing sexual battery and "mind control." Ed-

wards, who appealed the verdict, said that the couple was "manipulated by our adversaries in the white Mississippi establishment." His contention is supported by Elizabeth Wright, New York editor of *Issues and Views*, a newsletter that follows self-help black enterprises nationwide. After an "exhaustive investigation" she concluded that the charges resulted from "a vicious alliance by jealous adversaries." Edwards understood that "[t]he bigger we get, the more vulnerable we are to rock-throwing. We recognize this as an attempt to break our concentration, but we've got to go on building something our children can thrive on instead of blaming someone else because they're poor."[51]

A slightly different vision of community outreach inspires Bishop Phillip Coleman, pastor of the Greater Bethlehem Temple Apostolic Faith Church in Jackson. One of the largest and fastest-growing congregations in the state, the fourteen-hundred-member congregation, up from one hundred fifty members fourteen years ago, recently constructed a three-million-dollar church with a seating capacity of three thousand. According to Bishop Coleman, the church seeks to minister to both spiritual and physical needs. To that end Greater Bethlehem owns about fifteen houses rented to needy families and students at Jackson State University, an insurance agency, and a tax service.

Perkins, Edwards, and Coleman are examples of forceful black religious leaders who have found innovative ways to address the serious economic and social problems that confront blacks in the state. It should be noted that all three of them operate outside the traditional black churches, although their tactics and theology are clearly drawn from the black historical experience. The Great Migration of blacks from the rural South to northern industrial cities brought dramatic changes to the black churches. This trend is most visible in the Delta, where over thirty-three thousand nonwhites left the region between 1970 and 1980. Once centered in the plantation districts, black churches in those areas folded as more and more blacks left rural areas. Statistics from Baptist churches in the Mississippi Delta reveal the depth of this transformation. In Bolivar County in 1906 there were 8,594 members of churches affiliated with the National Baptist Convention; in 1990 6,458 blacks belonged to all-black Baptist churches in the county; in Sharkey County, National Baptist churches reported 2,806 members in 1906 while all-black Baptist churches reported only 1,605 members in 1990.[52]

In county after county, the story has been the same: young blacks abandoned the depressed region, leaving behind an older, poorer community. The Reverend J. M. Roach, pastor of the Glover Grove Baptist Church near Walls, Mississippi, on the northern edge of the Delta, recalled, "There was a time when the churchyard would be so crowded after services that you couldn't move around there."[53] By 1976 the once-overcrowded church had only twelve regular members, many of them elderly, who could no longer afford to keep the leaky, sagging structure in repair. The Holly Grove Baptist Church, located on a plantation near Cary, Mississippi, once had more members than could fit inside the church. Mrs. Julia Thomas, who has attended the church since 1907, said, "It's not nothin' like it was. . . . We used to have services on Sunday night, and you couldn't get in for all the people. Now, none of the churches are open at night."[54] Along with reducing the number of services, some churches responded by combining their shrinking congregations; for example, three churches near Blanton merged to survive. The weakened black churches were left to minister to impoverished black communities increasingly characterized by "dislocation, disparity, and dependence."[55] Across the Delta, a higher percentage of the population lived below the poverty line than anywhere else in the state (53 percent in Tunica County, for example, in 1988), government transfer payments were the chief source of income, and poor health conditions rivaled and sometimes even surpassed those in third world countries.

In this setting, the churches serve as a rock in a weary land. Clifton L. Taulbert, who grew up in Glen Allan, wrote about the church in his moving memoir:

> It was closer to our hearts than our homes—the colored church. It was more than an institution, it was the very heartbeat of our lives. Our church was all our own, beyond the influence of whites, with its own societal structure. . . . [F]ield hands were ushers, mothers of the church, or trustees. The church transformed the ordinary into an institution of social and economic significance. Our lives centered around the colored church. It provided the framework for civic involvement,

the backdrop for leadership, a safe place for social gatherings, where our babies were blessed, our families married and our dead respected. Yes, the colored church became the sanctuary for our dreams and the closet for our secrets.[56]

However humble they might appear, these "Cottonfield Cathedrals"[57] served as the focal point of a vibrant black culture and community.

Given the centrality of music in the African American religious tradition and the rich musical heritage of blacks in Mississippi, it is no surprise that the state has continued to produce some of the most renowned gospel singers in contemporary American sacred music. Gospel music has provided talented black performers with a respected means of improving their skills without special training, an opportunity to travel and earn an income and recognition when many other avenues of advancement were closed, and a means of publicly professing their deep faith.[58] Among the most successful of the Mississippi gospel groups are the Southernaires, formed in Jackson in 1942 and still actively performing, having had many changes of performers. Over the years the group has recorded over a dozen albums, all of which have landed on *Billboard* magazine's Top 10 list of gospel hits. By the 1980s the group commanded anywhere from three thousand to six thousand dollars per performance. Like many of the more successful gospel groups, the Southernaires have been approached by commercial labels to sing blues or soul music, but they remain firmly committed to their gospel message. Indeed, while justifiably proud of their success, gospel groups like the Southernaires have not been motivated by a desire for fame; for these performers, music is another form of witness for the Lord. Frank Williams, a twenty-year veteran with the Southernaires—their lead singer, manager, and guitarist—is the son of Leon Williams, a farmer and bricklayer who discovered that his sons had a remarkable gift for music and formed the Williams Brothers. Frank began performing as a child and stood on a chair to do his solos. He said, "We've been blessed. . . . We're singing for God. . . . We learned early that God is everything. . . . We give God all the praise. . . . To be successful, you must be humble."[59]

That same spirit animates the most acclaimed gospel group in the state, the Mississippi Mass Choir, no doubt in part because the choir was organized by Frank Williams. He attributes the inspiration for the choir to divine influence. "It's a vision that God gave to me," he said. In 1988 Williams enlisted the assistance of David Curry, a Jackson songwriter, and Leon Williams issued a call for auditions from his gospel program on a McComb radio station. Soon cassette tapes came pouring in from across the state. "They came from everywhere," recalled the Reverend Ben Cone, the choir's spiritual advisor, and soon Williams had assembled a remarkably talented group of singers from around the state. The singers were people like Lillian Lilly, a resident of Brookhaven, who worked on an assembly line in a lawn mower company. As the child of a preacher in Sontag, Mississippi, Lilly began singing gospel at the age of ten. She wed in 1970, became the mother of three children, performed with a group called the Traveling Stars, and had a career as a solo artist. When people asked what she charged to sing, she replied, "Whatever you might give." She explained that "I've never been a person to charge for this gift. . . . I can't read a note. Everything you see comes from the Lord." The auditions took place at the Jackson studios of Malaco Records, which signed the choir to a contract.[60]

The choir, which numbers from fifty-five to eighty members, set out across the state to Tupelo, Columbus, and Vicksburg. The size varies, since the teachers, students, homemakers, policewomen, and factory workers who make up the group cannot always get time off from their regular jobs. Their first album, entitled *The Mississippi Mass Choir*, was recorded at the Jackson City auditorium before an audience of three thousand, while another fifteen hundred were turned away at the doors. The album, from an unknown group and a minor studio, shot to the number-one position on *Billboard*'s gospel chart in five short weeks and stayed there for a record-setting forty-nine weeks, a record that brought them a special achievement award from the magazine. The group's second album, *It Remains to Be Seen*, spent fifty-three weeks in the number-one position. Their rapid success is easy for Williams to explain. "This is God's choir," he said simply. "God anointed this choir."[61]

As important as the music and the success have been, the choir still sees its mission as a ministry. They shun the word "concert," for example, and prefer to call their performances "services." Their service ends with a long sermon that usually has the altar crowded with converts. Their official motto is "Serving God through song," a vision that steadily guides the group. The Reverend Milton Biggham, a gospel singer, songwriter, and producer in New York City said, "I have worked with choirs all over America and there is something special about the Mississippi Mass Choir. . . . I have come to the conclusion that the difference is in the attitude of the people involved. This choir minors in music and majors in ministry."[62] Jimmy Anthony, program director for WOAD, one of three full-time gospel radio stations in Jackson, reached the same conclusion about the choir's motivation: "As far as I can remember, from the first album, the choir had taken its ministry seriously. It's no show or performance for them. They want to reach some soul for Christ."[63] In their tours across America the choir attempts to change perceptions about the Magnolia State and its racist, discriminatory, and violent past; as Lilly said, "It is really up to us to bury that legacy. . . . It is up to us, when we go out of state, to show them the new Mississippi."[64] When he was governor, Ray Mabus presented the choir with the Heritage Award (one of the Governor's Awards for Excellence in the Arts) for their work as ambassadors for the state.

Unfortunately, the state's tragic legacy is a difficult one to escape, and the new Mississippi remains tied to its past, a link revealed in the many cases of arson against African American churches in the 1990s. As during the Reconstruction period and the civil rights era, black churches in Mississippi and across the South once more went up in flames. Before church arson became a matter of national concern in 1996, churches in Mississippi were being put to the torch, usually by young white racists. In 1993 three white teenagers were sentenced to four years in federal prison, ordered to pay $138,000 in restitution, and required to write ten-page reports on the civil rights movement after they were convicted of burning two black churches, the Springhill Freewill Baptist Church and the Rocky Point Missionary Baptist Church near Smithdale. The teens lit the fires on April 4, the anniversary of the assassination of Dr. Martin Luther King, Jr., and shouted racial epithets as the flames rose. For many blacks in the area the fires rekindled memories of the 1960s when such occurrences were commonplace in the area; Bernice Dixon, whose uncle was lynched in 1922 and lies buried in the Rocky Point church cemetery, said, "When this happened, it scared people and it still scares them." Following the blazes, about a hundred fifty volunteers, black and white, from thirty-eight churches helped rebuild the Springhill Church with funds raised by dona-tions. Though such interracial cooperation stood in stark contrast to the situation in the 1960s when law enforcement and others in the white pop-ulation turned a blind eye to such cases, the fires indicate the depth of racism in the state. Frank Lee, a leader in the Rocky Point church, said, "The idea you hear is that Mississippi has moved away from much of the hatred of the past. . . . But beneath the surface, the same hatred that was present then, is present today."[65]

In June 1996 two black churches, the Mount Pleasant Missionary Bap-tist Church and the Central Grove Baptist Church, located near Kossuth in the northeastern portion of the state, went up in flames on the same night within minutes of one another. While many residents of both races found it difficult to believe that the fires were set by local residents, others pointed out that a Ku Klux Klan rally had been held on the steps of the nearby Corinth courthouse only two months before. Still, a small group of blacks and whites countered the KKK rally with a prayer vigil, and the Lighthouse Foundation, a local multiracial religious group, raised over twenty-two thousand dollars to help rebuild the churches and offered a five-thousand-dollar reward for the arrest of the culprits.[66] While the cases of arson indicate that racial hatreds continue to fester, the level of interra-cial cooperation involved in rebuilding the churches offers hope for the state's future. W. A. Mathis, a black restaurant owner, compared the racial climate of the 1960s to the 1990s. "I was here in the 1960s," he said. "All the bombing and church burning and what have you, I was here. And this is different altogether, as different than daylight and dark. There's room for improvement. But it's 90 percent better than it used to be."[67]

Another bright spot of racial cooperation was Mission Mississippi, or-ganized in 1992 in Jackson by over one hundred pastors of both races. The group planned a dramatic rally for October 1993 at the city's sports sta-dium, and it was attended by thousands of people of both races. The Rev-erend Hosea Hines, a board member for the group, saw the mission as a path to racial reconciliation. In his view, the biracial, interdenominational group could serve to "bring harmony among sisters and brothers in the state of Mississippi." He said, "I believe Mission Mississippi is providence. As we look at the rest of the country and how it views our state, what better place is there to start a project like this than Mississippi?"[68]

Perhaps the most surprising departure from traditional values in contemporary Mississippi is the rise of casino gambling. In 1998 the state had thirty casinos with revenues of two billion dollars and trailed only Nevada in square feet of gambling space. The campaign to bring legalized gambling to the state began in the mid-1980s. Casino executives predicted that the state would legalize it for three reasons: first, the state's poverty meant that the economic argument in favor of gambling would carry considerable weight; second, the religious community was divided over the issue; and third, businessmen would support the measure and bring the mainline denominations with them. As one casino executive confidently put it, "Mississippi is probably as good an example of cultural Christianity as we have ever seen anywhere. We'll get the businessmen, and once we've got them, we'll silence the church."[69]

Scandal surrounded the initiative from the start, and churches fought against it. In 1985 the president pro tem of the state senate was convicted of taking a fifty-thousand-dollar bribe to help enact gambling legislation; his arrest spread fears of the corrosive effects of the industry and contributed to its defeat. In 1989 Governor Ray Mabus called for the creation of a state lottery to help fund educational programs, but Baptists and other religious groups helped kill that measure. In 1992 the legislature enacted a bill creating the Mississippi Gaming Commission (at a time when Southern Baptist and Methodist preachers were away for annual meetings). The law allowed counties along the Gulf Coast and the Mississippi River to vote on gambling. That strategy removed the issue from the state level and made it more difficult for the churches to organize effective opposition, especially in economically depressed areas. The law also allowed gambling proponents to put the issue before the voters year after year, in effect wearing down the opposition. Once legalized, there was no mechanism for reversing the choice.[70]

Casinos first opened along the Gulf Coast in 1992. At one time a popular tourist destination, the coast was in an economic slump. The area was also home to a large Catholic population, who are historically less opposed to gambling than are evangelical Protestants. The huge floating casinos brought rapid economic change but confirmed many of the religious leaders' worst fears. Pastor Kiely Young of the First Baptist Church of Gulfport reported that the church's charity work among the needy had tripled since the casinos arrived. One prominent church member lost his law practice and family to gambling and alcohol addiction. An elementary school teacher was arrested for embezzling eighteen hundred dollars from Adopt-a-School funds to support her habit. Those stories could be multiplied hundreds of times over, but the new jobs, higher real estate prices, and busy construction projects have overshadowed—in the media—individual stories of hardship and loss. A Mississippi State University study found between 46,400 and 88,700 "problem gamblers" in the state; unable to control their habit, they, like the elementary school teacher, often resort to crime or fall victim to bankruptcy. Other surveys have found that the poor residents of gambling counties—those people making less than ten thousand dollars per year—spend over 10 percent of their income on gambling.[71]

Nowhere is that statistic more evident than in Tunica County, once the nation's poorest, but now home to a booming gambling industry with more jobs than county residents. The numbers on the welfare rolls have plummeted, and tax revenues are rolling in faster than the county can spend them. Despite those gains, local religious leaders tell a different story. W. C. Johnson, director of missions for North Delta Baptists, reports more and more calls for assistance. Church attendance and offerings are down, which religious leaders attribute to the lure of the bright casino lights. Along with casinos, pawnshops do a thriving business. Local preachers feel paralyzed, given gambling's popularity; as Johnson said, "Most of them have decided that preaching is not going to work." Gambling's popularity and economic impact make it difficult for religious groups to fight. It would have been impossible to predict such an outcome in one of the nation's most conservative and religious states, but, as a writer in *Memphis* magazine said, "The skeptics who said 'the nation's fiftieth state' was too small, too conservative, too religious, too isolated . . . were wrong."[72]

One refrain that has emerged over and over again in this chapter, coming from gambling opponents, from Episcopal priests, from black Baptists, from leaders of the Moral Majority, from a former governor of the state, is a cry for a return to traditional values. The words have become so clichéd that it is difficult to unravel exactly what is meant by them. What do concerned Mississippians mean when they say that do not want the state to become another San Francisco or be subject to the wilds of urban living? In part, such sentiments represent a profound disillusionment with American culture and society that grew out of the changes of the 1960s. Mississippi was shaken to its very foundations and held up to ridicule across the nation and around the world. Many whites developed a siege mentality, a deep distrust of the federal government and of the nation's intellectual, religious, and cultural elites and a general dislike for the wide variety of civil rights movements that grew out of that tumultuous decade. Given the widespread perception that many mainline national denominations supported the civil rights movements and other liberalizing trends, it is hardly surprising that more and more white Mississippians joined fundamentalist churches or Southern Baptist churches, which are similarly decentralized and congregational in outlook. Such churches thrive on their democratic, populist orientation, and reflect most directly the values of their membership, not the values of a distant episcopacy or presbytery. Even when such churches enter the mainstream, as many Holiness and Pentecostal churches in Mississippi have, they continue to define themselves as outsiders who challenge the dominant culture. David K. Bernard of the First Pentecostal Church in Jackson said that his church "has made the transition to acceptability. Our college choir sings at the mayor's prayer breakfast, but the congregation still lives a separate lifestyle. We sponsor storefront churches. We may have arrived, but we're still involved with those who haven't arrived. We're fighting it."[73]

The appeal of fundamentalist churches to black Mississippians derives from very different sources. While blacks celebrated the gains of the civil rights movement, the very success of that movement and the opportunities it created for blacks helped revolutionize the African American experience in the state. The increased opportunities for blacks only accelerated the mass migration of blacks off the land, while those who remained behind continued to be mired in poverty. With the end of sharecropping, tenancy, and agricultural employment, blacks were forced to relocate to urban areas where opportunities still remained limited. Fundamentalism, with its focus on a message aimed at the poor and downtrodden, its openness to innovation and to charismatic leadership, its potential to create moral communities out of the dislocations of urban life, and its offer of positions of leadership to virtually anyone deemed worthy by their fellow members, resonated powerfully in African American communities buffeted by the economic and social changes of the past two decades.

Historian Nathan O. Hatch described the rise of fundamentalism over the past twenty years as "a populist crusade, a revolt of people who feel they are being disfranchised from the core institutions of American culture"—a description that certainly applies to many Mississippians.[74] The emergence of the most recent culture wars follows a pattern established in Mississippi's territorial days, a strategy that relies on a perception that religious folk are a righteous minority surrounded by a hostile culture. Even the current divisions among the opposing sides that pit North against South or rural against urban have deep roots in Mississippi's past. On the national level, some observers have warned that the cultural conflict may become so virulent that compromise may be impossible and the very civility of American democracy may be threatened.[75] Given the homogeneity among most religious groups in Mississippi, however, the result may well be different. The conflict serves to maintain religious vitality, to diminish sectarian conflict, and even to make common cause among black and white Christians.

The inevitable hypocrisy, which is associated with all of the collective activities of the human race, springs chiefly from this source: that individuals have a moral code which makes the actions of collective man an outrage to their conscience. . . . As individuals, men believe that they ought to love and serve each other and establish justice between each other. As racial, economic and national groups they take for themselves, whatever their power can command.

—REINHOLD NIEBUHR[1]

Epilogue

When denominational historians began to chart the histories of Mississippi's churches in the nineteenth century, they portrayed the remarkable expansion of religious bodies in numbers, wealth, prestige, and influence as a story of triumph. Statistics on baptisms, new members, the construction of new churches, and growing budgets gave evidence of religion's steady increase. With the expanding interest in southern religious history among professional historians since the 1960s, a more critical examination of southern religion has been under way. Scholars have sought to explain the near-dominance of evangelical Protestantism in the region and the complex relationship that emerged between religion and southern society. Professional historians have confronted what denominational historians and most southern churchgoers tried to ignore—the startling contradictions between religious ethics and a society plagued by racism, slavery, segregation, and other social ills.

Even in the colonial period the relationship between religion and the rapacious, racist, and violent colonization enterprise was fraught with contradictions and ambiguities. The European religious model, linked closely to the nation-state, did not provide a clear pattern for planting religion in the New World. While the colonial powers, particularly the French, attempted to use the church and her emissaries as instruments of empire, the church and priests were more often than not at odds with the secular government. The French found religious sanction for their colonial enterprise, and priests were sometimes useful among Native American tribes, but the conflicts between the priests and settlers, as well as those among various religious orders, probably did more to hamper colonization than to promote it. Even after decades of working among the Native Americans, the French missionaries had little to show for their efforts, and, as the dramatic Natchez uprising demonstrated, Christianity had done little to win the loyalty of the hard-pressed tribes. The English proved no more successful in introducing their own state church, though the number of Protestant settlers, including a small number of evangelicals, emigrated to the Natchez region. Surprisingly, the Spanish proved more adaptable than the French in attempting to find creative ways of bypassing the exclusive state church tradition by bringing in Protestant settlers and then gradually converting them to the true faith, though even those innovative plans ended in disaster. One reason that the clever Spanish plan failed was the presence of those evangelicals on the frontier. In one sense, they brought the revolutionary zeal of the Reformation and its challenge to the state church with them to colonial Mississippi.

Still, when the United States acquired the Mississippi Territory in 1797, the region was virtually a religious wilderness, without Christian symbols and practice. Natchez's Catholic Church for all practical purposes collapsed after the Spanish withdrawal, and no Protestant houses of worship stood there. Territorial status brought a rapid influx of settlers, including large numbers of African American slaves, who quickly made up a substantial portion of the population. Natchez's position as a freewheeling river town made it unusually irreligious, and, despite the Protestant missionaries' best efforts, evangelical churches in Mississippi attracted only a few hundred members before 1810. There were hopeful signs, however, even on the Mississippi frontier, and, by the early nineteenth century, the denominations that would dominate the state through much of its history—Baptists, Methodists, and Presbyterians—were firmly established.

On the surface, the early Mississippi evangelicals appeared weak indeed; they were primarily from the lower class, they were poor, and they did not control the government. That apparent weakness masked a dynamic religious movement, and their ideology proved to have enormous appeal in their society. Like any successful ideology, theirs brought converts, in this case through a dramatic and life-altering "New Birth." This integrative experience brought converts a sense of empowerment and prepared them to do battle with the local elites. That ideology spread through words, sermons, songs, and voices, which were now given new powers of social definition, especially as the Great Revival reached Mississippi. Through their emotional services, especially in the camp meetings, evangelicals created new identities for themselves, their region, and ultimately for the entire nation.

Evangelicals had several advantages over their more powerful elite opponents. Evangelicals reached out to all members of society, but especially to those most alienated from elite culture. In a wide variety of ways, evangelicals challenged social stability by upsetting the prevailing hierarchical social relationships. Their message of spiritual equality resonated with women and blacks, who joined in large numbers. Husbands and fathers often opposed the conversion of the women in their households, and sometimes pressured women in their families to stay away from religious services or to withdraw their memberships.

Older men bristled at young men who challenged their authority and threatened to upset social relations. Masters often opposed the conversion of their slaves and remained suspicious of evangelicals' equivocal stand on slavery. The mingling of blacks and whites in camp meetings and other evangelical services challenged their society's racial mores and the control masters attempted to exert over their slaves. The evangelical emphasis on the equality of believers led white evangelicals toward an acceptance of blacks as individuals with souls equal to their own, a concept with revolutionary potential so great that many masters refused to allow evangelicals to preach to their slaves.

Despite the opposition of their masters, and probably in part because of it, slaves converted to Christianity in increasing numbers and organized independent "African" churches under their own control. African churches were among Mississippi's largest, and, while their exact number is unknown, the scattered references suggest that they were not uncommon. These independent black churches also had black preachers who were among the most respected and dynamic leaders of the black community and whose influence often extended to white evangelicals as well. Throughout the antebellum period, both blacks and whites worshiped under the ministry of black preachers. But in terms of the future development of Mississippi's religious heritage, the emergence of black Christianity must be considered one of the defining moments.

Mississippi's slave society was firmly grounded in patriarchy, inequality, and domination. While evangelicals challenged some aspects of their society, ultimately they made no attempt to topple the asymmetrical relations of power either between masters and slaves or between men and women. Evangelicals preached equality in Christ, and blacks and women attempted, with some success, to force the white men who governed the churches to face the true meaning of their creed. But they could go only so far. Although preachers were eager to spread the Word to everyone— regardless of gender, race, or class—as white men of the master race they had a stake in the hierarchical slave system that they were unwilling to surrender.

Despite the dramatic culture wars that divided the plain folk from the pillared folk, their cultural systems were not completely at odds. Indeed, the two groups found common ground on several fundamental issues that, over time, bridged the gulf separating them. Again, the force of the cotton revolution cannot be ignored in this context. The wealth it created was not limited to the great planters. Unlike the revolutions tied to sugar or rice, it linked small farmers and planters together in a web of common economic interests. The high profits associated with cotton meant that many of the evangelical plain folk quickly rose into the ranks of the slaveholders. With the commitment to cotton came a commitment to slavery. While few of the early evangelicals were rabid abolitionists, they had been critical of the institution and the abuses masters often inflicted on their slaves. White evangelicals had not equated the spiritual freedom they offered slaves with freedom from physical bondage, but some slaves and many masters did make such a connection. After the 1820s, white evangelicals brought independent black churches under their control, limited the activities of black preachers, and provided racially segregated seating or separate services for black members of biracial churches.

As more of the evangelicals joined the slaveholders' ranks, they became vocal defenders of the institution of slavery. Proslavery ministers emphasized the centrality of hierarchical, patriarchal households governed by white men as the foundations of their republican society. Here, again, their doctrine meshed with that of the planter elite who also idealized a society composed of households presided over by independent white men. An article of faith for white men of all social classes was their determination to maintain their authority over their own households. Even the most devout white evangelical preachers sometimes resented influential women or slaves whose spiritual gifts exceeded their own. Increasingly, the ministers attempted to rein in evangelical women by depriving them of the right to vote in church conferences and the right to exhort or otherwise lead religious services and by celebrating their subordinate role in the churches and in society. Proslavery ministers offered domestic and social harmony, rather than cultural revolt, to a region divided by class and race, and their equation of evangelical virtue with a slaveholding republic sealed their alliance with the planter elite.

By the 1830s the evangelical cultural revolt had ended; for evangelicals the decades after 1830 were a time of triumph, when their membership, wealth, and influence grew dramatically. Many ministers moved into the ranks of the southern professional elite and separated themselves from the laity. Thus, the period after 1830 saw a major shift in evangelical theology and organization as most evangelicals abandoned their traditional emphasis on the equality of believers in favor of a more hierarchical, corporate view of the religious community. The denominational model redefined the place of women and blacks in evangelical culture. While this idealized religious vision of southern society imposed certain duties and limitations on the power of the patriarchs, it gave strong religious sanction to their mastery over their households and, by extension, over southern society, an exalted position that most white men defended by every possible means.

As sectional tensions rose during the antebellum period, religious leaders contributed to the growing divisions between the sections and to the tragic war that followed. Once averse to political activism, preachers and churches rallied to the southern cause. Through their proslavery theology, their sectional divisions, and their denunciation of northern abolitionists, they encouraged white Mississippians to see themselves as God's chosen people engaged in mortal combat with a godless enemy. A few courageous ministers raised their voices in opposition to secession, but by and large churches and their ministers rallied to the Confederacy and promoted southern nationalism. Preachers became willing allies of the Confederate government and tried to nurture patriotism among the faithful by proclaiming God's rebel sympathies. Drawing on their experience in church societies, women worked to supply troops and nurse the sick and wounded as many churches filled with mourners or were used as hospitals. Black southerners saw the war and the growing certainty of a Union victory as an answer to their prayers for freedom. Paradoxically, more and more blacks joined the biracial churches during the war, even as the preachers called for a Confederate victory and churches tried to use their moral courts to enforce obedience from increasingly assertive slaves and runaways.

The Reconstruction era marks a major turning point in the history of

Mississippi religion. That period saw the racial segregation of religious life as the biracial churches collapsed. It became clear that many blacks sought either complete control over their religious lives or complete equality within the biracial churches, neither of which white Christians would grant without a struggle. With few resources other than their deep and abiding faith, blacks set about creating their own religious institutions; churches and preachers quickly came to hold a central position in the black community, and churches became the largest institutions under black control. Faced with a devastating defeat, white clergy issued a clarion call for a renewed covenant. They were forced to admit that God had visited a terrible punishment on white southerners, but they quickly snatched victory from the jaws of defeat by fashioning a brilliant theological apologia that emphasized southern virtues and moral victory and promoted postbellum revivals. Through the Religion of the Lost Cause, Mississippi's white clergymen helped assuage the painful defeat and ease the transition from the Old South to the New.

As Mississippi approached the twentieth century, white Christians looked back reverently to the past but increasingly reentered the national mainstream. Women's work became even better organized and funded, and was officially recognized by denominational bodies. Women rebuilt churches, funded missions, provided charity, built hospitals and orphanages, promoted temperance, and fought lynching. Some white women and prominent preachers condemned racial violence and discrimination and worked to promote better race relations at a time when such relations reached their lowest ebb, but the white churches failed to provide effective leadership on the state's most compelling moral issue.

Despite the overwhelming evangelical majority in the state, "outsider" religious groups, including especially Catholics and Jews, also gained an important foothold in Mississippi. The roots of the Catholic and Jewish presence date back to the colonial period, and so long as they followed the state's racial code, they were tolerated and even welcomed. In fact, many outsider groups relied on that racial code to facilitate their own integration into a society that focused its persecution on blacks and defined all others as white. Catholic and Jewish communities flourished in the Delta, in Jackson, and in other parts of the state, and their members played important roles in civic life.

The twentieth century ushered in dramatic social, cultural, and economic change, though the extent of those transformations was not always evident at the time. On the surface, religious life ran in familiar channels as the major denominations continued to grow in wealth, membership, and influence. By the 1930s the black Baptists had become by far the state's largest denomination, with more than twice the membership of white Baptist churches. One of the hallmarks of American Christianity is its populist appeal, its innovative character, and its churning creativity. While the mainline denominations dominated the state's religious life, powerful challenges to their hegemony arose from the bottom rungs of the socioeconomic ladder as fundamentalist churches sprang up among both black and white Christians. Those churches continued to grow during the Great Depression, but most mainline denominations saw their membership and revenues plummet. Neither private charity nor federal programs were adequate to meet the needs of Mississippi's poor, and innovative Christian responses to the depression like the establishment of cooperative farms met with a hostile reception.

Only World War II managed to pull the nation out of the depression; it brought changes to the South greater than any other event since the Civil War. Many whites became more sensitive to calls for racial justice as they confronted the horrors of Hitler's racist ideology, and blacks, particularly black veterans, were even more empowered to confront segregation. Finally, Mississippians confronted their greatest moral dilemma; religion infused the movement and defined the struggle. Black churches served as meeting places and freedom schools, and civil rights activists relied on church networks. For over a century, black Christians had believed in racial equality, divine justice, and religious brotherhood. The role of leaders like Fannie Lou Hamer cannot be understood apart from their faith. Many moderate white Christians sympathized with black demands for equal rights, but those voices of moderation were quickly overwhelmed by a hate-filled chorus of opposition. White denominational bodies tried to lead their members toward an acceptance of equal rights, but their lukewarm efforts were hardly equal to the task. Churches and their leaders divided over the issue, segregationists launched a vicious and sometimes violent campaign against any minister or religious group that refused to tow the line, moderate ministers fled for their lives, and moderate religious leaders were all but paralyzed. Only after a horrible decade of violence and bloodshed did the state move toward racial justice.

As Mississippi enters the twenty-first century, evangelical Christianity continues to dominate the state's religious life, an outcome that could hardly have been predicted from the fledgling churches that appeared on the Mississippi frontier two centuries before. Many of the characteristics of those early churches—their antielitism, their localism, their dynamic leaders, and their populist orientation—help explain that continued success. Confronted by the rapid social and economic changes of the twentieth century, grassroots religious movements including the Holiness movement, fundamentalism, and Pentecostalism arose to challenge traditional denominations among both blacks and whites. Their success can be measured by their rapid growth, their remarkable cultural creativity (especially their music), and the influence of their political mobilization. Still sharply divided by race, these churches and their political crusades over abortion and the constellation of issues loosely defined as family values have found support across racial lines and even among mainline denominations.

To some extent, the populist nature of religion in Mississippi has been the source of its greatest strength and its greatest weakness. From their very inceptions, evangelical Christian sects measured success by growth in numbers. Their democratic structure, their openness to innovation, and their close connection to their membership and to the larger community fueled their remarkable growth but wedded them closely to the larger society. Observers have often characterized southern religion as monolithic, dominated by mainline denominations whose similarities far outweighed any differences. But in a search for religious uniformity such people have overlooked the importance of sectarian divisions, the lengths to which religious groups often go to exaggerate the differences between themselves and others, and the cracks appearing within denominations that have spawned new religious movements.

Southern, and American, religious life has been characterized by energetic antagonisms, struggles over definition, and popular upsurges. But few, if any, religious groups in Mississippi have followed the path of the early Quakers, who saw themselves as a holy remnant motivated by a critical stance toward the larger society. Most religious groups in Mississippi have been motivated by a providential mission to spread their beliefs as far as possible, fed by an unquenchable expansionism deeply ingrained in American society. In that sense, they have been prisoners of their own success, focused on individual conversion and denominational growth rather than on the larger evils in southern society. That is not to argue that churches have had no impact on the larger society; one of the major themes of this book is that they have, but they have been unable to effectively confront the problems that have plagued Mississippi society. Whether we consider the slavery question, discrimination and racial violence in the postbellum period, or the movement for civil rights, the churches as institutions have failed to provide effective leadership. Here we confront the "inevitable hypocrisy" to which Neibuhr made reference, a tragic weakness endemic, perhaps, in American religious life that has prevented the genuine faith, love, and brotherhood espoused by individual Christians from redeeming an oppressive, discriminatory society. That rather gloomy assessment of collective failure should not obscure the power of religious folk to effect dramatic change, though often outside church structures. They continue to heed St. Paul's call to "fight the good fight of faith" (1 Timothy 6:12).

Notes

Barker—Eugene C. Barker Texas History Center, University of Texas, Austin, Texas

Cain Archives—J. B. Cain Archives, Millsaps College, Jackson, Mississippi

Evans Memorial Library—Evans Memorial Library, Aberdeen, Mississippi

MBHC—Mississippi Baptist Historical Commission, Mississippi College, Clinton, Mississippi

MDAH—Mississippi Department of Archives and History, Jackson, Mississippi

MSU—Special Collections, Mississippi State University, Starkville, Mississippi

SBHC—Southern Baptist Historical Commission, Nashville, Tennessee

Introduction

1. H. Richard Niebuhr, *The Kingdom of God in America* (1937; reprint, Middletown, Conn.: Wesleyan University Press, 1988), 164–84.

Chapter 1

1. Dunbar Rowland and A. G. Sanders, eds. and trans., *Mississippi Provincial Archives: French Dominion, 1701–1743*, 3 vols. (Jackson, Miss.: Press of the Mississippi Department of Archives and History, 1932), II, 241 (hereinafter cited as *MPA:FD*).

2. Ibid., 488.

3. *MPA:FD*, III, 541.

4. J. F. H. Claiborne, *Mississippi, as a Province, Territory and State.* . . . (1880; reprint, Baton Rouge: Louisiana State University Press, 1964), 14; *MPA:FD*, II, 13.

5. *MPA:FD*, III, 17, 31 (first quotation).

6. Ibid., 27, 31; II, 13.

7. *MPA:FD*, III, 38; II, 27, 347.

8. *MPA:FD*, III, 27, 40; II, 28.

9. *MPA:FD*, II, 43 (first quotation), 242 (fourth quotation), 414, 518 (second quotation), 594 (third quotation), 613; III, 148.

10. *MPA:FD*, II, 25 (first quotation), 643.

11. *MPA:FD*, I, 155–63, 194 (second quotation), 209 (third and fourth quotations), 245, 270; II, 28 (first quotation), 488.

12. *MPA:FD*, II, 509–10.

13. Ibid., II, 13, 512 (first quotation); III, 17 (second quotation), 150, 541 (third quotation); Plan for New Biloxi reproduced in Richard Aubrey McLemore, ed., *A History of Mississippi*,

2 vols. (Hattiesburg, Miss.: University and College Press of Mississippi, 1973), I, following 130.

14. *MPA:FD*, II, 26 (first quotation), 29, 30 (second quotation).

15. Ibid., 26–27 (first quotation), 167 (second quotation).

16. Ibid., 28, 169 (first and second quotations), 31 (fourth quotation), 32, 43 (third quotation), 58, 171, 241 (fifth quotation), 571 (sixth quotation); *MPA:FD*, III, 135, 140–41.

17. *MPA:FD*, II, 49 (first quotation), 53 (second quotation), 69 (third quotation); Daniel H. Usner, Jr., *Indians, Settlers, and Slaves in a Frontier Exchange Economy: The Lower Mississippi Valley Before 1783* (Chapel Hill and London: University of North Carolina Press, 1992), 235 (fourth quotation).

18. Usner, *Indians, Settlers, and Slaves*, 47–50; *MPA:FD*, II, 28, 70, 73 (fourth quotation), 253, 279 (first quotation), 494 (second quotation), 502, 558 (third quotation), 560 (fourth quotation); *MPA:FD*, III, 24–25.

19. *MPA:FD*, II, 531–32.

20. Ibid., 525–28.

21. Ibid., 471–72.

22. Ibid., 569–72, 631; *MPA:FD*, III, 701–2.

23. *MPA:FD*, II, 28 (first quotation); *MPA:FD*, III, 47, 53 (second quotation), 62, 129, 141 (third quotation), 246, 255, 356, 372–74, 493, 521 (fifth and sixth quotations), 523 (fourth quotation), 524–25, 645; Walter G. Howell, "The French Period, 1699–1763," in McLemore, ed., *History of Mississippi*, I, 127; Usner, *Indians, Settlers, and Slaves*, 32–33; Claiborne, *Mississippi*, 40; Russell R. Menard, "Economic and Social Development of the South," in Stanley L. Engerman and Robert E. Gallman, eds., *The Cambridge Economic History of the United States*, vol. I, *The Colonial Era* (Cambridge and New York: Cambridge University Press, 1996), 289–90.

24. *MPA:FD*, II, 465, 488 (second quotation), 490 (first quotation), 520 (fourth and fifth quotations), 528 (third quotation), 531 (sixth quotation), 532 (seventh quotation).

25. Ibid., 526–27 (first quotation).

26. *MPA:FD*, III, 493 (first quotation).

27. *MPA:FD*, I, 54–136 (first quotation on p. 63, second quotation on p. 58).

28. Ibid., 102 (first quotation), 103 (second quotation).

29. *MPA:FD*, III, 604–5 (quotation on p. 605), 681–782; Usner, *Indians, Settlers, and Slaves*, 77–104, 276–79; Howell, "French Period," 130–33.

30. *MPA:FD*, III, 13.

31. Robert R. Rea, "British West Florida: Stepchild of Diplomacy," in Samuel Proctor, ed., *Eighteenth-Century Florida and Its Borderlands* (Gainesville, Fla.: University of Florida Press, 1975), 69 (first quotation); Byrle A. Kynerd, "British West Florida," in McLemore, ed., *History of Mississippi*, I, 134–44 (second quotation on p. 144), 145 (third quotation), 154 (fourth quotation); Jack D. L. Holmes, *Gayoso: The Life of a Spanish Governor in the Mississippi Valley, 1789–1799* (Baton Rouge: Louisiana State University Press, 1968), 22.

32. Claiborne, *Mississippi*, 115 (first quotation), 116, 127–34; Usner, *Indians, Settlers, and Slaves*, 112–13.

33. Holmes, *Gayoso*, 23, 68 (first and second quotations), 69–72; Usner, *Indians, Settlers, and Slaves*, 280.

34. Holmes, *Gayoso*, 71–77.

35. Ibid., 73, 76–77.

36. Ibid., 77.

37. John G. Jones, *A Concise History of the Introduction of Protestantism into Mississippi and the Southwest* (St. Louis: P. M. Pinckard, 1866), 20–21, 23–24, 27–47, 70–71; Daniel S. Farrar, ed., "Alexander K. Farrar's Deed to Kingston Church, 1874," *Journal of Mississippi History* XVII (January–October 1955): 135–41; Jack D. L. Holmes, "Spanish Religious Policy in West Florida: Enlightened or Expedient?" *Journal of Church and State* XV (spring 1973): 259–69; Claiborne, *Mississippi*, 106–7, 209, 210, 342, 528 (quotation).

38. Jones, *Concise History*, 20–21, 23–24, 27–47, 70–71 (quotation on p. 31); Charles H. Otken, "Richard Curtis in the Country of the Natchez," *Publications of the Mississippi Historical Society* (hereinafter cited as *PMHS*), III (1900): 147–53; Walter Brownlow Posey, *The Baptist Church in the Lower Mississippi Valley, 1776–1845* (Lexington: University of Kentucky Press, 1957), 5–7; Richard Aubrey McLemore, *A History of Mississippi Baptists, 1780–1970* (Jackson: Mississippi Baptist Convention Board, 1971), 6–7.

39. Jones, *Concise History*, 33 (first quotation); James, *Antebellum Natchez*, 39; Jack D. L. Holmes, "Barton Hannon in the Old Southwest," *Journal of Mississippi History* XLIV (February 1982), 69–79 (second quotation on p. 79); Holmes, *Gayoso*.

40. Jones, *Concise History*, 35–45; Holmes, *Gayoso*, 83 (second quotation).

41. Holmes, "Barton Hannon," 69–73 (first quotation on p. 69, second quotation on p. 71); Holmes, *Gayoso*, 189–91.

42. Holmes, "Barton Hannon," 73–79; James, *Antebellum Natchez*, 70–72; Holmes, *Gayoso*, 191–99; Terry Alford, *Prince Among Slaves* (New York and London: Oxford University Press, 1977), 62. Hannon became an American citizen and landowner, though there is no evidence of further religious activity on his part.

Chapter 2

1. John F. Schermerhorn and Samuel J. Mills, *A Correct View of That Part of the United States Which Lies West of the Allegany Mountains, with Regard to Religion and Morals* (Hartford, Conn.: Peter B. Gleason, 1814).

2. Laurner Blackman Journal, January 16, 1813, Cain Archives.

3. *Rab & Jane: A Legendary Tale, (and True)*. By Peter Pindar's Cousin Pindar (Natchez, Miss. [?]: n.p., 1805), 18–19. A few years later a different poet made similar charges in "The Loud Call or Disinterested Parson," another light verse that described a preacher who warned his "snoring flock" that they were doomed "If they would not abjure the world / And count as dross its filthy mammon, Gold." But the preacher took another pulpit, one that doubled his salary. In his farewell sermon, "He ply'd them long, in righteous strain, / Bade them from darling sins refrain, . . . / To hate the world, in holy ways be bold, / And shun the soul's seducer, *glitt'ring gold.*" While most members of the congregation praised

him as "a Saint on *earth*," a slave named Caesar saw through the contradictions in his message and taunted him for hearing such a loud call.

4. David S. Shields has recently brought the world of elite Anglo-American culture brilliantly to life in *Civil Tongues & Polite Letters in British America* (Chapel Hill and London: University of North Carolina Press, 1997). On verse such as this one, see pp. 46–48.

5. Ira Berlin, "The Plantation Revolution and the Chronology of African American Slavery," paper presented at the 63rd Annual Meeting of the Southern Historical Association, November 7, 1997; Ira Berlin, *Many Thousands Gone: The First Two Centuries of Slavery in North America* (Cambridge, Mass., and London: Harvard University Press, 1998), 325–57; Bernard Bailyn, *Voyagers to the West: A Passage in the Peopling of America on the Eve of the Revolution* (New York: Knopf, 1986), 490 (quotation).

6. Randy J. Sparks, *On Jordan's Stormy Banks: Evangelicalism in Mississippi, 1773–1876* (Athens, Ga. and London: University of Georgia Press, 1994), 7, 14; James Hebron Moore, *The Emergence of the Cotton Kingdom in the Old Southwest: Mississippi, 1770–1860* (Baton Rouge and London: Louisiana State University Press, 1988), 8–12, 75–77; James, *Antebellum Natchez*, 45, 48; Charles Sydnor, *A Gentleman of the Old Natchez Region* (Durham, N.C.: Duke University Press, 1938), 9–13; Claiborne, *Mississippi*, I, 208 (quotation).

7. Sparks, *On Jordan's Stormy Banks*, 11–12; John G. Jones, *A Complete History of Methodism in the Mississippi Conference* (Nashville, Tenn.: Publishing House of the M. E. Church, South, 1908), 164 (first quotation). Jacob Young, *Autobiography of a Pioneer. . . .*(Cincinnati: Cranston and Curts, 1857), 222–23.

8. Sparks, *On Jordan's Stormy Banks*, 14; Morton Rothstein, " 'The Remotest Corner': Natchez on the American Frontier" in Noel Polk, ed., *Natchez before 1830* (Jackson, Miss.: University Press of Mississippi, 1989), 96 (first quotation); Levi Weeks to Ed Hoyt, September 27, 1812, Levi Weeks and Family Papers, MDAH.

9. Ellicott quoted in Holmes, *Gayoso*, 109.

10. Holmes, *Gayoso*, 111 (first and fourth quotations), 126–27; ? to Rev'd Brother, April 1, 1833, Tobias Gibson Subject File (third quotation), MDAH; Claiborne, *Mississippi*, 198 (second quotation); *The Louisiana and Mississippi Almanack . . . 1813* (Natchez, Miss.: n.p., 1813), 49 (final quotation). For an example of dancing school advertisements, see *Mississippi Republican*, October 27, 1813; Rhys Isaac, *The Transformation of Virginia, 1740–1790* (Chapel Hill: University of North Carolina Press, 1982), 98–101, 118–19, 132; Shields, *Civil Tongues*, 141.

11. Shields, *Civil Tongues*, 26 (first quotation), 301–7; James, *Antebellum Natchez*, 100 (second quotation), 227; *Washington Republican and Natchez Intelligencer*, November 20, 1816 (third quotation); Blackman Journal, 39.

12. "Minutes of the Mississippi Baptist Association, 1818" in Albert E. Casey, comp., *Amite County, Mississippi, 1699–1865* (Birmingham, Ala.: Amite County Historical Fund, 1948), II, 120; Jeanne Middleton Forsythe, "Education in Natchez before 1830," in Polk, ed., *Natchez before 1830*, 130–31. For a Masonic response to criticism, see *Washington Republican and Natchez Intelligencer*, September 6, 1817. Evangelicals helped create an Antimasonic political party in the Burned Over District of New York in 1826 that swept briefly across the Northeast. See Steven C. Bullock, *Revolutionary Brotherhood: Freemasonry and the Transformation of the American Social Order, 1730–1840* (Chapel Hill: University of North Carolina Press, 1996); Paul Goodman, *Towards a Christian Republic: Antimasonry and the Great Transition in New England, 1826–1836* (New York: Oxford University Press, 1988).

13. James, *Antebellum Natchez*, 231, 247; Shields, *Civil Tongues*, xiii–xvi, xxvii–xxx, 175–208; *Mississippi Republican*, December 1, 1818 (first quotation), February 18 (remaining quotations), March 18, 1819; *Minutes and Resolutions of the Religious Convention of Christian Denominations Held at Washington [Miss.], on November 19, 1818* (Natchez, Miss.: n.p., 1818).

14. Winans Autobiography, 164, Cain Archives; Holmes, *Gayoso*, 119 (second quotation), 120, 111 (fourth quotation), 112 (fifth quotation); James Pearse, *A Narrative of the Life of James Pearse* (Rutland, Vt.: W. Fay, 1825), 51 (third quotation), 52 (fourth quotation).

15. Young, *Autobiography of a Pioneer*, 241–43; Sparks, *On Jordan's Stormy Banks*, 36–37, 153–59.

16. Winans Journal, Cain Archives, December 20, 1820 (second quotation), May 6, 1821 (first quotation); Salem Baptist Church Records, July 1820, MBHC; Young, *Autobiography of a Pioneer*, 241–43; Sparks, *On Jordan's Stormy Banks*, 36–37, 153–59.

17. Sparks, *On Jordan's Stormy Banks*, 16–19; Perry Miller, *The Life of the Mind in America from the Revolution to the Civil War* (New York: Harcourt, Brace & World, 1965), 6; Isaac, *Transformation of Virginia*, passim; Nathan O. Hatch, *The Democratization of American Christianity* (New Haven and London: Yale University Press, 1989); Jon Butler, *Awash in a Sea of Faith: Christianizing the American People* (Cambridge, Mass., and London: Harvard University Press, 1990), 212–24.

18. Pearse, *Narrative*, 9–10, 51–57, 72; Sparks, *On Jordan's Stormy Banks*, 13–15.

19. *Rab & Jane*, 22.

20. Sparks, *On Jordan's Stormy Banks*, 11–12; Jones, *History of Methodism*, 164; Young, *Autobiography of a Pioneer*, 222–23; Henry G. Hawkins, *Methodism in Natchez* (Jackson, Miss.: Hawkins Foundation, 1937), 38 (third quotation); see also Winans Autobiography, 56–57, Cain Archives; Samuel J. Mills and Daniel Smith, *Report of a Missionary Tour. . . .* (Andover, Mass.: Flagg and Gould, 1815), 26; Timothy Flint, *Recollections of the Last Ten Years. . . .* (Boston: Cummings, Hilliard, 1826), 295.

21. Sparks, *On Jordan's Stormy Banks*, 10, 18.

22. Ibid.

23. ? to Rev'd Brother, April 1, 1833, Tobias Gibson Subject File, quotation, MDAH; Sparks, *On Jordan's Stormy Banks*, 10–11.

24. Sparks, *On Jordan's Stormy Banks*, 11.

25. Samuel S. Hill, ed., *Encyclopedia of Religion in the South* (Macon, Ga.: Mercer University Press, 1984), 487.

26. Blackman Journal, 5–6; Sparks, *On Jordan's Stormy Banks*, 11–12.

27. Sparks, *On Jordan's Stormy Banks*, 18–19; Asbury quoted in Hatch, *Democratization*, 49.

28. Lorenzo Dow, *History of the Cosmopolite: or the Writings of Rev. Lorenzo Dow. . . .* (Cincinnati: Anderson, Gates & Wright, 1857), 217–18.

29. Winans Autobiography, 94 (first quotation); Winans Journal, October 5, 1823 (second quotation); Samuel Sellers Diary, June 1, 1814, Cain Archives; Pearse, *Narrative*, 70 (third quotation); Frances Allen Cabiness and James Allen Cabiness, "Religion in Ante-Bellum Mississippi," *Journal of Mississippi History* VI (October 1944): 202 (remaining quotations); Sparks, *On Jordan's Stormy Banks*, 19.

30. "Notes on Yellow Fever in Natchez," Charles Kimball Marshall Papers, MDAH.

31. Quotations from clippings in Winans Scrapbook, Cain Archives; Sparks, *On Jordan's Stormy Banks*, 20–21.

32. Mary Douglas, *Natural Symbols: Explorations in Cosmology* (New York: Random House, 1973), 118; Hatch, *Democratization*, 37 (second quotation); Jones, *Concise History*, 175 (second quotation); Winans Journal, December 20, 1820, April 12, May 6, July 15, 16, 1821, July 22, 1823 (third quotation); Winans Autobiography, 132; Sellers Diary, June 21, 1816 (fourth quotation); Sparks, *On Jordan's Stormy Banks*, 21.

33. Douglas, *Natural Symbols*, 15–18, 39, 74, 118–19 (first quotation on p. 93, second and third quotations on p. 114); John G. Jones Autobiography, 131, 132 (fourth and fifth quotations), 136 (sixth and seventh quotations), 138, MDAH; Winans Journal, May 19, 1812, May 28, 1815, May 13, 1821; Winans Autobiography, 81 (quotation); Sparks, *On Jordan's Stormy Banks*, 21–23.

34. Jones Autobiography, 135–37 (quotations); Sparks, *On Jordan's Stormy Banks*, 22.

35. Drake Sermon, July 6, 1825, Drake-Satterfield Papers, MDAH.

36. Winans Autobiography, 27 (second quotation), 64 (second quotation); Sparks, *On Jordan's Stormy Banks*, 22–23.

37. Jones, *Complete History*, 145; Sparks, *On Jordan's Stormy Banks*, 23.

38. Pearse, *Narrative*, 70–71 (second quotation); New Orleans *Christian Advocate*, September 9, 1854 (first quotation); Sparks, *On Jordan's Stormy Banks*, 23–24.

39. Jones, *Concise History*, 48, 63 (second quotation), 55, 66, 71, 76, 209–10; Jones, *Complete History*, I, 61, 79, 145 (first quotation), 327, 334, 409, 447, II, 220, 159; L. S. Foster, *Mississippi Baptist Preachers* (St. Louis: National Baptist Publishing Co., 1895), 493, 495 (third quotation); Winans Journal, May 28, 1815, July 27, 1821, May 13, June 14, 1823, July 22, 1823; Bruce Rosenberg, *The Art of the American Folk Preacher* (New York: Oxford University Press), 4, 5, 9–10 (third quotation on p. 10); Gerald L. Davis, *I got the Word in me and I can sing it, you know: A Study of the Performed African-American Sermon* (Philadelphia: University of Pennsylvania Press, 1985), 8–9, 25; Sparks, *On Jordan's Stormy Banks*, 24.

40. Rosenberg, *American Folk Preacher*, 7, 14, 35–36, 105 (quotation); Winans Journal, June 6, 1812; Davis, *I got the Word in me*, 25, 27; Albert J. Raboteau, *Slave Religion: The 'Invisible Institution' in the American South* (Oxford: Oxford University Press, 1978), 236–37; *Sacred Harp* hymnal (1869 edition), 59; E. B. Cobb, Jr., *The Sacred Harp: A Tradition and Its Music* (Athens, Ga.: University of Georgia Press, 1978), appendix B.

41. Sparks, *On Jordan's Stormy Banks*, 24; Mississippi Baptist Association, *A Republication of the Minutes of the Mississippi Baptist Association, from Its Organization in 1806 to the Present Time* (New Orleans: Mississippi Baptist Association, 1849), 167 (quotation).

42. Peter Van Der Merwe, *Origins of the Popular Style: The Antecedents of Twentieth-Century Popular Music* (Oxford: Clarendon Press, 1989), 34 (first quotation), 77–78, 139–40; *South-Western Religious Luminary*, February 1838 (second quotation); Winans Journal, May 26, 1823 (third quotation); Mechal Sobel, *The World They Made Together: Black and White Values in Eighteenth-Century Virginia* (Princeton, N.J.: Princeton University Press, 1987), 205–6; "Shouting Song," *Sacred Harp* (1869 edition), 80; Sparks, *On Jordan's Stormy Banks*, 26–28.

43. Hatch, *Democratization*, 146 (first and second quotations); Watts quoted in Stephen Marini, "Rehearsal for Revival: Sacred Singing and the Great Awakening in America," in Joyce

L. Irwin, ed., *Sacred Sound: Music in Religious Thought and Practice* (Chico, Calif.: Scholars Press, 1983), 80. Marini considers Watts "the most widely-published and read writer in eighteenth-century America." Jones, *Complete History*, 256 (fourth quotation); January 12, 1815, Sellers Diary (fifth quotation); Sparks, *On Jordan's Stormy Banks*, 26, 28; Raboteau, *Slave Religion*, 233; Ramsey, *Autobiography*, 86 (second quotation); Gene Ramsey Miller, *A History of North Mississippi Methodism, 1820–1900* (Nashville, Tenn.: Parthenon Press, 1966), 43–44 (third and fourth quotations); Flint, *Recollections*, 343 (final quotation).

44. Jones, *Complete History*, I, 61 (first quotation); A. B. Amis, Sr., *Recollections of Social Customs in Newton and Scott Counties, Mississippi Fifty Years Ago* (Meridian, Miss.: Dement Printing Co., 1934), 7–8 (remaining quotations); Sparks, *On Jordan's Stormy Banks*, 27–28.

45. Sparks, *On Jordan's Stormy Banks*, 28.

46. Marini, "Rehearsal for Revival," 76 (first quotation); Augustus Harvey Mecklin Autobiography, 3 (second quotation), MDAH; Jones Autobiography, 91. The hymn "New Britain" is the shape-note version of "Amazing Grace." See *Sacred Harp* (1869 edition), 45; Sparks, *On Jordan's Stormy Banks*, 29.

47. Gordon A. Cotton, *Of Primitive Faith and Order: A History of the Mississippi Primitive Baptist Church, 1780–1974* (Raymond, Miss.: Keith Press, 1974), 87 (first quotation); Amis, *Recollections*, 5 (second quotation); Harris Autobiography, 20, MDAH; Hatch, *Democratization*, 153 (third and fourth quotations); Sparks, *On Jordan's Stormy Banks*, 29.

48. Dow, *History of the Cosmopolite*, 218; Young, *Autobiography*, 235 (quotation), 236–39; Sparks, *On Jordan's Stormy Banks*, 19–20.

49. Sellers Diary, March 11, 1814. Though the itinerancy is usually associated with Methodists, in 1813 the Baptists appointed fifteen itinerant preachers. Mississippi Baptist Association, *Republication of the Minutes of the Mississippi Baptist Association, From Its Organization in 1806 to the Present Time* (New Orleans: The Association, 1849), 35; Winans Autobiography, 76–79; Jones Autobiography, 128; Jones Journal, March 20, 1835 (first quotation); Langford Autobiography, 14, 22, Cain Archives; Sparks, *On Jordan's Stormy Banks*, 30.

50. Isaac, *Transformation*, 263–64; Norvelle Robertson, Sr., Autobiography, MDAH; Sparks, *On Jordan's Stormy Banks*, 30–31.

51. Osmon C. Baker, *Guide-Book in the Administration of the Discipline of the Methodist Episcopal Church* (New York: Carlton & Phillips, 1855), 54 (first quotation); *The Doctrines and Discipline of the Methodist Episcopal Church, South* (Charleston, S.C.: n.p., 1851), 72 (second quotation); Jones Journal, March 20, 1835; Winans Journal, May 19, 1812 (quotation); ? to Elijah Steele, June 14, 1838, Steele Letters, Cain Archives; John Burruss to B. M. Drake, May 1, 1826, Drake Papers (second quotation), Cain Archives; Sparks, *On Jordan's Stormy Banks*, 31.

52. Winans Journal, February 18 (quotation), July 22, August 12, 1821, July 22, 1823; B. M. Drake, *A Sketch of the Life of Rev. Elijah Steele* (Cincinnati: Methodist Book Concern, 1843), 16; Jean Strickland, ed., *The Autobiography of A. C. Ramsey* (Moss Point, Miss.: J. Strickland, 1980), 31; New Orleans *Western Methodist*, December 27, 1833; Sparks, *On Jordan's Stormy Banks*, 31–32.

53. Kate M. Power, "Centennial Celebration of Old Bethany Church," *Minutes of the Presbyterian Historical Society of the Synod of Mississippi* (Jackson, Miss.: Clarion Steam Printing Establishment, 1908), 29 (second quotation); Ernest Trice Thompson, *Presbyterians in the South*,

Volume One: 1607–1861, 3 vols. (Richmond, Va.: John Knox Press, 1963), 226–29; Sparks, *On Jordan's Stormy Banks*, 32.

54. Mississippi Baptist Association, *Republication of the Minutes*, 20 (first and second quotations); Sellers Diary, July 11, 1814 (third quotation); Salem Church Records, June and July, 1819 (fourth quotation), SBHC; Sparks, *On Jordan's Stormy Banks*, 32–33.

55. Jones, *Concise History*, 102, 110; "Comparative Statement of the Condition of the Churches composing the Mississippi Baptist Association, from 1807 to 1847 inclusive," in Mississippi Baptist Association, *Republication of the Minutes*, 264; Mills and Smith, *Report of a Missionary Tour*, 26; Schermerhorn and Mills, *Correct View*, 29; Sparks, *On Jordan's Stormy Banks*, 29–30.

56. Winans Autobiography, 94, 154; Winans Journal, October 5, 1823 (first quotation); Sellers Diary, June 1, 1814; Pearse, *Narrative*, 70 (second quotation); Cabiness and Cabiness, "Religion in Ante-Bellum Mississippi," 202; Sparks, *On Jordan's Stormy Banks*, 19, 49–50; *Mississippi Republican*, February 18, 1819 (first quotation); Carroll Smith-Rosenberg, "Women and Religious Revivals: Emergence of the American Bourgeoisie," in Leonard I. Sweet, ed., *The Evangelical Tradition in America* (Macon, Ga.: Mercer University Press, 1984), 215–16. From 1800 to 1820 between 65 and 80 percent of Mississippi's population was under the age of twenty-four. See Bureau of the Census, *Historical Statistics of the United States: Colonial Times to 1970* (Washington, D.C.: U.S. Government Printing Office, 1975), 28, 30, 34; Christine Leigh Heyrman, *Southern Cross: The Beginnings of the Bible Belt* (New York: Knopf, 1997), 25–26.

57. E. Hearn to Benjamin Drake, June 6, 1823; De Vinne to Drake, August 22, 1823, Drake Correspondence, Cain Archives; G. M. Montgomery to Joseph A. Montgomery, May 2, 1839, Joseph A. Montgomery Papers, MDAH; "Religion Is a Fortune," McCurry, *Social Harp*, 42 (the hymn, entitled "Greenwich," can be found in McCurry, *Social Harp*, 173); Sparks, *On Jordan's Stormy Banks*, 36.

58. Donald Mathews, *Religion in the Old South* (Chicago and London: University of Chicago Press, 1977), 48; Joseph Campbell, *The Masks of God*, vol. 4, *Creative Mythology* (New York: Viking Press, 1968), 84; Sparks, *On Jordan's Stormy Banks*, 39–40.

59. Dow, *History of the Cosmopolite*, 593.

Chapter 3

1. "Duties of Heads of Families" (1835) in Mississippi Baptist Association, *A Republication of the Minutes*, 164.

2. James Bradley Finley, *Sketches of Western Methodism. . . .* (Cincinnati: Methodist Book Concern, 1854), 532.

3. Mathews, *Religion in the Old South*, 101–24 (quotation on p. 102).

4. Sparks, *On Jordan's Stormy Banks*, 44.

5. Ibid., 44–45.

6. Heyrman, *Southern Cross*, 166–69; Sparks, *On Jordan's Stormy Banks*, 45.

7. Jones, *Complete History*, II, 295 (quotations); Dickson D. Bruce, *And They All Sang Hallelujah* (Ithaca, N.Y., and London: Cornell University Press, 1985), 86–87.

8. Jones, *Complete History*, II, 205 (first and second quotations); Jones Autobiography, 90

(third quotation); n.a., *Biographical and Historical Sketches of Mississippi*, 2 vols. (Spartanburg, S.C.: n.p., 1978), I, 949 (fourth quotation); Finley, *Sketches*, 536 (fifth quotation); Sparks, *On Jordan's Stormy Banks*, 45–46.

9. Amis, *Recollections of Social Customs*, 5 (first quotation); Sparks, *On Jordan's Stormy Banks*, 47–48.

10. Sellers Diary, May 4, July 9, 1814 (quotation), October 1, 1816, Cain Archives; Sparks, *On Jordan's Stormy Banks*, 48–49; Heyrman, *Southern Cross*, 173–89.

11. Flint, *Recollections*, 294; Isham Howze to Elizabeth Howze, January 5, 1847; Isham Howze Journal, January 11, February 25, 27, August 26, 1854, March 20, 1857, MDAH.

12. Sophia Andrews to Matilda Boyd, January 18, 1854, Hayes, Ray, Webb Collection, MSU.

13. New Orleans *Christian Advocate*, September 5, 1851 (first quotation), June 14, 1851 (fifth quotation); *Mississippi Baptist*, July 15, 1858 (second quotation), September 22, 1859 (third and fourth quotations); Heyrman, *Southern Cross*, 200–201.

14. *Mississippi Baptist*, October 5, 1859 (first quotation).

15. New Orleans *Christian Advocate*, April 10, 1852 (quotation), February 5, 1853, June 24, 1854; *Mississippi Baptist*, November 8, 1860.

16. Winans, "Substance of a Funeral Sermon Occasioned by the Death of Miss Mary Magruder . . . September 23, 1824," Winans Funeral Sermons, 1825–41, Winans Papers; New Orleans *Christian Advocate*, May 10, 31, 1851.

17. Elizabeth C. Irion Journal, September 6, 1852 (first quotation), Irion-Neilson Family Papers, MDAH; Lewis Hobbs to Winans, December 29, 1813, Drake Correspondence (third quotation), MDAH; Jones Autobiography, 105–6 (fourth quotation); Jones to Drake, May 6, 1840, Drake Papers; Winans Journal, June 10, 1812 (quotation); Winans Autobiography, 7, 17; Heyrman, *Southern Cross*, 162–65.

18. Agnew Diary, February 13, 1857; Academy Baptist Church Records, September 5, 25, November 10, 1852 (quotation), March 1853, February, August, October, 1854, MDAH; Jones Autobiography, 8.

19. Sophia B. Andrews to Matilda Boyd, August 22, 1851, Hays, Ray, Webb Collection.

20. Rev. Henry J. Harris Autobiography, 20–24, 32, MDAH; Jones Autobiography, 8; Sparks, *On Jordan's Stormy Banks*, 102.

21. Obituary in the New Orleans *Christian Advocate*, November 17, 1866; Sparks, *On Jordan's Stormy Banks*, 50.

22. Galilee Baptist Church, Amite County, in Casey, *Amite County*, II, 211 (first quotation). For similar examples, see Line Creek and East Fork Baptist churches, Casey, *Amite County*, II, 54, 78. The 1839 Rules of Decorum for Enon Primitive Baptist Church stipulated that "[a]ll male & female members shall have privileges in church government. . . ." Enon Church, Itawamba County, MSU. Some churches put limits on women's voting rights; Concord Baptist Church, for example, allowed women to vote only on the choice of a pastor and the reception of members. Concord Church, Choctaw County, MSU. Church records rarely give names for votes taken in conference, but a few examples do show women voting in church trials. See Salem Baptist Church, Jefferson County, November 1822, SBHC; Bogue Chitto Baptist Church, September 1860, MSU. See also Jean E. Friedman, *The Enclosed*

Garden: Women and Community in the Evangelical South (Chapel Hill and London: University of North Carolina Press, 1985), 13; Heyrman, *Southern Cross*, 168–69.

23. Sarepta Baptist Church, Franklin County, 1810, August 1816, June 1834, MSU. For another example of a church denying women the right to vote, then reversing that decision, see Bethesda Baptist Church, Hinds County, May 1846, September 1850, SBHC. At Bethesda in 1850 there were thirty white female and eighteen white male members. A. A. Worrell, *Review of Corrective Church Discipline* (Nashville, Tenn.: Southwestern Baptist Publishing House, 1860), 208–10 (quotation), 214; Sparks, *On Jordan's Stormy Banks*, 50–51.

24. *Annual Report of the Managers and Officers of the Natchez Orphan Asylum.* . . . (Natchez, Miss.: Natchez Orphan Asylum, 1855), 15 (first quotation); Joseph B. Stratton, D.D., *Memorial of a Quarter-Century's Pastorate* (Philadelphia: Lippencott 1869), 52–53; Sparks, *On Jordan's Stormy Banks*, 51–52.

25. Natchez Orphan Asylum, *Annual Report*, 1855, 9–26 (first quotation on p. 14, third quotation on p. 25); "An Act to Incorporate the Female Charitable Society of Natchez," Official Archives of the State of Mississippi. Legislature, First and Second Sessions, 1816–19; Petitions and Memorials to the Legislature and Bills, 1823–26 (second quotation); Natchez Orphan Asylum Records, Natchez Trace Collection, Barker; Sparks, *On Jordan's Stormy Banks*, 52.

26. C. T. Stiles to W. Winans, March 11, 1820, Winans Correspondence; Winans Journal, November 1, 1823, Cain Archives; First Methodist Church, Columbus, Second Conference, 1837, MSU; Jones, *Complete History*, II, 388 (second quotation); *Tennessee Baptist*, June 12, 1847 (final quotation); Sparks, *On Jordan's Stormy Banks*, 52–53.

27. Baptist State Convention, *Second Annual Report . . . 1824* (Natchez, Miss.: n.p., 1825), 3; Mississippi Baptist State Convention, *Proceedings of A Meeting*, 21 (third quotation); Woman's Missionary Union of Mississippi, *Hearts the Lord Opened: The History of Mississippi Woman's Missionary Union* (Jackson, Miss.: Woman's Missionary Union, 1954), 13, 14–18, 21 (first quotation on p. 14, second on p. 15, fourth on p. 17); James Adair Lyon Journal, October–December, 1854 (quotation), MSU; Boyd, *Popular History*, 277–78; *Mississippi Baptist*, April 14, 28, November 3, 1859; John Hebron Moore, *The Emergence of the Cotton Kingdom: Mississippi, 1770–1860* (Baton Rouge and London: Louisiana State University Press, 1988), 199–200 (final quotation on p. 200); Sparks, *On Jordan's Stormy Banks*, 53.

28. Sparks, *On Jordan's Stormy Banks*, 53–54.

29. Mathews, *Religion in the Old South*, 110; Sparks, *On Jordan's Stormy Banks*, 54.

30. *Tennessee Baptist*, May 8, 1847; April 27, 1848 (first quotation); July 13, 1848 (third quotation); *South-Western Religious Luminary*, March 1835 (second quotation); *Mississippi Baptist*, March 10, 1860; Sparks, *On Jordan's Stormy Banks*, 55.

31. *Tennessee Baptist*, July 13, 1848; November 16, 27, 1848 (third quotation). See also October 12, 1848. *Mississippi Baptist*, July 22, 1858; New Orleans *Christian Advocate*, February 6, 1860 (first and second quotations).

32. Charles F. Deems, *Annals of Southern Methodism* (New York: J. A. Gray, 1856), 279–80 (quotation on p. 279); *Tennessee Baptist*, June 1, 1848; Charles B. Galloway, "Elizabeth Female Academy—The Mother of Female Colleges," *Publications of the Mississippi Historical Society* II (1899): 169–78; Winans Autobiography, 91–92; *Natchez Gazette*, March 11, 1826 (article typescript in Elizabeth Female Academy Subject File, MDAH); Sparks, *On Jordan's Stormy Banks*, 55–56.

33. Galloway, "Elizabeth Female Academy," 177 (first and third quotations); *Tennessee Baptist*, March 6, 1848 (second quotation); New Orleans *Christian Advocate*, April 2, 1853; February 7, 1852 (fifth quotation), December 22, 1866; Mathews, *Religion in the Old South*, 111 (fourth quotation); Sparks, *On Jordan's Stormy Banks*, 56.

34. Ruth H. Bloch, "The Gendered Meanings of Virtue in Revolutionary America," *Signs: Journal of Women in Culture and Society* XIII (autumn 1987): 37–58; Jan Lewis, "The Republican Wife: Virtue and Seduction in the Early Republic," *William and Mary Quarterly* XLIV (October 1987): 689–72; Catherine Clinton, *The Plantation Mistress: Woman's World in the Old South* (New York: Pantheon Books, 1982), 130 (quotations); Sparks, *On Jordan's Stormy Banks*, 56–57.

35. Galloway, "Elizabeth Female Academy," 177; Sparks, *On Jordan's Stormy Banks*, 57–58.

36. Synod of Mississippi *Extracts*, 423. Ownby's statistics from ninety-seven churches across the South closely resemble my sample. See Ownby, *Subduing Satan*, 119, 134–35.

37. *Mississippi Baptist*, September 1836.

38. Spring Hill Baptist Church, June 1858, MSU; Bethany Baptist Church, September 1831, SBHC; Sparks, *On Jordan's Stormy Banks*, 159–63.

39. Elizabeth Fox-Genovese, "Religion in the Lives of Slaveholding Women of the Antebellum South," in Lynda L. Coon, Katherine J. Haldane, and Elisabeth W. Sommers, eds., *That Gentle Strength: Historical Perspectives on Women in Christianity* (Charlottesville and London: University of Virginia Press, 1990), 208; Sparks, *On Jordan's Stormy Banks*, 162–63.

40. Cynthia Lynn Lylerly, *Methodism and the Southern Mind, 1770–1810* (New York and Oxford: Oxford University Press, 1998), 101.

41. Cullen Murphy, *The Word According to Eve: Women and the Bible in Ancient Times and Our Own* (Boston: Houghton Mifflin, 1998), 16, 134.

Chapter 4

1. J. F. H. Claiborne, *Mississippi, As a Province, Territory, and State. . . .* (1880; reprint, Baton Rouge: Louisiana State University Press, 1964), I, 144–45.

2. W. E. B. Du Bois, *The Souls of Black Folk* (New York: Fawcett Publishers, 1961), 142.

3. Butler, *Awash in a Sea of Faith*; Sobel, *The World They Made Together*.

4. Sylvia Frey and Betty Wood, *Come Shouting to Zion: African American Protestantism in the American South and British Caribbean to 1830* (Chapel Hill and London: University of North Carolina Press, 1988), 33, 40, 117.

5. Ibid., 118, 140, 181.

6. Daniel De Vinne to Benjamin Drake, August 22, 1823, Drake Correspondence, Cain Archives; James E. Davis, *Frontier America 1800–1840: A Comparative Demographic Analysis of the Settlement Process* (Glendale, Calif.: A. H. Clark, 1977), 128; Sparks, *On Jordan's Stormy Banks*, 61.

7. Bogue Chitto Baptist Church, November, December 1818 (quotation), MBHC; Sparks, *On Jordan's Stormy Banks*, 62; Butler, *Awash in a Sea of Faith*, 250.

8. Church records reproduced in Casey, *Amite County*, II, 413, 56, 251, 315, 59, 212, 173, 251–53, 315–20.

9. Kenneth M. Stampp, *The Peculiar Institution: Slavery in the Ante-Bellum South* (New York: Vintage, 1956), 158–61; John W. Blassingame, *The Slave Community: Plantation Life in the Antebellum South* (New York and Oxford: Oxford University Press, 1979), 84–87; Eugene D. Genovese, *Roll, Jordan, Roll: The World the Slaves Made* (New York: Vintage Books, 1976), 202–9; Du Bois, *Souls of Black Folk*, 141.

10. Mathews, *Religion in the Old South*, 202 (first quotation); Casey, *Amite County*, II, 315, 321 (second and third quotations), 323 (fourth quotation), 324, 330 (remaining quotations); Sparks, *On Jordan's Stormy Banks*, 66.

11. Sydnor, *Slavery in Mississippi*, 219, 220, 223, 224, 234; Jones, *Complete History*, II, 300; Beulah Baptist Church, Tippah County, May 1859, SBHC; Winans Journal, August 3 (first quotation), August 24 (second quotation), 1845; George P. Rawick, ed., *The American Slave: A Composite Biography*, 41 vols. (Westport, Conn., 1972–79), Supp., Ser. 1, vol. 6, pt. 1, 58 (third and fourth quotations); *Mississippi Baptist*, August 26, 1858 (remaining quotations); Nancy M. Robinson Diary, January 1, 1859, MDAH; Sparks, *On Jordan's Stormy Banks*, 66–67, 132–33.

12. Hopewell Church, Franklin County, November 1825 (first quotation), July, November 1827, October 1829 (second quotation), MBHC; Bogue Chitto Baptist Church, Pike County, September, December 1827, February 1828, MBHC; New Hope Baptist Church, December 1830 (third quotation), March, June 1832, June, November 1834, September 1839 (fourth quotation); Magnolia Baptist Church, Claiborne County, April 1853 (fifth quotation), SBHC; First Baptist Church, Louisville, August 1851; Bethany Baptist Church, Jefferson Davis County, June 1858 (final quotation), SBHC; Sparks, *On Jordan's Stormy Banks*, 133–34.

13. New Orleans *Christian Advocate*, February 6, 1860 (quotation); Sparks, *On Jordan's Stormy Banks*, 133.

14. Foster, *Mississippi Baptist Preachers*, 19; Sparks, *On Jordan's Stormy Banks*, 66–67.

15. Rawick, ed., *American Slave*, Supp., Ser. 1, 8, pt. 3, p. 1111; 9, pt. 4, 1664–65; 9, pt. 4, 1610; 10, pt. 5, 1913.

16. See John Thornton, *Africa and Africans in the Making of the Atlantic World, 1400–1680* (Cambridge, Eng.: Cambridge University Press, 1992), 235–71.

17. Rawick, ed., *American Slave*, Supp., Ser.1, 7, pt. 2, 757; 6, pt. 1, 311; 8, pt. 3, 1110; 9, pt. 4, 1502, 1868.

18. Ibid., Supp., Ser. 1, 8, pt. 3, 1307 (first quotation); 10, pt. 5, 2402–3 (remaining quotations).

19. Ibid., Supp., Ser. 1, 8, pt. 3, 1307 (first quotation); 10, pt. 5, 2403 (second quotation). See also Lucindy Hall Shaw interview, 10, pt. 5, 1926; Lucy Galloway interview, 8, pt. 3, 804.

20. Susan Snow interview, ibid., 10, pt. 5, 2009.

21. Ibid., 7, pt. 2, 785.

22. Sobel, *Trabelin' On*, 99–135; Sparks, *On Jordan's Stormy Banks*, 61.

23. John B. Boles, *Black Southerners, 1619–1869* (Lexington, Ky.: University Press of Kentucky, 1984), 140–55 (first quotation on p. 154); Mathews, *Religion in the Old South*, 188–98. In an argument reminiscent of one made by Stanley Elkins, Jon Butler described "a holocaust

that destroyed collective African religious practice in colonial America." See Butler, *Awash in a Sea of Faith*, 129–63 (quotation on p. 157). Some African slaves in the South were Moslem and may not have found Christianity as foreign as other native Africans did. Though their numbers and influence are difficult to measure, there were Moslem slaves in Mississippi. See, for example, Jordan, *Prince Among Slaves*; Jones, *Complete History*, I, 105.

24. Winans Journal, February 11 (first and second quotation), April 1, August 12, July 22, 1821 (third and fourth quotations); July 22, 1823 (fifth and sixth quotations); Sparks, *On Jordan's Stormy Banks*, 62.

25. Jones Journal, July 31, 1836. Campbellites, followers of Alexander Campbell, were otherwise known as the Disciples of Christ.

26. Sparks, "Religion in Amite County, Mississippi, 1800–1861," in John B. Boles, ed., *Masters and Slaves in the House of the Lord: Race and Religion in the American South, 1740–1870* (Lexington, Ky.: University Press of Kentucky, 1988), 69. This was also the pattern in Georgia. See Frederick A. Bode, "The Formation of Evangelical Communities in Middle Georgia: Twiggs County, 1820–1861," *Journal of Southern History* LX (November 1994): 729–34.

27. Winans Autobiography, 10 (quotations); Mary G. Barker, Mavis Oliver Feltus, and Diane A. Stockfelt, comps., *Early Will Records of Adams County, Mississippi* (Natchez, Miss.[?]: n.p., 1975), 77; Sparks, *On Jordan's Stormy Banks*,

28. Bethlehem Baptist Church, Choctaw County, Rules of Decorum, 1835, MSU; New Hope Baptist Church, Monroe County, Rules of Decorum, 1819, Evans Memorial Library; Sparks, *On Jordan's Stormy Banks*, 62–63.

29. First Baptist Church, Louisville, Miss., August 1836 (first and second quotations), SBHC; Liberty Baptist Church, Jackson, Miss., August 1851, SBHC; Mars Hill Baptist Church, Summit, Miss., October 15, 1864, SBHC; East Fork Baptist Church Records in Casey, *Amite County*, II, 21; Sparks, *On Jordan's Stormy Banks*, 65.

30. Jones Autobiography, 75 (first and second quotations); Jones, *Concise History*, 240 (third and fourth quotations), 116; Talley to William Winans, March 28, 1826 (fifth quotation); diary of Jacob Young reproduced in Casey, *Amite County*, II, 540; Lewis Hobbs to Winans, December 29, 1813, Drake Papers, MDAH; Jones, *Complete History*, II, 488; Sparks, *On Jordan's Stormy Banks*, 67.

31. Pisgah Church Records in Casey, *Amite County*, II, 94; ibid, II, 102, 106; Sarepta Baptist Church, Franklin County,1810 (second quotation), MSU; Sparks, *On Jordan's Stormy Banks*, 68.

32. Casey, *Amite County*, II, 123–25; Sparks, *On Jordan's Stormy Banks*, 68.

33. McLemore, ed., *History of Mississippi*, I, 238, 252, 254, 276; Claiborne, *Mississippi*, 391; Sparks, *On Jordan's Stormy Banks*, 70, 134–35; Patrick H. Thompson, *The History of the Negro Baptists in Mississippi* (Jackson, Miss.: R. W. Bailey Print Co., 1898), 25–36; Bethany Church, May 1829 (first and second quotations); J. L. Boyd, Sr., "History of the Baptists in Rankin County," *Journal of Mississippi History* XII (July 1950), 165 (third quotation); Z. T. Leavell and T. J. Bailey, *A Complete History of Mississippi Baptists, From the Earliest Times*, 2 vols. (Jackson, Miss.: n.p., 1904), I, 77; Jesse Laney Boyd, *A Popular History of the Baptists in Mississippi* (Jackson, Miss.: n.p., 1930), 70; Mt. Moriah Baptist Church, April 1848, MSU; Bethesda Baptist Church, November 1848.

34. McLemore, ed., *History of Mississippi*, 234; Winans Autobiography, 166 (quotations); William Sumner Jenkins, ed., *Records of the States of the United States*, Miss. B1, Reel 1, 1807–

1823, "Statutes of the Mississippi Territory. . . ." (1816), 382; "The Revised Code of the Laws of Mississippi. . . ." (1824), 390; B2 Reel 2, 1805–1822, "Laws of the State of Mississippi. . . ." (1822), 184.

35. Winans Autobiography, 166 (quotation), 167, 172; *Minutes of the Mississippi Baptist Association*, 87; Leavell and Bailey, *Complete History*, I, 129; Claiborne, *Mississippi*, 391; "Laws of the State of Mississippi" (1822), 184; Sparks, *On Jordan's Stormy Banks*, 70–71.

36. *Minutes of the Mississippi Baptist Association*, pp. 167–68 (emphasis added); Sparks, *On Jordan's Stormy Banks*, 71.

37. Sparks, *On Jordan's Stormy Banks*, 71.

38. Thompson, *History of the Negro Baptists*, 25–36; James, *Antebellum Natchez*, 249 (first quotation); Bethany Church, May 1829 (second and third quotations), SBHC; J. L. Boyd, Sr., "History of the Baptists in Rankin County," *Journal of Mississippi History* XII (July 1950): 165 (fourth quotation); Leavell and Bailey, *Complete History of Mississippi Baptists*, I, 77; Jesse Laney Boyd, *A Popular History of the Baptists in Mississippi* (Jackson, Miss.: The Baptist Press, 1930), 70; Mt. Moriah Baptist Church, April 1848, MSU; Bethesda Baptist Church, November 1848, SBHC; Sparks, *On Jordan's Stormy Banks*, 135.

39. Aberdeen Baptist Association, *Minutes of the Second Anniversary of the Aberdeen Baptist Association . . . 1845* (Aberdeen, Miss.: The Association, 1845), 8 (quotations). See also the detailed suggestions from a similar committee appointed by the Columbus Baptist Association in the same year. *Minutes of the Columbus Baptist Association . . . 1845* (n.p., n.d. [1845]), 2–3. Sparks, *On Jordan's Stormy Banks*, 135.

40. *Proceedings of the Third Annual Meeting of the Convention of the Baptist Denomination of the State of Mississippi . . . 1839* (Natchez, Miss.: n.p., 1839), 10; Sparks, *On Jordan's Stormy Banks*, 135.

41. Clear Creek Church, January 20, 1845 (first quotation), SBHC; May 1846; Concord Baptist Church, Choctaw County, January 1846, February 1854, MSU; Academy Baptist Church, July 1848, April 1850, MDAH; Dr. John Hunter Diary, p. 2 in Jackson First Presbyterian Church Papers, MDAH; Bethesda Baptist Church, January 1855, SBHC; Liberty Baptist Church, June 1860, SBHC.

42. Rawick, ed. *The American Slave*, Supp., Ser. 1, vol. 10, pt. 5, p. 2237; Sparks, *On Jordan's Stormy Banks*, 136.

43. Liberty Baptist Church, June 1860, SBHC; Concord Church, February 1854, MSU; Sydnor, *Slavery in Mississippi*, 55; W. A. Evans, *A History of First Baptist Church, Aberdeen, Mississippi, 1837 to 1945. . . .* (Aberdeen, Miss.: First Baptist Church, 1945), 25; "Reminiscences & Stories: No. 11, Dr. J. M. Heard," Evans Memorial Library; Thompson, *Negro Baptists*, 32; Sparks, *On Jordan's Stormy Banks*, 136–37.

44. Thompson, *History of the Negro Baptists*, 24–29; James, *Natchez*, 251; Port of Aberdeen Clippings File, 52, Evans Memorial Library; Mathews, *Religion in the Old South*, 199–207; Sobel, *Trabelin' On*, 314–31, 355–56; Raboteau, *Slave Religion*, 188–207; *Minutes of the Thirty-Fifth Anniversary of the Union Baptist Association . . . 1856* (New Orleans: The Association, 1856), 12 (quotation).

45. Port of Aberdeen Clippings File, 52, Evans Memorial Library. The Aberdeen Church employed white ministers. Jonathan Beasley, "Blacks—Slave and Free—Vicksburg, 1850–1860," *Journal of Mississippi History* XXXVIII (February 1976): 12; Sparks, *On Jordan's Stormy Banks*, 137–38.

46. *Mississippi Baptist*, January 7, 1858 (quotations); Sparks, *On Jordan's Stormy Banks*, 139.

47. Winans Journal, August 12, 1821; First Presbyterian Church, Holly Springs, Miss., November 7, 1842, MDAH; Louisville First Baptist Church, June 1849 (first quotation), SBHC; Academy Baptist Church, December 1859 (second quotation), MDAH; Sparks, *On Jordan's Stormy Banks*, 139–40.

48. Academy Church, July 1854, MDAH; Casey, *Amite County*, II, 300 (second quotation); Bethany Baptist Church, August, October 1833 (third quotation), SBHC; Bethesda Baptist Church, January 1856, August 1849, SBHC; Magnolia Baptist Church, August 1853, SBHC; Liberty Baptist Church, August 1853, March 1858, January 1860, SBHC; Rawick, *American Slave*, Supp., Ser. 1, vol. 8, pt. 3, p. 1062 (fourth quotation); Sparks, *On Jordan's Stormy Banks*, 140.

49. Concord Baptist Church, January 1845, MSU; Liberty Baptist Church, May 1854, SBHC; Milton C. Sernett, *Black Religion and American Evangelicalism: White Protestants, Plantation Missions, and the Flowering of Negro Christianity, 1787–1865* (Metuchen, N.J.: Scarecrow Press, 1975), 96–97 (final quotation); Sparks, *On Jordan's Stormy Banks*, 140–41.

50. New Orleans *Christian Advocate*, August 23, 1856.

51. Rawick, ed., *American Slave*, Supp., Ser. 1, vol. 7, pt. 2, 615 (first quotation); vol. 6, pt. 1, 157; vol. 7, pt. 2, 757, 744, 784, 623, 537, 345, 749, 594–95 (second quotation); vol. 8, pt. 3, 1212 (third quotation), 1325, 1197, 1171, 1128–29, 1062, 845; vol. 9, pt. 4, 1588–89, 1567, 1411, 1381; vol. 10, pt. 5, 2410–11, 2370–71, 2337, 2315, 2251, 2237, 2233, 2107–8, 1984; Sparks, *On Jordan's Stormy Banks*, 141–42.

52. Rawick, ed., *American Slave*, Supp., Ser. 1, vol. 7, pt. 2, 797 (first quotation); vol. 8, pt. 3, 1321 (second quotation); vol. 9, pt. 4, 1779, vol. 10, pt. 5, 2087; Sparks, *On Jordan's Stormy Banks*, 142–43.

53. Rawick, ed., *American Slave*, Supp., Ser. 1, vol. 6, pt. 1, 58–59 (first and second quotation), 285 (fourth quotation); vol. 9, pt. 4, 1772 (third quotation); 1488 (fifth quotation), 1489, 1779; vol. 8, pt. 3, 1171, 823, 1321; vol. 10, pt. 5, 2058–59, 2048, 2087.

54. Sparks, *On Jordan's Stormy Banks*, 71–72.

55. Ibid., 72.

56. Ibid.

57. Ibid., 72–73.

58. Ibid., 73.

59. Jones, *Complete History*, II, 240; Sydnor, *Slavery in Mississippi*, 216–217n (quotation), 215–17; Sparks, *On Jordan's Stormy Banks*, 74–75.

60. Clear Creek Church, April 24, 1836.

61. Genovese quoted in Drew Gilpin Faust, ed., *The Ideology of Slavery: Proslavery Thought in the Antebellum South, 1830–1860* (Baton Rouge and London: Louisiana State University Press, 1981), 9.

62. Boles, *Black Southerners*, 158.

Chapter 5

1. Thomas Jefferson Lowry Memoranda, 1844, 6, typescript, MDAH.

2. Nathan J. Fox Papers, January 18, 1855, MDAH.

3. Charles F. Deems, ed., *The Southern Methodist Pulpit* (Richmond, Va.: Richmond Christian Advocate, n.d. [1850]), III, 227.

4. Joseph G. Baldwin, *The Flush Times of Alabama and Mississippi: A Series of Sketches* (New York: D. Appleton & Co., 1854); Moore, *Emergence of the Cotton Kingdom*, 16, 28; Sparks, *On Jordan's Stormy Banks*, 76.

5. *Tennessee Baptist* (Nashville, Tenn.), May 1835 (first quotation); *Proceedings of a Meeting to Consider the Propriety of Forming a Baptist State Convention*, 10 (second quotation); Sparks, *On Jordan's Stormy Banks*, 77.

6. Newton Haskin James, "Josiah Hinds: Versatile Pioneer of the Old Southwest," *Journal of Mississippi History* II (January 1940): 25 (quotation); Sparks, *On Jordan's Stormy Banks*, 78–79.

7. *South-Western Religious Luminary*, May 1837; Aberdeen Baptist Association, *Minutes of the Second Anniversary*, 8; Sparks, *On Jordan's Stormy Banks*, 79.

8. Butler, *Awash in a Sea of Faith*, 268–70; Sparks, *On Jordan's Stormy Banks*, 87–88.

9. Membership figures for Methodists and Baptists cited in Samuel Hill, ed., *Encyclopedia of Religion in the South* (Macon, Ga.: Mercer University Press, 1984), 486–87. Figures for Presbyterians in Thompson, *Presbyterians in the South*, I, 175, 433; Sparks, *On Jordan's Stormy Banks*, 88.

10. Sparks, *On Jordan's Stormy Banks*, 88–89.

11. Ibid., 89–90.

12. Griffin, *History of Primitive Baptists*, 177–78. By 1844 at least 900 antimissionary preachers, 1,622 churches, and 68,000 members had left the Baptist Church in the South. Bertram Wyatt-Brown, "The Antimission Movement in the Jacksonian South: A Study in Regional Folk Culture," *Journal of Southern History* XXXVI (November 1970): 527.

13. James E. Tull, *A History of Southern Baptist Landmarkism in the Light of Historical Baptist Ecclesiology* (New York: Arno Press, 1980), 154–231, 413–15 (first quotation on p. 155, second quotation on p. 156); Sparks, *On Jordan's Stormy Banks*, 90.

14. Sparks, *On Jordan's Stormy Banks*, 91.

15. N.a., *Biographical and Historical Memoirs of Mississippi*, 2 vols. (Spartanburg, S.C.: n.p., 1978), I: 364–65.

16. Sparks, *On Jordan's Stormy Banks*, 91–92.

17. Ibid., 92.

18. Sparks, "Mississippi's Apostle of Slavery: James Smylie and the Biblical Defense of Slavery," *Journal of Mississippi History* LI (summer 1989): 89–106; Sparks, *On Jordan's Stormy Banks*, 92–93.

19. Sparks, *On Jordan's Stormy Banks*, 93.

20. *Extracts from the Records of the Synod* 16 (first quotation), 22, 118; Sparks, *On Jordan's Stormy Banks*, 94–95.

21. *Mississippi Baptist*, September 16, 1858 (first quotation); Sparks, *On Jordan's Stormy Banks*, 95–96.

22. Robert Rogers, "From Alienation to Integration: A Social History of Baptists in Antebel-

lum Natchez" (Ph.D. diss., New Orleans Baptist Theological Seminary, 1990), 43–48 (*Luminary* quoted on p. 47); Sparks, *On Jordan's Stormy Banks*, 96–97.

23. Sparks, *On Jordan's Stormy Banks*, 97.

24. Elijah Steele to Henry H. Bridges, August 10, 1837 (first quotation), Steele Papers, MDAH; Winans Journal, February 3, 1855 (second quotation); Memoirs of Edwina Burnley (typescript), Cid Ricketts Sumner Papers, 19 (third quotation), 25 (fourth and fifth quotations), MDAH; New Orleans *South-Western Baptist Chronicle*, January 22, 1848 (sixth quotation), July 8, 1848; Sparks, *On Jordan's Stormy Banks*, 99–100.

25. New Orleans *Christian Advocate*, September 22, 1855; Jones, *Complete History*, II, 274–76, 286; Boyd, *Popular History*, 104, 121; *Mississippi Baptist*, September 17, 1857, July 22, 1858; *South-Western Religion Luminary*, September, October, 1836; E. Brooks Holifield, *The Gentlemen Theologians: American Theology in Southern Culture, 1795–1860* (Durham, N.C.: Duke University Press, 1978), 17–31, 39–49; Hatch, *Democratization*, 193–209; Scott, *From Office to Profession*, 64–65; Jones Autobiography, 60 (first quotation); Bridges to Steele, December 29, 1836 (second, third, and fourth quotations), Elijah Steele Letters, MDAH; New Orleans *Christian Advocate*, March 2, 1859; Sparks, *On Jordan's Stormy Banks*, 102–3.

26. Fontaine Autobiography, MSU; Hill, ed., *Encyclopedia of Religion in the South*, 487; David L. Holmes, *A Brief History of the Episcopal Church* (Valley Forge, Penn.: Trinity Press, 1993), 66–68, 82; McLemore, ed., *History of Mississippi*, I, 385–89.

27. E. Brooks Holifield, *Gentlemen Theologians*, 29, and "The Penurious Preacher? Nineteenth-Century Clerical Wealth: North and South," *Journal of the American Academy of Religion* LVIII (spring 1990): 17–36 (first quotation on p. 17). Holifield found that in 1860 the average wealth of southern urban ministers was $10,177 compared to $4,376 for the same group in the North. Sparks, *On Jordan's Stormy Banks*, 102–3.

28. R. H. Rivers, *The Life of Robert Paine, D. D., Bishop of the Methodist Episcopal Church, South* (Nashville, Tenn.: Southern Methodist Publishing House, 1884), 102 (first quotation); Jones, *Concise History*, 135–37, 139; Winans to Drake, August 15, 1834 (second quotation), February 10, 1857, Drake Papers, Cain Archives; John Buford Cain, *Methodism in the Mississippi Conference, 1846–1870* (Jackson: The Hawkins Foundation, 1939), 187–88 (third and fourth quotations); undated clipping from the Nashville *Christian Advocate*, Winans Scrapbook, Winans Papers (fifth quotation); New Orleans *Christian Advocate*, July 10, 1850 (seventh quotation); Winans Journal, February 10, 1855; Drake Autobiography, Drake Papers (sixth quotation); Hawkins, *Methodism in Natchez*, 42; Sparks, *On Jordan's Stormy Banks*, 102–3.

29. *South-Western Religious Luminary*, October 1836 (first, second, and third quotations); Jones, *Concise History*, 63; Robinson Diary, June 7, 1854; Robert B. Alexander Diary, March 19, 1854 (fourth quotation), June 13, 1861, MDAH; New Orleans *Christian Advocate*, March 10, 1855; Sparks, *On Jordan's Stormy Banks*, 104–5.

30. Amis, *Recollections of Social Customs*, 4–11.

31. *South-Western Religious Luminary*, February 1838 (first quotation); *Mississippi Baptist*, March 18, 1858; Jones, *Complete History*, I, 61, 447, 448 (second quotation), II, 220, 320–21; Tynes Diary, 10, MDAH; Sparks, *On Jordan's Stormy Banks*, 106.

32. Jones, *Complete History*, I, 334 (quotation), 459; Sparks, *On Jordan's Stormy Banks*, 105–6.

33. Jones, *Complete History*, II, 408 (first quotation); New Orleans *Christian Advocate*, April 12, 1851; February 5, 1853; Winans Journal, February 10, 1855; "Church Music," *Western Messenger* I (June 1835): 134–37; Sparks, *On Jordan's Stormy Banks*, 106.

34. New Orleans *Christian Advocate*, August 9, 1851; July 5, 1856; May 20, 1854; August 19, 1854 (first quotation); May 5, 1866; Sparks, *On Jordan's Stormy Banks*, 107–98.

35. Cotton, *Of Primitive Faith*, 29 (first quotation); Tombigbee Baptist Association of the Primitive Order, *Minutes of the Annual Sessions, 1846–1884*, microfilm, Circular Letters of 1848 (second, third, and fourth quotations) and 1852 (fifth quotation), MSU; New Orleans *Christian Advocate*, March 13, 1852 (final quotation); August 13, 1853; Sparks, *On Jordan's Stormy Banks*, 110–11.

36. Jones, *Concise History*, 240 (first quotation); Jones, *Complete History*, II, 488 (second quotation); Sparks, *On Jordan's Stormy Banks*, 115–17.

37. Sparks, *On Jordan's Stormy Banks*, 117.

38. Jones Journal, April 7, 1835 (third and fourth quotations), April 12, 1835 (second quotation), May 8, 1835, June 6, 21, 1835, December 5, 1836; Jones, *Complete History*, II, 488; Winans to Daniel De Vinne, August 31, 1841, Winans Collection. Winans's letters clearly show that he, too, moved from being antislavery to being proslavery. Sparks, *On Jordan's Stormy Banks*, 117–18.

39. Sparks, "Mississippi's Apostle," 89–91; Sparks, *On Jordan's Stormy Banks*, 119.

40. Sparks, *On Jordan's Stormy Banks*, 118–19.

41. Sparks, "Mississippi's Apostle," 97–98 (third quotation).

42. On the curse of Ham, see Robin Blackburn, "The Old World Background to European Colonial Slavery," *William and Mary Quarterly*, 3d ser., LIV (January 1997): 90–97; Benjamin Braude, "The Sons of Noah and the Construction of Ethnic and Geographic Identities in the Medieval and Early Modern Periods," *William and Mary Quarterly*, 3d ser., LIV (January 1997): 103–42.

43. Sparks, "Mississippi's Apostle," 98.

44. Sparks, "Mississippi's Apostle," 98–99 (first, second, third, and fourth quotations); *Christian Herald*, October 1, 1836 (final quotation); Walter Brownlow Posey, *Frontier Mission: A History of Religion West of the Southern Appalachians to 1861* (Lexington, Ky.: University of Kentucky Press, 1966), 342; E. N. Elliott, ed., *Cotton is King, and pro-Slavery Arguments. . . .* (Augusta, Ga.: Prichard, Abbott & Loomis, 1860), x; James Smylie, *A Review of a Letter from the Presbytery of Chillicothe, to the Presbytery of Mississippi, on the Subject of Slavery. . . .* (Woodville, Miss.: William A. Norris & Co., 1836); Gerrit Smith, *Letter of Gerrit Smith to Rev. James Smylie, of the State of Mississippi* (New York: R. G. Williams, 1837); Synod of Mississippi and South Alabama, *Extracts from the Records of the Synod of Mississippi and South Alabama, From 1829 to 1835* (Jackson, Miss.: Clarion Steam Publishing Establishment, 1880), 278–83; Sparks, *On Jordan's Stormy Banks*, 119–20.

45. Sparks, *On Jordan's Stormy Banks*, 121–22.

46. Mitchell Snay, "American Thought and Southern Distinctiveness: The Southern Clergy and the Sanctification of Slavery," *Civil War History* XXXV (December 1989): 322 (second quotation); Sparks, "Mississippi's Apostle," 103 (first quotation); S. G. Winchester, *The Religion of the Bible, The Only Preservation of Our Civil Institutions. . . .* (Natchez, Miss.: Oakland College, 1838), 17–23 (third quotation on p. 23); Sparks, *On Jordan's Stormy Banks*, 122–23.

47. *Mississippi Baptist*, July 14, 1859 (first quotation); Daniel Baker, *A Series of Revival Sermons* (Pennfield, Ga.: J. S. Baker, 1847), 28 (second quotation); Sparks, *On Jordan's Stormy Banks*, 122.

48. Winans to De Vinne, August 31, 1841, Winans Papers; Sparks, *On Jordan's Stormy Banks*, 123.

49. New Orleans *Christian Advocate*, October 5, 1859 (quotation); Smylie, *Review of a Letter*, 74; Sparks, *On Jordan's Stormy Banks*, 123.

50. Rawick, *American Slave*, Supp., Ser. 1, vol. 9, pt. 4, 1597 (first quotation), 1571 (second quotation); vol. 10, pt. 5, 2337; Sparks, *On Jordan's Stormy Banks*, 144.

51. *Liberty Advocate*, March 31, 1838 (quotations). The *Advocate* was published in Amite County, and one of Smylie's family members was an editor. Sparks, *On Jordan's Stormy Banks*, 123–24.

52. Sparks, *On Jordan's Stormy Banks*, 124–26.

Chapter 6

1. "Prayer to be used during the present trouble," William M. Green Papers, MDAH.

2. Eliza Lucy Irion Journal, Book II, January 3–4, 1861, typescript, MDAH; Lyon Journal, June 1861, MSU.

3. McLemore, ed., *History of Mississippi*, I, 529–31 (first quotation on p. 529); Rev. Walter Edwin Tynes Diary, 11 (second quotation), MDAH; New Orleans *Christian Advocate*, January 12, October 5, 1859; *Mississippi Baptist*, October 13 (third quotation), March 24, 1859; November 25, 1858; February 16 (fourth quotation), March 1, 22, 1860; Ray Holder, ed., "On Slavery: Selected Letters of Parson Winans, 1820–1844," *Journal of Mississippi History* VXLVI (November 1984): 341 (fifth and sixth quotations); Sparks, *On Jordan's Stormy Banks*, 175.

4. Robert B. Alexander Diary, June 13, 1861 (first quotation), February 28, 1862 (second quotation), August 21, 1863, MDAH; James W. Silver, *Confederate Morale and Church Propaganda* (New York: Norton, 1957), 64 (third quotation), 65 (fourth quotation), 66, 95; Sparks, *On Jordan's Stormy Banks*, 177–78.

5. Augustus H. Mecklin Diary, February 14–15, 17, 1862 (first quotation), MDAH; Lyon Journal, 33 (second and third quotations); Eliza Lucy Irion Journal, April 1862; Cordelia Scales to "Dearest Darling Loulie," May 15, 1862, Scales Letters, MDAH; Sophia Boyd Hays Diary, May 1862, MSU; McLemore, ed., *History of Mississippi*, 531; Sparks, *On Jordan's Stormy Banks*, 178–79.

6. Anonymous Diary, September, November 1863, MDAH; Cain, *Methodism in the Mississippi Conference*, 297; Sparks, *On Jordan's Stormy Banks*, 179.

7. Beulah Baptist Church, Tippah County, January 1862, SBHC; Bethlehem Church, June 1862, August 1861, November 8, 1864, MSU; Crawfordsville Methodist Circuit, September 3, 1861, January 24, 1862, MSU; Minutes of the Quarterly Conference of the Methodist Episcopal Church South, Port Gibson Station, April 29, 1848, to December 31, 1872, June 18, 1864 (quotation), Cain Archives; Jackson First Presbyterian Church Records, 24–25, MDAH; Liberty Baptist Church, May 1861, SBHC; Samuel A. Agnew Diary, June 1, 6, August 31 (quotation), October 26, December 21, 1862; February 1, August 12, 16, 1863; June 16, 1864 (quotation), MSU; Sparks, *On Jordan's Stormy Banks*, 179.

8. Rawick, ed., *American Slave*, Supp., Ser. 1, vol. 6, pt. 1, 202 (first quotation); vol. 7, pt. 2, 785 (second quotation); vol. 8, pt. 3, 899; Agnew Diary, July 30, August 18, October 29,

October 30 (third quotation), November 1, 1862; May 25, 1865 (fourth quotation); Anonymous Natchez Diary, July 30, 1863, MDAH; Robert B. Alexander Diary, 1863, 1864, MDAH; W. Maury Darst, ed., "The Vicksburg Diary of Mrs. Alfred Ingraham (May 2–June 13, 1863)," *Journal of Mississippi History* LXIV (May 1982): 168 (fourth quotation); James L. Roark, *Masters Without Slaves: Southern Planters in the Civil War and Reconstruction* (New York: Norton, 1977), 81–85 (fifth quotation on p. 82); Sparks, *On Jordan's Stormy Banks*, 179.

9. Line Creek Baptist Church Records, Casey, comp., *Amite County*, II, 91; Sparks, *On Jordan's Stormy Banks*, 164–67, 169–70.

10. Walter Edwin Tynes Diary, 11, MDAH; Sparks, *On Jordan's Stormy Banks*, 179–80.

11. Lyon Diary, 30 (quotation); Sparks, *On Jordan's Stormy Banks*, 180–81.

12. College Hill Church Records reproduced in Brown, "What Desolations!," Maude M. Brown Papers, 105–8, MDAH; Sparks, *On Jordan's Stormy Banks*, 181.

13. Anonymous Diary, July 16, 28 (quotation), MDAH; Sparks, *On Jordan's Stormy Banks*, 182.

14. Strong River Baptist Association, *Minutes of the Eleventh Annual Session . . . 1863* (Brandon, Miss.: The Association, 1863), appendix C (first quotation); Strong River Baptist Association, *Minutes of the Ninth Anniversary of the Strong River Baptist Association . . . 1861* (Jackson, Miss.: The Association, 1861), 14; Cain, *Methodism in the Mississippi Conference*, 339; Aberdeen Baptist Association, *Minutes of the Twenty-first Anniversary of the Aberdeen Baptist Association . . . 1864* (N.p.: The Association, 1864), appendix B (second quotation); New Orleans *Christian Advocate*, January 27, 1866 (final quotation); Sparks, *On Jordan's Stormy Banks*, 182–83.

15. Silver, *Confederate Morale*, p. 64 (first quotation); Strong River Baptist Association, *Minutes . . . 1863*, appendix D (second quotation); Sparks, *On Jordan's Stormy Banks*, 183.

16. Cain, *Methodism in the Mississippi Conference*, 296 (quotation), 339; Jones Autobiography, 117; Sparks, *On Jordan's Stormy Banks*, 183–84.

17. Tynes Diary, 11 (first quotation); New Orleans *Christian Advocate*, January 27, 1866 (second quotation); Casey, *Amite County*, II, 40 (third quotation); Sparks, *On Jordan's Stormy Banks*, 184–85.

18. Lyon Journal, 102 (first and second quotations), 107 (third quotation); Mississippi Baptist State Convention, *Proceedings of the Twenty-Seventh Session of the Baptist State Convention . . . 1866* (Jackson, Miss.: The Association, 1866), 22 (fourth and fifth quotations); Cain, *Methodism in the Mississippi Conference*, 386; Sparks, *On Jordan's Stormy Banks*, 184–85.

19. "The Cause and Design of the War of Southern Independence," Fontaine Sermons, Fontaine Collection, MSU.

20. Salem Baptist Association, *Minutes of the Fifth Annual Meeting . . . 1866* (Jackson, Miss.: The Association, 1866), 10 (first quotation); Sparks, *On Jordan's Stormy Banks*, 185.

21. Sparks, *On Jordan's Stormy Banks*, 187.

22. Ibid., 186–88.

23. A. T. Morgan, *Yazoo; or, on the Picket Line of Freedom in the South* (Washington, D.C.: A. T. Morgan, 1884), 108.

24. Agnew Diary, July 21–24, August 3, 19, September 8, 24, 29, 1867, April 19, August 9,

23, 1868, April 18, June 6, July 4, August 8, 16, 29, October 30, 31, 1869, April 10, July 20, 30, 31, August 21, 27, September 20, 23, 1870, April 2, 17, July 29, 30, October 28, 29, 1871, February 15 (first quotation), December 14 (second quotation), 1872; Sparks, *On Jordan's Stormy Banks*, 195.

25. Casey, *Amite County*, II, 310 (first quotation), 56–76; Rawick, *American Slave*, Supp., Ser. I, vol. 9, pt. 4, 1601 (second quotation); Bethany Church, July 1871, SBHC; Sparks, *On Jordan's Stormy Banks*, 198–99.

26. Academy Church, November 1865, August 1869, August 1870; Magnolia Baptist Church, July 1867, December 23, 1871; Liberty Church, May 1866, July, August 1867, May 1872; Hopewell Baptist Church Records, August 1871, MBHS; Sparks, *On Jordan's Stormy Banks*, 198–99.

27. Salem Baptist Association, *Minutes of the Ninth Annual Session of the Salem Baptist Association . . . Jasper County, Mississippi . . . 1870* (Lauderdale Station, Miss.: The Association, 1870), 6 (quotation), 11; Salem Baptist Association, *Minutes . . . 1865* (Mobile, Ala.: The Association, 1865), 11; Salem Baptist Association, *Minutes . . . 1872* (Enterprise, Miss.: The Association, 1872), 7, 11. See also Statistical Tables in Aberdeen Baptist Association, *Minutes of the Aberdeen Baptist Association . . . 1865* (Jackson, Tenn.: The Association, 1865); *Minutes . . . 1868* (N.p.: The Association, 1868); Fellowship Baptist Church, May 1874, January 1876, SBHC.

28. New Orleans *Christian Advocate*, August 11, 1866 (first quotation); December 15, 1866 (second and third quotations); Cain, *Methodism in the Mississippi Conference*, 441, 457; Sparks, *On Jordan's Stormy Banks*, 198–99.

29. Morgan, *Yazoo*, 103–9 (quotations on p. 108); Sparks, *On Jordan's Stormy Banks*, 188–89.

30. Thompson, *Black Baptists*, 79 (first quotation); 44 (second quotation); Morgan, *Yazoo*, 271 (third quotation); Sparks, *On Jordan's Stormy Banks*, 188.

31. Mt. Olivet Baptist Association *Minutes*, 1871, 10 (second quotation); Michael William Fitzgerald, "The Union League Movement in Alabama and Mississippi: Politics and Agricultural Change in the Deep South During Reconstruction" (Ph.D. diss., University of California, Los Angeles, 1986), 39–40, 78 (first quotation), 140; Sparks, *On Jordan's Stormy Banks*, 188–89.

32. Sparks, " 'The White People's Arms Are Longer Than Ours': Blacks, Education, and the American Missionary Association in Reconstruction Mississippi," *Journal of Mississippi History* LIV (February 1992): 16 (first quotation), 5 (second quotation); Sparks, *On Jordan's Stormy Banks*, 189.

33. Sparks, "White People's Arms," 16–20 (first quotation on p. 16); *Minutes of the Twenty-First Annual Session of the Central Baptist Association . . . 1866* (Jackson, 1866), appendix D (second quotation); *Minutes of the Twenty-Third Annual Session of the Central Baptist Association . . . 1868* (Jackson, 1868); Sparks, *On Jordan's Stormy Banks*, 189.

34. Sparks, "White People's Arms," 19 (first quotation); Sparks, *On Jordan's Stormy Banks*, 189–90.

35. Waterbury, *Seven Years*, 118–120 (quotations); see also 41, 154–55. Another northerner recorded a similar examination meeting where visionary experiences were related. See George C. Benham, *A Year of Wreck: A True Story By a Victim* (New York: Harper & Brothers, 1880), 303–4; Sparks, *On Jordan's Stormy Banks*, 190–91.

36. Waterbury, *Seven Years*, 195–96; Sparks, *On Jordan's Stormy Banks*, 191.

37. Thompson, *History of the Negro Baptists*, 41, 519–20.

38. *Minutes of the First Annual Session of the Mount Olivet Baptist Association . . . 1869* (n.p., 1869); *Minutes of the Third Annual Session of the Mt. Olivet Baptist Association . . . 1871* (Columbus, Miss., 1871), 5–6 (first quotation); *Minutes of the Fourth Annual Session of the Mt. Olivet Baptist Association . . . 1872* (Columbus, 1872); 14–15; *Proceedings of the Mt. Olive Baptist Association . . . 1877* (Meridian, Miss., 1877); Thompson, *Negro Baptists*, 49 (second quotation), 62, 81, 84, 109, 127–28, 135–36, 371. See also *Minutes of the First Session of the Sardis Missionary Baptist Association . . . 1870* (Memphis, 1870); Sparks, *On Jordan's Stormy Banks*, 192.

39. Thompson, *Black Baptists*, 92 (first quotation), 108 (second quotation).

40. Ibid., 62–65 (quotation), 327, 360–61; Sparks, *On Jordan's Stormy Banks*, 193.

41. Sparks, "White People's Arms," 2–3, 6, 16; Thompson, *Negro Baptists*, 32, 52, 58, 99–100, 157 (quotation); Sparks, *On Jordan's Stormy Banks*, 197.

Chapter 7

1. New York *Sun*, August 1, 1897, Craig Scrapbook, MDAH.

2. Brookhaven *Leader* (n.d.), Craig Scrapbook, MDAH ; New York *Sun*, August 1, 1897, Craig Scrapbook, MDAH.

3. "Intemperance" sermon (1876), Charles B. Galloway, Galloway Papers, Cain Archives.

4. W. B. Jones, *Methodism in the Mississippi Conference, 1870–1894* (Jackson, Miss.: Hawkins Foundation, 1951), 135.

5. George Leftwich to "Dear Pa & Ma," April 14, 1890; Leftwich to "Dear Mother," April 27, 1890, George Jabez Leftwich Papers, MDAH; Johnny Parrott Diary, July 18, 1887, MDAH.

6. Boyd, *Popular History of the Baptists*, 138, 191–92, 215–16; Jackson *Clarion-Ledger*, June 27, 1893; "Influence and Missions of Southern Womanhood," Charles B. Galloway Papers, MDAH.

7. Belle Kearney, *A Slaveholder's Daughter* (1900; reprint, New York: Negro Universities Press, 1969), 20, 21.

8. Ibid., 30–41 (first quotation on p. 41, second and third quotations on p. 44, fourth quotation on p. 45).

9. Ibid., 46 (first quotation), 47 (second quotation), 55 (third quotation), 69 (fourth quotation).

10. Ibid., 107–31 (first quotation on p. 130, second quotation on p. 118).

11. Ibid., 131–48 (first quotation on p. 134, second quotation on p. 136, third quotation on p. 148).

12. Ibid., 155–207 (first quotation on p. 164, second quotation on p. 206).

13. Winnie Phillips, *A History of Methodist Women* (Clinton, Miss.: Mississippi Conference, United Methodist Church, 1980), 18, 144–45; Mrs. John Rundle, comp., *History of Grenada County Baptist Association, 1921–1960* (Grenada, Miss.: Baptist Press, 1961), 17, 25–27; Christian Citizens League Subject File, MDAH.

14. Baltimore *Christian Advocate*, August 2, 1899, Galloway Papers, Cain Archives; Kearney, *Slaveholder's Daughter*, 223.

15. Charles Reagan Wilson, *Baptized in Blood: The Religion of the Lost Cause, 1865–1920* (Athens, Ga.: University of Georgia Press, 1980), 10–11 (first quotation); Gaines M. Foster, *Ghosts of the Confederacy: Defeat, the Lost Cause, and the Emergence of the New South, 1865 to 1913* (New York and Oxford: Oxford University Press, 1987); *Confederate Veteran*, March 1901, 111 (second quotation).

16. Wilson, *Baptized in Blood*, 109 (first quotation); *Confederate Veteran*, March 1901, 119 (second quotation); March 1901, 120 (third quotation).

17. *Journal of the One Hundred and Fourth Session of the Mississippi Annual Conference of the Methodist Episcopal Church, South . . . 1917* (Jackson, Miss.: The Conference, n.d.), 25; Bratton quoted in Wilson, *Baptized in Blood*, 167.

18. *Confederate Veteran*, July 1901, 304; Boyd, *Popular History*, 225, 320; Baptist Hospital Subject File, MDAH.

19. International Order of King's Daughters and Sons Subject File, MDAH.

20. Boyd, *Popular History*, 182–83; Baptist Children's Village Subject File, MDAH.

21. "Influence and Missions of Southern Womanhood," Galloway Papers, MDAH.

22. Mrs. Rolfe Hunt, *Mississippi Missionaries* (Meridian, Miss.: n.p., n.d. [1933]), 8–12; Boyd, *Popular History*, 150–52; Leavell and Bailey, *Complete History of Mississippi Baptists*, 115–17, 310; "Report of Woman's Missionary Society, June 1880," Charles Kimball Marshall Papers, MDAH.

23. Maude Morrow Brown, "A Preliminary Report on the History of the First Presbyterian Church of Oxford . . . ," unpublished manuscript in Brown Papers, MDAH.

24. Phillips, *Methodist Women*, 20, 23.

25. *Southwestern Christian Advocate*, May 19, 1904; undated and untitled manuscripts [1890s]; Sermon 51 [1870s]; "Unauthorized Justice" [1890s], Galloway Papers, Cain Archives; New Orleans *Christian Advocate*, May 10, 1900; Baltimore *Christian Advocate*, August 2, 1899; May 21, 1909.

26. Theodore DuBose Bratton, *Wanted—Leaders! A Study of Negro Development* (New York: Department of Missions and Church Expansion, 1922), 212, 216, 227–28.

27. T. C. Schilling, *Abstract History of the Mississippi Baptist Association for One Hundred Years* (New Orleans: J. G. Hauser, 1908), 247; C. Vann Woodward, *Origins of the New South, 1877–1913* (Baton Rouge: Louisiana State University Press, 1951), 352.

28. Bessie C. Alford Biography, Winnie Ellis Phillips Papers, Cain Archives; Mississippi Council on Interracial Cooperation Subject File, MDAH; Bratton to Anslem J. Finch, February 10, 1944, Finch Papers, MDAH.

29. Phillips, *Methodist Women*, 135–36; Woman's Missionary Society, *Twentieth Annual Report of the Woman's Missionary Society of the Mississippi Conference, Methodist Episcopal Church, South . . . 1931* (n.p., n.d.), 31, 35, 55.

30. "Mississippi Synodical, 1935–40," 5; "History of Mississippi Synodical Auxiliary, October 3, 1940–October 4, 1945," 1; "History of Women's Auxiliary, Synod of Mississippi, October 4, 1944–October 3, 1945," Presbyterian Auxiliaries Papers, Synod of Mississippi, Presbyterian Church, United States, MDAH.

31. Phillips, *Methodist Women*, 136–37; Woman's Missionary Society, *Twenty-Third Annual Report of the Woman's Missionary Society of the Mississippi Conference, Methodist Episcopal Church, South . . . 1934* (n.p., n.d.), 50–51.

32. Phillips, *Methodist Women*, 197–98.

33. Ibid., 25, 137–38; New Orleans *Christian Advocate*, October 30, 1930; January 11, 18, August 2, 1934; *Mississippi Methodist Advocate*, June 18, 1947.

34. Leon F. Litwack, *Trouble in Mind: Black Southerners in the Age of Jim Crow* (New York: Knopf, 1998), 297–98.

35. Galloway to unnamed Vardaman supporter, undated [1900?], Galloway Papers, Cain Archives.

36. Gavin Wright, *Old South, New South: Revolutions in the Southern Economy Since the Civil War* (New York: Basic Books, 1986), 55; Boyd, *Popular History*, 209–18.

Chapter 8

1. Richard Wright, *12 Million Black Voices* (New York: Viking Press, 1941), conclusion.

2. Boyd, *Popular History*, 211–14.

3. U.S. Bureau of the Census, Religious Bodies, 1936, vol. I (Washington, D.C., 1941), pp. 374–423. The three major black Methodist denominations were the Colored Methodist Episcopal Church, the African Methodist Episcopal Church, and the African Methodist Episcopal Church, Zion.

4. John Morant, *Mississippi Minister* (New York: Vantage Press, 1958), 9–25.

5. Ibid., 25–28.

6. Ibid., 31–46.

7. Ibid., 47–51.

8. Richard Wright, *Black Boy* (New York: Harper and Brothers, 1945), 166–67.

9. U.S. Bureau of the Census, Religious Bodies, 1936, 374–423.

10. Jackson *Clarion-Ledger*, March 4, 1979.

11. Ibid.; Boyd, *Popular History*, 24; Edward Ayers, *The Promise of the New South: Life After Reconstruction* (New York and Oxford: Oxford University Press, 1992), 399–405; Ian MacRobert, *The Black Roots and White Racism of Early Pentecostalism in the USA* (New York: St. Martin's Press, 1988), 6–7, 37–41.

12. Jackson *Clarion-Ledger*, March 4, 1979.

13. Wright, *Black Boy*, 113.

14. Ibid., 123–24.

15. Seventh-Day Adventist Church Subject File, MDAH.

16. Gary Don McElhany, "Fire in the Pines: A History of the Assemblies of God in Mississippi, 1900–1936" (M.A. thesis, Mississippi State University, 1992), 47.

17. Ibid., 101–8, 139.

18. Ibid., 119, 127.

19. Ibid., 62–63.

20. Ibid., 150, 162.

21. Bernice Johnson Reagon, "Pioneering African American Gospel Music Composers: A Smithsonian Institution Research Project," in Bernice Johnson Reagon, ed., *We'll Understand It Better By and By* (Washington, D.C.: Smithsonian Institution Press, 1992), 5.

22. *Congressional Record*, October 27, 1990.

23. Horace Clarence Boyer, *How Sweet the Sound: The Golden Age of Gospel* (Washington, D.C.: Elliott & Clark, 1995), 64.

24. Ibid., 124.

25. James C. Cobb, *The Most Southern Place on Earth: The Mississippi Delta and the Roots of Regional Identity* (New York and Oxford: Oxford University Press, 1992), 286; B. B. King, Oral History Interview by John Jones, Gentry High School, Indianola, Miss., June 5, 1980, 2–5, MDAH.

26. King, interview by Jones, 2–5; Ayers, *Promise of the New South*, 393; Cobb, *Most Southern Place*, 277–302.

27. Bill C. Malone, *Southern Music, American Music* (Lexington, Ky.: University Press of Kentucky, 1979), 67; J. P. Wright, Oral History Interview by Carl A. Ray, July 30, 1972, Webster County, Mississippi, MDAH; Ayers, *Promise of the New South*, 397–98.

28. Wright, interview by Ray; Malone, *Southern Music*, 67–69; Ayers, *Promise of the New South*, 397–98.

29. Cobb, *Most Southern Place*, 281; Malone, *Southern Music*, 68–69.

30. Bob McRaney, Sr., *A History of Radio in Mississippi* (N.p.: Mississippi Broadcasters Association, 1979), 14–22; Howard Williams Subject File, MDAH.

31. *The Gospel Messenger* (Scooba, Miss.), August 1925 (first quotation); George E. Webb, *The Evolution Controversy in America* (Lexington, Ky.: University Press of Kentucky, 1994), 63.

32. Webb, *Evolution Controversy*, 94.

33. Wright, *Old South, New South*, 56–57.

34. E. L. Stanford, *The History of Calvary Baptist Church, Jackson, Mississippi* (Jackson, Miss.: The Church, 1980), 120–23; U.S. Bureau of the Census, Religious Bodies, 1936, 374–423.

35. Stanford, *History of Calvary Baptist*, 123.

36. Sherwood Eddy, *A Door of Opportunity or An American Adventure in Cooperation with Sharecroppers* (New York: Eddy and Page, 1937), 9.

37. Ibid., 10.

38. Ibid., 28.

39. Ibid., 32–33.

40. H. L. Mitchell, *Mean Things Happening in This Land: The Life and Times of H. L. Mitchell, Co-Founder of the Southern Tenant Farmers Union* (Montclair, N.J.: Allanheld, Osmun, 1979), 133.

41. Reinhold Niebuhr, "Meditations from Mississippi," *Christian Century* (February 10, 1937), 183–84.

42. Mitchell, *Mean Things*, 134.

43. Hortense Powdermaker, *After Freedom: A Cultural Study in the Deep South* (New York: Viking Press, 1939), 17–18, 26.

44. Ibid., 18, 35.

45. Ibid., 223, 233–34.

46. Ibid., 234–35.

47. Ibid., 236–37.

48. Ibid., 243–448.

49. Ibid., 246–48.

50. Ibid., 248–49.

51. Chalmers Archer, Jr., *Growing Up Black in Rural Mississippi: Memories of a Family, Heritage of a Place* (New York: Walker, 1992), 66.

52. Ibid., 225–29.

53. Ibid., 331–53.

54. Ibid., 363.

55. Dema Chauncy Alcott, "A Eulogy," 1954, Wharton Collection, MDAH.

56. See, for example, her undated lessons entitled "The War Against Beverage Alcohol" and "The Christian War—Temperance" in Wharton Collection. The extent to which the Social Gospel movement affected the South has been the subject of considerable debate. J. Wayne Flynt has argued forcefully for the existence of an important southern reform movement, particularly among Wharton's fellow Presbyterians. See Flynt, " 'Feeding the Hungry and Ministering to the Broken Hearted': The Presbyterian Church in the United States and the Social Gospel, 1900–1920" in Charles Reagan Wilson, ed., *Religion in the South* (Jackson, Miss.: University Press of Mississippi, 1985), 83–137. See also John P. McDowell, *The Social Gospel in the South: The Woman's Home Mission Movement in the Methodist Episcopal Church South, 1886–1939* (Baton Rouge: Louisiana State University Press, 1982); Dewey W. Grantham, *Southern Progressivism: The Reconciliation of Progress and Tradition* (Knoxville, Tenn.: University of Tennessee Press, 1983), 200–45; Eighmy, *Churches in Cultural Captivity*, 80–82; Jones, *Methodism in the Mississippi Conference*, 135.

57. "When We Work with God," Wharton Collection.

58. "A Nation Demands a King," Wharton Collection.

59. "Christian Relations Among Races," Wharton Collection.

60. "The Christian and the Race Problem," Wharton Collection.

61. "Two Brothers Learn Tolerance," Wharton Collection.

62. John Egerton, *Speak Now Against the Day: The Generation Before the Civil Rights Movement in the South* (New York: Knopf, 1994), 289.

63. Cobb, *Most Southern Place on Earth*, 196–97.

64. Chester M. Morgan, "At the Crossroads: World War II, Delta Agriculture, and Modernization in Mississippi," *Journal of Mississippi History* LVII (winter 1995): 361–62; Nan Elizabeth Woodruff, "Mississippi Delta Planters and Debates over Mechanization, Labor, and Civil Rights in the 1940s," *Journal of Southern History* LX (May 1994): 263, 278–79.

65. Wright, *12 Million*, conclusion.

66. Youth of the Rural Organizing and Cultural Center, *Minds Stayed on Freedom: The Civil Rights Struggle in the Rural South, an Oral History* (Boulder, Colo.: Westview Press, 1991), 65, 94.

67. "Pillars of Peace" (undated sermon), Bishop Marvin A. Franklin Collection, Cain Archives.

68. Ibid.; "That Freedom May Not Perish" (quotations), Bishop Marvin A. Franklin Collection, Cain Archives.

69. *Jackson Daily News*, February 20, 1949.

70. Ibid., November 30, 1948.

71. Ibid., June 4 (remaining quotations), 11 (fourth quotation), 1946; James W. Silver, *Mississippi: The Closed Society* (New York: Harper, Brace & World, 1966), 134.

Chapter 9

1. Charles E. Nolan, *St. Mary's of Natchez: The History of a Southern Catholic Congregation, 1716–1988* (Natchez, Miss.: St. Mary's Catholic Church, 1992), 125.

2. Jackson *Clarion-Ledger*, July 14, 1985.

3. David E. Harrell, "Religious Pluralism: Catholics, Jews, and Sectarians," in Wilson, ed., *Religion in the South*, 60–62. Historian R. Laurence Moore coined the term "religious outsiders" and argued that members of these groups used that "outsiderness" to invent their "Americanness." See R. Laurence Moore, *Religious Outsiders and the Making of Americans* (New York and Oxford: Oxford University Press, 1986).

4. Mills and Smith, *Report of a Missionary Tour*, 26.

5. Nolan, *St. Mary's*, 120.

6. Ibid, 122.

7. Richard Oliver Gerow, *Catholicity in Mississippi* (Natchez, Miss.: n.p., 1939), 52.

8. Nolan, *St. Mary's*, 128–29.

9. Gerow, *Catholicity in Mississippi*, 52.

10. Nolan, *St. Mary's*, 96–97.

11. Randall M. Miller, "Slaves and Southern Catholicism," in Boles, ed., *Masters and Slaves in the House of the Lord*, 127.

12. Nolan, *St. Mary's*, 139.

13. Gerow, *Catholicity in Mississippi*, 61.

14. Richard Oliver Gerow, *Cradle Days of St. Mary's at Natchez* (Natchez, Miss.: n.p., 1941), 219–24.

15. Ibid., 247–57, 265–70.

16. Nolan, *St. Mary's*, 152–53.

17. Ibid., 270–72; "Holy Family Is Oldest Black Parish," *Mississippi Today*, September 25, 1987; Nolan, *St. Mary's*, 26.

18. Nolan, *St. Mary's*, 271–75.

19. Gerow, *Catholicity in Mississippi*, 190.

20. Ibid., 351.

21. Ibid., 352.

22. Ibid., 263.

23. Ibid., 307.

24. Cobb, *Most Southern Place on Earth*, 110–11.

25. Nolan, *St. Mary's*, 208.

26. Ibid., 192.

27. Ibid., 193.

28. Ibid., 198.

29. Ibid., 211.

30. Ibid., 216.

31. Ibid., 218.

32. Ibid., 225.

33. Martin E. Marty, *Pilgrims in Their Own Land: 500 Years of Religion in America* (Boston: Little, Brown, 1984), 289.

34. *New York Times*, September 29, 1991.

35. *Jackson Daily News*, May 12, 1940.

36. Fulton *Itawambian* quoted in *The Southron* (Jackson), December 17, 1845.

37. "Southern States Mission," *Liahona: The Elders' Journal* 36 (January 24, 1939): 379.

38. Ibid.

Chapter 10

1. Martin Luther King, Jr., *Stride Toward Freedom: The Montgomery Story* (San Francisco: Harper & Row, 1986), 205.

2. Ibid., 205, 208.

3. Silver, *Mississippi*, 22, 283.

4. Jackson *Capital Reporter* June 5, 1980; John Dittmer, *Local People: The Struggle for Civil Rights in Mississippi* (Urbana and Chicago: University of Illinois Press, 1994), 28–29.

5. Florence Mars, *Witness in Philadelphia* (Baton Rouge and London: Louisiana State University Press, 1977), 42.

6. Nan Elizabeth Woodruff, "Mississippi Delta Planters and Debates over Mechanization, Labor, and Civil Rights in the 1940s," *Journal of Southern History* LX (May 1994): 272, 279.

7. Youth of the Rural Organizing and Cultural Center, *Minds Stayed on Freedom*, 23–24, 28–29, 151; Anne Moody, *Coming of Age in Mississippi* (New York: Dell Publishers, 1968), 248.

8. Youth of the Rural Organizing and Cultural Center, *Minds Stayed on Freedom*, 23–24; Charles M. Payne, *I've Got the Light of Freedom: The Organization Tradition and the Mississippi Freedom Struggle* (Berkeley, Los Angeles, London: University of California Press, 1995), 188–90.

9. Youth of the Rural Organizing and Cultural Center, *Minds Stayed on Freedom*, 15.

10. Moody, *Coming of Age*, 254.

11. Payne, *I've Got the Light*, 249, 266–67; Vicki Crawford, "Race, Class, Gender, and Culture: Black Women's Activism in the Mississippi Civil Rights Movement," *Journal of Mississippi History* LVIII (spring 1996): 1, 18–21; Dittmer, *Local People*, 433; Kay Mills, *This Little Light of Mine: The Life of Fannie Lou Hamer* (New York: Dutton, 1993), 17–21.

12. Mills, *This Little Light*, 238; Moody, *Coming of Age*, 281, 283.

13. Depositions, 1964, Council of Federated Organizations Records, MDAH.

14. *Jackson Daily News*, June 1, 6, 1954, March 10, 1955; Memphis *Commercial Appeal*, November 26, 1954; First Methodist Church of Clarksdale, Resolutions (undated [1954]), Garland Holloman Papers, Special Collections, MSU.

15. Silver, *Mississippi*, 8, 36 (quotation), 40–43; *Jackson Daily News*, July 7, 10; December 30, 1960.

16. C. C. Smith, "WAKE UP!" (n.d., n.p.), Citizens' Council Subject File, MDAH. Noah became drunk on wine and lay naked in his tent. Ham saw his father lying exposed, but, rather than cover him, Ham went out and told his brothers, who then came, averted their eyes, and covered their father. When Noah awoke he aimed his curse not at Ham, but at Ham's son. Noah said, "Cursed be Canaan; a servant of servants shall he be unto his brethren." The story appears in Genesis 9–10. Benjamin Braude, "The Sons of Noah and the Construction of Ethnic and Geographical Identities in the Medieval and Early Modern Periods," *William and Mary Quarterly*, 3d ser., LIV (January 1997): 103–4; "Is Segregation Unchristian?" (Greenwood, Miss., n.d.); R. B. Eleazer, *"The Curse of Ham"* (Nashville, Tenn.: n.p., n.d.); Gillespie, *A Christian View of Segregation*, 9.

17. *Jackson Daily News*, February 21, 1956 (first quotation); Silver, *Mississippi*, 36 (second quotation), 107–14; Dittmer, *Local People*, 61–64.

18. D. M. Nelson, *Conflicting Views on Segregation* (Greenwood, Miss.: Educational Fund of the Citizens' Council, 1954), 5, 10. The Reverend G. T. Gillespie, president emeritus of Belhaven College, a school in Jackson supported by the Presbyterian Church, also published a segregationist tract through the Citizens' Council. See G. T. Gillespie, *A Christian View on Segregation* (Greenwood, Miss.: Educational Fund of the Citizens' Council, 1954).

19. Caskey, "Inaugural Invocation, Mississippi College, 1960," W. M. Caskey Subject File, MDAH.

20. Caskey to Coody, October 3, 1957, Coody Papers, MDAH.

21. Stimson Coody to "Dear Mother," April 13, 1951, Coody Papers, MDAH.

22. Archibald S. Coody, *The Race Question from the White Chief: A Story of the Life and Times of James K. Vardaman* (N.p.: A. S. Coody, 1944), 13–14, 23–24.

23. "A Search for Life's Meaning," June 4, 1961, Coody Papers, MDAH.

24. "Our Problem—How to Meet It," May 1, 1958, Coody Papers, MDAH.

25. Coody to Marilyn R. Allen, June 14, 1956, Coody Papers, MDAH.

26. Coody to "Dear Sonny," February 21, 1956, Coody Papers, MDAH.

27. "Jesus Questioned," February 1, 1959, Coody Papers, MDAH.

28. *Jackson Daily News*, January 3, 1947 (first quotation); Samuel S. Hill, Jr., "The South's Two Cultures," in Samuel S. Hill, Jr., ed., *Religion and the Solid South* (Nashville and New York: Abingdon Press, 1972), 51.

29. Bilbo to Coody, May 29, 1945, Coody Papers, MDAH.

30. On his popularity as a teacher, see W. Henry Holman to Coody, June 21, July 15, 1954. He was invited to teach at other churches, including Galloway Methodist Church. See Coody to "Dear Katherine," March 8, 1957; Jones to Coody, October 31, 1960; Nelson to Coody, February 27, 1956; March 20, 1957; Florence Sillers Ogden to Coody, July 30, 1958; Archibald B. Roosevelt to Coody, October 5, 1960; February 10, 1961; Erle Johnston to Coody, January 17, 1957; Horace Sherman Miller to Coody, October 5, 1957; Ku Klux Klan Certificate of Merit, 1958.

31. *Jackson Daily News*, January 30, 1958, June 1, 6, 29, 1954; *Christian Conservative Communique*, May 17, 1966; *Information Bulletin of the Mississippi Association of Methodist Ministers and Laymen*, January 1959, June 1960; Francis B. Stevens, "Splinter Group Develops in Mississippi," Letters and Documents, Social Struggles, 1960s, Cain Archives.

32. Stevens, "Splinter Groups," 1 (first quotation); Clarice Campbell to "Jean and Don," February 3, 1961 (final quotation), Campbell Papers, MDAH; National Council, Protestant Episcopal Church, Department of Social Relations, "Sowing Dissensions in the Churches," 15–16, Letters and Documents, Social Change, Cain Archives.

33. *Mississippi Methodist Advocate*, April 22, 1964; Stevens, "Splinter Group," 1; Margrit and John B. Garner to "Dear Friends," March 1963, Garner Papers, MDAH; *Jackson Daily News*, March 24, 1956, March 18, 1963; Hodding Carter III, "Citadel of the Citizens Council," *New York Times Magazine*, November 12, 1961, 23; Silver, *Mississippi*, 54.

34. *The Citizens' Council*, November 1956, July, August 1957; "WAKE UP!," Citizens' Council Subject File, 1954–55, MDAH; Jefferson County Citizens' Council to "All Members," January 30, 1956; W. J. Simmons to John Bell Williams, March 27, 1956; John Bell Williams to Honorable Francis E. Walter, Chairman, House Committee on Un–American Activities, March 30, 1956, John Bell Williams Papers, MDAH.

35. Egerton, *Speak Now*, 289; Phillips, *Methodist Women*, 135–43.

36. *Mississippi Methodist Advocate*, October 10, 1962.

37. "Born of Conviction," *Mississippi Methodist Advocate*, January 2, 1963; Silver, *Mississippi*, 58–60.

38. "Mississippi Methodists Lead in Attack on Segregation," *The Presbyterian Outlook*, January 21, 1963.

39. John and Margrit Garner to "Dear Friends," March 1963, Garner Papers, MDAH;

Stevens, "Splinter Groups," 4; Jackson *Clarion-Ledger*, November 12, 1972; Eighmy, *Churches in Cultural Captivity*, 197; Silver, *Mississippi*, 58–60, 286–88; Francis B. Stevens, Associate Conference Lay Leader, Mississippi Conference, Report, November 9, 1964, John D. Humphrey Papers, Special Collections, MSU.

40. John B. Garner to "Dear Friends," June 16, 1964, Garner Papers, MDAH; Jackson *Free Press*, December 14, 1963; *Jackson Daily News*, November 26, 1963; Rev. Gerald O. Trigg, "Who Killed President Kennedy," *Mississippi Methodist Advocate* (December 4, 1963), 8–9.

41. Silver, *Mississippi*, 57–58.

42. Reed Massengill, *Portrait of a Racist: The Man Who Killed Medgar Evers?* (New York: St. Martin's Press, 1994), 215–18, 256–58; Jackson *Clarion-Ledger*, September 23, November 22, 1967; *Jackson Daily News*, September 22, 1967, November 21, 23, 1967.

43. Silver, *Mississippi*, 282.

44. Dittmer, *Local People*, 128–29, 143–53.

45. Payne, *I've Got The Light of Freedom*, 324–42; "A Delta Discussion—Issue V of a Series," Letters and Documents, Social Struggle, Cain Archives.

46. Jackson *Clarion-Ledger*, April 12, 1968; Mark Newman, "The Mississippi Baptist Convention and Desegregation, 1945–1980," *Journal of Mississippi History* LIX (spring 1997): 26.

47. MAMML *Information Bulletin*, June 1960; Silver, *Mississippi*, 289–90; Robert W. Spike to John D. Humphrey, October 2, 1963, Humphrey Papers, Special Collections, MSU.

48. Ben R. Hartley, "Progress in Mississippi?," March 1966, Tombigbee Council on Human Relations Papers, Special Collections, MSU; John D. Humphrey, "Statement Regarding the Delta Ministry," August 9, 1966; Smith to Bishop Marvin Franklin, June 9, 1964, Humphrey Papers, Special Collections, MSU; Dittmer, *Local People*, 336–37; Silver, *Mississippi*, 290–91.

49. Humphrey, "Statement Regarding the Delta Ministry," August 9, 1966; Francis B. Stevens, Associate Conference Lay Leader to Bishop Edward J. Pendergrass, April 27, 1965, Humphrey Papers, Special Collections, MSU.

50. Hartley, "Progress in Mississippi," 1965 Report to National Council of Churches, Delta Ministries Subject File, MDAH; "Goals for the Delta Ministry," July 7, 1966, Tombigbee Council on Human Relations Papers; Jackson *Clarion-Ledger*, September 30, October 1, 1966.

51. Hartley, "Progress in Mississippi," 1965 Report to National Council of Churches, Delta Ministries Subject File, MDAH; "Goals for the Delta Ministry," July 7, 1966, Tombigbee Council on Human Relations Papers.

52. John and Margrit Garner to "Dear Friends," November 17, 1963, December 19, 1966, Garner Papers, MDAH; MAMML *Information Bulletin*, February 1964; Clarice Campbell to ?, May 9, 1964, Campbell Papers, MDAH; *Jackson Daily News*, March 30, 1964.

53. John and Margrit Garner to "Dear Friends," November 17, 1963, December 19, 1966, Garner Papers, MDAH; John Herbers, "The Churches and Race in Mississippi," *Concern* (February 1, 1964), 11–12; "Why the Methodist Church," *Mississippi Methodist Advocate* (April 22, 1964), 3; Bishop Edward J. Pendergrass, "Evaluation of Methodism in the Jackson Area" (n.d. [1964]), Humphrey Papers; Clarice Campbell to ?, May 9, 1964, Campbell Papers, MDAH; *Jackson Daily News*, March 30, 1964.

54. "To Mississippi Methodists," *Mississippi Methodist Advocate*, December 2, 9, 1967; *Jackson*

Daily News, November 21, 23, 1967; Jackson *Clarion-Ledger*, November 22, 1967; John and Margrit Garner to "Dear Friends," December 19, 1966 [1967?], Garner Papers, MDAH; Silver, *Mississippi*, 247–48; Mars, *Witness in Philadelphia*, 269.

55. Hartley, "Progress in Mississippi," 1.

Chapter 11

1. Jackson *Clarion-Ledger*, December 12, 1993.

2. *Jackson Daily News*, March 11, 1983.

3. Memphis *Commercial Appeal Mid-South Magazine*, October 28, 1984.

4. Jackson *Clarion-Ledger*, March 11, 1989.

5. Ibid.

6. On the concept of "culture wars," see James Davison Hunter, *Culture Wars: The Struggle to Define America* (New York: Basic Books, 1991) and Robert Wuthnow, *The Restructuring of American Religion* (Princeton, N.J.: Princeton University Press, 1988).

7. R. Stephen Warner, "Work in Progress Toward a New Paradigm for the Sociological Study of Religion in the United States," *American Journal of Sociology* XCVIII (March 1993): 1056.

8. Webb, *Evolution Controversy in America*, 153.

9. Samuel S. Hill, "Religion and Politics in the South," in Wilson, ed., *Religion in the South*, 141.

10. Douglas W. Johnson, Paul R. Picerd, and Bernard Quinn, *Churches and Church Membership in the United States . . . 1971* (Washington, D.C.: Glenmary Research Center, 1974), 10. The survey underestimates membership and omits many small denominations. Though imprecise, it probably accurately reflects larger trends in religious affiliation.

11. Martin B. Bradley, et al., *Churches and Church Membership in the United States 1990 . . .* (Atlanta: Glenmary Research Center, 1992), 23.

12. *New York Times Magazine*, October 30, 1994, 49.

13. Jackson *Clarion-Ledger*, March 9, 1986.

14. Ibid., August 15, 1990.

15. *New York Times Magazine*, September 2, 1990, 24.

16. *New York Times Magazine*, September 2, 1990.

17. Jackson *Clarion-Ledger*, January 20, 1983.

18. Wells to "Dear Family Member," March 7, 1983, Moral Majority Subject File, MDAH.

19. *Jackson Daily News*, April 28, 1983.

20. Nolan, *St. Mary's*, 275; Brenda and Wanda Henson, "How the Spirit Moves," September 9, 1999; <http://www.echonyc.com/~onissues/sp97spirit.html>.

21. *Jackson Daily News*, November 10, 1982.

22. Ibid., November 15, 1978.

23. Jackson *Clarion-Ledger*, November 2, 1994.

24. Ibid., April 30, 1980.

25. Biloxi-Gulfport *Sun-Herald*, February 13, 1997; "FTM News Briefs: Mississippi," September 9, 1999; ; "Marriage," "About MFC," September 9, 1999; <www.freedomtomarry.org/usa/sates/ms>; "Marriage," "About MFC," September 9, 1999; <http://www.msfamily.org/News/Archive/Spring97/Marriage.htm>.

26. *Jackson Daily News*, March 17, 1986.

27. Jackson *Clarion-Ledger*, August 30, 1991.

28. Ibid., October 19, 1991.

29. Ibid., January 26, 1975.

30. "Address by the Rev. Thomas H. Waggener to the 150th Annual Council of the Episcopal Diocese of Mississippi, Oxford, Mississippi, January 29, 1977," Episcopal Church, Diocese of Mississippi Subject File, MDAH.

31. Holmes, *Brief History of the Episcopal Church*, 168.

32. *Jackson Daily News*, October 24, 1984.

33. Jackson *Clarion-Ledger*, February 15, 1986.

34. Ibid., December 20, 1993.

35. Ibid., December 12, 1993.

36. Grant Scrapbook, Cain Archives; Jackson *Clarion-Ledger*, February 27, 1994 (second quotation).

37. *Good News*, December 1975, 1.

38. Ibid., 3.

39. Ibid., April/May, 1979, 1.

40. Ibid.

41. Jackson *Clarion-Ledger*, October 19, 1991.

42. Ibid., August 4, 1990.

43. *Good News*, December 1975, 1.

44. Jackson *Clarion-Ledger*, July 5, 1980.

45. Ibid.

46. Ibid.

47. *Jackson Daily News*, June 3, 1986.

48. Ibid.

49. *Sunbelt*, July 1980, 21; *Christianity Today*, March 2, 1998, 73.

50. *Washington Post*, September 29, 1992.

51. Ibid.

52. Department of Commerce and Labor, Bureau of the Census, Thirteenth Census of the United States, 1910, *Population by States and Territories* (Washington, D.C.: U.S. Government Printing Office, 1910), 99–100; Bradley, et al., *Churches and Church Membership*, 219–27.

53. *Good News*, May 1976, 6.

54. Ibid.

55. Cobb, *Most Southern Place on Earth*, 273.

56. Clifton L. Taulbert, *Once Upon a Time When We Were Colored* (Tulsa, Okla.: Council Oak Books, 1989), 91, 94.

57. Memphis *Commercial Appeal Mid-South Magazine*, October 28, 1984.

58. Boyer, *How Sweet the Sound*, 31.

59. Jackson *Clarion-Ledger*, September 1, 1984.

60. *The Boston Globe Magazine*, December 9, 1990.

61. Ibid.

62. Vicksburg *Evening Post*, December 1, 1990.

63. Jackson *Clarion-Ledger*, October 29, 1994.

64. Ibid.

65. *New York Times*, June 3, 1994.

66. Ibid., June 19, 1996.

67. Ibid., June 3, 1994.

68. "Mission: Reconciliation," Jackson *Clarion-Ledger* [October 1993], Race Relations Subject File, MDAH; Jackson *Clarion-Ledger*, January 16, October 25, 1993.

69. "None Dare Call It Sin: How Mississippi's Bible Belt Succumbed So Quickly and So Completely to the Gambling Industry," *Christianity Today*, May 18, 1998.

70. Ibid.

71. Ibid.

72. Ibid.

73. *Jackson Daily News*, August 12, 1985.

74. Hatch, *Democratization of American Christianity*, 218.

75. See Hunter, *Culture Wars*, passim.

Epilogue

1. Reinhold Niebuhr, *Moral Man and Immoral Society* (New York and London: C. Scribner's, 1932), 8–9.

Selected Bibliography

Unpublished Sources

Church Records

Academy Baptist Church. Tippah County. MDAH.

Bethany Baptist Church. Jefferson Davis County. SBHC.

Bethesda Baptist Church. Hinds County. SBHC.

Bethlehem Baptist Church. Choctaw County. MSU.

Beulah Baptist Church. Tippah County. SBHC.

Bogue Chitto Baptist Church. Pike County. MBHC.

Carolina Presbyterian Church. Session Book. MDAH.

Carthage Circuit Record Book. Methodist Episcopal Church. Cain Archives.

Clear Creek Baptist Church. Adams County. SBHC.

Concord Baptist Church. Winston-Choctaw Counties. MSU.

Crawfordville Methodist Church. Crawford, Mississippi. MSU.

Crystal Springs Circuit. Methodist Episcopal Church. MDAH.

Enon Baptist Church. Itawamba County. MSU.

Fellowship Baptist Church. Lauderdale County. SBHC.

First Baptist Church. Louisville, Mississippi. SBHC.

First Methodist Church. Columbus, Mississippi. MSU.

First Methodist Church. Jackson, Mississippi. "Recording Steward's Book," 1847–1849, 1865–1874. Cain Archives.

First Presbyterian Church. Jackson, Mississippi. MDAH.

First Presbyterian Church. Natchez, Mississippi. MDAH.

First Presbyterian Church. Port Gibson, Mississippi. MDAH.

First Presbyterian Church. Vicksburg, Mississippi. MDAH.

Hopewell Baptist Church. Franklin County. MBHS.

Liberty Baptist Church. Jackson, Mississippi. SBHC.

Magnolia Baptist Church. Claiborne County. SBHC.

Mars Hill Baptist Church. Summit, Mississippi. SBHC.

Montrose Presbyterian Church. Jasper County. MDAH.

Mt. Moriah Baptist Church. Choctaw County. MSU.

Mt. Pisgah Baptist Church. Choctaw County. MSU.

New Hope Baptist Church. Monroe County. Evans Memorial Library.

New Zion Baptist Church. Choctaw County. MSU.

Old Lebanon Presbyterian Church. Choctaw County. MSU.

Philadelphia Missionary Baptist Church. Choctaw County. MSU.

Port Gibson Station. Quarterly Conference Minutes. Methodist Episcopal Church. Cain Archives.

Prairie Hill Circuit. Methodist Episcopal Church. MSU.

Salem Baptist Church. Jefferson County. SBHC.

Sarepta Baptist Church. Franklin County. MSU.

Spring Hill Baptist Church. Choctaw County. MSU.

Woodville Methodist Church. Woodville, Mississippi. MDAH.

Manuscript Collections

Agnew, Samuel Andrew. Diary. MSU.

Alexander, Robert B. Diary and Account Ledger. MDAH.

Amite and Florida Auxilliary Bible Society. Minutes. MDAH.

Anonymous Diary. Natchez. MDAH.

Bachman, G. W. "Sketches and Incidents of Life, 1839–1914." MSU.

Baptist Children's Village. Subject File. MDAH.

Baptist Hospital. Subject File. MDAH.

Blackman, Learner [Laurner]. Journal. Cain Archives.

Boddie Family. Papers. MDAH.

Bond, T. M. and Family. Biography File. MBHC.

Brown, Maude M. Papers. MDAH.

Campbell, Clarice. Papers. MDAH.

Caskey, W. M. Subject File. MDAH.

Chamberlain-Hyland-Gould Papers. Barker.

Chapman Family Papers. MDAH.

Christian Citizens League. Subject File. MDAH.

Citizens' Council. Subject File. 1954–1955. MDAH.

Coody, Archibald S. Papers. MDAH.

Cook, Mrs. Jared Reese. Diary. MDAH.

Council of Federated Organizations. Records. MDAH.

Craig. Scrapbook. MDAH.

Dana, Charles B. Papers. MDAH.

DeHay, Elizabeth Norton. Papers. MDAH.

Delta Ministries. Subject File. MDAH.

Downs, Lettie Vick. Journal. MDAH.

Drake, Benjamin M. Papers. Cain Archives.

Drake, Benjamin M. and Family. Papers. MDAH.

Elizabeth Female Academy. Subject File. MDAH.

Episcopal Church. Diocese of Mississippi. Subject File. MDAH.

Evans, Dr. Holder Garthur. Diary. MDAH.

Finch, Anslem J. Papers. MDAH.

Fontaine, Charles D. and Family. Papers. MDAH.

Fontaine, Edward. Papers. MSU.

Fox, Nathan J. Papers. MDAH.

Franklin, Bishop Marvin A. Collection. Cain Archives.

Galloway, Charles B. Galloway Papers. Cain Archives.

Garner, Margrit and John B. Papers. MDAH.

Gibson, Tobias. Subject File. MDAH.

Gordon, Robert. Diary. MDAH.

Grafton, Cornelius W. Papers. MDAH.

Grant Scrapbook. Cain Archives.

Green, William M. Papers. MDAH.

Hargrove, Allan. Papers. MDAH.

Harris, Rev. Henry J. Autobiography. Cain Archvies.

Hays, Sophia Boyd. Diary. Hays-Ray-Webb Collection. MSU.

Holloman, Garland. Papers. MSU.

Howze, Isham Robertson. Papers. MDAH.

Humphrey, John D. Papers. MSU.

International Order of King's Daughters and Sons. Subject File. MDAH.

Irion-Nelson Family. Papers. MDAH.

Jones, John G. Journal. MDAH.

Kennedy, Rev. J. Whitmer. Manuscripts. MDAH.

Kiger Family Papers. Natchez Trace Collection. Barker.

King, B. B. Oral History Interview. MDAH.

Langford, Lorenzo Dow. Autobiography. Cain Archives.

Leftwich, George Jabez. Papers. MDAH.

Lipscomb, W. L. and Family. Letters. MDAH.

Lomax, Alexander A. Notebook. MDAH.

Lowry, Rev. Thomas Jefferson. Memoranda. MDAH.

Lyon, James A. Papers. MSU.

McNabb, Eliza R. Letters. MDAH.

Marshall, Charles Kimball. Papers. MDAH.

Mecklin, Augustus Harvey. Papers. MDAH.

Mississippi Council on Interracial Cooperation. Subject File. MDAH.

Montgomery, Joseph A. and Family. Papers. MDAH.

Moral Majority. Subject File. MDAH.

Natchez Orphan Asylum Records. Natchez Trace Collections. Barker.

Nicholson, Flavellus G. Diary-journal. MDAH.

Nicholson, James M. Diary. MDAH.

Official Archives of the State of Mississippi. Legislature. MDAH.

Parrott, Johnny. Diary. MDAH.

Phillips, Winnie Ellis. Papers. Cain Archives.

"Port of Aberdeen." Clippings. Evans Memorial Library.

Presbyterian Auxiliaries Papers. Synod of Mississippi. Presbyterian Church, United States. MDAH.

Rabb, Matilda C. Letters. MDAH.

Randolph-Sherman Family. Papers. MSU.

Reminiscences and Stories. Evans Memorial Library.

Rice, Augusta H. Letters. Rice Collection. MSU.

Robertson, Norvelle, Sr. Autobiography. MDAH.

Robinson, Nancy M. Diary. MDAH.

Rollins, Bertie Shaw. Papers. MSU.

Sager, Sarah Knox Harris. Recollections. Sager Collection. MDAH.

Scales, Cordelia Lewis. Letters. MDAH.

Scofield, Lorenzo. Diary. MBHC.

Sellers, Samuel. Diary. Cain Archives.

Seventh-Day Adventist Church. Subject File. MDAH.

Social Struggles. Letters and Documents. 1960s. Cain Archives.

Steele, Elijah. Letters. MDAH.

Stockwell, Eunice J. Papers. MDAH.

Strickland, Belle. Diary. MDAH.

Sumner, Cid Ricketts. Papers. MDAH.

Tombigbee Council on Human Relations. Papers. MSU.

Tynes, Walter Edwin. Diary. MDAH.

Wade, Walter. Plantation Diary. MDAH.

Weeks, Levi and Family. Papers. MDAH.

Wharton, Mary. Collection. MDAH.

Williams, Howard. Subject File. MDAH.

Williams, John Bell. Papers. MDAH.

Winans, William. Papers. Cain Archives.

Winston, E. T. and Family. Papers. MDAH.

Wright, J. P. Oral History Interview. MDAH.

Theses, Dissertations and Other Sources

Archer, Kate. "History of the Methodist Ladies Co-operative Association, Methodist Church, Port Gibson, Mississippi." Microfilm, Mississippi State University.

Berlin, Ira. "The Plantation Revolution and the Chronology of African American Slavery." Paper presented at the 63rd Annual Meeting of the Southern Historical Association, November 7, 1997.

Bolton, Charles Clifton. "The Failure of Yeoman Democracy: Poor Whites in the Antebellum South." Ph.D. diss., Duke University, 1989.

Downey, J. C. "The Music of American Revivalism, 1740–1800." Ph.D. diss., Tulane University, 1968.

Ellington, C. L. "The Sacred Harp Tradition of the South: Its Origin and Evolution." Ph.D. diss., Florida State University, 1969.

Fitzgerald, William. "The Union League Movement in Alabama and Mississippi: Politics and Agricultural Change in the Deep South During Reconstruction." Ph.D. diss., University of California, Los Angeles, 1986.

Harper, Louis Keith. "The Historical Context for the Rise of Old Landmarkism." M.A. thesis, Murray State University, 1986.

McElhany, Gary Don. "Fire in the Pines: A History of the Assemblies of God in Mississippi, 1900–1936." M.A. thesis, Mississippi State University, 1992.

Miller, Gene Ramsey. "A History of South Mississippi Methodism, 1820–1900." Ph.D. diss., Mississippi State University, 1964.

Rich, Charles A. "The History of the French Camp Presbyterian Church." M.A. thesis, Mississippi State University, 1967.

Sims, J. N. "The Hymnody of the Camp Meeting Tradition." Ph.D. diss., Union Theological Seminary, 1960.

Published Sources

Aberdeen Baptist Association. *Minutes of the Second Anniversary . . . 1845*. Aberdeen, Miss.: Aberdeen Baptist Association, 1845.

————. *Minutes of the Fifth Annual Meeting . . . 1848*. Houston, Miss.: Aberdeen Baptist Association, 1848.

————. *Minutes of the Sixth Annual Meeting . . . 1849*. Pontotoc, Miss.: Aberdeen Baptist Association, 1849.

————. *Minutes of the Seventh Annual Meeting . . . 1850*. Aberdeen, Miss.: Aberdeen Baptist Association, 1850.

————. *Minutes of the Ninth Annual Session . . . 1852*. Aberdeen, Miss.: Aberdeen Baptist Association, 1852.

————. *Minutes of the Tenth Annual Session . . . 1853*. Philadelphia, Miss.: Aberdeen Baptist Association, 1853.

————. *Minutes of the Eleventh Annual Session . . . 1854*. Aberdeen, Miss.: Aberdeen Baptist Association, 1854.

————. *Minutes of the Twelfth Session . . . 1855*. Aberdeen, Miss.: Aberdeen Baptist Association, 1856.

————. *Minutes of the Eighteenth Anniversary . . . 1861*. Greensboro, Miss.: Aberdeen Baptist Association, 1862.

————. *Minutes of the Nineteenth Session . . . 1862*. Greensboro, Miss.: Aberdeen Baptist Association, 1862.

————. *Minutes of the Twenty-First Anniversary . . . 1864*. N.p.: Aberdeen Baptist Association, 1864.

————. *Minutes of the Twenty-Second Session . . . 1865*. Jackson, Tenn.: Aberdeen Baptist Association, 1865.

————. *Minutes of the Twenty-Fourth Annual Session . . . 1867*. Atlanta, Ga.: Aberdeen Baptist Association, 1868.

————. *Minutes of the Twenty-Fifth Annual Session . . . 1868*. N.p.: Aberdeen Baptist Association, 1868.

————. *Minutes of the Thirty-Seventh Annual Session . . . 1880*. Jackson, Miss.: Aberdeen Baptist Association, 1880.

Adams, Revels A. *Cyclopedia of African Methodism in Mississippi*. Natchez, Miss.: n.p., 1902.

Alford, Terry. *Prince Among Slaves*. New York and London: Oxford University Press, 1977.

Alho, Olli. *The Religion of the Slaves: A Study of the Religious Tradition and Behavior of the Plantation Slaves in the United States, 1830–1865*. Helsinki, Finland: Academia Scientiarum Fennica, 1976.

American Colonization Society. *Annual Reports.* New York: Negro Universities Press, 1908–1910.

Amis, A. B., Sr. *Recollections of Social Customs in Newton and Scott Counties, Mississippi Fifty Years Ago.* Meridian, Miss.: Dement Printing Co., 1934.

Amite Primitive Baptist Association. *Minutes of the Amite Primitive Baptist Association . . . 1885.* Middletown, N.Y.: Amite Primitive Baptist Association, 1885.

Appleby, Joyce. *Capitalism and a New Social Order: The Republican Vision of the 1790s.* New York and London: New York University Press, 1984.

Archer, Chalmers, Jr. *Growing Up Black in Rural Mississippi: Memories of a Family, Heritage of a Place.* New York: Walker, 1992.

Aughey, John H. *The Fighting Preacher.* Chicago: Rhodes and McClure, 1899.

———. *The Iron Furnace: or, Slavery and Secession.* Philadelphia, Penn.: Alfred Martien, 1863.

Ayers, Edward L. *The Promise of the New South: Life After Reconstruction.* New York and Oxford: Oxford University Press, 1992.

Bailey, David T. *Shadow on the Church: Southwestern Evangelical Religion and the Issue of Slavery, 1783–1860.* Ithaca, N.Y., and London: Cornell University Press, 1985.

Bailyn, Bernard. *Voyagers to the West: A Passage in the Peopling of America on the Eve of the Revolution.* New York: Knopf, 1986.

Baird, E. T. *Historical Sketch of the Bethel Presbyterian Church, Lowdnes County, Miss. . . .* Columbus, Miss.: Bethel Presbyterian Church, 1885.

Baker, Daniel. *A Series of Revival Sermons.* Pennfield, Ga.: J. S. Baker, 1847.

Baker, Osmon C. *Guide-Book in the Administration of the Discipline of the Methodist Episcopal Church.* New York: Carlton & Phillips, 1855.

Baklanoff, Joy Driskell. "The Celebration of a Feast: Music, Dance, and Possession Trance in the Black Primitive Baptist Footwashing Ritual." *Ethnomusicology* XXXI (fall 1987): 381–94.

Baldwin, Joseph G. *The Flush Times of Alabama and Mississippi: A Series of Sketches.* New York: D. Appleton, 1854.

Baptist State Convention. *Second Annual Report . . . 1824.* Natchez, Miss.: Baptist State Convention, 1825.

Barker, Mary G., Mavis Oliver Feltus, and Diane A. Stockfelt, comps. *Early Will Records of Adams County, Mississippi.* Natchez, Miss.[?]: n.p., 1975.

Barnes, William Wright. *The Southern Baptist Convention, 1845–1953.* Nashville, Tenn.: Broadman Press, 1954.

Barney, William L. *The Secessionist Impulse: Alabama and Mississippi in 1860.* Princeton, N.J.: Princeton University Press, 1974.

Bassett, Ancel Henry. *A Concise History of the Methodist Protestant Church. . . .* Baltimore, Md.: William McCracken, Jr., 1887.

Bartley, Numan V. *The Evolution of Southern Culture.* Athens, Ga., and London: University of Georgia Press, 1988.

Beasley, Jonathan. "Blacks—Slave and Free—Vicksburg, 1850–1860." *Journal of Missis-sippi History* XXXVIII (February 1976): 1–32.

Benham, George C. *A Year of Wreck: A True Story By a Victim.* New York: Harper & Brothers, 1880.

Beringer, Richard, Herman Hattaway, Archer Jones, and William N. Still, Jr. *The Ele-ments of Confederate Defeat: Nationalism, War Aims, and Religion.* Athens, Ga., and London: University of Georgia Press, 1988.

Berlin, Ira. *Many Thousands Gone: The First Two Centuries of Slavery in North America.* Cambridge, Mass., and London: Harvard University Press, 1998.

Berthoff, Rowland. *An Unsettled People: Social Order and Disorder in American History.* New York: Harper and Row, 1971.

Bettersworth, John K. *Confederate Mississippi: The People and Policies of a Cotton State in Wartime.* Baton Rouge: Louisiana State University Press, 1943.

———. *Mississippi in the Confederacy: as they saw it.* Baton Rouge: Louisiana State Uni-versity Press, 1961.

———. "Mississippi Unionism: The Case of the Reverend James A. Lyon." *Journal of Mississippi History* I (January 1939): 37–52.

Biographical and Historical Sketches of Mississippi. 2 vols. Spartanburg, S.C.: n.p., 1978.

Blackburn, Robin. "The Old World Background to European Colonial Slavery." *Wil-liam and Mary Quarterly,* 3d ser., LIV (January 1997): 90–97.

Blassingame, John W. *The Slave Community: Plantation Life in the Antebellum South.* New York and Oxford: Oxford University Press, 1979.

Blesser, Carol. *In Joy and In Sorrow: Women, Family, and Marriage in the Victorian South.* New York and Oxford: Oxford University Press, 1991.

Bloch, Ruth H. "The Gendered Meanings of Virtue in Revolutionary America." *Signs: Journal of Women in Culture and Society* XIII (autumn 1987): 37–58.

Boles, John B. *Black Southerners, 1619–1869.* Lexington, Ky.: University Press of Ken-tucky, 1984.

———. *The Great Revival, 1787–1805.* Lexington, Ky.: University Press of Kentucky, 1972.

———. *Masters and Slaves in the House of the Lord: Race and Religion in the American South, 1740–1870.* Lexington, Ky.: University Press of Kentucky, 1988.

Bowen, O. D. *Gospel Ministry of Forty Years.* Handsboro, Miss.: O. D. Bowen, 1911.

Boyd, J. L., Sr. "History of the Baptists in Rankin County." *Journal of Mississippi History* XII (July 1950): 162–68.

Boyd, Jesse Laney. *A Popular History of the Baptists in Mississippi.* Jackson: The Baptist Press, 1930.

Boyer, Clarence Horace. *How Sweet the Sound: The Golden Age of Gospel.* Washington, D.C.: Elliott & Clark, 1995.

Boylan, Anne. *Sunday School: The Formation of an American Institution, 1790–1880.* New Haven, Conn.: Yale University Press, 1988.

Bradley, Martin B., et al. *Churches and Church Membership in the United States 1990.* . . . Atlanta, Ga.: Glenmary Research Center, 1992.

Bratton, Theodore DuBose. *Wanted—Leaders! A Study of Negro Development.* New York: Department of Missions and Church Expansion, 1922.

Braude, Benjamin. "The Sons of Noah and the Construction of Ethnic and Geographical Identities in the Medieval and Early Modern Periods." *William and Mary Quarterly,* 3d ser., LIV (January 1997): 103–42.

Bruce, Dickson D. *And They All Sang Hallelujah: Plain-Folk Camp-Meeting Religion, 1800–1845.* Knoxville, Tenn.: University of Tennessee Press, 1974.

Bullock, Steven C. *Revolutionary Brotherhood: Freemasonry and the Transformation of the American Social Order, 1730–1840.* Chapel Hill: University of North Carolina Press, 1996.

Burger, Nash K., ed. "An Overlooked Source for Mississippi Local History: The Spirit of Missions, 1836–1854." *Journal of Mississippi History* VII (July 1945): 171–78.

Butler, Jon. *Awash in a Sea of Faith: Christianizing the American People.* Cambridge, Mass., and London: Harvard University Press, 1990.

Cabiness, Allen. *Life and Thought of a Country Preacher, C. W. Grafton.* . . . Richmond, Va.: John Knox Press, 1941.

Cabiness, Frances Allen, and James Allen Cabiness. "Religion in Ante-Bellum Mississippi." *Journal of Mississippi History* VI (October 1944): 191–224.

Cain, John Buford. *Methodism in the Mississippi Conference, 1846–1870.* Jackson: The Hawkins Foundation, 1939.

———. *The Cradle of Mississippi Methodism.* N.p., n.d.

Calhoon, Robert M. *Evangelicals and Conservatives in the Early South, 1740–1861.* Columbia, S.C.: University of South Carolina Press, 1988.

Campbell, Joseph. *The Masks of God.* Vol. 4, *Creative Mythology.* New York, Viking Press, 1968.

Carr, Anne E. *Transforming Grace: Christian Tradition and Women's Experience.* San Francisco, Calif.: Harper & Row, 1988.

Casey, Albert E., comp. *Amite County Mississippi, 1699–1865.* 2 vols. Birmingham, Ala.: Amite County Historical Fund, 1948.

Cashin, Joan E. *A Family Venture: Men & Women in the Southern Frontier.* New York and Oxford: Oxford University Press, 1991.

Central Baptist Association. *Minutes of the Eighth Annual Session . . . 1853.* Jackson, Miss.: Central Baptist Association, 1853.

———. *Minutes of the Fifteenth Annual Session . . . 1860.* Jackson, Miss.: Central Baptist Association, 1860.

———. *Minutes of the Sixteenth Annual Session . . . 1861.* Jackson, Miss.: Central Baptist Association, 1861.

———. *Minutes of the Twenty-First Annual Session . . . 1866.* Jackson, Miss.: Central Baptist Association, 1866.

————. *Minutes of the Twenty-Third Annual Session . . . 1868*. Jackson, Miss.: Central Baptist Association, 1868.

————. *Minutes of the Twenty-Fourth Annual Session . . . 1869*. Jackson, Miss.: Central Baptist Association, 1869.

————. *Minutes of the Twenty-Ninth Annual Session . . . 1874*. Vicksburg, Miss.: Central Baptist Association, 1875.

Citizens' Council. *Is Segregation Unchristian?* Greenwood, Miss.: Citizens' Council Educational Fund, n.d.

Claiborne, J. F. H. *Mississippi, As a Province, Territory and State. . . .* Baton Rouge: Louisiana State University Press, 1964.

Clark, Norman H. *Deliver Us from Evil: An Interpretation of American Prohibition.* New York: Norton, 1976.

Clark, Thomas D., and John D. W. Guice. *Frontiers in Conflict: The Old Southwest, 1795–1830.* Alburquerque, N.M.: University of New Mexico Press, 1989.

Clinton, Catherine. *The Plantation Mistress: Woman's World in the Old South.* New York: Pantheon Books, 1982.

Cmiel, Kenneth. *Democratic Eloquence: The Fight Over Popular Speech in Nineteenth-Century America.* New York: W. Morrow, 1990.

Cobb, E. B., Jr. *Sacred Harp: A Tradition and Its Music.* Athens, Ga.: University of Georgia Press, 1978.

Cobb, James C. *The Most Southern Place on Earth: The Mississippi Delta and the Roots of Regional Identity.* New York and Oxford: Oxford University Press, 1992.

Cold Water Baptist Association. *Minutes of the Twentieth Annual Session . . . 1861.* Memphis, Tenn.: Cold Water Baptist Association, 1861.

Columbus Baptist Association. *Minutes of the Eleventh Anniversary . . . 1848.* Houston, Miss.: Columbus Baptist Association, 1848.

Connelly, Thomas L., and Barbara L. Bellows. *God and General Longstreet: The Lost Cause and the Southern Mind.* Baton Rouge and London: Louisiana State University Press, 1982.

Coody, Archibald S. *The Race Question from the White Chief: A Story of the Life and Times of James K. Vardaman.* N.p.: A. S. Coody, 1944.

Coon, Lynda L., Katherine J. Haldane, and Elisabeth W. Sommers, eds. *That Gentle Strength: Historical Perspectives on Women in Christianity.* Charlottesville, Va., and London: University of Virginia Press, 1990.

Cornelius, Janet Duitsman. *When I Can Read My Title Clear: Literacy, Slavery, and Religion in the Antebellum South.* Columbia, S.C.: University of South Carolina Press, 1991.

Cotton, Gordon A. *Of Primitive Faith and Order: A History of the Mississippi Primitive Baptist Church, 1780–1974.* Raymond, Miss.: Keith Press, 1974.

Crawford, Vicki. "Race, Class, Gender, and Culture: Black Women's Activism in the Mississippi Civil Rights Movement." *Journal of Mississippi History* LVIII (spring 1996): 1–21.

Currie, James T. *Enclave: Vicksburg and Her Plantations, 1863–1870*. Jackson, Miss.: University Press of Mississippi, 1980.

Daniel, W. Harrison. *Southern Protestantism in the Confederacy*. Bedford, Va.: Virginia Baptist Historical Society, 1989.

Darst, W. Maury, ed. "The Vicksburg Diary of Mrs. Alfred Ingraham (May 2–June 13, 1863)." *Journal of Mississippi History* LXIV (May 1982): 148–79.

Davis, Gerald L. *I got the Word in me and I can sing it, you know: A Study of the Performed African-American Sermon*. Philadelphia: University of Pennsylvania Press, 1985.

Davis, James E. *Frontier America, 1800–1840: A Comparative Demographic Analysis of the Settlement Process*. Glendale, Calif.: A. H. Clark, 1977.

Davis, Reuben. *Recollections of Mississippi and Mississippians*. Boston and New York: Houghton, Mifflin & Co., 1890.

Deems, Charles F. *Annals of Southern Methodism*. New York: J. A. Gray, 1856.

———. *The Southern Methodist Pulpit*. Richmond, Va.: Richmond Christian Advocate, n.d. [1849?].

Degler, Carl N. *The Other South: Southern Dissenters in the Nineteenth Century*. New York: Harper & Row, 1974.

Department of Commerce and Labor. Bureau of the Census. Thirteenth Census of the United States, 1910. *Population by States and Territories*. Washington, D.C.: U.S. Government Printing Office, 1910.

———. *Religious Bodies, 1936*. Vol. I. Washington, D.C.: U.S. Government Printing Office, 1941.

De Vinne, Daniel. *The Methodist Episcopal Church and Slavery*. . . . New York: Francis Hart, 1857.

Dittmer, John. *Local People: The Struggle for Civil Rights in Mississippi*. Urbana and Chicago: University of Illinois Press, 1994.

Donald, David. "The Proslavery Argument Reconsidered." *Journal of Southern History* XXXVII (February 1971): 3–31.

Dorgan, Howard. *Giving Glory to God in Appalachia: Worship Practices of Six Baptist Subdenominations*. Knoxville, Tenn.: University of Tennessee Press, 1987.

Douglas, Mary. *Natural Symbols: Explorations in Cosmology*. New York: Random House, 1971.

Dow, Lorenzo. *History of the Cosmopolite: or the Writings of Rev. Lorenzo Dow*. . . . Cincinnati, Oh.: Anderson, Gates & Wright, 1857.

Drake, Benjamin M. *A Funeral Sermon Preached . . . On the Death of Mrs. A. F. W. Speer*. . . . Vidalia, La.: N.p., [1849].

———. *A Sketch of the Life of Rev. Elijah Steele*. Cincinnati, Oh.: Methodist Book Concern, 1843.

Drake, Winbourne Magruder. "The Mississippi Constitutional Convention of 1832." *Journal of Southern History* XXIII (August 1957): 354–70.

———, ed. "The Road to Freedom." *Journal of Mississippi History* III (January 1941): 44–45.

Du Bois, W. E. B. *The Souls of Black Folk: Essays and Sketches*. New York: Fawcett Publishers, 1961.

Dumond, Dwight L. *Letters of James Gillespie Birney, 1831–1857.* 2 vols. Gloucester, Mass.: P. Smith, 1966.

Dunn, Durwood. *Cades Cove: The Life and Death of a Southern Appalachian Community, 1818–1937.* Knoxville, Tenn.: University of Tennessee Press, 1988.

Eaton, Clement. *Freedom of Thought in the Old South*. Durham, N.C.: Duke University Press, 1940.

Economic Research Department. *Mississippi Statistical Summary of Population, 1800–1980*. N.p.: Mississippi Power and Light Co., 1983.

Eddy, Sherwood. *A Door of Opportunity or An American Adventure in Cooperation with Sharecroppers*. New York: Eddy and Page, 1937.

Egerton, John. *Speak Now Against the Day: The Generation Before the Civil Rights Movement in the South*. New York: Knopf, 1994.

Eighmy, John Lee. *Churches in Cultural Captivity: A History of the Social Attitudes of Southern Baptists*. Knoxville, Tenn.: University of Tennessee Press, 1972.

Eleazer, R. B. *"The Curse of Ham."* Nashville, Tenn.: n.p., n.d.

Elliott, E. N., ed. *Cotton is King, and Pro-Slavery Arguments*. . . . Augusta, Ga.: Prichard, Abbott & Loomis, 1860.

Engerman, Stanley L., and Robert E. Gallman. *The Cambridge Economic History of the United States*. Vol. 1, *The Colonial Era*. Cambridge and New York: Cambridge University Press, 1996.

Epstein, Barbara L. *The Politics of Domesticity: Women, Evangelicalism, and Temperance in Nineteenth-Century America*. Middletown, Conn.: Wesleyan University Press, 1981.

Essig, James D. *The Bonds of Wickedness: American Evangelicals Against Slavery, 1770–1808*. Philadelphia, Penn.: Temple University Press, 1982.

Evans, W. A. *A History of First Baptist Church, Aberdeen, Mississippi, 1837 to 1945*. . . . Aberdeen, Miss.: First Baptist Church, 1945.

Farrar, Daniel S., ed. "Alexander K. Farrar's Deed to Kingston Church, 1874." *Journal of Mississippi History* XVII (January–October 1955): 135–41.

Faust, Drew Gilpin. "Christian Soldiers: The Meaning of Revivalism in the Confederate Army." *Journal of Southern History* LIII (February 1987): 63–90.

——— *The Creation of Confederate Nationalism: Ideology and Identity in the Civil War South*. Baton Rouge and London: Louisiana State University Press, 1988.

———. *The Ideology of Slavery: Proslavery Thought in the Antebellum South, 1830–1860*. Baton Rouge and London: Louisiana State University Press, 1981.

Finley, James Bradley. *Sketches of Western Methodism*. . . . Cincinnati, Oh.: Methodist Book Concern, 1854.

Flint, Timothy. *Recollections of the Last Ten Years.* . . . Boston: Cummings, Hillard, 1826.

Foner, Eric. *Reconstruction: America's Unfinished Revolution, 1863–1877.* New York: Harper & Row, 1988.

Foote, Henry S. *Casket of Reminiscences.* New York: Negro Universities Press, 1968.

Formisano, Ronald P. *The Birth of Mass Political Parties, Michigan, 1827–1861.* Princeton, N.J.: Princeton University Press, 1971.

Foster, Gaines M. "Guilt Over Slavery: A Historiographical Analysis." *Journal of Southern History* LVI (November 1990): 665–94.

———. *Ghosts of the Confederacy: Defeat, the Lost Cause, and the Emergence of the New South, 1865 to 1913.* New York and Oxford: Oxford University Press, 1987.

Foster, L. S. *Mississippi Baptist Preachers.* St. Louis: National Baptist Publishing Co., 1895.

Fox-Genovese, Elizabeth. *Within the Plantation Household: Black and White Women of the Old South.* Chapel Hill and London: University of North Carolina Press, 1988.

Fox-Genovese, Elizabeth, and Eugene Genovese. "The Divine Sanction of Social Order: Religious Foundations of the Southern Slaveholders' World View." *Journal of the American Academy of Religion* LV (summer 1987): 226–27.

Freehling, William W. "James Henry Thornwell's Mysterious Antislavery Moment." *Journal of Southern History* LVII (August 1991): 383–406.

———. *Prelude to Civil War: The Nullification Controversy in South Carolina, 1816–1836.* New York: Harper & Row, 1965.

Friedman, Jean E. *The Enclosed Garden: Women and Community in the Evangelical South, 1830–1900.* Chapel Hill and London: University of North Carolina Press, 1985.

Fry, Sylvia R., and Betty Wood. *Come Shouting to Zion: African American Protestantism in the American South and British Caribbean to 1830.* Chapel Hill and London: University of North Carolina Press, 1998.

Fulkerson, H. S. *Random Recollections of Early Days in Mississippi.* Baton Rouge: Otto Claitor, 1937.

Galloway, Charles B. "Elizabeth Female Academy: The Mother of Female Colleges." *Publications of the Mississippi Historical Society* III (1899): 169–78.

Genovese, Eugene D. *Roll, Jordan, Roll: The World the Slaves Made.* New York: Vintage Books, 1976.

———. *The World the Slaveholders Made: Two Essays in Interpretation.* New York: Pantheon Books, 1969.

Genovese, Eugene D., and Elizabeth Fox-Genovese. "The Religious Ideals of Southern Slave Society." *Georgia Historical Quarterly* LXX (spring 1986): 1–16.

Gerow, Richard Oliver. *Catholicity in Mississippi.* Marrero, La.: Hope Haven Press, 1939.

Gillespie, G. T. *A Christian View on Segregation.* Greenwood, Miss.: Educational Fund of the Citizens' Councils, 1954.

Goen, C. C. *Broken Churches, Broken Nation.* Macon, Ga.: Mercer University Press, 1985.

Goodman, Paul. *Towards a Christian Republic: Antimasonry and the Great Transition in New England, 1826–1836.* New York: Oxford University Press, 1988.

Gordon, Michael, ed. *The American Family in Social-Historical Perspective.* New York: St. Martin's Press, 1978.

Grantham, Dewey W. *Southern Progressivism: The Reconciliation of Progress and Tradition.* Knoxville, Tenn.: University of Tennessee Press, 1983.

Graves, Fred R., comp. and ed. *The Presbyterian Work in Mississippi.* Jackson, Miss.: Sentinel Press, 1927.

Griffin, Benjamin. *A History of the Primitive Baptists of Mississippi. . . .* Jackson, Miss.: Barksdale & Jones, 1853.

Gusfield, Joseph R. *Symbolic Crusade: Status Politics and the American Temperance Movement.* Urbana, Ill.: University of Illinois Press, 1963.

Gutman, Herbert G. *The Black Family in Slavery and Freedom, 1750–1925.* New York: Vintage Books, 1976.

Haber, Samuel. *The Quest for Authority and Honor in the American Professions, 1750–1900.* Chicago and London: University of Chicago Press, 1991.

Halsell, Willie D., ed. "A Stranger in a Strange Land." *Alabama Historical Quarterly* XXX (summer 1968): 61–75.

Hamer, T. L. "Beginnings of Presbyterianism in Mississippi." *Publications of the Mississippi Historical Society* X (1909): 203–21.

Hamrick, William Lee. *The Mississippi Conference of the Methodist Protestant Church.* Jackson, Miss.: Hawkins Foundation, 1957.

Harris, William C. *The Day of the Carpetbagger: Republican Reconstruction in Mississippi.* Baton Rouge: Louisiana State University Press, 1979.

Hatch, Nathan O. *The Democratization of American Christianity.* New Haven and London: Yale University Press, 1989.

Hawkins, Henry G. *Methodism in Natchez.* Jackson, Miss.: Hawkins Foundation, 1937.

Hawks, Joanne V., and Shelia L. Skemp. *Sex, Race, and the Role of Women in the South.* Jackson, Miss.: University Press of Mississippi, 1983.

Hermann, Janet Sharp. *The Pursuit of a Dream.* New York and Oxford: Oxford University Press, 1981.

Heyrman, Christine Leigh. *Southern Cross: The Beginnings of the Bible Belt.* New York: A. A. Knopf, 1997.

Hill, Samuel S. *Religion in the Southern States: A Historical Study.* Mercer, Ga.: Mercer University Press, 1983.

———, ed. *Encyclopedia of Religion in the South.* Macon, Ga.: Mercer University Press, 1984.

———, ed. *Varieties of Southern Religious Experience.* Baton Rouge and London: Louisiana State University Press, 1988.

Holder, Ray, ed. "On Slavery: Selected Letters of Parson Winans, 1820–1844." *Journal of Mississippi History* VXLVI (November 1984): 323–54.

Holifield, E. Brooks. *The Gentlemen Theologians: American Theology in Southern Culture, 1795–1860.* Durham, N.C.: Duke University Press, 1978.

———. "The Penurious Preacher? Nineteenth-Century Clerical Wealth: North and South." *Journal of the American Academy of Religion* LVIII (spring 1990): 17–36.

Holmes, David L. *A Brief History of the Episcopal Church.* Valley Forge, Penn.: Trinity Press International, 1993.

Holmes, Jack D. L. "Barton Hannon in the Old Southwest." *Journal of Mississippi History* XLIV (February 1982): 69–79.

———. *Gayoso: The Life of a Spanish Governor in the Mississippi Valley, 1789–1799.* Baton Rouge: Louisiana State University Press, 1965.

———. "Spanish Religious Policy in West Florida: Enlightened or Expedient?" *Journal of Church and State* XV (spring 1973): 259–69.

Howe, Daniel Walker. "The Evangelical Movement and Political Culture in the North during the Second Party System." *Journal of American History* LXXVII (March 1991): 1216–39.

Hunt, Mrs. Rolfe. *Mississippi Missionaries.* Meridian, Miss.: N. p., n. d. [1933].

Hunter, James Davison. *Culture Wars: The Struggle to Define America.* New York: Basic Books, 1991.

Irwin, Joyce, ed. *Sacred Sound: Music in Religious Thought and Practice.* Chico, Calif.: Scholars Press, 1983.

Isaac, Rhys. "Evangelical Revolt: The Nature of the Baptists' Challenge to the Traditional Order of Virginia, 1765 to 1775." *William and Mary Quarterly,* 3d ser., XXXI (July 1974): 345–68.

———. *The Transformation of Virginia, 1740–1790.* Chapel Hill: University of North Carolina Press, 1982.

Ingraham, Joseph H. *The South-West, by a Yankee.* 2 vols. New York: Harper, 1835.

Jackson, George Pullen. *White Spirituals in the Southern Uplands.* 1933. Reprint, New York: Dover Publications, 1965.

———. *Spiritual Folk-Songs of Early America.* New York: J. J. Augustin, 1937.

James, D. Clayton. *Antebellum Natchez.* Baton Rouge: Louisiana State University Press, 1968.

James, Janet Wilson, ed. *Women in American Religion.* Philadelphia: University of Pennsylvania Press, 1980.

James, Newton Haskin. "Josiah Hinds: Versatile Pioneer of the Old Southwest." *Journal of Mississippi History* II (January 1940): 22–33.

Jenkins, William Summer, ed. *Records of the States of the United States.* Washington, D.C.: Library of Congress Photoduplication Service, 1949.

Johnson, Douglas W., Paul R. Picerd, and Bernard Quinn. *Churches and Church Mem-*

bership in the United States . . . 1971. Washington, D.C.: Glenmary Research Center, 1974.

Johnson, John. *Recollections of the Rev. John Johnson and His Home. . . .* Nashville, Tenn.: Southern Methodist Publishing House, 1869.

Jones, John G. *A Complete History of Methodism in the Mississippi Conference.* 2 vols. Nashville, Tenn.: Publishing House of the M. E. Church, South, 1908.

———. *A Concise History of the Introduction of Protestantism into Mississippi and the Southwest.* St. Louis, Mo.: P. M. Pinckard, 1866.

Jones, R. W. "Some Facts Concerning the Settlement and Early History of Mississippi." *Publications of the Mississippi Historical Society* I (1898): 86–89.

Jones, W. B. *Methodism in the Mississippi Conference, 1870–1894.* Jackson, Miss.: Hawkins Foundation, 1951.

Jordan, Winthrop. *White Over Black: American Attitudes Toward the Negro, 1550–1812.* Chapel Hill: University of North Carolina Press, 1968.

Journal of the One Hundred and Fourth Session of the Mississippi Annual Conference of the Methodist Episcopal Church, South . . . 1917. Jackson, Miss.: The Conference, n.d. [1917].

Judson Baptist Association. *Minutes of the Seventeenth Annual Session . . . 1869.* Tuscumbia, Ala.: The Association, 1869.

Juster, Susan. "In a Different Voice: Male and Female Narratives of Religious Conversion in Post-Revolutionary America." *American Quarterly* XLI (March 1989): 34–62.

Kearney, Belle. *A Slaveholder's Daughter.* 1900. Reprint, New York: Negro Universities Press, 1969.

Kerr, Norwood Allen. "The Mississippi Colonization Society (1831–1860)." *Journal of Mississippi History* XLIII (February 1981): 1–30.

King, Martin Luther, Jr. *Stride Toward Freedom: The Montgomery Story.* San Francisco: Harper & Row, 1986.

Kohl, Lawrence Frederick. *The Politics of Individualism: Parties and the American Character in the Jacksonian Era.* New York and Oxford: Oxford University Press, 1989.

Leavell, Z. T., and T. J. Bailey. *A Complete History of Mississippi Baptists: From the Earliest Times.* 2 vols. Jackson: Mississippi Baptist Publishing Co., 1904.

Levine, Lawrence W. *Black Culture and Black Consciousness: Afro-American Folk Thought from Slavery to Freedom.* New York: Oxford University Press, 1977.

———. *Highbrow/Lowbrow: The Emergence of Cultural Hierarchy in America.* Cambridge, Mass.: Harvard University Press, 1988.

Lewis, H. P. *An Autobiography of Rev. H. P. Lewis.* New Orleans: Press of the New Orleans Christian Advocate, 1913.

Lewis, Jan. "The Republican Wife: Virtue and Seduction in the Early Republic." *William and Mary Quarterly*, 3d ser., XLIV (October 1987): 689–721.

Litwack, Leon F. *Been in the Storm So Long: The Aftermath of Slavery*. New York: Knopf, 1979.

———. *Trouble in Mind: Black Southerners in the Age of Jim Crow*. New York: Knopf, 1998.

Loveland, Anne. *Southern Evangelicals and the Social Order, 1800–1860*. Baton Rouge and London: Louisiana State University Press, 1980.

Lumpkin, William L. *Baptist Foundations in the South: Tracing Through the Separates the Influence of the Great Awakening, 1754–1787*. Nashville, Tenn.: Broadman Press, 1961.

Lylerly, Cynthia Lynn. *Methodism and the Southern Mind, 1770–1810*. New York and Oxford: Oxford University Press, 1998.

Lynch, John Roy. *Reminiscences of an Active Life: The Autobiography of John Roy Lynch*. Edited by John Hope Franklin. Chicago and London: University of Chicago Press, 1970.

Lyon, James A. *A Lecture on Christianity and the Civil Laws*. Columbus, Miss.: Mississippi Democrat Print., 1859.

McCoy, Drew R. *The Elusive Republic: Political Economy in Jeffersonian America*. Chapel Hill: University of North Carolina Press, 1980.

McDowell, John P. *The Social Gospel in the South: The Woman's Home Mission Movement in the Methodist Episcopal Church South, 1886–1939*. Baton Rouge: Louisiana State University Press, 1982.

McLemore, Richard Aubrey, ed. *A History of Mississippi*. 2 vols. Hattiesburg, Miss.: University and College Press of Mississippi, 1973.

———. *A History of Mississippi Baptists, 1780–1970*. Jackson: Mississippi Baptist Convention Board, 1971.

McRaney, Bob, Sr. *A History of Radio in Mississippi*. N.p.: Mississippi Broadcasters Association, 1979.

MacRobert, Ian. *The Black Roots and White Racism of Early Pentecostalism in the USA*. New York: St. Martin's Press, 1988.

Maddox, Jack P., Jr. "From Theocracy to Spirituality: The Southern Presbyterian Reversal on Church and State." *Journal of Presbyterian History* LIV (winter 1976): 438–57.

———. "Proslavery Millennialism: Social Eschatology in Antebellum Southern Calvinism." *American Quarterly* XXXI (spring 1979): 46–62.

———. "The Southern Apostasy Revisited: The Significance of Proslavery Christianity." *Marxist Perspectives* II (fall 1979): 132–41.

Malone, Bill C. *Southern Music, American Music*. Lexington, Ky.: University Press of Kentucky, 1979.

Mars, Florence. *Witness in Philadelphia*. Baton Rouge and London: Louisiana State University Press, 1977.

Marsden, George M. *The Evangelical Mind and the New School Presbyterian Experience*. New Haven, Conn.: Yale University Press, 1970.

Marty, Martin E. *Pilgrims in Their Own Land: 500 Years of Religion in America.* Boston: Little, Brown, 1984.

Massengill, Reed. *Portrait of a Racist: The Man Who Killed Medgar Evers?* New York: St. Martin's Press, 1994.

Mathews, Donald G. *Religion in the Old South.* Chicago and London: University of Chicago Press, 1977.

———. "The Second Great Awakening as an Organizing Process, 1780–1830: An Hypothesis." *American Quarterly* XXI (spring 1969): 23–43.

———. *Slavery and Methodism: A Chapter in American Morality, 1780–1845.* Princeton, N.J.: Princeton University Press, 1965.

Mellen, T. L., ed. *In Memoriam: Life and Labors of the Rev. William Hamilton Watkins, D. D.* . . . Nashville: Southern Methodist Publishing House, 1886.

Methodist Episcopal Church, South. *The Doctrines and Discipline of the Methodist Episcopal Church, South.* Charleston, S.C.: Methodist Episcopal Church, South, 1851.

———. *Minutes of the Annual Conferences . . . 1845–1851.* Richmond, Va.: Methodist Episcopal Church, South, 1846–53.

Miles, Edwin A. "Franklin E. Plummer: Piney Woods Spokesman of the Jackson Era." *Journal of Mississippi History* XIV (January 1952): 1–34.

———. *Jacksonian Democracy in Mississippi.* New York: Da Capo Press, 1970.

Miller, Floyd J. *The Search for a Black Nationality: Black Emigration and Colonization, 1787–1863.* Urbana, Ill.: University of Illinois Press, 1975.

Miller, Gene Ramsey. *A History of North Mississippi Methodism, 1820–1900.* Nashville, Tenn.: Parthenon Press, 1966.

Miller, Perry. *The Life of the Mind in America from the Revolution to the Civil War.* New York: Harcourt, Brace & World, 1965.

Mills, Kay. *This Little Light of Mine: The Life of Fannie Lou Hamer.* New York: Dutton, 1993.

Mills, Samuel J., and Daniel Smith. *Report of a Missionary Tour . . .* Andover, Mass.: Flagg and Gould, 1815.

"Minutes of Zion Baptist Church of Bucatunna, Wayne County, Mississippi." *Mississippi Genealogical Exchange* IXX (winter 1973): 123–25.

Mississippi Baptist Association. *Abstract History of the Mississippi Baptist Association for One Hundred Years.* . . . New Orleans: Mississippi Baptist Association, 1906.

———. *Minutes of the Forty-Third Anniversary . . . 1849.* Natchez, Miss.: Mississippi Baptist Association, 1849.

———. *Minutes of the Forty-Fourth Anniversary . . . 1850.* Natchez, Miss.: Mississippi Baptist Association, 1850.

———. *Minutes of the Forty-Fifth Anniversary . . . 1851.* Natchez, Miss.: Mississippi Baptist Association, 1851.

———. *Minutes of the Forty-Sixth Anniversary . . . 1852.* Natchez, Miss.: Mississippi Baptist Association, 1852.

———. *Minutes of the Forty-Seventh Anniversary* . . . *1853*. Natchez, Miss.: Mississippi Baptist Association, 1853.

———. *Minutes of the Forty-Ninth Anniversary* . . . *1855*. Natchez, Miss.: Mississippi Baptist Association, 1855.

———. *Proceedings of the Fiftieth Anniversary* . . . *1856*. Nashville, Tenn.: Mississippi Baptist Association, 1856.

———. *Minutes of the Fifty-Second Anniversary* . . . *1858*. New Orleans, La.: Mississippi Baptist Association, 1858.

———. *Minutes of the Fifty-Third Anniversary* . . . *1859*. Jackson, Miss.: Mississippi Baptist Association, 1859.

———. *Minutes of the Fifty-Fourth Anniversary* . . . *1860*. Jackson, Miss.: Mississippi Baptist Association, 1860.

———. *Minutes of the Fifty-Fifth Anniversary* . . . *1861*. Jackson, Miss.: Mississippi Baptist Association, 1861.

———. *Minutes of the Fifty-Sixth Annual Session* . . . *1862*. Jackson, Miss.: Mississippi Baptist Association, 1862.

———. *Minutes of the Sixtieth Anniversary* . . . *1866*. Liberty, Miss.: Mississippi Baptist Association, 1866.

———. *Minutes of the Sixty-First Anniversary* . . . *1867*. Memphis, Tenn.: Mississippi Baptist Association, 1868.

———. *Minutes of the Sixty-Second Anniversary* . . . *1868*. Memphis, Tenn.: Mississippi Baptist Association, 1869.

———. *Minutes of the Sixty-Third Anniversary* . . . *1869*. Natchez, Miss.: Mississippi Baptist Association, 1869.

———. *Minutes of the Sixty-Fourth Anniversary* . . . *1870*. Summit, Miss.: Mississippi Baptist Association, 1870.

———. *Minutes of the Sixty-Seventh Anniversary* . . . *1873*. Natchez, Miss.: Mississippi Baptist Association, 1873.

———. *Minutes of the Sixty-Eighth Anniversary* . . . *1874*. Memphis, Tenn.: Mississippi Baptist Association, 1874.

———. *Minutes of the Sixty-Ninth Anniversary* . . . *1875*. Memphis, Tenn.: Mississippi Baptist Association, 1875.

———. *Republication of the Minutes of the Mississippi Baptist Association, From Its Organization in 1806 to the Present Time*. New Orleans: Mississippi Baptist Association, 1849.

Mississippi River Baptist Association. *Minutes of the Ninth Anniversary* . . . *1852*. Clinton, La.: The Association, 1852.

———. *Minutes of the Twelfth Anniversary* . . . *1854*. New Orleans, La.: The Association, 1854.

———. *Minutes of the Fourteenth Anniversary* . . . *1856*. Clinton, La.: The Association, 1856.

————. *Minutes of the Fifteenth Anniversary . . . 1857*. New Orleans, La.: The Association, 1857.

————. *Minutes of the Seventeenth Anniversary . . . 1859*. New Orleans, La.: The Association, 1859.

Mitchell, H. L. *Mean Things Happening in This Land: The Life and Times of H. L. Mitchell, Co-Founder of the Southern Tenant Farmers Union*. Montclair, N.J.: Allanheld, Osmun, 1979.

Miyakawa, T. Scott. *Protestants and Pioneers: Individualism and Conformity on the American Frontier*. Chicago and London: University of Chicago Press, 1964.

Mohr, Clarence L. "Before Sherman: Georgia Blacks and the War Effort, 1861–1865." *Journal of Southern History* XLV (August 1979): 331–52.

Moody, Anne. *Coming of Age in Mississippi*. New York: Dell Publishers, 1968.

Moore, John Hebron. "Two Documents Relating to Plantation Overseers of the Vicksburg Region, 1831–1832." *Journal of Mississippi History* XVI (January 1954): 31–32.

————. *The Emergence of the Cotton Kingdom in the Old Southwest: Mississippi, 1770–1860*. Baton Rouge and London: Louisiana State University Press, 1988.

————. "Local and State Governments of Antebellum Mississippi." *Journal of Mississippi History* XLIV (May 1982): 105–16.

Moore, Margaret Deschamps. "Religion in Mississippi in 1860." *Journal of Mississippi History* XXII (October 1960): 223–38.

Moore, R. Laurence. "Religion, Secularization, and the Shaping of the Culture Industry in Antebellum America." *American Quarterly* XLI (June 1989): 216–42.

————. *Religious Outsiders and the Making of Americans*. New York and Oxford: Oxford University Press, 1986.

Morant, John J. *Mississippi Minister*. New York: Vantage Press, 1958.

Morgan, A. T. *Yazoo: or on the Picket Line of Freedom in the South*. Washington, D.C.: A. T. Morgan, 1884.

Morgan, Chester M. "At the Crossroads: World War II, Delta Agriculture, and Modernization in Mississippi." *Journal of Mississippi History* LVII (winter 1995): 353–71.

Morgan, Edmund S. *Visible Saints: The History of a Puritan Idea*. Ithaca and London: Cornell University Press, 1963.

Morris, Willie. *North Toward Home*. Boston: Houghton Mifflin, 1967.

————. *Terrains of the Heart and Other Essays on Home*. Oxford, Miss.: Yoknapatawpha Press, 1981.

Mt. Olive Baptist Association. *Proceedings . . . 1877*. Meridian, Miss.: The Association, 1877.

Mt. Olivet Baptist Association. *Minutes of the First Annual Session . . . 1869*. N.p.: The Association, 1869.

————. *Minutes of the Fourth Annual Session . . . 1872*. Columbus, Miss.: The Association, 1872.

————. *Minutes of the Third Annual Session . . . 1871*. Columbus, Miss.: The Association, 1871.

Mount Pisgah Baptist Association. *Minutes of the Seventh Annual Meeting . . . 1843*. Brandon, Miss.: The Association, 1843.

Murphy, Cullen. *The Word According to Eve: Women and the Bible in Ancient Times and Our Own*. Boston: Houghton Mifflin, 1998.

Natchez Orphan Asylum. *Annual Report of the Managers and Officers of the Natchez Orphan Asylum. . . .* Natchez: Natchez Orphan Asylum, 1855.

Nelson, D. M. *Conflicting Views on Segregation*. Greenwood, Miss.: Educational Fund of the Citizens' Councils, 1954.

New Hope Primitive Baptist Association. *New Hope Primitive Baptist Association Minutes . . . 1877*. Corinth, Miss.: The Association, 1877.

Newman, Mark. "The Mississippi Baptist Convention and Desegregation, 1945–1980." *Journal of Mississippi History* LIX (spring 1997): 1–31.

Niebuhr, H. Richard. *The Kingdom of God in America*. Middletown, Conn.: Wesleyan University Press, 1988.

Niebuhr, Reinhold. *Moral Man and Immoral Society*. New York and London: C. Scribner's, 1932.

Nolan, Charles E. *St. Mary's of Natchez: The History of a Southern Catholic Congregation, 1716–1988*. Natchez: St. Mary's Catholic Church, 1992.

Oakes, James. *The Ruling Race: A History of American Slaveholders*. New York: Knopf, 1982.

————. *Slavery and Freedom: An Interpretation of the Old South*. New York: Knopf, 1990.

Olmsted, Frederick Law. *The Cotton Kingdom*. New York: Modern Library, 1984.

Osborn, George C. "Plantation Life in Central Mississippi as Revealed in the Clay Sharkey Papers." *Journal of Mississippi History* (October 1941): 277–88.

Otken, Charles H. "Richard Curtis in the Country of the Natchez." *Publications of the Mississippi Historical Society* III (1900): 147–53.

Owen, Christopher H. "By Design: The Social Meaning of Methodist Church Architecture in Nineteenth-Century Georgia." *Georgia Historical Quarterly* LXXV (summer 1991): 221–53.

Ownby, Ted. *Subduing Satan: Religion, Recreation, and Manhood in the Rural South, 1865–1920*. Chapel Hill and London: University of North Carolina Press, 1990.

Panola Baptist Association. *Minutes of the Fourth Anniversary of the Panola Baptist Association*. Panola, Miss.: The Association, 1847.

————. *Minutes of the Fifth Annual Meeting . . . 1848*. Panola, Miss.: The Association, 1848.

Payne, Charles M. *I've Got the Light of Freedom: The Organization Tradition and the*

Mississippi Freedom Struggle. Berkeley, Los Angeles, London: University of California Press, 1995.

Pearl River Baptist Association. *Minutes of the Twenty-Fifth Annual Meeting . . . 1844*. Monticello, Miss.: The Association, 1844.

———. *Minutes of the Forty-First Anniversary . . . 1860*. Monticello, Miss.: The Association, 1860.

Pearse, James. *A Narrative of the Life of James Pearse*. Rutland, Vt.: W. Fay, 1825.

Phillips, Winnie. *A History of Methodist Women*. Clinton, Miss.: Mississippi Conference, United Methodist Church, 1980.

Pitts, Walter. "Keep the Fire Burnin': Language and Ritual in the Afro-Baptist Church." *Journal of the American Academy of Religion* LVI (spring 1988): 377–97.

Powdermaker, Hortense. *After Freedom: A Cultural Study in the Deep South*. New York: Viking Press, 1939.

Polk, Noel, ed. *Natchez Before 1830*. Jackson and London: University Press of Mississippi, 1989.

Posey, Walter Brownlow. *The Baptist Church in the Lower Mississippi Valley, 1776–1845*. Lexington: University of Kentucky Press, 1957.

———. *The Development of Methodism in the Old Southwest, 1783–1824*. 1933. Reprint, Philadelphia: Procupine Press, 1974.

———. *Frontier Mission: A History of Religion West of the Southern Appalachians to 1861*. Lexington: University of Kentucky Press, 1966.

Power, Kate M. "Centennial Celebration of Old Bethany Church." *Minutes of the Presbyterian Historical Society of the Synod of Mississippi*. N.p.: Presbyterian Historical Society, 1908.

Prentiss, George Lewis., ed. *A Memoir of S. S. Prentiss*. 2 vols. New York: C. Scribner, 1855.

Proceedings of a Meeting to Consider the Propriety of Forming a Baptist State Convention Held . . . December, 1836. Natchez: n.p., 1837.

Proceedings of the Ninth Annual Meeting of the Convention of the Baptist Denomination of the State of Mississippi . . . 1845. Jackson: Baptist State Convention, 1845.

Proceedings of the Third Annual Meeting of the Convention of the Baptist Denomination of the State of Mississippi . . . 1839. Natchez: Baptist State Convention, 1839.

Proctor, Samuel, ed. *Eighteenth-Century Florida and Its Borderlands*. Gainesville, Fla.: University Press of Florida, 1975.

Rable, George C. *But There Was No Peace: The Role of Violence in the Politics of Reconstruction*. Athens, Ga.: University of Georgia Press, 1984.

Raboteau, Albert J. *Slave Religion: The "Invisible Church" in the American South*. New York: Oxford University Press, 1978.

Rainwater, Percy. "Conquistadors, Missionaries, and Missions." *Journal of Mississippi History* XXVII (April 1965): 123–47.

———. *Mississippi: Storm Center of Secession, 1856–1861*. Baton Rouge: O. Claitor, 1938.

Rawick, George P., ed. *The American Slave : A Composite Biography*. Westport, Conn., and London: Greenwood Press, 1977.

Reagon, Bernice Johnson, ed. *We'll Understand It Better By and By*. Washington, D.C.: Smithsonian Institution Press, 1992.

Richardson, Joe M. *Christian Reconstruction: The American Missionary Association and Southern Blacks, 1861–1890*. Athens, Ga., and London: University of Georgia Press, 1986.

Riley, Franklin L., ed. "A Contribution to the History of the Colonization Movement in Mississippi." *Publications of the Mississippi Historical Society* IX (1906): 396–99.

Rivers, R. H. *The Life of Robert Paine, P. D., Bishop of the Methodist Episcopal Church, South*. Nashville, Tenn.: Southern Methodist Publishing House, 1884.

Roark, James L. *Masters Without Slaves : Southern Planters in the Civil War and Reconstruction*. New York: Norton, 1977.

Rogers, Tommy W. "T. C. Thornton: A Methodist Educator of Antebellum Mississippi." *Journal of Mississippi History* XLIV (May 1982): 136–47.

Rorabough, W. J. *The Alcoholic Republic*. New York and Oxford: Oxford University Press, 1979.

———. "Estimated U.S. Alcoholic Beverage Consumption, 1790–1860." *Journal of Studies on Alcohol* XXVII (March 1976): 357–63.

Rosenberg, Bruce. *The Art of the American Folk Preacher*. New York: Oxford University Press, 1970.

Rowland, Dunbar, and A. G. Sanders, eds. and trans. *Mississippi Provincial Archives: French Dominion, 1701–1743*. Jackson, Miss.: Press of the Mississippi Department of Archives and History, 1932.

Rundle, John Mrs., comp. *History of Grenada County Baptist Association, 1921–1960*. Grenada, Miss.: Baptist Press, 1961.

Ryan, Mary. "The Power of Women's Networks: A Case Study of Female Moral Reform in Antebellum America." *Feminist Studies* V (spring 1979): 66–85.

———. *Womanhood in America: From Colonial Times to the Present*. New York: New Viewpoints, 1979.

Salem Baptist Association. *Minutes of the Fourth Annual Meeting . . . 1865*. Mobile, Ala.: Salem Baptist Association, 1865.

———. *Minutes of the Eighth Annual Meeting . . . 1869*. Lauderdale Springs, Miss.: Salem Baptist Association, 1869.

———. *Minutes of the Eleventh Annual Session . . . 1872*. Enterprise, Miss.: Salem Baptist Association, 1872.

———. *Minutes of the Fifth Anniversary . . . 1866*. Jackson, Miss.: Salem Baptist Association, 1866.

———. *Minutes of the Ninth Annual Session . . . 1870*. Lauderdale Station, Miss.: Salem Baptist Association, 1870.

Sardis Missionary Baptist Association. *Minutes of the First Session . . . 1870*. Memphis, Tenn.: Sardis Missionary Baptist Association, 1870.

Satcher, Buford. *Blacks in Mississippi Politics, 1865–1900*. Washington, D.C.: University Press of America, 1978.

Schermerhorn, John F., and Samuel J. Mills. *A Correct View of That Part of the United States Which Lies West of the Allegany Mountains, with Regard to Religion and Morals*. Hartford, Conn.: Peter B. Gleason, 1814.

Schilling, T. C. *Abstract History of the Mississippi Baptist Association for One Hundred Years*. New Orleans: J. G. Hauser, 1908.

Schmidt, Leigh Eric. "A Church-going People are a Dress-loving People: Clothes, Communication, and Religious Culture in Early America." *Church History* LVIII (March 1989): 36–51.

———. *Holy Fairs: Scottish Communions and American Revivals in the Early Modern Period*. Princeton: Princeton University Press, 1989.

Scott, Anne Firor. "The Ever Widening Circle: The Diffusion of Feminist Values from the Troy Female Seminary, 1822–1872." *History of Education Quarterly* XIX (spring 1979): 3–25.

Scott, Donald M. *From Office to Profession: The New England Ministry, 1750–1850*. Philadelphia: University of Pennsylvania Press, 1978.

Sellers, Charles G. *The Market Revolution: Jacksonian America, 1815–1846*. New York and Oxford: Oxford University Press, 1991.

———, ed. *The Southerner as American*. Chapel Hill: University of North Carolina Press, 1960.

Sernett, Milton C. *Black Religion and American Evangelicalism: White Protestants, Plantation Missions, and the Flowering of Negro Christianity, 1787–1865*. Metuchen, N. J.: Scarecrow Press, 1975.

Shields, David S. *Civil Tongues & Polite Letters in British America*. Chapel Hill and London: University of North Carolina Press, 1997.

Silver, James W. *Mississippi: The Closed Society*. New York: Harcourt, Brace, and World, 1966.

———. *Confederate Morale and Church Propaganda*. New York: Norton, 1957.

Smedes, Susan Dabney. *Memorials of a Southern Planter*. Jackson, Miss.: University Press of Mississippi, 1981.

Smith, Elwyn A. "The Role of the South in the Presbyterian Schism of 1837–1838." *Church History* XXIX (March 1960): 44–63.

Smith, Gerrit. *Letter of Gerrit Smith to Rev. James Smylie, of the State of Mississippi*. New York: R. G. Williams, 1837.

Smith, H. Shelton. *In His Image, But . . . : Racism in Southern Religion, 1780–1910*. Durham, N.C.: Duke University Press, 1972.

Smith, Timothy L. "Righteousness and Hope: Christian Holiness and the Millennial Vision in America, 1800–1900." *American Quarterly* XXXI (spring 1979): 21–45.

Smith-Rosenberg, Carroll. *Disorderly Conduct: Visions of Gender in America.* New York: Knopf, 1985.

Smylie, James. *A Review of a Letter from the Presbytery of Chillicoth, to the Presbytery of Mississippi, on the Subject of Slavery.* . . . Woodville, Miss.: William. A. Norris and Co., 1836.

Snay, Mitchell. "American Thought and Southern Distinctiveness: The Southern Clergy and the Sanctification of Slavery." *Civil War History* XXXV (December 1989): 311–28.

Sobel, Mechal. *Trabelin' On: The Slave Journey to an Afro-Baptist Faith.* Westport, Conn., and London: Greenwood Press, 1979.

———. *The World They Made Together: Black and White Values in Eighteenth-Century Virginia.* Princeton, N.J.: Princeton University Press, 1987.

Sparks, Randy J. "Mississippi's Apostle of Slavery: James Smylie and the Biblical Defense of Slavery." *Journal of Mississippi History* LI (May 1989): 89–106.

———. *On Jordan's Stormy Banks: Evangelicalism in Mississippi, 1773–1876.* Athens, Ga., and London: University of Georgia Press, 1994.

———. " 'The White People's Arms Are Longer Than Ours': Blacks, Education, and the American Missionary Association in Reconstruction Mississippi." *Journal of Mississippi History* LIV (February 1992): 1–27.

Springfield Baptist Association. *Minutes of the Fourth Annual Meeting . . . 1877.* Memphis, Tenn.: The Association, 1877.

———. *Minutes of the Second Annual Session . . . 1875.* Meridian, Miss.: The Association, 1875.

———. *Minutes of the Third Annual Session . . . 1876.* Morton, Miss.: The Association, 1876.

Spring Hill Baptist Association. *Minutes of the Fourth Annual Session . . . 1873.* Jackson, Miss.: The Association, 1874.

Stampp, Kenneth M. *The Peculiar Institution: Slavery in the Ante-Bellum South.* New York: Vintage, 1956.

Stanford, E. L. *The History of Calvary Baptist Church, Jackson, Mississippi.* Jackson: The Church, 1980.

Staudenraus, P. J. *The African Colonization Movement, 1816–1865.* New York: Columbia University Press, 1961.

Stratton, Joseph B. *Memorial of a Quarter-Century's Pastorate.* Philadelphia: Lippencott, 1869.

Strickland, Jean, ed. *The Autobiography of A. C. Ramsey.* Moss Point, Miss.: J. Strickland, 1980.

Striefford, David M. "The American Colonization Society: An Application of Republican Ideology to Early American Reform." *Journal of Southern History* XLV (May 1979): 201–20.

Strong River Baptist Association. *Minutes of the Seventh Anniversary . . . 1859.* Jackson, Miss.: The Association, 1859.

———. *Minutes of the Ninth Anniversary of the Strong River Baptist Association . . . 1861.* Jackson, Miss.: The Association, 1861.

———. *Minutes of the Eleventh Annual Meeting . . . 1863.* Brandon, Miss.: The Association, 1863.

———. *Minutes of the Twelfth Annual Meeting . . . 1864.* Brandon, Miss.: The Association, 1864.

———. *Minutes of the Sixteenth Annual Meeting . . . 1868.* Jackson, Miss.: The Association, 1868.

———. *Minutes of the Eighteenth Annual Meeting . . . 1870.* Jackson, Miss.: The Association, 1870.

———. *Minutes of the Nineteenth Annual Meeting . . . 1871.* Jackson, Miss.: The Association 1871.

Sumners, Thomas O., ed. *Autobiography of the Rev. Joseph Travis, A.M. . . .* Nashville: M. E. Church, South, 1855.

Swearingen, Mark. "Luxury at Natchez: A Ship's Manifest from the McDonough Papers." *Journal of Southern History* III (May 1937): 188–90.

Sweet, Leonard I., ed. *The Evangelical Tradition in America.* Macon, Ga.: Mercer University Press, 1984.

Sweet, William Warren. "The Churches As Moral Courts of the Frontier." *Church History* II (March 1933): 3–21.

———. *Men of Zeal: The Romance of American Methodist Beginnings.* New York: Abingdon Press, 1935.

———. *Revivalism in America.* New York: Abingdon Press, 1944.

———. *The Story of Religion in America.* New York and London: Harper & Brothers, 1939.

Sydnor, Charles S. *American Revolutionaries in the Making: Political Practices in Washington's Virginia.* New York: Free Press, 1952.

———. *A Gentleman of the Old Natchez Region: Benjamin L. C. Wailes.* Durham, N. C.: Duke University Press, 1938.

———. *Slavery in Mississippi.* New York and London: D. Appleton-Century Co., 1933.

Synod of Mississippi and South Alabama. *Extracts from the Records of the Synod of Mississippi and South Alabama, From 1829 to 1835.* Jackson, Miss.: Clarion Steam Publishing Establishment, 1880.

Taulbert, Clifton L. *Once Upon a Time When We Were Colored.* Tulsa, Okla.: Council Oak Books, 1989.

Thompson, Ernest Trice. *Presbyterians in the South, 1607–1861.* Richmond, Va.: The Knox Press, 1963.

Thompson, Patrick H. *The History of the Negro Baptists in Mississippi.* Jackson, Miss.: R. W. Bailey, 1898.

Thornton, John. *Africa and Africans in the Making of the Atlantic World, 1400–1680.* Cambridge, Eng.: Cambridge University Press, 1992.

Thornton, Thomas C. *An Inquiry into the History of Slavery*. . . . Washington, D.C.: W. M. Morrison, 1841.

Tise, Larry E. *Proslavery: A History of the Defense of Slavery in America, 1701–1840*. Athens and London: University of Georgia Press, 1987.

Tishomingo Baptist Association. *Proceedings of the Ninth Annual Session of the Tishomingo Baptist Association . . . 1869*. Memphis, Tenn.: The Associatioin, 1869.

Tull, James E. *A History of Southern Baptist Landmarkism in the Light of Historical Baptist Ecclesiology*. New York: Arno Press, 1980.

———. "The Landmark Movement: An Historical and Theological Appraisal." *Baptist History and Heritage* X (January 1975): 3–18.

Tyrrell, Ian R. "Drink and Temperance in the Antebellum South: An Overview and Interpretation." *Journal of Southern History* XLVIII (November 1982): 485–510.

Union Baptist Association. *Minutes of the Thirty-Third Anniversary . . . 1853*. New Orleans, La.: The Association, 1854.

———. *Minutes of the Thirty-Fourth Anniversary . . . 1854*. New Orleans, La.: The Association, 1854.

———. *Minutes of the Thirty-Fifth Anniversary . . . 1856*. New Orleans, La.: The Association, 1856.

———. *Minutes of the Thirty-Seventh Anniversary . . . 1857*. Jackson, Miss.: The Association, 1857.

———. *Minutes of the Thirty-Eighth Anniversary . . . 1858*. Jackson, Miss.: The Association, 1858.

———. *Minutes of the Thirty-Ninth Anniversary . . . 1859*. Jackson, Miss.: The Association, 1859.

———. *Minutes of the Fortieth Annual Session . . . 1860*. Jackson, Miss.: The Association, 1860.

———. *Minutes of the Forty-First Annual Session . . . 1861*. Jackson, Miss.: The Association, 1861.

———. *Minutes of the Fiftieth Annual Meeting . . . 1870*. Crystal Springs, Miss.: The Association, 1870.

———. *Minutes of the Fifty-First Annual Session . . . 1871*. Crystal Springs, Miss.: The Association, 1871.

———. *Minutes of the Fifty-Second Annual Session . . . 1872*. Crystal Springs, Miss.: The Association 1872.

Usner, Daniel H., Jr. "American Indians on the Cotton Frontier: Changing Economic Relations with Citizens and Slaves in the Mississippi Territory." *Journal of American History* LXXII (September 1985): 297–317.

———. *Indians, Settlers, & Slaves in a Frontier Exchange Economy: The Lower Mississippi Valley Before 1783*. Chapel Hill and London: University of North Carolina Press, 1992.

Van Der Merwe, Peter. *Origins of the Popular Style: The Antecedents of Twentieth-Century Popular Music.* Oxford: Clarendon Press, 1989.

Wailes, B. L. C. *Memoir of Leonard Covington by B. L. C. Wailes Also Some of General Covington's Letters.* Edited by Nellie Wailes Brandon and W. M. Drake. Natchez, Miss.: Natchez Printing and Stationery Co., 1928.

Walker, Clarence G. *A Rock in a Weary Land: The African Methodist Episcopal Church during the Civil War and Reconstruction.* Baton Rouge: Louisiana State University Press, 1982.

Wallace, Anthony F. C. *Religion: An Anthropological View.* New York: Random House, 1966.

Warner, R. Stephen. "Work in Progress Toward a New Paradigm for the Sociological Study of Religion in the United States." *American Journal of Sociology* XCVIII (March 1993): 1044–93.

Warren, Harris Gaylord. "Vignettes of Culture in Old Claiborne." *Journal of Mississippi History* XX (July 1958): 125–46.

Watson, Harry L. *Jacksonian Politics and Community Conflict: The Emergence of the Second Party System in Cumberland County, North Carolina.* Baton Rouge and London: Louisiana State University Press, 1981.

———. *Liberty and Power: The Politics of Jacksonian America.* New York: Hill & Wang, 1990.

Wayne, Michael. *The Reshaping of Plantation Society: The Natchez District, 1860–1880.* Baton Rouge and London: Louisiana State University Press, 1983.

Webb, George E. *The Evolution Controversy in America.* Lexington, Ky.: University Press of Kentucky, 1994.

Weidman, Judith L., ed. *Women Ministers.* San Francisco: Harper & Row, 1981.

Whittington, G. P., ed. "Dr. John Sibley of Natchitoches, 1757–1837." *Louisiana Historical Quarterly* X (October 1927): 474–97.

Wilson, Charles Reagan. *Baptized in Blood: The Religion of the Lost Cause, 1865–1920.* Athens, Ga.: University of Georgia Press, 1980.

———, ed. *Religion in the South.* Jackson, Miss.: University Press of Mississippi, 1985.

Winchester, S. G. *The Religion of the Bible, The Only Preservation of Our Civil Institutions.* . . . Natchez, Miss.: Oakland College, 1838.

Woman's Missionary Society. *Twenty-Third Annual Report of the Woman's Missionary Society of the Mississippi Conference, Methodist Episcopal Church, South . . . 1934 .* N.p., n.d.

———. *Twentieth Annual Report of the Woman's Missionary Society of the Mississippi Conference, Methodist Episcopal Church, South . . . 1931.* N.p., n.d.

Woman's Missionary Union of Mississippi. *Hearts the Lord Opened: The History of Mississippi Woman's Missionary Union.* Jackson, Miss.: Woman's Missionary Union of Mississippi, 1954.

Wood, Forrest G. *The Arrogance of Faith: Christianity and Race from the Colonial Era to the Twentieth Century.* New York: Knopf, 1990.

Wood, Gordon S. *The Creation of the American Republic, 1776–1787*. Chapel Hill: University of North Carolina Press, 1969.

Woodruff, Nan Elizabeth. "Mississippi Delta Planters and Debates over Mechanization, Labor, and Civil Rights in the 1940s." *Journal of Southern History* LX (May 1994): 263–84.

Woodward, C. Vann. *Origins of the New South, 1877–1913*. Baton Rouge: Louisiana State University Press, 1951.

Worrell, A. S. *Review of Corrective Church Discipline*. Nashville, Tenn.: Southern Baptist Publishing House, 1860.

Wright, David F. *The Bible in Scottish Life and Literature*. Edinburgh: St. Andrew Press, 1988.

Wright, Gavin. *Old South, New South: Revolutions in the Southern Economy Since the Civil War*. New York: Basic Books, 1986.

Wright, Richard. *Black Boy*. New York: Harper & Brothers, 1945.

———. *12 Million Black Voices*. New York: Viking Press, 1941.

Wuthnow, Robert. *The Restructuring of American Religion*. Princeton, N.J.: Princeton University Press, 1988.

Wyatt-Brown, Bertram. "The Antimission Movement in the Jacksonian South: A Study in Regional Folk Culture." *Journal of Southern History* XXXVI (November 1970): 501–29.

———. "God and Honor in the Old South." *Southern Review* XXV (April 1989): 283–96.

———. *Southern Honor: Ethics and Behavior in the Old South*. New York and Oxford: Oxford University Press, 1982.

Young, Jacob. *Autobiography of a Pioneer. . . .* Cincinnati: Cranston & Curts, 1857.

Youth of the Rural Organizing and Cultural Center. *Minds Stayed on Freedom: The Civil Rights Struggle in the Rural South, an Oral History*. Boulder, Colo.: Westview Press, 1991.

Yazoo Baptist Association. *Proceedings of the Sixteenth Annual Session . . . 1867*. Memphis, Tenn.: The Association, 1867.

Zuckerman, Michael. "Holy Wars, Civil Wars: Religion and Economics in Nineteenth-Century America." *Prospects: The Annual of American Studies* (1992): 205–40.

Newspapers and Periodicals

Biloxi-Gulfport *Sun-Herald*

The Boston Globe Magazine

Capital Reporter (Jackson)

Christian Century

Christian Conservative Communique

Christianity Today

The Citizens' Council

Concern

Confederate Veteran

Congressional Record

Good News

The Gospel Messenger

Jackson Daily News

Jackson *Free Press*

Liahona: The Elders' Journal

Louisiana and Mississippi Almanack

Memphis *Commercial Appeal*

Mississippi Association of Methodist Ministers and Laymen *Information Bulletin*

Mississippi Baptist

Mississippi Methodist Advocate

Mississippi Today

Natchez *Messenger*

New Orleans *Christian Advocate*

New Orleans *South-Western Baptist Chronicle*

New Orleans *Western Methodist*

New York Times

New York Times Magazine

The Presbyterian Outlook

The Southron (Jackson)

Southwestern Christian Advocate

South-Western Religious Luminary

Sunbelt

Tennessee Baptist

Vicksburg *Evening Post*

Vicksburg *Post*

Washington *Post*

Washington Republican and Natchez Intelligencer

Western Messenger

Western Methodist (Nashville)

Index